LANDSCAPES OF WAR IN GREEK AND ROMAN LITERATURE

Also available from Bloomsbury

LUCAN'S IMPERIAL WORLD
edited by Laura Zientek and Mark Thorne

WAR AND PEACE IN THE WESTERN POLITICAL IMAGINATION
by Roger B. Manning

WAR AS SPECTACLE
edited by Anastasia Bakogianni and Valerie M. Hope

LANDSCAPES OF WAR IN GREEK AND ROMAN LITERATURE

Edited by Bettina Reitz-Joosse, Marian W. Makins and C. J. Mackie

BLOOMSBURY ACADEMIC
LONDON • NEW YORK • OXFORD • NEW DELHI • SYDNEY

BLOOMSBURY ACADEMIC
Bloomsbury Publishing Plc
50 Bedford Square, London, WC1B 3DP, UK
1385 Broadway, New York, NY 10018, USA
29 Earlsfort Terrace, Dublin 2, Ireland

BLOOMSBURY, BLOOMSBURY ACADEMIC and the Diana logo are trademarks of
Bloomsbury Publishing Plc

First published in Great Britain 2021
This paperback edition published 2022

Copyright © Bettina Reitz-Joosse, Marian W. Makins, C. J. Mackie & Contributors 2021

Bettina Reitz-Joosse, Marian W. Makins and C. J. Mackie have asserted their right under the Copyright, Designs and Patents Act, 1988, to be identified as Editors of this work.

For legal purposes the Acknowledgements on p. x constitute an extension of this copyright page.

Cover design: Terry Woodley
Cover image © *Battle of Lake Trasimene*, Léonard Thiry (*c.* 1500–1550). Universal Images Group / Getty

All rights reserved. No part of this publication may be reproduced or transmitted in any form or by any means, electronic or mechanical, including photocopying, recording, or any information storage or retrieval system, without prior permission in writing from the publishers.

Bloomsbury Publishing Plc does not have any control over, or responsibility for, any third-party websites referred to or in this book. All internet addresses given in this book were correct at the time of going to press. The author and publisher regret any inconvenience caused if addresses have changed or sites have ceased to exist, but can accept no responsibility for any such changes.

A catalogue record for this book is available from the British Library.

Library of Congress Cataloging-in-Publication Data
Names: Reitz-Joosse, Bettina, editor. | Makins, Marian W., editor. | Mackie, C. J. (Christopher J.), 1954– editor.
Title: Landscapes of war in Greek and Roman literature / edited by Bettina Reitz-Joosse, Marian W. Makins, and C. J. Mackie.
Description: London ; New York : Bloomsbury Academic, 2021. | Includes bibliographical references and index. | Summary: "In this volume, literary scholars and ancient historians from across the globe investigate the creation, manipulation and representation of ancient war landscapes in literature. Landscape can spark armed conflict, dictate its progress and influence the affective experience of its participants. At the same time, warfare transforms landscapes, both physically and in the way in which they are later perceived and experienced. Landscapes of War in Greek and Roman Literature breaks new ground in exploring Greco-Roman literary responses to this complex interrelationship. Drawing on current ideas in cognitive theory, memory studies, ecocriticism and other fields, its individual chapters engage with such questions as: how did the Greeks and Romans represent the effects of war on the natural world? What distinctions did they see between spaces of war and other landscapes? How did they encode different experiences of war in literary representations of landscape? How was memory tied to landscape in wartime or its aftermath? And in what ways did ancient war landscapes shape modern experiences and representations of war? In four sections, contributors explore combatants' perception and experience of war landscapes, the relationship between war and the natural world, symbolic and actual forms of territorial control in a military context, and war landscapes as spaces of memory. Several contributions focus especially on modern intersections of war, landscape and the classical past"– Provided by publisher.
Identifiers: LCCN 2020034851 (print) | LCCN 2020034852 (ebook) | ISBN 9781350157903 (hardcover) | ISBN 9781350157910 (ebook) | ISBN 9781350157927 (epub)
Subjects: LCSH: Classical literature–History and criticism. | War in literature. | Landscapes in literature.
Classification: LCC PA3015.W46 L36 2021 (print) | LCC PA3015.W46 (ebook) | DDC 880.09/3581—dc23
LC record available at https://lccn.loc.gov/2020034851
LC ebook record available at https://lccn.loc.gov/2020034852

ISBN: HB: 978-1-3501-5790-3
PB: 978-1-3501-9221-8
ePDF: 978-1-3501-5791-0
eBook: 978-1-3501-5792-7

Typeset by RefineCatch Limited, Bungay, Suffolk

To find out more about our authors and books visit www.bloomsbury.com
and sign up for our newsletters.

CONTENTS

List of Illustrations   vii
Notes on Contributors   viii
Acknowledgements   x

Introduction   *Marian W. Makins and Bettina Reitz-Joosse*   1

Part I   Perception and Experience of War Landscapes

1. Homer's Landscape of War: Spatial Mental Model and Cognitive Collage   *Elizabeth Minchin*   25
2. War, Weather and Landscape in Livy's *Ab Urbe Condita*   *Virginia Fabrizi*   38
3. The Challenge of Historiographic *Enargeia* and the Battle of Lake Trasimene   *Andrew Feldherr*   62

Part II   Landscapes of Ruin and Recovery

4. The Problems with Agricultural Recovery in Lucan's Civil War Narrative   *Laura Zientek*   91
5. Landscapes in Sophocles' *Oedipus at Colonus* and the Poetry of the First World War   *William Brockliss*   111
6. Dissenting Voices in Propertius's Post-War Landscapes   *Marian W. Makins*   131

Part III   Controlling Landscapes and the Symbolism of Power

7. Justifying Civil War: Interactions between Caesar and the Italian Landscape in Lucan's Rubicon Passage (*BC* 1.183–235)   *Esther Meijer*   157
8. Writing a Landscape of Defeat: The Romans in Parthia   *Bettina Reitz-Joosse*   177
9. Landscape and Character in Herodian's *History of the Roman Empire*: The War between Niger and Severus   *Karine Laporte*   193

Part IV   Memory in War Landscapes

10. Seascapes of War: Herodotus's Littoral Gaze on the Battle of Salamis   *J. Z. van Rookhuijzen*   213

Contents

11 War in a Landscape: The Dardanelles from Homer to Gallipoli
    C. J. Mackie   229

12 Mutable Monuments and Mutable Memories in Lucan's
    Bellum Civile and the Former Yugoslavia   *Jesse Weiner*   241

Index Locorum   262
Index   273

ILLUSTRATIONS

1.1	Wallace Anderson and Louis McCubbin (fabricators): Lone Pine (Gallipoli Peninsula) diorama (AWM ART41017).	26
6.1	Map showing parts of ancient Etruria, Umbria and Latium. Created by Marian W. Makins with Antiquity À-la-carte (Ancient World Mapping Center) http://awmc.unc.edu/awmc/applications/alacarte/ [Accessed: 8 June 2020]. Licensed under the Creative Commons Attribution 4.0 International Licence (CC BY 4.0).	141
10.1	Map of Salamis and a part of Attica showing locations in the battle of Salamis. Drawn by René Reijnen and J. Z. van Rookhuijzen.	215
11.1	Map of the Gallipoli Peninsula showing the main ancient and modern sites. C. J. Mackie, M. Atabay, R. Körpe and A. Sagona, 'Boundary and Divide: The Antiquity of the Dardanelles', in A. Sagona, M. Atabay, C. J. Mackie, I. McGibbon and R. Reid (eds), *Anzac Battlefield: A Gallipoli Landscape of War and Memory* (Melbourne: Cambridge University Press, 2016), 6. Reproduced with kind permission of Cambridge University Press.	231
12.1	Scene still from *Planet of the Apes,* dir. Franklin J. Schaffner. 20th Century Fox, 1968. Alamy.	243
12.2	*Monument to the Revolution of the People of Moslavina* (sculptor: Dušan Džamonja) in Podgarić, Croatia. Jan Kempenaers, *Spomenik #1* (2006). © Jan Kempenaers.	244
12.3	*Monument to the Uprising of the People of Kordun and Banija* (sculptor: Vojin Bakić) in Petrova Gora, Croatia. Jan Kempenaers, *Spomenik #2* (2006). © Jan Kempenaers.	245
12.4	Monument in Krusevo, Macedonia. Jan Kempenaers, *Spomenik #5* (2007). © Jan Kempenaers.	246
12.5	Destroyed monument in Kamenska, Croatia. Jan Kempenaers, *Spomenik #21* (2009). © Jan Kempenaers.	247
12.6	Graffiti-covered monument in Košute, Croatia. Jan Kempenaers, *Spomenik #12* (2007). © Jan Kempenaers.	248
12.7	Crumbling monument in Makljen, Bosnia and Herzegovina. Jan Kempenaers, *Spomenik #15* (2007). © Jan Kempenaers.	248

CONTRIBUTORS

William Brockliss is Associate Professor of Classics at the University of Wisconsin–Madison. He studies interactions between Greek and Roman texts and the natural environment, as reflected in his monograph, *Homeric Imagery and the Natural Environment* (Center for Hellenic Studies, 2019). He has also published on topics such as the nightmare (*Illinois Classical Studies* 2017), monstrosity (*Classical Journal* 2018) and the abject (D. Felton, ed., *Landscapes of Dread*, 2018), in preparation for a second book, *Horror in Ancient Epic*.

Virginia Fabrizi obtained her PhD at the University of Udine and held postdoctoral positions at the Freie Universität Berlin and the Ludwig-Maximilians-Universität of Munich. She is currently working as an Italian teacher in Munich and is affiliated with the University of Pavia as a 'Cultore della materia' in Classical Philology. She published a book on the representation of Roman history in Ennius's *Annales* entitled *Mores veteresque novosque: rappresentazioni del passato e del presente di Roma negli Annales di Ennio* (2012) as well as several articles on Livy, in particular on the narrative construction of space in the *Ab Urbe Condita*.

Andrew Feldherr (PhD Berkeley 1991) is Professor of Classics at Princeton University. He works on Latin Literature, with a particular interest in historiography and the poetry of the Augustan period. A main focus of his scholarship has been on how political and social forces transform conceptions of the function of literature during the Roman Republic and Empire.

Karine Laporte is a PhD candidate at Leiden University Centre for the Arts in Society. Her dissertation is on narrative patterns in ancient historiography and, in particular, how Herodian engages with this practice in the *History of the Roman Empire*. She has forthcoming articles further exploring Herodian's method of composition, specifically his use of imperial death notices (with O. J. Hekster) and of stock character types.

C. J. Mackie (PhD Glasgow) is Professor of Classics and Ancient History at La Trobe University. He has written widely on Greek and Roman topics, especially Vergil, Homer and Greek mythology. Much of his research focuses on the Trojan War, as told by the Greek and Roman sources, and the impact of these accounts on the later European tradition of war narratives. More recently he has developed interests in the Gallipoli region of western Turkey, and was on a three-nation team (Australia, New Zealand and Turkey) carrying out a historical and archaeological survey of the Anzac battlefield. He is a regular contributor to *The Conversation*.

Marian W. Makins (PhD University of Pennsylvania) is Assistant Professor of Instruction in Greek and Roman Classics at Temple University in Philadelphia. Her current research focuses on intersections between war, death and landscape in Roman culture and its reception. She has also published articles on classical receptions in the nonsense of Edward Lear, J. R. R. Tolkien's *The Lord of the Rings* and the Hunger Games trilogy.

Esther Meijer is a PhD candidate in Classics at Durham University (UK). She works on landscape and identity in Neronian and Flavian literature, with particular attention to intertextuality and rhetoric of empire. Further research interests include metapoetics, (poetic) geographies and Flavian panegyric, especially Statius's *Silvae*. She is currently co-editing a volume with Mark Heerink on Flavian responses to Nero's Rome.

Elizabeth Minchin is Emeritus Professor in the Centre for Classical Studies at the Australian National University, Canberra. Her research publications cover memory in its various aspects, whether personal, social or cultural, particularly as we observe its operations in the Homeric epics; landscape too is an interest, especially as it interlocks with memory. Her publications include *Homer and the Resources of Memory: Some Applications of Cognitive Theory to the Iliad and the Odyssey* (2001) and *Homeric Voices: Discourse, Memory, Gender* (2007) and numerous articles and book chapters.

Bettina Reitz-Joosse is Associate Professor of Latin Language and Literature at the University of Groningen (Netherlands). Her work focuses on the relationship between literary texts and material culture in the ancient Roman world and on the reception of Roman antiquity under Italian Fascism.

J. Z. van Rookhuijzen is a researcher and lecturer at the universities of Utrecht and Leiden (Netherlands) and member of the National Research School of Classical Studies (OIKOS). His doctoral work examined the role of memory in Herodotus's account of the Persian Wars, resulting in the monograph *Herodotus and the Topography of Xerxes' Invasion* (2018). He currently investigates the archaeology and reception history of the Acropolis of Athens. This project, funded by the Dutch Research Council (NWO), traces the role of narratives in current ideas of the Acropolis temples and has been featured in National Geographic.

Jesse Weiner is Assistant Professor of Classics at Hamilton College (USA). He publishes broadly on Greek and Latin literature and its reception, with special interests in monumentality and memory, sexuality and gender, and aesthetics. In public humanities, his work has appeared in *History Today* and *The Atlantic*. He is co-editor of *Frankenstein and Its Classics: The Modern Prometheus from Antiquity to Science Fiction* (Bloomsbury Academic, 2018).

Laura Zientek is Visiting Assistant Professor of Classics and Humanities at Reed College. Her research focuses on the intersection of landscape representation and natural philosophy in Roman literature, with special interests in ecocriticism, biocosmology and horror. Her publications include analyses of the sublime, landscape aesthetics and depictions of mining. She is co-editor of *Lucan's Imperial World: The Bellum Civile in Its Contemporary Contexts* (Bloomsbury Academic, 2020).

ACKNOWLEDGEMENTS

This book began as a panel on 'Landscapes of War' which we organized for the Celtic Conference in Classics (CCC) in Montréal in July 2017. We are grateful to the organizers of the conference for hosting our panel, and to all panel participants for extraordinarily lively, enthusiastic and productive discussions. We would like to mention specially those speakers who were unable to contribute to this volume, but whose insights benefited all of us in the writing and editing process: Jake Butera, Debbie Felton, Andrew Fox, Josie Rae and Roy van Wijk. We are also immensely grateful to Jenny Strauss Clay, who concluded our panel with a magisterial response that helped us draw the threads together and provided a great deal of inspiration for our introduction to this volume.

Both the CCC panel and this volume received generous funding from the Nederlandse Organisatie voor Wetenschappelijk Onderzoek (NWO) as part of Bettina Reitz-Joosse's Veni project 'Landscapes of War in Roman Literature' (project number 016.164.057). Finally, we would like to thank the editors and anonymous readers for Bloomsbury for their constructive feedback on our proposal and manuscript; Andrew Devine for his meticulous copy-editing of our manuscript; and Hylke de Boer for his invaluable assistance with the Index Locorum.

Bettina Reitz-Joosse, Marian W. Makins and C. J. Mackie
(Groningen, Philadelphia and Melbourne, June 2020)

INTRODUCTION
Marian W. Makins and Bettina Reitz-Joosse

1 The 'landscape of war'

In 1917, the journal *Zeitschrift für angewandte Psychologie* published an article entitled 'Kriegslandschaft', later translated into English as 'The Landscape of War'.[1] The article's author, a Berlin-educated Polish Jew named Kurt Lewin, would later flee Nazi Germany for the USA and come to prominence there as a pioneering social psychologist. In 1917, however, he was just twenty-six years old, a newly minted PhD whose studies had been interrupted by the First World War. Despite marked anti-militaristic and anti-nationalistic leanings, Lewin – along with both of his brothers and their brother-in-law – had enlisted as a private in the German army in 1914. By the time of his discharge at war's end, he had risen to the rank of lieutenant and received the Iron Cross for bravery.[2]

Lewin wrote 'Kriegslandschaft' during a long hospital stay while he was convalescing from wounds received in action. Psychological work, fueled by what biographer Alfred J. Marrow has called Lewin's 'unquenchable curiosity', seems to have offered a refuge from the horrors and tedium of war, both in hospital and at the front.[3] Yet the observations set forth in the article stem directly from those experiences of combat. He describes with great clarity, for example, how soldiers in the field experience the landscape differently as they move in the direction of the front.[4] As long as the front remains distant, Lewin observes, the landscape seems to extend 'to infinity in all directions alike'. But this expansiveness – typical of peacetime landscapes – disappears as the soldiers continue their march. A new sense of restriction, of *boundedness*, sets in; 'the area seems to come to an end somewhere in the direction of the Front'. And whereas previously they had experienced the landscape as *round*, it now appears to be *directed*, with 'a front and behind that do not relate to those marching, but firmly pertain to the area itself'. This impression both increases and shifts when the boundary, the invisible but all-important line between 'our' territory and 'theirs', comes into view:[5]

---

[1] Lewin (1917); English translation in Lewin (2009). We thank Jenny Strauss Clay for directing our attention to this fascinating text during her response at the 'Landscapes of War' panel at the Celtic Conference in Classics in Montréal in 2017, at which this volume originated.
[2] On Lewin's early life and military service, see Marrow (1969: 3–12); with Lewin (1992: 15–21).
[3] Marrow (1969: 10–11); cf. Lewin (1992: 21).
[4] Lewin (2009: 201–2).
[5] Lewin (2009: 202).

The area presents itself as a *zone* running roughly parallel to the boundary. While in the previous region the direction *towards* the boundary was experienced as the direction of the landscape, now the expansion along the boundary defines the direction of the landscape. A border zone emerges, whose character as such intensifies rapidly in the direction of the enemy.

The foregoing represents only a small portion of Lewin's observations about war landscapes.[6] And it is important to note, as Lewin himself does, that the specifics of his account reflect his experience as a field artilleryman; other types of soldiers, or soldiers fighting in other combat settings, would experience the landscape in other ways. But one of the crucial points implied by Lewin's work is precisely that war landscapes will *always* be experienced differently than peacetime ones. Or – seeing as phenomenology is only one of many approaches to the study of landscape – we might even say that war landscapes possess distinctive properties, which impact both how they are experienced and the ways they might be imagined or represented. Lewin's work also illustrates two fundamental aspects of landscape in general: that subjective human experience is an important part of what constitutes a landscape (as opposed to 'land' or 'terrain'), and that landscape is essentially a dynamic and shifting phenomenon. By adopting these premises, Lewin points forward to recent critical trends in landscape studies that have informed our own approach to landscapes of war in this book.

Neither the Latin nor the Greek language has a word equivalent to the German 'Landschaft' or the English 'landscape'.[7] Unlike 'space' or 'environment', the word 'landscape' foregrounds human perspective and human experience. Following Cosgrove's influential definition, we take 'landscape' broadly to mean 'the external world mediated through subjective human experience'.[8] Landscape encompasses the natural world, its cultural overlay and human experiences of it: 'not merely the world we see, ... [but] a construction ... of that world'.[9]

Essential to our understanding of landscape is its dynamic nature. Landscapes are far more than simply a static setting or backdrop for human activity. A landscape is constantly in flux, and 'never inert, [as] people interact with it, re-work it, appropriate and contest it'.[10] One of the ways in which landscapes are contested and re-worked is through military conflicts and their memories. Landscapes are often the object of military conflict, as their ownership is contested and reestablished. As the result of war, landscapes can be physically altered, damaged, or re-zoned. But they are more than only the passive objects of war: landscapes act on those within them. The nature of the terrain impacts the course of fighting and the strategic decisions of combatants, and the surroundings influence combatants' experience of war, their actions, and their memories.

---

[6] See below for an application of some of Lewin's concepts to a passage from the *Iliad*.
[7] On the etymology of the word 'landscape' and its uses in different languages and contexts, see Antrop (2018).
[8] Cosgrove (1984: 13).
[9] Cosgrove (1984: 13).
[10] Bender (1993: 3).

This book is dedicated to exploring this complex interrelationship between landscape and armed conflict in the ancient world of Greece and Rome. To do so, we offer neither military-historical nor topographical accounts of ancient wars. Instead, we focus on the representations of war landscapes in ancient literature. We believe that this allows access to insights no less essential than the exact locality of battles or the probable movement of troops: namely, how war and its spaces were perceived and experienced, what they meant and what they were made to mean in antiquity.[11] Individual chapters in this book deal with questions such as: How did the Greeks and Romans represent the effects of war on the natural world? What distinctions did they see between spaces of war and other landscapes? How did they encode different experiences of war in literary representations of landscape? And how did memory become tied to landscape in wartime or its aftermath? By answering these questions, we will gain a better understanding of ancient 'lived space' and ancient experiences of war.[12]

Within the term 'landscapes of war', we embrace not only battlefields proper, but all landscapes that have in some way been altered or impacted by armed conflict, physically or conceptually. By our definition, a landscape of war may be a particular site where fighting has occurred, but also a space which in some other way bears the traces of war, its commemoration or forgetting – or is perceived as doing so. Landscapes of war in this volume therefore include such well-known battlefields as Salamis and Pharsalus, but also the Rubicon (a famous landmark of the Roman civil wars, even if no fighting took place there) and even the Palatine Hill in Rome, where painful civil war memories were negotiated.[13]

Several chapters also discuss modern artistic responses to war landscapes, from British and Australian First World War literature to a series of post-Second World War monuments erected in former Yugoslav nations.[14] Such material appears in the volume both because ancient literary war landscapes have undeniably influenced later ones – and thereby also more recent experiences and representations of war – and secondly because comparison with modern examples can often yield fruitful approaches to understanding ancient texts.

2 The case of Scamander

Before delineating the individual sections and chapters of the volume, we first turn to one of the earliest and most influential war landscapes in western literature: the Trojan

---

[11] Larsen (2004: 470): 'Literature investigates the possibilities, the modalities, and the conditions of a relationship, or, to put it briefly: literature *constitutes* a relation between war and landscape, not on the conditions of war or of the landscape, but on the conditions of literature as a means, an *organon* in the original Greek sense, of the cultural interpretation of human life. Literature offers a perspective on the relationship at the same time that it constructs a specific version of it.' (Emphasis in the original.)

[12] On lived space in ancient literature, see Heirman/Klooster (2013: esp. 5–6).

[13] See the chapters of van Rookhuijzen (Salamis), Zientek (Pharsalus), Meijer (Rubicon) and Weiner (Palatine).

[14] See the chapters of Brockliss and Mackie (First World War literature) and Weiner (post-Second World War monuments).

plain.[15] Specifically, we offer here a reading of the Scamander episode in Book 21 of the *Iliad* to demonstrate key features of literary war landscapes, to introduce the main themes of this volume, and to show how literary texts can offer insights not accessible to strict military-historical or topographical accounts of ancient wars.[16]

In Book 18 of the *Iliad*, after killing Patroclus and seizing from him the armour of Achilles, Hector persuades his fellow Trojans to make a second strike against the Greek ships on the following morning. The folly of this plan becomes clear when Achilles, clad in the new armour made for him by Hephaestus, rejoins the fighting in a fury over the killing of his companion. Book 20 ends with a vivid description of a blood-spattered Achilles on the rampage, trampling men and armour beneath his chariot as he single-handedly repels the Trojan advance. It may come as a surprise, then, that the poet starts Book 21 by pulling back from his tight focus on Achilles and emplacing the action in the landscape to a degree rarely seen in the epic's battle sequences. This focus on landscape centres on the river Scamander, who is enraged at having his stream clogged with Trojan corpses and rises to do battle with Achilles. The Greek hero escapes with his life thanks to Hera and Hephaestus, who subdue Scamander by scouring the entire Trojan plain with fire.

A play of perspectives

The Scamander episode offers valuable insights into how combatants experience landscape during battle, and how literature can communicate those experiences to the audience. The first eleven lines are especially rich from this standpoint, and are worth quoting in full:[17]

Ἀλλ᾽ ὅτε δὴ πόρον ἷξον ἐϋρρεῖος ποταμοῖο
Ξάνθου δινήεντος, ὃν ἀθάνατος τέκετο Ζεύς,
ἔνθα διατμήξας τοὺς μὲν πεδίον δὲ δίωκε
πρὸς πόλιν, ᾗ περ Ἀχαιοὶ ἀτυζόμενοι φοβέοντο
ἤματι τῷ προτέρῳ, ὅτε μαίνετο φαίδιμος Ἕκτωρ.   5
τῇ ῥ᾽ οἵ γε προχέοντο πεφυζότες, ἠέρα δ᾽ Ἥρη
πίτνα πρόσθε βαθεῖαν ἐρυκέμεν· ἡμίσεες δὲ
ἐς ποταμὸν εἰλεῦντο βαθύρροον ἀργυροδίνην.
ἐν δ᾽ ἔπεσον μεγάλῳ πατάγῳ, βράχε δ᾽ αἰπὰ ῥέεθρα,
ὄχθαι δ᾽ ἀμφὶ περὶ μεγάλ᾽ ἴαχον· οἳ δ᾽ ἀλαλητῷ   10
ἔννεον ἔνθα καὶ ἔνθα ἑλισσόμενοι περὶ δίνας.

---

[15] On the interrelationship between war and landscape in the *Iliad* in general, see e.g. Minchin (in this volume), Bouvier (1986) and Brockliss (2018).
[16] Our subsequent analysis of the Scamander episode makes little claim to originality: its aim here is rather to draw out, through a necessarily brief reading of this endlessly rich episode, some of the thematic threads which will tie together the chapters of this volume.
[17] The text of the *Iliad* is taken from Munro and Allen (1920); translations from Green (2019), slightly adapted.

> But when they came to the ford of the swift-flowing River,
> eddying Xanthus, whom immortal Zeus engendered,
> Achilles now split the rout. Some he pursued across the plain
> towards the city, where the Achaians were fleeing in panic
> the day before, when faced with illustrious Hector's fury –   5
> they'd broken, fled in disorder, and Hera had spread
> a dense mist in front to confuse them – but half the Trojans
> were herded into the River, deep-flowing and silver-eddied.
> In they splashed with great outcry: the deep streambed resounded,
> both riverbanks echoed the tumult as they went swimming   10
> this way and that, still shouting, spun round by the eddies.

These lines help Homer's audience envision the action taking place on the battlefield and keep track of the participants' positions, in relation both to each other and to fixed topographical points such as the coastline, the river, and the city of Troy itself.[18] The passage highlights how different participants in war experience the landscape differently. Lines 1–5 point to what Lewin terms the 'directedness' of war landscapes. Unlike a rounded, expansive peacetime landscape, the Trojan plain during the siege has a front and behind, with a boundary zone running perpendicularly along the river. The orientation to front and rear is different for the Greeks than for the Trojans, however. Achilles, who is the grammatical subject of the first main verb (δίωκε), here propels himself with the same powerful *forward* momentum he possessed at the close of Book 20. For him, moving from the ships to the river and beyond, means advancing toward his ultimate (military) objective: Troy. The Trojans' intuitive understanding of forward and behind is the opposite of his, since their objective is to pin the Greeks back against their ships and destroy both along with the camp. Lines 4–5 reinforce this point. This morning, the Trojans are being put to flight, driven back across the plain toward the only secure refuge that remains to them. But we are reminded that yesterday – when Hector, not Achilles, was raging (ὅτε μαίνετο φαίδιμος Ἕκτωρ) – it was the Greeks who fled in terror over the same ground. The directionality of their flight, and their experience of it, was then the same as the Trojans' is now (away from danger, across the boundary, back to safety behind their own lines), although the absolute *direction* was the exact opposite.[19] The river, meanwhile, is a common element in both groups' orientations to the landscape, functioning as the

---

[18] A comprehensive spatial reading of the *Iliad* and its landscape and landmarks is Clay (2011) – see especially chapter 3 on the Trojan plain. Cf. also De Jong (2012a) for a narratological analysis of space in the Homeric epics.

[19] Clay (2011: 45–8) emphasizes that 'left' and 'right' remain stable throughout the poem, the narrator's self-positioning providing 'a fixed point for viewing the action' from the perspective of the Greek camp. 'In sharing that perspective with the poet, we, the audience, become active spectators of the events in his narrative' (48). However, this fixity of narratorial perspective does not prevent the poet from indicating, as in the scene cited, that the directionality of the landscape is contingent and closely related to an individual's experience.

boundary that divides the contested space between the city and the camp.[20] By mentioning the ford (πόρος) in line 1, however, Homer stresses the permeability of the boundary and the lability of perspective in a dynamic combat landscape. The ford permitted the Trojans to sally forth and approach the Greek camp this morning; but it may now permit Achilles to cut a swath of destruction all the way to their gates.

This is a type of insight afforded by literary representations of combat: a text can offer its audience the opportunity to share in the perceptions of multiple individuals, to understand the same terrain as, in effect, multiple landscapes corresponding to multiple subjective experiences. In lines 6–11 of this passage, Homer ceases to emphasize the freedom and velocity with which Achilles blazes across the plain, scattering the panicked Trojan warriors before him, and conveys instead the Trojans' experience of being driven, confined, and confused. First, we hear that Hera restrains (ἐρυκέμεν) the men who are fleeing toward the city by spreading a thick cloud in their path. Then we learn that the rest of the Trojans are being crammed into the river (ἐς ποταμὸν εἰλεῦντο), where they make no headway trying to swim 'this way and that' (ἔνθα καὶ ἔνθα) against a current literally spinning them in circles (ἑλισσόμενοι περὶ δίνας). The same river that has at other times helped organize the terrain, separate the armies, and orient us as the audience of the poem – the river that has perhaps played a part in limiting the extent of space the Greeks might safely occupy – now completely *dis*orients these men, and us along with them.

Literary texts can also make their audiences experience a landscape of war to some extent, by evoking the kinds of sensory impressions normally unavailable to anyone not present in the spatial and temporal zone of combat.[21] Throughout the Scamander episode, Homer employs a blend of description and metaphor to bring to life not only the harrowing sights of the battlefield, but also the ambient noise and other sensations experienced by the combatants. We 'hear' the resounding roar of the river and screams of the drowning (9–10), the groaning of men slashed by Achilles' sword (20–1), and, later, the terrible clanging of his bronze armour when he flees from an enraged Scamander (254–5). Then, when Hephaestus scours the entire plain with fire at Hera's command, a pungent simile likening the river to a cauldron of bubbling pork fat engages the senses of both hearing and smell (361–4):[22]

ὡς δὲ λέβης ζεῖ ἔνδον ἐπειγόμενος πυρὶ πολλῷ
κνίσην μελδόμενος ἁπαλοτρεφέος σιάλοιο
πάντοθεν ἀμβολάδην, ὑπὸ δὲ ξύλα κάγκανα κεῖται,
ὣς τοῦ καλὰ ῥέεθρα πυρὶ φλέγετο, χέε δ' ὕδωρ.   365

---

[20] Clay (2011: 108) argues that the Scamander episode 'dramatically mark[s] the crucial point in Achilles' advance' when Achilles for the first time starts slaughtering Trojans on the 'Trojan' side of the river.
[21] On the spatial and temporal dimensions of the 'war zone', see McLaughlin (2011: chapter 3). On sense impressions and the war landscape of the *Iliad*, see Minchin (in this volume).
[22] Richardson (1993: *ad loc.*) also draws attention to the onomatopoeic effects of lines 363–4, suggesting first the 'sizzling of fat in the cauldron' and then the 'dry crackling' of wood.

> As a cauldron will boil over when forced by a hot fire,
> that's rendering down the lard of a fattened porker,
> bubbling up all round, dry firewood stacked beneath it –
> so the River's sweet streams blazed, and their water bubbled.   365

Although this simile is directly applied to the river, it suggests as well the twin odours of charred flesh and wood-smoke, which would have been present on the battlefield thanks to Hephaestus's having just set fire to both the bodies of Achilles' victims (343–4) and the many trees and plants growing along the banks of the Xanthus (350–2).

War and the natural world

In addition to illustrating the capacity of literary texts to convey experiential dimensions of war landscapes, the Scamander episode dramatizes the relationship between war and the natural world. The potentially devastating impact of war on the natural environment emerges strongly here as first Achilles, and then Hephaestus do violence to the non-human elements in the landscape. The fact that Scamander is a deity, empowered to speak and act in some ways like a person (212–13), means that we get to hear a river describe its own experience of being dammed up and polluted.[23] In an initial plea to Achilles to cease throwing bodies into the water, Scamander explains the discomfort he is feeling (218–20):

> πλήθει γὰρ δή μοι νεκύων ἐρατεινὰ ῥέεθρα,
> οὐδέ τί πη δύναμαι προχέειν ῥόον εἰς ἅλα δῖαν
> στεινόμος νεκύεσσι, σὺ δὲ κτείνεις ἀϊδήλως.   220

> 'My lovely streams are currently all awash with corpses;
> I can't get to discharge my waters into the bright sea,
> I'm so choked with the dead, while you ruthlessly keep on killing!'   220

Scamander later experiences pain of a different kind when, after first cremating the bodies of the men slain by Achilles, Hephaestus 'turn[s] his blazing flames' against Scamander (349). The river is set alight (356; καίετο); his water seethes (361; ἔφλυε) and boils (365; ζέε); and he halts once again, lacking the will to flow on (365; οὐδ᾽ ἔθελε προρέειν, ἀλλ᾽ ἴσχετο).

The onslaught of intense heat causes other sorts of damage as well. While Hera's principal aim in deploying her flame-throwing son is to punish Scamander, who has angered her with his assault on Achilles, she also explicitly commands Hephaestus to burn the trees along the river's banks (337–8; σὺ δὲ Ξάνθοιο παρ᾽ ὄχθας | δένδρεα καῖ᾽,

---

[23] Holmes (2015: 38).

ἐν δ' αὐτὸν ἵει πυρί).²⁴ Hephaestus complies, and the effect on the landscape is described in a catalogue of environmental destruction remarkable in its detail (350–5):

καίοντο πτελέαι τε καὶ ἰτέαι ἠδὲ μυρῖκαι,	350
καίετο δὲ λωτός τε ἰδὲ θρύον ἠδὲ κύπειρον,	
τὰ περὶ καλὰ ῥέεθρα ἅλις ποταμοῖο πεφύκει·	
τείροντ' ἐγχέλυές τε καὶ ἰχθύες οἳ κατὰ δίνας,	
οἳ κατὰ καλὰ ῥέεθρα κυβίστων ἔνθα καὶ ἔνθα	
πνοιῇ τειρόμενοι πολυμήτιος Ἡφαίστοιο.	355

The elms caught fire, and the willows and tamarisks,	350
the celandine burned, the rushes, the galingale – everything	
that grew in abundance along the sweet course of the River,	
and the eels and fish in the eddies were sorely distressed,	
somersaulting this way and that along the sweet streams,	355
tormented by the fire blast that wily Hephaestus discharged.	

These lines challenge our assumptions about Scamander's nature by showing his punishment shared out among the many species of plant and animal life that depend on him for their existence. It is as if 'Scamander' in a sense embodies an entire riparian ecosystem, the vulnerability of which undercuts our previous understanding of him as an immortal god.²⁵ The river will survive the conflagration, but without the trees that shade his banks, the rushes that grow where his waters are shallowest, the fish and eels that swim in his depths – we might wonder if he will truly be the same river as before.²⁶

Earlier in the episode, the poet makes a similar point in a different way. When describing Achilles' panicked flight from the river in the moments before Hera's intervention, he compares the murderous Scamander to an irrigation ditch that gets away from a farmer seeking to shape it with a mattock (21.257–66):

---

²⁴ It is important to remember that the struggle between Scamander and Hera/Hephaestus is part of the Theomachy ('Battle of the gods'), which commenced at the beginning of Book 20 and only concludes late in Book 21 (513). Compared to the other main pairings of Olympian oppositions (Poseidon vs. Apollo; Ares vs. Athena; Hera vs. Artemis; and Leto vs. Hermes), which never really amount to much, the brutal domination of Scamander by Hephaestus illustrates the defeat of the pro-Trojan gods in a particularly graphic way. From a narrative standpoint, it also removes one last barrier to the destruction of Troy, since Scamander vows under duress never to try to protect the city again (Holmes 2015: 44).

²⁵ Against such devastation, some of the other environmental impacts mentioned in the Scamander episode – a spear that pierces the earthen riverbank up to 'half its length' (169–72; μεσσοπαγές), for example, or a soldier's guts spilling out onto the sand at the river's edge (180–1) – may seem minor; yet it is difficult, amidst such a strong use of personification, not to feel the impact of that hard-thrown spear as a kind of wound. The burning of Scamander here also prefigures the city's actual burning and destruction, which lies in the future, though not within the scope of the poem (Holmes 2015: 47).

²⁶ Scamander appears almost eerily quiet at 24.349–51, when Hermes and Priam stop to water their mules and horses on their way to Achilles' encampment. Cf. Holmes (2015: 51) on Scamander's 'narrative dormancy' after Book 21, and Mackie (1999: 488–91) on Scamander's Stygian overtones in Book 24.

ὡς δ' ὅτ' ἀνὴρ ὀχετηγὸς ἀπὸ κρήνης μελανύδρου
ἂμ φυτὰ καὶ κήπους ὕδατι ῥόον ἡγεμονεύῃ
χερσὶ μάκελλαν ἔχων, ἀμάρης ἐξ ἔχματα βάλλων·
τοῦ μέν τε προρέοντος ὑπὸ ψηφῖδες ἅπασαι   260
ὀχλεῦνται· τὸ δέ τ' ὦκα κατειβόμενον κελαρύζει
χώρῳ ἔνι προαλεῖ, φθάνει δέ τε καὶ τὸν ἄγοντα·
ὣς αἰεὶ Ἀχιλῆα κιχήσατο κῦμα ῥόοιο . . .

As a man who digs a channel from a dark-water spring
to the plants in his garden will guide the water's flow,
mattock in hand to clear obstructions from the channel,
and, as the rill flows on, all the pebbles that litter its bed   260
are swept along with it while it chuckles quickly down
a slope in the channel, even getting ahead of its guide –
just so did the River's bore keep overtaking Achilles . . .

The inadequacy of this comparison to the situation at hand ironically highlights the very great distance that lies between the landscapes of war and peace, and raises the question of when or even whether the inhabitants of the Troad will be able to return to the agricultural and pastoral tasks that animate the peacetime landscape.[27] Nor is this the first time a simile has been used to raise such a question. In Book 2, in a passage immediately preceding the Catalogue of Ships, we hear that as the Greek tribes poured forth from their ships and shelters onto Scamander's plain (465–8),

αὐτὰρ ὑπὸ χθὼν   465
σμερδαλέον κονάβιζε ποδῶν αὐτῶν τε καὶ ἵππων.
ἔσταν δ' ἐν λειμῶνι Σκαμανδρίῳ ἀνθεμόεντι
μυρίοι, ὅσσά τε φύλλα καὶ ἄνθεα γίγνεται ὥρῃ.

Beneath the tread   465
of men and horses the earth re-echoed, a fearsome sound,
and they halted and stood, in Scamander's flowery meadow,
thousands strong, like leaves and blossoms in their season.

This apparently charming simile comparing the Greeks to leaves and flowers has a darker side. Whereas the meadow between the Xanthus and the sea is customarily filled with leaves and flowers 'in their season', it is now filled instead with armed invaders,

---

[27] Edwards (1987: 24–41) offers an excellent overview of the function of similes in Homer. De Jong (2012b: 22) notes that the majority of Iliadic similes show men engaged in a struggle against hostile nature (e.g. storms, flooding rivers, wild animals); peaceful subjects like irrigating a garden are the exception, which heightens the contrast between this simile's subject and the grim battlefield situation in this particular instance. See also Minchin, pp. 33–4 below, on the description at 22.153–6 of the two springs and adjacent stone washing tanks 'where the wives and lovely daughters | of the Trojans would formerly wash their glistening garments | in the days of peace, before the Achaeans' sons arrived'.

for whom one assumes there *is* no proper season – and whose continued active presence there may well prove detrimental to the native flora.[28] The dominant feature of the plain after nine years of fighting is, after all, dust.[29]

Fighting for control

Implicit in much of the foregoing discussion have been issues relating to the control of landscape. Combatants in a war tend to evaluate and make use of whatever features of their environment help them stay alive and achieve their objectives. In this episode, for example, we can see how the ford in the river has become a 'combat formation', something that was once part of the normal peacetime landscape and is now defined chiefly by its use to the soldier.[30] In that, it resembles the tamarisk bushes Achilles uses as a spear-rest when preparing to leap into the river carrying only his sword (21.17–18; δόρυ μὲν λίπεν αὐτοῦ ἐπ᾽ ὄχθῃ | κεκλιμένον μυρίκῃσιν). But of course, this landscape demonstrates in no uncertain terms that it will not willingly submit to being used or controlled by anyone, least of all Achilles. 'Scamander's agency is a force that, unchecked, threatens to derail the plot.'[31]

Confronted with Achilles in his fury, Scamander reveals himself to be a formidable opponent, and one loyal to the Trojans. He exhibits this partiality in various ways throughout the episode, as when, angered by Achilles' scornful flinging of Lycaon's corpse into the water, he 'ponder[s] in his mind how to make noble Achilles | stop his war work, how to fend off calamity from the Trojans' (136–8; ποταμὸς δὲ χολώσατο κηρόθι μᾶλλον, | ὅρμηνεν δ᾽ ἀνὰ θυμὸν ὅπως παύσειε πόνοιο | δῖον Ἀχιλλῆα, Τρώεσσι δὲ λοιγὸν ἀλάλκοι); or when he instils courage in the Trojan Asteropaeus, himself the grandson of the river Axios (145–7; μένος δε οἱ ἐν φρεσὶ θῆκε | Ξάνθος, ἐπεὶ κεχόλωτο δαϊκταμένων αἰζηῶν, | τοὺς Ἀχιλεὺς ἐδάϊζε κατὰ ῥόον οὐδ᾽ ἐλέαιρεν); or when, at last, he calls upon his brother-river Simois to help protect 'King Priam's great city' (309; ἄστυ μέγα Πριάμοιο ἄνακτος) from destruction at Achilles' hand. Then, when at last he is roused to face Achilles in physical combat, Scamander displays all the might one would expect from a son of Zeus. Not only does he forcibly eject from his waters all the corpses Achilles has deposited there, heaving them up onto dry land *en masse* while simultaneously sheltering living Trojans underwater 'in his eddies, which were both large and deep' (238–9; ζωοὺς δὲ σάω κατὰ καλὰ ῥέεθρα, | κρύπτων ἐν δίνῃσι βαθείῃσιν μεγάλῃσι), he also puts Achilles to flight and causes the seemingly invincible hero to fear for his life.

There is an oddly personal dimension to the way Achilles struggles for dominance over the river. Even before Scamander rises against him, Achilles shows a marked

---

[28] On the 'impossible season' of the *Iliad*, see Bouvier (1986: 238–41). Cf. also Holmes (2015: 29–30 with n. 4), on the natural forces' evacuation of the Trojan plain, leaving behind a 'weatherless space'; and Minchin below, p. 31 with n. 26.
[29] See Minchin below, p. 31; Bouvier (1986: 241–6).
[30] Lewin (2009: 205): 'That which lies within the combat zone belongs to the soldier as his rightful property, not because it has been captured … but because, as a combat formation, it is a military thing, which is naturally there for the soldier's benefit'.
[31] Holmes (2015: 48).

contempt for rivers. While taunting and despoiling the mortally wounded Asteropaeus, Achilles repeatedly denigrates the other man's descent from a river, especially when compared to his own Olympian lineage (21.190–3):

τῷ κρείσσων μὲν Ζεὺς ποταμῶν ἁλιμυρηέντων,	190
κρείσσων αὖτε Διὸς γενεὴ ποταμοῖο τέτυκται.	
καὶ γὰρ σοὶ ποταμός γε πάρα μέγας, εἰ δύναται τι	
χραισμεῖν: ἀλλ' οὐκ ἔστι Διὶ Κρονίωνι μάχεσθαι.	

'So, as Zeus is mightier than all seaward-flowing rivers,	190
Zeus's line likewise outranks a River's ancestry!	
You may have a great River beside you – always supposing	
it can protect you: but still there's no fighting Cronus's son Zeus!'	

This scornful attitude soon resurfaces when Achilles fears he will die in the sudden, violent flooding. Scamander harries him on, one moment beating down on him from above, the next moment tiring out his legs with strong current, and all the while pulling the ground from beneath his feet (21.268–71). At last Achilles cries out to Zeus, complaining of the disgraceful death he now faces. According to him, it seems, it is honourable neither to be born from a river, nor to be killed by one (279–83):

ὥς μ' ὄφελ' Ἕκτωρ κτεῖναι ὃς ἐνθάδε γ' ἔτραφ' ἄριστος:	
τῷ κ' ἀγαθὸς μὲν ἔπεφν', ἀγαθὸν δέ κεν ἐξενάριξε:	280
νῦν δέ με λευγαλέῳ θανάτῳ εἵμαρτο ἁλῶναι	
ἐρχθέντ' ἐν μεγάλῳ ποταμῷ ὡς παῖδα συφορβόν,	
ὅν ῥά τ' ἔναυλος ἀποέρσῃ χειμῶνι περῶντα.	

'If only Hector had killed me, the best-bred warrior here,	
then noble had been the slayer, noble the man he slew –	280
whereas now it's my wretched fate to perish miserably,	
trapped in a great river, like some swineherd's boy	
who's swept away by the torrent he tries to cross in winter.'	

In this moment, we watch Achilles come to grips with the fact that the landscape has established mastery over him, and not the reverse.[32] His outrage at losing control of his destiny may be familiar to soldiers who have worried about dying in some similarly 'inglorious' or 'unheroic' way.[33] Achilles' words, and especially the simile he uses to

---

[32] Holmes (2015) explores Scamander's 'objectifying powers': see esp. 31–2.
[33] Such concerns are often articulated in diaries and literary accounts of the Western Front during the First World War, where soldiers spent much of their time underground and where the inescapable mud, already saturated with the dead, claimed not a few soldiers' lives through drowning. As Saunders (2004: 9) writes: 'By smothering soldiers with debris, or sucking them down into glutinous mud, it seemed as if the earth itself was alive.' See also Gilbert (2013) on this and other antipastoral themes in First World War poetry.

describe himself dying in the torrent ('like some swineherd's boy'), suggest that such a death would erode his reputation as a brave man and perhaps even his identity as a warrior. It would also entail a loss, not just of bodily autonomy – death always takes that from us – but of his body, and with it the chance of receiving proper funeral rites.

Landscape and memory

We now come to the last key aspect of war landscapes illuminated by the Scamander episode, namely their association with memory. The struggle between Achilles and Scamander demonstrates especially clearly how the landscape of war may be implicated in an individual soldier's concern for his memory. In the culture of the *Iliad*, it was crucial that a fallen warrior's body be found and returned to his comrades or family for funerary rites and that a tomb or σῆμα be built to provide a focus for cult and remembrance later. This tomb would anchor his body, his name, and the orally transmitted record of his deeds in the (cultural) landscape, not unlike the Tomb of Ilus, the eponymous hero of Ilium (Troy), mentioned repeatedly in the poem.[34] To have one's tomb built in the landscape of war itself might not be a bad thing, as the known associations of the site would add luster to the burial even as the presence of a hero's monument would influence the way later visitors would navigate and interpret the site.[35]

In battle, however, the landscape itself may pose a threat to any who desire such an outcome. If a soldier's body cannot be recovered from the landscape of war, there will be no focus for mourning by his community, no natural locus for commemoration. That is the danger the river presents in this episode to those who die in or beside his waters. Achilles voices this threat initially when he taunts Lycaon, whom he has just run through with his sword and thrown into the river (122–7):

ἐνταυθοῖ νῦν κεῖσο μετ᾽ ἰχθύσιν, οἵ σ᾽ ὠτειλὴν
αἷμ᾽ ἀπολιχμήσονται ἀκηδέες· οὐδέ σε μήτηρ
ἐνθεμένη λεχέεσσι γοήσεται, ἀλλὰ Σκάμανδρος
οἴσει δινήεις εἴσω ἁλὸς εὐρέα κόλπον·   125
θρῴσκων τις κατὰ κῦμα μέλαιναν φρῖχ᾽ ὑπαΐξει
ἰχθύς, ὅς κε φάγῃσι Λυκάονος ἀργέτα δημόν.

'Lie there now with the fishes, that'll lick the blood
from your wound, quite indifferent to you; nor will your mother
lay you out on a bier and wail over you: rather will Scamander
roll you away in its eddies to the wide gulf of the sea,   125
and fish darting through the waves will surface amid
their black ripples to nibble Lycaon's white lustrous fat!'

---

[34] 10.415; 11.166, 372; 20.232, 236; 24.349. The last of these references is particularly important because the tomb of Ilus is part of series of markers that identify the boundary of the city of Troy beyond which Priam must venture to ransom the body of his son Hector.

[35] On *tumuli* in the Trojan landscape and the accretion of social memory around them, see Minchin (2016).

The very fate here described soon befalls Asteropaeus, when Achilles abandons his body at the water's edge and fish and eels begin to tear at the flesh (203–4); it seems not even the river's partiality for the Trojans can prevent nature from taking its course in this way. And Scamander himself is clearly aware of the potent threat he poses, since he says in his appeal to Simois (316–23):

> φημὶ γὰρ οὔτε βίην χραισμησέμεν οὔτέ τι εἶδος
> οὔτε τὰ τεύχεα καλά, τά που μάλα νειόθι λίμνης
> κείσεθ᾿ ὑπ᾿ ἰλύος κεκαλυμμένα· κὰδ δέ μιν αὐτὸν
> εἰλύσω ψαμάθοισιν ἅλις χέραδος περιχεύας
> μυρίον, οὐδέ οἱ ὀστέ᾿ ἐπιστήσονται Ἀχαιοὶ   320
> ἀλλέξαι· τόσσην οἱ ἄσιν καθύπερθε καλύψω.
> αὐτοῦ οἱ καὶ σῆμα τετεύξεται, οὐδέ τί μιν χρεὼ
> ἔσται τυμβοχόης, ὅτε μιν θάπτωσιν Ἀχαιοί.

> 'For I tell you, neither [Achilles'] violence nor his good looks will save him,
> nor his fine armour, which in some flooded pool of mine
> will lie, all coated with mud; while the man himself
> I'll wrap in sand, pour over him an abundance of shingle.
> That way the Achaeans will have no idea where to gather   320
> his bones, under such a mass of silt I shall entomb him!
> Here will his grave be prepared, and he'll have no need
> of a burial mound, when Achaeans perform his funeral rites.'

Scamander thus proposes to bury Achilles under his own version of a tumulus, one that would not memorialize the hero but rather condemn him to the same kind of erasure, of both body and memory, that Achilles has already tried to inflict on his many Trojan victims.

Memory and commemoration function in this part of the poem in more abstract ways as well. For example, we might read Achilles' entire killing spree, his strewing of the plain and stuffing of the river with dead Trojans, as an attempt to construct a gruesome kind of landscape memorial to Patroclus. Homer's audience knows that Patroclus would not have wanted such a tribute, and even Lycaon intimates as much when he mentions Patroclus's gentleness (96; ἑταῖρον ... ἐνηέα) to try and elicit pity from Achilles. But as we have seen, Achilles' attempt to construct any such 'memorial' is doomed to fail, since Scamander and Hephaestus together deprive him of its 'monuments' or *topoi* by first removing the bodies of his victims from the river and then incinerating them. In a similar way, we know from Book 12 that the Trojan rivers will eventually join forces to tear down the Achaean wall, an act that has been interpreted as an attempt to ensure that the Trojan landscape will not be dominated by memories of the Greek invaders.[36] And even hundreds of years later, we can see the Roman poet Lucan

---

[36] Holmes (2015: 35).

renegotiate the dynamics of remembrance and forgetting in this same landscape of war, when Caesar tours the Trojan plain in Book 9 of the *Bellum Civile*. This Scamander is indeed a very different river from the one who rose to stand against Achilles; Caesar steps right over him without recognizing or even seeming to notice the trickle of a stream beneath his feet.[37]

3 This volume

I. Perception and experience of war landscapes

People experience landscape differently in wartime. Combatants, for example, will tend to interpret landscape features from a tactical standpoint, valuing them according to the extent to which they offer help or hindrance, hazard or refuge.[38] Equally, people experience different things in wartime landscapes than they do in peacetime ones, inasmuch as combat involves a complex multisensory experience unavailable to anyone outside the war zone.[39] Moreover, landscapes of war often provoke intense emotions less often encountered in peacetime landscapes, such as rage, fear and dread.[40]

Authors of literary texts are able to communicate some of these perceptions and experiences of war landscapes to their audiences, whether that means reminding combat veterans of their experiences, or giving people who have never been in combat the merest hint of what it might be like. The chapters in this section deal with just such issues of perception and experience in literary war landscapes, focusing in particular on questions such as: What impressions and experiences from war landscapes do Greek and Roman authors communicate to their audiences? What techniques do they use to do so? And what purposes, literary or metaliterary, do such representations serve?

In the first article in the section, Minchin uses theories from the work of cognitive psychologists H. A. Taylor and B. Tversky to explore techniques used by Homer to bring his audience into the landscape of the Trojan War. She explains how he provides, on the one hand, sparse but economical/strategic 'locative information' (selected topographical landmarks) for the audience to use in creating a 3D 'spatial mental model', and on the other, 'nonlocative information' pertaining to the realm of experience (e.g. visual and auditory impressions, similes, descriptions of contrasting landscapes) from multiple points of view, with which the audience builds a 'cognitive collage'. In this way, Homer is able to create an immersive experience, analogous to

---

[37] Lucan, *BC* 9.974–5. See Weiner (in this volume) with further references. Cf. also Labate (1991: 182–3) on Lucan's debt to the scene in the *Aeneid* where Aeneas visits the 'little Troy' (3.349; *parvam Troiam*) – complete with 'a dried-up stream going by the name of Xanthus' (350; *arentem Xanthi cognomine rivum*) – mapped onto the Chaonian landscape by Helenus and Andromache.
[38] Appleton (1996) with McLoughlin (2011: 91–5). See also Lewin (1917).
[39] McLoughlin (2011: chapter 3).
[40] On fear, see Tuan (1979); on dread, Felton and Gilhuly (2018).

that available in the First World War galleries of the Australian War Memorial, but using only words.

In the second chapter, Fabrizi takes up another important dimension of war landscapes, namely atmospheric phenomena. While far less durable than topography and other landscape features, weather conditions nonetheless exert a powerful influence on how combatants perceive and experience the landscapes they fight in. Fabrizi focuses in particular on representations of atmospheric phenomena in Livy's battle narratives. She takes an essentially narratological approach, in that she is interested not only in how these phenomena condition soldiers' experiences of landscape in the *AUC*, but also in how including these details helps Livy achieve his narrative goals. She shows that Livy's depictions of the dynamic relationship between topography and weather reveal the war landscape to be a living environment that not only can help or hinder human action 'on the ground', but which an author can use to reflect characters' morals or psychological states and to involve the reader more deeply through focalization or by creating suspense.

The last chapter in the section, by Feldherr, continues the focus on weather conditions and narrative technique in Livy's history. Feldherr focuses primarily on one battle narrative (Lake Trasimene) and compares it closely with Polybius's account of the same battle. In a similar vein to Fabrizi, Feldherr reads the mist in Livy's account of Lake Trasimene – or, rather, Livy's representation of the Roman soldiers' *experience of the landscape in* the mist – as symbolizing something about the Roman army as a whole, namely the lack of strategic cognition and strong leadership that led to the men's lack of preparedness and, ultimately, many deaths by drowning. But Feldherr's main interest lies in the way Livy and Polybius use their representations of the same event to make different metaliterary points about historiography and the extent to which it can – or even should – attempt to make the reader see events like they were there themselves. Lake Trasimene makes a powerful case study for Feldherr's study of *enargeia* and the challenges it posed to ancient readers, precisely because of the way the internal audience experienced the landscape of battle: making readers see Trasimene like they were participants, would mean blinding them (and, in Livy's case, making them experience complete sensory disorientation).

These three chapters thus furnish fruitful examples – both Roman and Greek, in both poetry and prose – of literary war landscapes that give readers some sense of what it might have been like to be there in the landscape themselves. Furthermore, Minchin, Fabrizi and Feldherr are united in their interest in the *how* and especially the *why* of this: *How* did writers like Homer and Livy communicate soldiers' perceptions and experiences to their audiences; *why* did they do it; and *why* did they do it in the way that they did? It turns out that literary war landscapes were sometimes shaped by the nature of literature as much as by that of war.

II. Landscapes of ruin and recovery

The relationship of war to the natural world is both vexed and complex. This is the territory staked out by the chapters in this section, all of which approach ancient literary landscapes of war from an ecocritical perspective.[41] In general, war tends to exert a negative and destructive influence on the environment. This was true even in antiquity, when military operations caused environmental problems such as wildfires, deforestation, the diversion and pollution of water courses, and the destruction of crops.[42] These and other environmental impacts could last beyond the duration of the conflict, delaying or preventing the inhabitants' return to farming and other peacetime activities. Ancient writers crafted powerful responses to such concrete environmental consequences: for example, Zientek in this volume studies Lucan's treatment of agricultural fertility as it is compromised by armed conflict.

All three authors in this section also deal to some extent with representations of war's impact on landscape that veer from the realistic into the symbolic. Idealized conceptions of landscape often come into play during war, not because warfare makes landscapes idyllic, but because, on the contrary, it brings the threat of land being seized, ruined, or rendered hateful by association with painful memories. Just so, Brockliss finds in modern war poetry a useful model for understanding an ancient text that presents an exaggeratedly idealized version of what was in fact a landscape of tension and violence. Makins, like Zientek, deals with poems depicting the lingering effects of war on the natural world; but here, as in the text treated by Brockliss, the impact of the depiction derives from its fantastical nature.

The chapters in this section thus demonstrate the range of effects authors can achieve by engaging, either implicitly or explicitly, with images of idealized landscapes in the context of war and its aftermath. Such images can inspire and console; they can elicit painful longing and nostalgia; and, especially when the failure of environmental recovery is emphasized, they can express concerns about the lingering impact of conflict on the broader social landscape as well.

Laura Zientek's chapter, the first in the section, explores the theme of agricultural recovery in Lucan's war landscapes. After discussing key literary and historical precursors, ranging from Aeschylus to Plutarch, Zientek shows how Lucan both alludes to and departs from his predecessors: he disrupts the war-recovery cycle enshrined in earlier literature by highlighting the desolation and toxicity of post-war landscapes, as well as the self-perpetuating nature of war.

William Brockliss adopts an innovative approach in his chapter, arguing that comparison with First World War poetry can yield valuable insights into Sophocles' treatment of landscape in *Oedipus at Colonus*. By reading the landscapes of the *Oedipus at Colonus* alongside poems by Wilfred Owen, Ivor Gurney and others, Brockliss reveals the idealized nature of Sophocles' descriptions of the Attic countryside and explores how a contemporary audience might have reacted to them in the aftermath of the Deceleian War.

---

[41] 'Simply put, ecocriticism is the study of the relationship between literature and the physical environment' (Glotfelty 1996: xix). Recent work applying ecocritical approaches to Greek and Roman literature can be found in Felton (2018) and Schliephake (2017).
[42] Hughes (2013).

In the third and final chapter, Marian Makins examines post-war landscapes in the *Elegies* of Propertius through an ecocritical lens. Focusing on landscape descriptions associated with the Perusine War, the Roman conquest of Veii and the battle of Actium, Makins looks at how personification allows these literary landscapes to express positions that challenge both the dominant narrative of Augustan peace and the poet's own authoritative voice.

III. Controlling landscapes and the symbolism of power

Landscapes are fought over in a bid to gain control over a territory and its inhabitants. Such control may be established in a variety of ways, both physical and symbolic. In this section of the volume, we investigate how literary texts represent attempts to control landscapes, and the ways in which such control can fail. We also investigate how texts themselves can play a part in establishing and challenging such control over landscapes.

Control of landscape is at issue in combat on a tactical level: soldiers attempt to master the terrain in which they fight, while the make-up of the terrain influences armies' strategy and tactics. The chapters in this section explore the underlying reasons which authors suggest for failed efforts at control, such as inadequate geographic understanding or a lack of moral fibre in an army or commander in the face of natural challenges.

Establishing control over terrain is often made more challenging when aspects of the landscape appear to 'fight back'. Language used in combat often hints at this, as we hear of terrain 'aiding' or 'hindering' one side or the other, even at times appearing to switch allegiances or betray one group when their positions and objectives change. Such resistance can come in the form of seemingly intractable elements of the terrain, such as marshes, or even inclement weather conditions like rain or fog.[43] But authors of war literature frequently amplify this type of conflict between humans and landscape through personification and other types of metaphor. We have seen already how a river's defiance, usually regarded as figurative, becomes literal in the Scamander episode. The chapters in this section further investigate how and why landscapes themselves are depicted as resisting their would-be conquerors' efforts at controlling them.

Finally, control over landscape can be expressed and established symbolically. Literary texts reflect on such symbolically charged displays of control, which include the erection of trophies or the construction of bridges.[44] Texts can also themselves be part of efforts to communicate and thereby establish territorial control, for example when geographical or ethnographical exploration functions as a tool for the expression of control, or when literary authors manipulate or overwrite historical narratives connected with particular places.

In the first chapter in this section, Esther Meijer focuses on Caesar's crossing of the Rubicon in Lucan's *Bellum Civile*. She explores the general's superficially successful

---

[43] Biggs (2019), Östenberg (2018), Van Broeck (2018).
[44] See generally Hölscher (2006).

attempt to control the landscape physically: the river swells in protest, but cannot prevent the illegal crossing. Through the performance of a mock-fetial ritual, Caesar attempts to transform the river from a legal boundary into a material obstacle. Even though he momentarily seems to achieve physical and legal control over this liminal landscape, Meijer argues that Lucan in fact turns Caesar's crossing of the Rubicon into an emblem of the geographic and political disorder and lawlessness that forms the theme of the entire *Bellum Civile*.

Bettina Reitz-Joosse discusses Roman literary representations of Parthia as a 'landscape of defeat' during the principate. She argues that Roman authors construct inadequacy of geographic and ethnographic understanding as the basis of Roman military failures in Parthia, and considers how these writers envisage the lasting effect of Roman defeat on the landscape of Parthia. In writing Parthia as a 'landscape of defeat', Ovid, Propertius and other authors depict the failures of established Roman modes of understanding, conquering and controlling landscapes in Parthia.

Finally, Karine Laporte argues that in Herodian's *History of the Roman Empire*, the depiction and staging of war landscapes and their manipulation in the course of fighting are made to symbolize the individual characters of his protagonists. Focusing on the war between Pescennius Niger and Septimius Severus in 193–194 CE, she investigates how Herodian uses landscapes of war to build his story and reveal the key features of the main characters. Herodian's representation of the city of Byzantium, a pass at Mount Taurus and a plain near Issus are used to articulate the characteristics of the contenders and, more generally, the nature of imperial power.

IV. Memory in war landscapes

Landscapes play an important role in the processes of remembering and forgetting armed conflicts, and the papers in this section explore the way in which literary texts and their narratives participate in and reflect on these processes. 'Memory studies' have now been flourishing for decades, and the chapters in this section build on some of the central tenets of the field: that memories are not only individual but also created and formed collectively and across generations; that such communal memories are constitutive for identity formations of groups and societies; and – most importantly in the context of this volume – that such memories often crystallize around certain 'sites'.[45]

An understanding of the working of memory is crucial to an investigation of landscapes in the richest sense. Schama, in his seminal study on 'Landscape and Memory',

---

[45] For an introduction to the field see e.g. Erll and Nünning (2010); for a recent overview of memory studies and the Classics see e.g. the introduction to Galinsky (2016). The strong relationship between place and memory has been inherent in the field of inquiry from its inception: cf. Maurice Halbwachs's trailblazing study on collective memory and the sites of the Holy Land (Halbwachs (1941)). Pierre Nora's influential 'lieux de mémoire' conceive of 'sites' in a metaphorical rather than topographical sense, but the concept has often been developed as a means of considering the relationship between place and memory specifically: for example, Winter (2010: 61), writing about the 'shadow of war', defines 'sites of memory' as 'physical sites where commemorative acts take place'.

famously writes that '... landscape is a work of the mind. Its scenery is built up as much from strata of memory as from layers of rock.'[46] In their investigation of war landscapes and their memory, van Rookhuijzen and Weiner both deploy Assmann's concept of the 'mnemotope', a term which Assmann originally introduced to describe an entire landscape serving as the medium of cultural memory.[47] While this concept and terminology might initially be thought to foreground the stability and situatedness of memory across time, all three authors of this section in fact stress, in line with more recent trends in memory studies, the essentially dynamic nature of memory formation in relation to places.[48] In their investigations they explore, for example, processes of layering (Mackie), reinvention and resituation (van Rookhuijzen), and overwriting and 'mutation' (Weiner) in war landscapes, foregrounding the agency of texts and narratives in these processes.[49]

In his chapter, van Rookhuijzen interrogates the relationship between landscape and war memory in a case where the 'landscape' is, in fact, the sea. Focusing on the battle of Salamis, he elucidates the process of the creation of mnemotopes of the battle, which grew up around the peculiarities of the coastal terrain, community practices of commemoration, physical monumentalization, and storytelling and literary engagement with topographic features of the coastline.

Mackie's chapter focuses on the landscape of the Dardanelles, which he reads as a landscape 'defined by war more than any other single area of the ancient Mediterranean world'.[50] His chapter moves beyond the often stressed Homeric war topography in the region, emphasizing how the landscape of the Dardanelles was already in antiquity the site of many (mythical and actual) conflicts: from the precursors of the Trojan War to the Persian campaigns, the Peloponnesian War and Alexander's Macedonian campaigns. The memories of these conflicts and their physical and literary memorials already overlay, reinforce and jostle one another in antiquity. Mackie also looks forward to the Gallipoli campaign, showing how striking continuities of conflict in the area inform our understanding of ancient war narratives; and, conversely, how ancient sites of

---

[46] Schama (1995: 7). An excellent overview of the relationship between memories and landscapes, with a focus on its dynamic nature, is Holtorf and Williams (2006)'s exploration of 'accumulative landscapes'.
[47] Assmann (1992: 60): 'Sogar und gerade *ganze Landschaften* können als Medium des kulturellen Gedächtnisses dienen ... die konkrete Verortung von Erinnerungen in einer erinnerungsträchtigen, bedeutungsgeladenen Landschaft' (our emphasis).
[48] For example, ten years ago, Erll and Rigney (2009: 2) sensed in the field 'a shift towards understanding cultural memory in more dynamic terms: as an ongoing process of remembrance and forgetting in which individuals and groups continue to reconfigure their relationship to the past and hence reposition themselves in relation to established and emergent memory sites'.
[49] Rigney (2010: 350–2) argues that we should think of texts as both 'agents' and 'monuments': texts can be agents, in that they relay, stabilize or destabilize memories, and they can also (and often at the same time) be the objects of recollection, which, by virtue of being recalled, are continually revised and recoded. Holtorf and Williams (2006) argue that 'in landscapes where people experienced war, migration or death, all of which are largely invisible and easily "forgotten", selected memories can distil in other media ... Memories can be present in landscapes of the imagination' (239–40). Makins (2013) and Reitz-Joosse (2016) specifically investigate instances of ancient literature shaping the power of landscape to recall wars and their consequences.
[50] Mackie (in this volume: p. 229).

war and their mnemonic power impinged on the experience of participants in the grim battles of the First World War.

Finally, Weiner's contribution concludes the volume with an investigation of particularly divisive *loci* of memory production: civil war landscapes. Through a reading of monuments in Lucan's *Bellum Civile*, contrasted and compared to Yugoslav war monuments and their contemporary and later reception, Weiner argues that wars and their monuments create landscapes of memory that are dynamic and unstable. He shows how Lucan's depiction of a number of Roman monuments both problematizes and performs their 'mutability', comparing this process to the way that Tito's *Spomeniks*, designed to commemorate the Second World War in a unifying and healing way, soon engendered anger and neglect in a changed political situation of renewed civil war. While monuments remain mnemotopes, the memories they anchor and produce can change drastically.

The themes explored in these four sections are naturally not confined only to their respective chapters. For example, the theme of memory and its relation to landscape is explored most fully in the final section of the volume, but also discussed in the chapters of Makins, Meijer and Reitz-Joosse; the interrelation between landscape and the personality and character of those engaging with it is especially explored by Feldherr, Fabrizi and Laporte; and the agency of landscapes in war and conflict surfaces in all four sections and almost every chapter, explored from a variety of different angles. Indeed, we hope that upon reading this volume, it will become clear that the chapters are interconnected by a whole web of thematic threads. We and all authors have aimed to translate some of the spirited debates which engendered this book at the 2017 Celtic Conference in Classics onto the printed page, and we hope that our readers will feel inspired to join the conversation and continue it into the future.

Bibliography

Antrop, M. 2018. 'A Brief History of Landscape Research.' In *The Routledge Companion to Landscape Studies*, edited by P. Howard, I. Thompson, E. Waterton and M. Atha, 1–15. London: Routledge.
Appleton, J. 1996. *The Experience of Landscape*. Rev. edn. New York: John Wiley & Sons.
Assmann, J. 1992. *Das kulturelle Gedächtnis*. Munich: C. H. Beck.
Bender, B. 1993. *Landscape. Politics and Perspectives*. Providence, RI: Berg.
Biggs, T. 2019. 'Campania at War in Silius Italicus' *Punica*.' In *Campania in the Flavian Poetic Imagination*, edited by A. Augoustakis and R. J. Littleman, 201–17. Oxford: Oxford University Press.
Bouvier, D. 1986. 'La tempête de la guerre. Remarques sur l'heure et le lieu du combat dans l'*Iliade*.' *Métis* 1: 237–57.
Brockliss, W. 2018. 'Abject Landscapes in the *Iliad*.' In *Landscapes of Dread in Classical Antiquity: Negative Emotion in Natural and Constructed Spaces*, edited by D. Felton, 15–37. Oxford and New York: Routledge.
Cosgrove, D. 1984. *Social Formation and Symbolic Landscape*. London: Croom Helm.
Edwards, M. 1987. *Homer, Poet of the Iliad*. Baltimore: Johns Hopkins University Press.
De Jong, I. J. F. 2012. 'Homer.' In *Space in Ancient Greek Narrative*, edited by I. J. F. de Jong, 22–38. Leiden: Brill.
De Jong, I. J. F. 2012b. *Homer: Iliad. Book XXII*. Cambridge and New York: Cambridge University Press.

Erll, A. and A. Nünning, eds. 2010. *A Companion to Cultural Memory Studies: An International and Interdisciplinary Handbook*. Berlin and Boston: De Gruyter.

Erll, A. and A. Rigney. 2009. 'Introduction: Cultural Memory and Its Dynamics.' In *Mediation, Remediation, and the Dynamics of Cultural Memory*, edited by A. Erll and A. Rigney, 1–11. Berlin and Boston: De Gruyter.

Felton, D., ed. 2018. *Landscapes of Dread in Classical Antiquity: Negative Emotion in Natural and Constructed Spaces*. Oxford and New York: Routledge.

Felton, D. and K. Gilhuly. 2018. 'Dread and the Landscape.' In *Landscapes of Dread in Classical Antiquity: Negative Emotion in Natural and Constructed Spaces*, edited by D. Felton, 1–11. Oxford and New York: Routledge.

Galinsky, K., ed. 2016. *Memory in Ancient Rome and Early Christianity*. Oxford and New York: Oxford University Press.

Gilbert, S. M. 1999. '"Rats' Alley": The Great War, Modernism, and the (Anti)Pastoral Elegy.' *New Literary History* 30 (1): 179–201.

Glotfelty, C. 1996. 'Introduction: Literary Studies in an Age of Environmental Crisis.' In *The Ecocriticism Reader: Landmarks in Literary Ecology*, edited by C. Glotfelty and H. Fromm, xv–xxxvii. Athens, GA and London: University of Georgia Press.

Green, P., trans. *Homer. The Iliad*. Berkeley: University of California Press.

Halbwachs, M. 1941. *La topographie légendaire des évangiles en terre sainte: Étude de mémoire collective*. Paris: Presses Universitaires de France.

Holmes, B. 2015. 'Situating Scamander: "Natureculture" in the *Iliad*.' *Ramus* 44 (1/2): 29–51.

Hölscher, T. 2006. 'The Transformation of Victory into Power: From Event to Structure.' In *Representations of War in Ancient Rome*, edited by S. Dillon and K. E. Welch, 27–48. Cambridge: Cambridge University Press.

Holtorf, C. and H. Williams. 2006. 'Landscapes and Memories.' In *The Cambridge Companion to Historical Archaeology*, edited by D. Hicks and M. C. Beaudry, 235–54. Cambridge: Cambridge University Press.

Hughes, J. D. 2013. 'Warfare and Environment in the Ancient World.' In *The Oxford Handbook of Warfare in the Classical World*, edited by B. Campbell and L. A. Tritle, 128–39. Oxford and New York: Oxford University Press.

Labate, M. 1991. 'Città morte, città future: un tema della poesia augustea.' *Maia* 43: 167–84.

Larsen, S. E. 2004. 'Landscape, Identity, and War.' *New Literary History* 35 (3): 469–90.

Lewin, K. 1917. 'Kriegslandschaft.' *Zeitschrift für angewandte Psychologie* 12: 440–7.

Lewin, K. 2009. 'The Landscape of War', trans. J. Blower. *Art in Translation* 1 (2): 199–209.

Lewin, M. 1992. 'The Impact of Kurt Lewin's Life on the Place of Social Issues in His Work.' *Journal of Social Issues* 48 (2): 15–29.

Mackie, C. J. 1999. 'Scamander and the Rivers of Hades in Homer.' *American Journal of Philology* 120 (4): 485–501.

Marrow, A. J. 1992. *The Practical Theorist: The Life and Work of Kurt Lewin*. New York and London: Basic Books.

Mayo, J. M. 1988. 'War Memorials as Political Memory.' *Geographical Review* 78 (1): 62–75.

McLaughlin, K. 2011. *Authoring War: The Literary Representation of War from the Iliad to Iraq*. Cambridge: Cambridge University Press.

Makins, M. 2013. 'Monumental Losses: Confronting the Aftermath of Battle in Roman Literature.' PhD diss., University of Pennsylvania.

Minchin, E. 2012. 'Commemoration and Pilgrimage in the Ancient World: Troy and the Stratigraphy of Cultural Memory.' *Greece & Rome* 59 (1): 76–89.

Minchin, E. 2016. 'Heritage in the Landscape: The "Heroic Tumuli" in the Troad Region.' In *Valuing Landscape in Classical Antiquity: Natural Environment and Cultural Imagination*, edited by J. McInerney and I. Sluiter, 255–75. Leiden and Boston: Brill.

Munro, D. B. and T. W. Allen, eds. 1920. *Homeri Opera*, 2 vols. 3rd edn. Oxford: Oxford University Press.

Östenberg, I. 2017. 'Defeated by the Forest, the Pass, the Wind: Nature as an Enemy of Rome.' In *Brill's Companion to Military Defeat in Ancient Mediterranean Society*, edited by J. Clark and B. Turner, 240–61. Leiden and Boston: Brill.

Reitz-Joosse, B. L. 2016. 'Land at Peace and Sea at War: Landscape and the Memory of Actium in Greek Epigrams and Propertius.' In *Valuing Landscape in Classical Antiquity: Natural Environment and Cultural Imagination*, edited by J. McInerney and I. Sluiter, 276–96. Leiden and Boston: Brill.

Rigney, A. 2010. 'The Dynamics of Remembrance: Texts between Monumentality and Morphing.' In *A Companion to Cultural Memory Studies*, edited by A. Erll and A. Nünning, 345–53. Berlin and Boston: De Gruyter.

Rossi, A. 2001. 'Remapping the Past: Caesar's Tale of Troy (Lucan *BC* 9.964–999).' *Phoenix* 55 (3/4): 313–26.

Saunders, N. J. 2004. 'Material Culture and Conflict: The Great War, 1914–2003.' In *Matters of Conflict: Material Culture, Memory and the First World War*, edited by N. J. Saunders, 5–25. London and New York: Routledge.

Schama, S. 1995. *Landscape and Memory*. London: HarperCollins.

Schliephake, C., ed. 2017. *Ecocriticism, Ecology, and the Cultures of Antiquity*. London: Lexington Books.

Stein-Hölkeskamp, E. and K. Hölkeskamp, eds. 2006. *Erinnerungsorte der Antike: Die römische Welt*. München: Beck.

Tuan, Y.-F. 1979. *Landscapes of Fear*. New York: Pantheon Books.

Van Broeck, L. 2018. 'Wily Wetlands: Imperialism and Resistance in Tacitus' Batavian Revolt.' in *Landscapes of Dread in Classical Antiquity: Negative Emotion in Natural and Constructed Spaces*, edited by D. Felton, 145–62. Oxford and New York: Routledge.

Winter, J. 2010. 'Sites of Memory and the Shadow of War.' In *A Companion to Cultural Memory Studies*, edited by A. Erll and A. Nünning, 61–74. Berlin and Boston: De Gruyter.

PART I
PERCEPTION AND EXPERIENCE OF WAR LANDSCAPES

CHAPTER 1
HOMER'S LANDSCAPE OF WAR: SPATIAL MENTAL MODEL AND COGNITIVE COLLAGE
Elizabeth Minchin

1 Introduction

This discussion begins in the Australian War Memorial (AWM) in Canberra. Here in the galleries devoted to the First World War we find a series of dioramas representing significant battles in which Australian forces had been involved: on the Western Front (e.g. the battlefields of the Somme, Pozières and Passchendaele (Ypres)) and on the Gallipoli Peninsula (Lone Pine), not so distant from the plain of Troy across the strait (Fig. 1.1).[1] As we study these fabricated landscapes of war our attention is held by two aspects of these representations: by the *topography* itself and by the evidence of human presence, of *life experienced*. The battlefields represented here are, as we would expect, uniformly bleak and desolate: the terrain is irregular, eaten away by shelling; buildings have been reduced to rubble; instead of the trees and grasses that had once covered the land we see nothing but mud; and here in the mud our eyes linger for a moment on the bodies of the wounded and the dead. Our attention is drawn away, inevitably, to the figures of fighting men, arrested, as it were, in the midst of action: we see them, picked out by subtle lighting effects, moving around below ground level in the trenches – the trenches that characterize First World War operations – and, on the surface, hurling grenades, attending to their guns, striking out across no man's land or being overwhelmed by enemy fire.[2]

When they were first displayed, in Melbourne and then Sydney in the 1920s, and eventually, in 1941, in the newly built Australian War Memorial in Canberra, these

---

[1] These dioramas of distant fields of war represent the vision of Charles Bean, the Australian official war correspondent for the First World War and subsequently the founder of the Australian War Memorial. They were created for Australians in the 1920s, at a time when overseas travel was neither relatively affordable nor easy, whereas for Europeans, should they so wish, it would be possible to visit sites and cemeteries, and to remember the sacrifices of war now inscribed in the landscape. The dioramas under discussion here, fabricated in Melbourne by a team led by hand-picked artists and sculptors, would show the conditions under which Australian troops fought and would interpret significant battles in detail. With Australian visitors in mind they would help tell the full story of the war (Back and Webster 2008: 7–8). This chapter has benefited from the comments and suggestions of a number of participants in the Landscapes of War panel at the 10th Celtic Conference in Classics, in Montréal. I am very grateful to them all.
[2] This is not surprising: psychology tells us that human figures (and their faces) are given special and sustained perceptual attention by viewers of scenes of all kinds: Fletcher-Watson, Findlay, Leekam and Benson (2008: 580–2). For further discussion of the importance of figures in a landscape, see below.

Figure 1.1 Wallace Anderson and Louis McCubbin (fabricators): Lone Pine (Gallipoli Peninsula) diorama (AWM ART41017).

dioramas were on view in the hush of a museum gallery.[3] Intended for silent contemplation they were devised to give the viewer a sense of what had actually occurred (this was the reality of war) and to have an emotional impact.[4] More recently, however, in a rejection of stillness and silence, the experience has been extended beyond the visual. The galleries in which these models are displayed were refurbished in 2015; they are now filled with recorded sound: the sharp shock of gunfire, the resonance of exploding shells.[5] Each diorama is now accompanied too by interactive electronic displays that contextualize the battle, evaluate its significance and list casualty numbers. And, for those who wish to learn more, trained guides make themselves available to answer questions and to share their deeper knowledge. The experience of the diorama – the scene before one's eyes, the sounds playing in one's ears, the signage, and the oral commentary – is now more than instructive; it is immersive, absorbing.[6] This is as close as many of us will come to a landscape of war.

The first literary work that has survived to us in the Western tradition was also preoccupied with warfare, with its glory, with its pathos and with its consequences for the lives of those caught up in its wake. Like the creators of the AWM dioramas, the poet of the *Iliad* creates a grim and desolate terrain; *unlike* the creators of the dioramas, his principal tools are words. My aim in this chapter is to analyse how a traditional poet succeeds in creating, in the minds of his audience members, a landscape as grim and as

---

[3] Back and Webster (2008: 29, 34–5, 74–5).
[4] To this end Bean insisted that these dioramas should aspire to be 'high art', on the same level as painting or sculpture: Back and Webster (2008: 16 and 22).
[5] Ryan Johnston, at the time head of art at the Australian War Memorial, assured me that the soundscape is a mélange of 'historical artillery fire'. I thank Ryan for giving up time to talk to me about the First World War dioramas from a curatorial perspective.
[6] In recently constructed galleries of the AWM, and in war museums elsewhere, visitors can experience the battlefield landscape even more intimately: for tactile experiences, for example, as well as visual and auditory, visitors may walk through First World War trenches or they can climb aboard Vietnam war helicopters and 'operate' them in simulated conditions. There has even been the brief opportunity, in an exhibition at the Deutschen Militärhistorischen Museum in Dresden, to explore the smell of war: www.deutschlandfunkkultur.de/geruchsforschung-im-museum-der-gestank-von-schlachtfeldern.1008.de.html?dram:article_id=418999. I thank Marian Makins for drawing my attention to this latter exhibition.

desolate as the small-scale representations we can see in a war museum – and how, using the poetic strategies at his disposal, he can evoke in his audiences powerful emotional responses to those representations of a landscape in which nature is denatured and men suffer and die.[7]

For the poet of the *Iliad*, landscape is not simply a neutral backdrop to action. It plays a dual role – in his narration and in his narrative. The poet recognized that one element of landscape is an essential *topography*, for example the series of landmarks that he marks out between the walls of Troy and the ships of the Achaeans. This 'locative' information, to use Holly Taylor and Barbara Tversky's term, will give necessary order and coherence to his telling.[8] The second element of landscape comprises 'nonlocative' information: the landscape is represented as a *realm of experience*, in which heroes engage in grim warfare and terrible fighting (πόλεμόν τε κακὸν καὶ φύλοπιν αἰνὴν, *Il.* 4.15). This realm of experience is structured as a series of overlays, each of which offers images that assist us in visualizing this landscape. In considering these two related aspects of the Iliadic landscape of war I draw on some useful insights from cognitive psychology on how we process, and how we generate, narratives that describe spatial environments: I am interested in what it is that we construct in our mind's eye and how we transmit this image to others.[9]

2 The topography of the Trojan plain: Homer's locative information

Despite the fact that most of the action of the *Iliad* takes place on the battlefield, the epic itself is by no means a 'one-scene' tale, to use David Rubin's phrase.[10] The principal events in Homer's battle-narrative occur in different locations within the confines of the plain – between strong-founded Ilion with its high walls (4.33–4) and the beach (1.34), where we find the ships (1.12) and the shelters (1.306). The plain itself, like the battlefields of the First World War as they are represented in the AWM, is almost, but not entirely – and this is significant – devoid of landmarks: in the expanse between the walls of Troy and the Achaean ditch there is, apart from the Scamander and its ford (14.433) and the rise on the plain (10.160), a fig tree (or possibly two: 6.433; 11.167); an oak tree (or possibly two: 7.22 and 60); Callicolone, a hill adjacent to the Simoeis (20.53 and 151);

---

[7] I acknowledge too that the poet, at the first performances of the epic, would have used gesture and facial expression to add weight to his words. That is, performative strategies would at that time have assisted him in evoking the responses he desired.

[8] For the terms 'locative' and 'nonlocative', see Taylor and Tversky (1992a: 263): locative information comprises information about spatial relationships; elaborative details about the environment (those elements that I describe under the heading 'realm of experience') are classified as nonlocative information.

[9] It is interesting to me that the AWM recognized these two complementary notions carried within the term 'landscape', just as I do. In the early years of these displays, 'topographical plan models' were created to show the positions of troops and the obstacles they faced, to complement the 'picture models', the dioramas, which describe conditions more intimately. Only one of those topographical models has survived the passing of time: the model of the battle of Lone Pine (Gallipoli) (Back and Webster 2008: 91).

[10] Rubin (1995: 62). Rubin claims, indeed, that there are *no* 'one-scene epics'.

a watching-post (22.145); and the grave of Ilos (11.166).[11] This near-desolation is plausible, in the light of years of hand-to-hand fighting; and, by virtue of its economy, it is eminently functional.

An economical representation of landscape is what we should expect of a practising oral poet, who makes it his task to hold in memory all the locations that he identifies in his song. He should be able to recall each location independently and, more importantly, place it in relation to the others within what is referred to in popular parlance as a mental 'map', or, as Taylor and Tversky more accurately describe it, a 'spatial mental model'.[12] Each of these locations serves a double purpose: each one in some way represents a narrative 'staging post', the appropriate setting in which some element of the action unfolds; and each one simultaneously operates as a retrieval cue for the material of his tale, in the same way that Cicero used *loci* and *imagines* as a mnemonic system.[13] I shall address these points separately.

Jenny Strauss Clay, in *Homer's Trojan Theater*, demonstrates the high degree of visualization on the part of the poet, who calls up in his mind's eye the spatial dimensions of the action he describes.[14] Although *exact* spatial references (so critical to the fabricant of a diorama) are not important to the poet, or to his audience, it is clear that the poet knows the Trojan plain well – perhaps as intimately as do Homer's Trojan horses (ἐπιστάμενοι πεδίοιο ... διωκέμεν ἠδὲ φέβεσθαι, cf. 5.222–3 = 8.106–7). He knows it so well that he can lead his audience in a linear fashion along a variety of routes, moving back and forth across the plain from Troy to the ships of the Achaeans, and from side to side: we can follow the short route taken by the Embassy, as they walk along the shore from Agamemnon's hut to Achilles' ships and his shelter (9.177–85), Priam and Idaeus's longer journey from the city to that same shelter (24.322–447) or, as Clay has set out so well, the movement of the opposing forces, and even of individual heroes, back and forth across the battlefield at any one point of time.[15]

A route description, as outlined above, offers one perspective on landscape.[16] But the poet asks us to adopt as well a bird's eye, or survey, perspective, as he does when Priam and the Trojan elders sit on the tower at the Scaean gates, overlooking the Trojan plain, and ask Helen to identify individual Achaean heroes assembled there (3.146–244); or when Achilles, standing on the stern of his ship and looking back across the plain at the

---

[11] The poet has created an occasionally fluid space that allows him sufficient landmarks to which he can tie his narrative: on this see Minchin (2007: 23). For a useful discussion of these 'locus-images', as he calls them, see Tsagalis (2012: 78–93). It is true that the poet's physical landscape is economical; but the poet gives us a sense of landscape through other strategies, as I shall demonstrate.

[12] My use here of the term 'map' reflects popular usage. For the preferred term, see Taylor and Tversky (1992a: 289). They argue for the more nuanced 'spatial mental model', which captures spatial relations and allows for different perspectives. It is this term that I shall use henceforth. On the misunderstandings that the term 'map' can create, see Tversky (1993: 14).

[13] For a discussion of this Roman contribution to the art of memory, see Small (1997: 95–105): the Roman orator Cicero used a mnemonic spatial system to prompt his memory for individual sections of his long speeches. See below for further reference to landmarks as retrieval cues for narrative.

[14] Clay (2011: 110).

[15] These routes are demonstrated in Clay's careful analysis (2011: 56–95) of the action of Books 12–17.

[16] Taylor and Tversky (1992a: 261).

fighting, sees Nestor coming away from the conflict with Machaon, wounded (11.599–601); or when Menelaus, responding to Ajax's suggestion, goes in search of Antilochus, who will bear the news of Patroclus's death to Achilles (17.651–81).[17] The poet compares Menelaus to an eagle hovering in the air, seeking its prey: indeed a bird's-eye view. Later in the poem, Priam takes his place again on the walls (22.25) and watches as the Trojans retreat in flight to the safety of the city, with Achilles behind them, sweeping across the plain (ἐπεσσύμενον πεδίοιο, 22.26). Priam is joined by Hecuba, and together they beg their son from above to leave his position outside the walls in front of the gates (38–91); and from here they watch as Hector meets his death. Later still Andromache hurries to the wall, full of foreboding (447–61). She too stands here and gazes out (ἔστη παπτήνασ', 463) over the plain, only to see the body of her husband now being dragged away behind Achilles' chariot towards the ships (463–5).

The long-range, even telescopic, perspective of the gods completes the mental model. Sometimes they view the contest from the lofty vantage point on Olympus (24.23), or, at other times, they come down to earth to watch from Mount Ida, behind Troy (Zeus, at 8.47–52, 11.181–4), or from the nearby island of Samothrace (Poseidon, at 13.10–14):

οὐδ᾽ ἀλαοσκοπιὴν εἶχε κρείων ἐνοσίχθων·   10
καὶ γὰρ ὁ θαυμάζων ἧστο πτόλεμόν τε μάχην τε
ὑψοῦ ἐπ᾽ ἀκροτάτης κορυφῆς Σάμου ὑλήσσης
Θρηϊκίης· ἔνθεν γὰρ ἐφαίνετο πᾶσα μὲν Ἴδη,
φαίνετο δὲ Πριάμοιο πόλις καὶ νῆες Ἀχαιῶν.

And the earthshaker did not keep a blind watch. He sat and wondered at the fighting and the battle, high on the topmost peak of wooded Samos, the Thracian place. And from there all Ida appeared before his eyes, and he saw the city of Priam and the ships of the Achaeans.

And we must include in our mental model the depths of the sea, Poseidon's own realm, where Achilles' mother Thetis also dwells (1.357–8). Thus, through both route and survey information, the poet enables us to do more than develop a two-dimensional 'map' of the Trojan plain; we slowly build up something more or less like the poet's own three-dimensional spatial mental model, and this will be a crucial resource for us as we follow the tale.[18]

The features of the landscape identified by the poet serve as the bases for the organization of his narrative.[19] Unlike many storytellers who compose in writing, the

---

[17] On survey descriptions: Taylor and Tversky (1992a: 261).
[18] Clay's 'overviews' of Troy (2011: 47, 50, 104) are necessarily two-dimensional; but it is clear that she 'envisions' Troy, just as Homer intended, in three dimensions (cf. the reproduction of the *Teichomachy* by W. Andrae reproduced at 46). For other (by necessity, two-dimensional) plans see, for example, Thornton (1984: 50), Minchin (2007: 32).
[19] For important observations from cognitive psychology, see, for example, Taylor and Tversky (1992b: 484), Rubin (1995: 46). The poet introduces settings at the very moment that he needs them: de Jong (2012: 21–2).

oral poet takes pains to establish a setting, minimal as it may be, for each episode and he notes each change of scene.[20] It is by these means that he counters the potential for confusion, for himself as he tells his tale and for his audience as they follow him. Indeed, Clay persuasively demonstrates the poet's control of his material, which enables us, the poet's audience, to track the movements of his characters as he (the poet) focuses on different zones of action on the Trojan plain.[21] Finally, as I mentioned above and as I have demonstrated elsewhere, the oral poet who works in this epic tradition uses both visual memory (of particular landmarks) and spatial memory (of relations between them) to prompt recall of appropriate story material.[22]

Thus, for example, the tomb of Ilos serves as a focus for action: the Trojan elders, according to Dolon, hold council here on the battlefield by night (10.414–16); the tomb serves as the waymark as the Trojans flee in panic back to the safety of the city walls (11.166–8) and, in the other direction, as Priam sets out on his night-time journey to Achilles (24.349). The ford on the Scamander is another such site: when Hector is struck by the rock Ajax hurls he collapses (14.409–13). He is carried from the fighting in his chariot. It is not until the horses are stopped at the ford on the Scamander that the hero regains consciousness (433–9).[23] It is here (although the location is not now specified) that Apollo later finds him and restores his strength (15.239–42); it is here too that Priam and Idaeus encounter Hermes (24.350–3) and where Hermes, the next morning, leaves them (24.692–4). In each of the above cases, the landmark not only serves to keep the story in good order; it also prompts the poet's memory of the episode itself. A similar use, in this case of a manufactured landmark, appears in *Iliad* 10. Odysseus and Diomedes, having killed Dolon, place the spoils on a tamarisk bush and pull reeds and tamarisk together, making a clear sign (δέελον δ'ἐπὶ σῆμα τ'ἐθήκε, 466) that they can locate in the dark on their return. And, indeed, on their way back to the camp, after their slaughter of the sleeping Thracians, they stop at this point, at the place where they had killed Dolon (526), gather up the spoils (528–9) and continue on their way. Using this landmark to bookend his tale, the poet launches himself into an episode of slaughter and subsequently brings that sequence, quite neatly, to a close.

---

[20] To compare the poet of the *Iliad*'s practice with that of a storyteller who works in writing: Jane Austen, for example, feels no need to be precise about location (cf. the first memorable – but unlocated – conversation in *Pride and Prejudice*, between Mr and Mrs Bennet).
[21] See Clay (2011: 68) on theatres of war.
[22] '[T]he setting *cues* the actions that arise ... Homer's concern for location is an indicator of a memory-based strategy developed for sustained oral performance' (Minchin 2007: 22–3); cf. Taylor and Tversky (1992b: 484): the features of the landscape noted in the narrative serve as bases for organization. See also van Rookhuijzen (in this volume) for his discussion of 'mnemotopes'.
[23] The poet is notoriously inconsistent on the sources of the Scamander: on this see, briefly, de Jong (2012: 97). One might argue, however, that the sources of the river are not an essential element of the Iliadic landscape of war. The poet therefore has not 'fixed' them so firmly in his mental model.

3 Landscape as a realm of experience: Homer's nonlocative information

George Miller, the cognitive psychologist, tells us that, as he reads a detailed description of a landscape, the 'image' (as he calls it) that he conjures up in his mind's eye cannot correspond in all its details to what is set out in the text; according to Miller, what he 'sees' is in many respects a generic representation of landscape; he doesn't fill in all the details.[24] We all recognize Miller's economical approach to the evocation of landscape. It seems to me that the poet of the *Iliad* also recognized this, although intuitively. He has not invested poetic energy in locating and generating detailed material of a purely descriptive kind. His landscape is bleak and bare. He gives us only a little *explicit* nonlocative information about the Trojan plain.[25] He insists, however, on those details that he has chosen to share. At several points the poet tells us that the plain is dusty (no rain, we notice, falls during the fighting).[26] So, as the Achaeans rush to the ships in response to Agamemnon's test of their will (2.149–51), they raise the dust (κονίη, 150); they are white with dust (κονίσαλῳ, 5.503) as their horses wheel about on the plain; Asios in death claws at the bloody dust (13.393); Hector, overwhelmed by Ajax, drops in the dust (14.418); a dust-storm (ἀέλλη, 16.374–5) is stirred up by the Trojans in their terror; the horse Pedasos goes down into the dust, screaming (16.469); Sarpedon falls and claws the bloody dust (16.486), as does Phorkys (17.315); and, finally, Hector drops in the dust (ἤριπε δ'ἐν κονίης, 22.330); as he is dragged behind the hero's chariot, dust is raised behind him (22.402–3); his whole head is covered in dust (405). Even in the course of the funeral games for Patroclus, held on the plain, the poet evokes its dusty surface (23.365–6). During the days of fighting this dusty surface at times runs with the blood of the wounded (ῥέε δ'αἵματι γαῖα, 4.451; see also 10.298; 11.163–4; 13.392–3; 13.655; 15.715; 16.486, 639–40; 17.360–1). The only natural feature here, apart from the landmark trees noted above, are the stones that serve as useful missiles: 3.79–80 (λάεσσί τ' ἔβαλλον); see also 4.518–19; 12.154–5, 380–1, 445; 14.409–11; 16.734–5, 774–5.[27]

Blood and dust are the defining qualities of this terrain, strewn with stones. And, as is clear from the examples above, any descriptive material is presented incidentally; all descriptors are built into the narrative: a dying hero claws at the bloody dust; another is felled by a stone casually taken up from the ground; as Hector's body is dragged off to the ships it stirs up the dust. As is the case with the dioramas of the AWM, however, the

---

[24] Miller (1993) offers us an 'experiment in self-observation' (358), as he describes the mental processes involved as he reads a sustained description of landscape. He notes (360) that it is the 'vagueness' of the representation that is critical to its utility.

[25] Cf. Andersson (1976: 16, 36), Tsagalis (2012: 460), who notes the 'absence of landscape description in the *Iliad*'.

[26] Cf. Fränkel (1921: 102) on the 'weatherless' space of Troy: '[i]n der Ilias gibt es keine Jahreszeit und fast kein Wetter'. The poet, however, twice reports an unnatural 'rain' of blood, on each occasion Zeus's doing: 11.52–5 (dew dripping with blood, a foreshadowing of the death and destruction that is about to be visited on the battlefield) and 16.459–61 (the god's tears as his son Sarpedon is killed). By contrast with the weatherless landscapes of the battle narrative, see below on the landscapes of Homer's similes.

[27] Equally terse are the poet's accounts of the Scamander, which cuts the plain: its eddies are silvery (21.8); its banks are sandy (21.202); and on its banks are trees, reeds and rushes (21.350–2).

landscape assumes a more complex – and grimmer – character when the poet includes the presence of the Achaean and Trojan heroes and sets them in motion.[28] The army of the Achaeans hastens to assemble (2.86); the bronze of their armour gleams (2.457–8; 4.431–2; 20.156) as they advance in serried ranks (4.427–9) – an image at once impressive and terrible. In the press of fighting we see in our mind's eye the tangled knot of men (17.679–80); we see weapons hurled (e.g. 4.459–62, 473, 490, 495–8, 527–8), horses brought down (16.467–9), men falling (e.g. 4.462, 482, 493, 504, 522–6, 536–8); we see shocking wounds (e.g. 11.97–8; 12.383–6; 16.321–4; 17.616–18),[29] and contests over the dead (4.463–72), whose bodies are pulled and tugged in all directions (17.389–95). And, at some points of the narrative, we see the terrain strewn (ἅλις, 21.344) with the corpses of the fallen.

These images of action in the landscape are intensified by the poet's similes that compare the gathering of the fighting men to swarms of bees (2.87–90), or of wasps by the roadside (16.259–62), or that compare the force of the attack of one or the other side to a blazing fire (11.596; 17.736–9). At some moments Achaeans and Trojans are evenly matched: comparison with the battle between the east and south wind (16.765–9), for example, allows us to envisage the closeness of the contests.[30] At other moments it is one side that carries the day: Hector comes on against the Achaeans like a rolling stone on a rock face, 13.137–42. As battle rages, we observe the lust for slaughter, as a hero moves through the throng like a wolf amongst lambs (16.352–5) or a lion amongst cattle (11.172–6; 15.630–6). These similes, by virtue of their readily pictureable images of the destructive force of nature, and by virtue of repetition (the essential repetition of the central narrative idea),[31] assist us in building up a more complex mental representation of the Trojan plain under siege.

In discussing how an individual builds a scene in his or her mind's eye using nonlocative information, Tversky proposes the metaphor of a 'cognitive collage'; she describes such a collage as a sequence of 'thematic overlays of multimedia from different points of view'.[32] Like the elements of a collage, this information may be multiform and partial, representing the focalization now of the narrator, now of one of his characters; it is unlikely, Tversky notes, that it could be organized into a single coherent maplike cognitive structure. I propose that Homer's accounts of action in the landscape of the

---

[28] See also Hellwig (1964: 32). Just as our attention as viewers of scenes in the real world, or in the AWM, is inevitably drawn to human figures (cf. Fletcher-Watson, Findlay, Leekam and Benson (2008: 580–2), noted in n. 2 above, so, when we construct scenes in our mind's eye, we pause over human figures and human action. It is this attention that contributes to the fixing of that image in memory. Grethlein and Huitink (2017: 4–5) take this discussion further: introducing an 'enactive' approach into Classics, and using the chariot race of *Iliad* 23 as a test-case, they argue that we do not 'see' a mental picture of the action but we visualize a scene through enacting it in our minds. The experience is 'undergone' rather than 'seen' in the mind's eye. It is this experiential aspect that contributes to Homer's 'imageability'.
[29] For an excellent survey of (non-fatal) wounds, see Neal (2006).
[30] Alex Purves (2010: 323) notes that the landscapes of Homer's similes are 'storm-tossed and windswept', and that they add complexity to the landscapes of the Troy-story, which are never touched by wind or rain (cf. above). On similes as a 'boundary-crossing experience', see Tsagalis (2102: 360–3).
[31] Minchin (2016: 24–6).
[32] Tversky (1993: 15).

Trojan plain (such as we have seen above) and the similes that describe them could be viewed as separate overlays of just such a cognitive collage. It is in this way that the poet counters his audience's unwillingness to process and to work with detailed description. These multimedia overlays in their variety invite us to create for ourselves a richer mental representation of this landscape of war.

But the poet does not rely on visual effects alone. He presents us also with a soundscape. We hear the thunder (κτύπος, 19.363–4) of an army on the move; the thunder of horses on the run (μεγάλα στενάχοντο, 16.393; ἀζηχὴς ὀρυμαγδός, 17.740–1); the 'unearthly clamour' of men (ἠχῇ θεσπεσίῃ, 8.159 = 12.252 = 13.834 = 15.590); the calling of man to man in the thick of battle (8.346–7; 15.424, 658), their appeals to the gods (8.346–7); the shouts that go skywards (ἀϋτή, 12.338; 14.60); shouts and threats and vaunts in the thick of the contest (εὐχωλή, 4.450; δεινὸν ἀΰσαντες, 16.565–6); the notes of terror in their voices (ἰαχῇ τε φόβῳ τε | πάσας πλῆσαν ὁδούς, 16.373–4; οὖλον κεκλήγοντες, 17.756, 759); the battering and clashing of shields by spears (4.447; κτύπος, 12.338), by swords, by arrows and by stones (ἐστυφέλιξαν, 16.774); the screams of horses – and men – as they are killed (οἰμωγή, 4.450; ἔβραχε ... μακών, 16.468–9); and the crash of armour as a great hero falls (δούπησεν δὲ πεσών, ἀράβησε δὲ τεύχε' ἐπ' αὐτῷ, 4.504 = 5.42 = 13.187). A certain amount of onomatopoeia – in expressions that capture the battering and clattering, the shrieking and shouting (οἰμωγή, 4.450; σμερδνὸν βοόων, 15.732), the whistling of arrows and the thump of spears (ὀϊστῶν τε ῥοῖζον καὶ δοῦπον ἀκόντων, 16.361) and the impact of battle action on the earth beneath – ensures that the din of battle resonates, automatically, in our senses. The soundtrack of the *Iliad* is as important to our engagement with this landscape of war as the poet's visual effects.[33] This was brought home to me quite emphatically after I had viewed the dioramas of the AWM – allowing the recorded sounds of combat to play in my ear – and then re-read Homer's descriptions of battle.[34]

Was the landscape of the Trojan plain always like this? What was it like before the Achaeans came?[35] Although the poet on one occasion refers to the plain of Troy as 'bountiful earth' (3.89), it is hard to reconcile this descriptor with that trampled terrain. The Trojan plain, rather than a source of life, is now in its tenth year a witness to death. And the poet plays with this idea. Just as he builds pathos into the lives and fates of the heroes, so, through a range of strategies, he builds pathos into the landscape itself.[36]

Let us turn to a critical moment late in the poem. When Achilles pursues Hector around the city, the two men run a little way out from the wall (τείχεος ... ὕπεκ, 22.146),[37]

---

[33] Cf. Andersson (1976: 25).
[34] Although our other senses, of taste and smell, are rarely, if ever, engaged as we read the *Iliad*, there is scope for enactive engagement with the land itself, when heroes make an impact on the ground beneath them as they fall, for example (4.504 = 5.42 = 13.187) or when they 'bite' the dust (ὀδὰξ ἕλον οὖδας: 11.749, 19.61, 24.738). I thank Bettina Reitz-Joosse for raising with me the possibility that other senses are also engaged as we read or listen to the text.
[35] For another perspective on the relationship between a fertile landscape and the landscape of war, see Zientek (in this volume).
[36] Griffin (1980: 21–2).
[37] Note the spatial indicator here. The poet expects us to plot this chase within our mental model.

past the watch-post, past the fig tree and, now away from the plain, past the two springs – one hot, one cold – that feed the city's washing pools (147–56):

κρουνὼ δ' ἵκανον καλλιρρόω· ἔνθα δὲ πηγαὶ
δοιαὶ ἀναΐσσουσι Σκαμάνδρου δινήεντος.
ἣ μὲν γάρ θ' ὕδατι λιαρῷ ῥέει, ἀμφὶ δὲ καπνὸς
γίγνεται ἐξ αὐτῆς ὡς εἰ πυρὸς αἰθομένοιο·   150
ἣ δ' ἑτέρη θέρεϊ προρέει ἐϊκυῖα χαλάζῃ,
ἢ χιόνι ψυχρῇ ἢ ἐξ ὕδατος κρυστάλλῳ.
ἔνθα δ' ἐπ' αὐτάων πλυνοὶ εὐρέες ἐγγὺς ἔασι
καλοὶ λαΐνεοι, ὅθι εἵματα σιγαλόεντα
πλύνεσκον Τρώων ἄλοχοι καλαί τε θύγατρες   155
τὸ πρὶν ἐπ' εἰρήνης πρὶν ἐλθεῖν υἷας Ἀχαιῶν.

They came to two clear-flowing springs. Here two fountains gush up, fed by the whirling Scamander. One of these runs with hot water and all around it there is steam, like smoke from a blazing fire. The other in summer runs cold like hail, or chilly snow, or ice that has formed from water. Beside these, close by, in this place, are wide washing pools of stone, splendid ones, where the wives of the Trojans and their lovely daughters washed their shining clothes in former times, in the days of peace before the sons of the Achaeans came.

The narrator, remarkably, lingers, first, over a description of these springs, and, then, over a description of the pools, insisting on their proximity to the marvellous springs. Now introducing human action into the scene, to fix it in our minds, he goes on to tell us that the wives and daughters of the Trojans used to come here to wash their garments.[38] But that was in the past, when there was peace, before the Achaeans came (πρὶν ἐλθεῖν υἷας Ἀχαιῶν, 22.147–56, at 156). This is the pathos of contrasts: the natural wonder of the setting and the memory of the orderly and companionable activities once carried out here in carefree security are overlaid on the scene before our eyes, a vision of desperation in what is now a hostile environment. And, soon in the telling, the poet will bring Hector once more to this very spot, for the last time (208), to meet his death.

Even in a time of war, however, there are moments when the landscape of the Trojan plain takes on a kinder guise. When the Trojans have pursued the Achaeans back to their ships at nightfall, Hector pauses by the river and calls an assembly in a place relatively clear of the fallen (ὅθι δὴ νεκύων διεφαίνετο χῶρος, 8.491). He proposes to his men that they make camp right there, on the open ground. The Trojans free their horses from their harness, tethering each one to his chariot, and throw down fodder (543–4). For themselves, they bring out from the city oxen and fat sheep, and, from their houses, they

---

[38] As I noted above, our attention to (and enactive experience of) figures of men and women in action fixes that scene in memory.

bring wine and provisions (545–7). They light their fires, make sacrifice and prepare their meal (549). And the poet, comparing the blaze of their watch-fires to the numberless stars in the night sky, when the 'endless bright air (ἄσπετος αἰθήρ) spills from the heavens', 558, creates a scene poignant in its serenity.[39] We imagine the crackling of flames, the sound of flutes and pipes, the murmur of voices (10.13) and the rustle of men as they move about (10.189). This break in the chaotic routines of battle offers respite to the Trojans, and a brief but wary glimpse of a different way of living. But even as we take in the grandeur of this nocturnal landscape and its gentler soundscape, we understand that this is temporary respite for the Trojan heroes; the din of battle, we know, will inevitably resume.

Finally, the poet, throughout the *Iliad*, suggests alternatives to the landscape of war that confronts us on the Trojan plain. He achieves this by two means, the first of which is a particular selection of similes. These are not the similes that I discussed above, which recreate scenes of violence and terror. I am referring here to similes that remind us of the productive aspects of nature and of the men and women who harness it. Through their pointed contrast with the action of the Trojan plain, these unexpected glimpses of 'what is not' allow us to see 'what might have been', or 'what once was'; they highlight the tragic consequences of making war. In the sheep pens in spring, as the pails froth with milk, thousands of insects swarm around them (so the Achaeans gather in their thousands to take up the fight once more, 2.469–73); on the threshing floor the wind scatters the chaff and separates it from the grain, and the piles of chaff mount up, all white (so the Achaeans are whitened by the dust as their horses drive across the plain) (5.499–502); a donkey who has strayed into a field of grain cannot be shifted by a cluster of young boys – not until it has eaten its fill (so Ajax retreats very reluctantly in the face of the Trojans) (11.558–62); on the threshing floor, again, the black-skinned beans and chickpeas bounce high beneath the winnowing fan (so Helenus's arrow bounced back from Menelaus's chest) (13.588–90). These images open a window, for a brief moment, onto a landscape under cultivation, a landscape of productive activity, a landscape that observes cycles of seasons and that works with, not against, nature.[40] And then that window is shut, and we are returned to engage with the fighting once more. Through a telling juxtaposition of the worlds of peace and war, the narrator, with no further commentary, makes his point: war will destroy the land that supports us.[41] These evocations of nature's bountiful landscapes are drawn together and recapitulated with a certain unique intensity in the tightly focused series of scenes the god Hephaestus works on the shield of Achilles: the triple-ploughed field, where teams of ploughmen work (18.541–9); the field at a later point of time, where men reap and bind the sheaves (550–60); the vineyard with its cluster of grapes ready for the harvest

---

[39] I draw here on the translation by Lattimore (1951).
[40] Redfield (1975: 186–8). Note too his comment (at 187) that the 'rhetorical purpose' of the similes is not to describe the world of peace but 'to make vivid' the world of war. On the image of the simile as a window, see Tsagalis (2012: 347).
[41] The poet exercises great restraint: without explicit evaluation on his part he allows his similes to carry this message. This is a fine example of the poet's *apparent* objectivity: cf. Minchin (2001: 127–8).

(561–72); the cattle at pasture by the river (573–86) and the sheepflocks in their meadow (587–9).[42]

4 Conclusions: language as a surrogate for experience

What has interested me as I have compared my immersive experience of landscapes of war as represented in the AWM's sound-and-light dioramas and as represented through words alone in the *Iliad* is the remarkable capacity of the poet to generate information that allows listeners or readers to recreate in their own mind's eye a three-dimensional topographical model. If we audience members are to follow the narrative in all its detail, it is essential that we work up such a model in our mind. With respect to the terrain, the poet remarks on it only too briefly. And yet he leaves us with a vivid impression. Just as the creator of a diorama brings his scenes to life through the depiction of human action, so the poet offers an account of action in the landscape. And he intensifies his scene through a strategic use of vivid comparisons, especially with phenomena of the natural world. Like the exhibition designers in the diorama galleries at the AWM, the poet of the *Iliad* ensures that the soundscape of warfare rings in our ears. But he can offer more. He has devised strategies for conveying affect: through the comparisons, the images and the memories that he evokes, he encourages us to observe for ourselves what happens to a landscape subjected to the destructive power of war; he invites us to register pathos, poignancy and the pain of loss. Responding to the multiform cues that the poet has offered us, we create our own 'cognitive collage', which represents that Iliadic landscape of war in all its complexity. Herein lies the special power of *this* immersive experience.

Bibliography

Andersson, T. M. 1976. *Early Epic Scenery: Homer, Virgil, and the Mediaeval Legacy*. Ithaca and London: Cornell University Press.
Austen, J. 1951. *Pride and Prejudice*. London: Macdonald.
Back, L. and L. Webster. 2008. *Moments in Time: Dioramas at the Australian War Memorial*. Sydney: New Holland Publishers.
Clay, J. S. 2011. *Homer's Trojan Theater: Space, Vision, and Memory in the Iliad*. Cambridge: Cambridge University Press.
Edwards, M. 1991. *The Iliad: A Commentary*, Vol. 5. Cambridge: Cambridge University Press.
Fletcher-Watson, S., J. Findlay, S. Leekam and V. Benson. 2008. 'Rapid Detection of Person Information in a Naturalistic Scene.' *Perception* 37: 571–83.
Fränkel, H. 1921. *Die homerischen Gleichnisse*. Göttingen: Vandenhoek & Ruprecht.
Grethlein, J. and L. Huitink, 2017. 'Homer's Vividness: An Enactive Approach'. *Journal of Hellenic Studies* 137: 67–91.

---

[42] The description of the images on the shield is achieved through a narration of its construction Minchin (2001: 128–9); see also Minchin (forthcoming). As Edwards (1991: 209) notes, it is ironic that Achilles, a hero who is now fated to die, should carry into battle depictions of 'the continuing life of ordinary human folk'.

Griffin, J. 1980. *Homer on Life and Death*. Oxford: Clarendon Press.
Hellwig, B. 1964. *Raum und Zeit im homerischen Epos*. Hildesheim: Georg Olms.
De Jong, I. J. F. 2012. 'Homer.' In *Space in Ancient Greek Narrative*, edited by I. J. F. de Jong, 22–38. Leiden: Brill.
Lattimore, R., trans. 1951. *The Iliad of Homer*. Chicago: The University of Chicago Press.
Miller, G. 1993. 'Images and Models, Similes and Metaphors.' In *Metaphor and Thought*, 2nd edn, edited by A. Ortony, 357–400. Cambridge: Cambridge University Press.
Minchin, E. 2001. *Homer and the Resources of Memory: Some Applications of Cognitive Theory to the Iliad and the Odyssey*. Oxford: Oxford University Press.
Minchin, E. 2007. 'Spatial Memory and the Composition of the *Iliad*.' In *Orality, Literacy, Memory in the Ancient Greek and Roman World*, edited by E. Anne Mackay, 9–34. Leiden: Brill.
Minchin, E. 2016. 'Repetition in Homeric Epic: Cognitive and Linguistic Perspectives.' In *Oral Poetics and Cognitive Science*, edited by M. Antović and C. Pagán Cánovas, 12–29. Berlin: De Gruyter.
Minchin, E. forthcoming. 'Visualizing the Shield of Achilles: Approaching its Landscapes via Cognitive Paths.' *Classical Quarterly*.
Neal, T. 2006. *The Wounded Hero: Non-Fatal Injury in Homer's Iliad*. New York: Peter Lang.
Purves, A. 2010. 'Wind and Time in Homeric Epic.' *Transactions of the American Philological Association* 140: 323–50.
Redfield, J. 1975. *Nature and Culture in the Iliad: The Tragedy of Hector*. Chicago: University of Chicago Press.
Rubin, D. 1995. *Memory in Oral Traditions: The Cognitive Psychology of Epic, Ballads, and Counting-out Rhymes*. New York: Oxford University Press.
Taylor, H. and B. Tversky. 1992a. 'Spatial Mental Models Derived from Survey and Route Descriptions.' *Journal of Memory and Language* 31: 261–92.
Taylor, H. and B. Tversky. 1992b. 'Descriptions and Depictions of Environments.' *Memory and Cognition* 20: 483–96.
Tsagalis, C. 2012. *From Listeners to Viewers: Space in the Iliad*. Washington: Center for Hellenic Studies.
Tversky, B. 1993. 'Cognitive Maps, Cognitive Collages, and Spatial Mental Models.' In *Spatial Information Theory: A Theoretical Basis for GIS*, edited by A. U. Frank and I. Campari, 14–24. Springer: Berlin.

CHAPTER 2
WAR, WEATHER AND LANDSCAPE IN LIVY'S *AB URBE CONDITA*[1]

Virginia Fabrizi

1 Introduction

What is a 'landscape of war' made of? First of all, of course, the topographic features of the area where military events take place – plains, hills, mountains, rivers. Topography is, however, but one component of a military landscape; just as crucial is the combatants' (or civilians') experience of the spaces involved in war. After all, it is the way people perceive, remember, or imagine their physical surroundings, as well as the symbolic meaning they attribute to them, that turns space into landscape.[2] These two aspects – topography and experience – also constitute, as Elizabeth Minchin's chapter in this volume shows, the organizing principles of verbal and visual representations of military events, as one finds for example in literary narratives and the visual arts.

Among the elements that affect combatants' experience of a landscape, an important role is played by climate, season and weather conditions. Such factors directly influence military operations both practically (as when rain curtails a battle or when snow makes marching harder)[3] and emotionally. For example, a landscape which is dimly perceived due to fog or pouring rain can appear threatening; severe cold or heat can be experienced by soldiers as enemies in their own right. For these reasons, such phenomena can also add pathos or drama to literary accounts of war.

My concern in this chapter is the literary representation of landscapes of war – and, in particular, of battle – as composed of both topography and weather. More specifically, I investigate how a literary narrative of Roman history, Livy's *Ab Urbe Condita*, uses atmospheric phenomena in battle accounts.

Ida Östenberg has recently shown that ancient writers used bad weather – alongside terrain and nature more generally – as an important factor in explaining Roman defeats.[4]

---

[1] This chapter is different from the paper I presented at the CCC panel 'Landscapes of War' in 2017, but it has in many respects profited from the discussion that took place during that conference. I wish to thank all participants for their input. In what follows, the text of the *AUC* is quoted from the following editions: Ogilvie (1974) for Books 1–5; Walters and Conway (1919) for Books 6–10; Briscoe 2016 for Books 21–5; Walsh (1989) for Books 26–7; Briscoe (1991) for Books 31–40; Briscoe (1986) for Books 41–5. Translations of Books 6–10 are taken from Yardley and Hoyos (2013), of Books 21–30 from Yardley and Hoyos (2006), of Books 31–4 from Yardley and Hoyos (2017), of Books 35–7 from Yardley (2018), and of Books 41–5 from Chaplin (2007).
[2] See e.g. Spencer (2010: 1-15) for a survey of modern approaches to landscape and experience.
[3] For the effects of weather on combat see e.g. Winters et al. (1998), Carter and Veale (2013).
[4] Östenberg (2018: esp. 249–51).

Moreover, as other scholars have stressed[5] and Andrew Feldherr's chapter in this volume further discusses, the narrated occurrence of certain atmospheric phenomena can take part in the complex web of symbolic meanings that characterizes at least some battle narratives in ancient historiography. In this respect, it should be borne in mind that ancient Roman culture saw such phenomena not merely as natural occurrences, but, in some cases, as omens – a fact that could enrich their potential to take on symbolic connotations.[6]

I first examine the role played by the weather in producing narrative suspense in battle narratives from the *Ab Urbe Condita* (§2). I then focus more specifically on how the weather shapes the settings of combat. I examine how atmospheric phenomena can come together with internal focalization as a way to direct the reader's gaze onto certain aspects of a setting and thus enhance the *enargeia* (vividness) of an account (§3). Subsequently, I turn my attention to the symbolic functions played by the weather in battle narratives – in particular, to its role in characterizing armies and commanders (§4) and in conveying ideas about the strengths and weaknesses of armies (§5). I then examine, more specifically, the role of fog and rain in some accounts of ambushes (§6). The final section (§7) attempts to draw some conclusions as to the very notion of 'landscapes of war' as it emerges from the *Ab Urbe Condita*.

2 Suspense and prefiguration

Livy's ability to create vivid military accounts is well known. While not always accurate from a technical point of view, his narratives capture the attention of readers because of their richness in emotional colouring, their dramatic turns of events, and the attention they devote to individual or collective shows of valour.

Among other things, the *Ab Urbe Condita* makes good use of the opportunities offered by weather conditions – especially extreme or unexpected ones – to construct gripping narratives. Some instances are very famous: one need only think of the snow and ice tormenting Hannibal's troops during their crossing of the Alps in 218 BCE,[7] or of the violent rainstorms that prevented the Carthaginian general from crossing the Apennines later in the same year.[8] In such cases, the weather forms an integral part of the threatening mountainous landscapes that act as enemies to the soldiers on the march.

There are several other cases, however, in which sudden changes of the weather work more subtly to enhance narrative suspense and/or prefigure the outcome of events. On a number of occasions, for example, combat is broken off by downpours of rain. This

---

[5] See e.g. Levene (2010: 269–70).
[6] On Livy's use of and attitude to prodigy lists see Levene (1993). For the complex issue concerning religion in the *AUC*, see the recent synthesis by Scheid (2015), which contains a history of the problem and further references.
[7] Livy 21.35.6–37.4. Cf. Clark (2014: 43–67), Fabrizi (2015) (with further bibliography).
[8] Livy 21.58.3–11. Cf. Levene (2010: 136–55), Clark (2014: 71–3).

phenomenon can delay the climactic moment of the action, as in the narrative of the battle at Nola between Romans and Carthaginians at 23.44 (215 BCE). Nola hosted a Roman garrison commanded by Marcus Claudius Marcellus. On seeing that the Carthaginians had surrounded the town from all directions, Marcellus ordered a sortie (23.44.4):

> aliquot primo impetu perculsi caesique sunt; dein concursu ad pugnantes facto aequatisque viribus atrox esse coepit pugna, memorabilisque inter paucas fuisset ni ingentibus procellis effusus imber diremisset pugnantes.

> A number of the enemy were taken by surprise and killed at the first onset. Then there was a rush to the scene of the fighting and, when both sides' forces evened up, it began to turn into a ferocious struggle, one that would have been memorable as few others had been, had not torrential rain arrived with gale-force winds to part the combatants.

Trans. J. C. Yardley

The falling of the rain is reported through a conditional sentence (*si ... pugnantes*), which frustrates readers' expectations at the very moment that they become aware of this battle's potential to be especially memorable. The reader, in other words, is made aware that the battle could have been one of those landmarks in the war to which the *Ab Urbe Condita* devotes elaborate accounts and might be slightly disappointed by the lost chance. The clashing of the two forces is further delayed, since the ongoing rain (23.44.6) causes the commanders to keep their men within their respective fortifications for the whole of the following day; further suspense is built up by mention of the willingness to fight that both sides feel (*quamquam utraque pars avidi certaminis erant*).

On the third day, at last, the battle takes place – and, as one might have expected, it turns out to be a very fierce combat, portrayed with the whole array of Livy's rhetorical tools (23.44.6–45.3). The text insists upon the role played by the two great commanders and grants each of them a speech to their troops. Both speeches revolve around the corrupting effects of Capua and *Campana luxuria* on the Carthaginian army;[9] as Levene (2010: 306) has pointed out, the emphasis placed on this theme serves to alert readers to the turning of the tide that Nola – the first major Roman victory in the war – comes to represent. Morale turns out to be the determining factor at Nola: the Romans become more and more emboldened as the fighting goes on, and the Carthaginians flee back to their camp.

In this account, the delay caused by the rain builds up a crescendo of suspense, which then climaxes in the symbolically charged second battle. The very fierceness of the latter, and thus its significance in the fortunes of the war, is prefigured by Livy's comment at 23.44.4.

---

[9] For an interesting variation on this theme, cf. Reitz-Joosse (in this volume).

On other occasions, rain interrupting a battle can produce a different kind of prefiguration. This is the case with 6.32.6, where rain breaks off a battle between the Romans and the joint forces of Volsci and Latins (378 BCE):

> ubi cum aciem instructam hostium loco aequo invenissent, extemplo pugnatum; et ut nondum satis claram victoriam, sic prosperae spei pugnam imber ingentibus procellis fusus diremit.

> At Satricum they found the enemy deployed on the even ground, and immediately went on the attack; and though victory was not yet quite assured, a heavy rainfall attended by high winds broke off what was a promising engagement.
> Trans. J. C. Yardley

The combat is said to be even, but for some reason (which is left unexplained) the Romans are optimistic about their chances. When fighting stops, the reader is thus invited to expect that a victory will take place – which, in fact, happens. After this first failed attempt at a military engagement, the two armies clash on the following day, and the Romans emerge victorious (6.32.7–9).

A similar turn of phrase is used at 6.8.7, where a battle against an alliance of Volsci, Latins and Hernici (386 BCE) is interrupted at the very moment in which the Romans are gaining the upper hand:[10]

> iam inclinata res erat, sed turba hostium et fuga impediebatur et longa caede conficienda multitudo tanta fesso militi erat, cum repente ingentibus procellis fusus imber certam magis victoriam quam proelium diremit.

> A rout had now begun, but even flight was impeded by the large numbers of the enemy, and there still remained a huge multitude for the exhausted Roman soldiers to finish off in a lengthy bloodbath when, suddenly, a cloudburst with heavy winds broke off what was a clear victory rather than a battle.
> Trans. J. C. Yardley

Here, the storm sanctions the Romans' victory, because it breaks out while the very proportions of the slaughter they are inflicting on their enemies is starting to cause trouble for the winning side. The text goes on to relate that, during the night, the alliance of Latins and Hernici comes apart, since each people, acknowledging the Romans' military superiority, decides to go back to their own city.

---

[10] Oakley (1998: 330–1) lists these and similar passages together with occurrences of the topos by which fighting is stopped by the coming of night – a topos which is frequent not just in Livy, but in ancient historiography more generally. Oakley argues that 'the annalists used the topos of the indecisive battle ended by darkness to give color to their battle–narratives' (331). Cf. e.g. 4.39.6 *Nox incertos diremit*; 7.33.15 *ni nox victoriam magis quam proelium dirimisset*.

At 8.1.4–5, a storm breaks off a battle between the Romans and the Volsci of Antium while the fortunes of the battle are still uncertain (341 BCE).[11] In this case, the storm itself, to some extent, decides the outcome of the military campaign:

> 4. inde victor exercitus Satricum contra Antiates ductus. ibi magna utrimque caede atrox proelium fuit; et cum tempestas eos neutro inclinata spe dimicantes diremisset, Romani nihil eo certamine tam ambiguo fessi in posterum diem proelium parant. 5. Volscis recensentibus quos viros in acie amisissent haudquaquam idem animus ad iterandum periculum fuit; nocte pro victis Antium agmine trepido sauciis ac parte impedimentorum relicta abierunt.

> 4. The victorious troops were led against the Antiates at Satricum, and there a fierce battle took place with much blood spilled on both sides, but a storm broke off the fight before hopes of success inclined to either side. The Romans, however, in no way demoralized by such an indecisive engagement, prepared for battle on the following day. 5. The Volsci, though, counting the men they had lost in the engagement, had no such enthusiasm for facing the danger once again, and they left fearfully for Antium during the night like beaten men, abandoning their wounded and part of their baggage.
>
> Trans. J. C. Yardley

Acting as a sort of touchstone for the troops' valour and morale, the storm reveals the Volscian lack of courage as opposed to the Romans' willingness to fight.[12]

The most famous episode in which a sudden rainfall (this time mixed with hail) prevents armies from fighting is, of course, Hannibal's attempt to attack Rome in 211 BCE (26.11.1–3):

> 1. postero die transgressus Anienem Hannibal in aciem omnes copias eduxit; nec Flaccus consulesque certamen detractavere. 2 instructis utrimque exercitibus in eius pugnae casum, in qua urbs Roma victori praemium esset, imber ingens grandine mixtus ita utramque aciem turbavit ut vix armis retentis in castra sese receperint, nullius rei minore quam hostium metu. 3. et postero die eodem loco acies instructas eadem tempestas diremit; ubi recepissent se in castra, mira serenitas cum tranquillitate oriebatur. 4. in religionem ea res apud Poenos versa est, auditaque vox Hannibalis fertur potiundae sibi urbis Romae modo mentem non dari, modo fortunam.

> 1. The next day Hannibal crossed the Anio and led out all his troops for battle; and Flaccus and the consuls did not decline the fight. 2. The two armies were now

---

[11] According to Oakley (1998: 393) the storm might have been an invention.
[12] In what follows, Livy goes on to relate that the consul (burnt and) dedicated the arms found in the Volscian camp and next to the corpses to a goddess named Lua Mater (see Oakley (1998: 397–8)) and plundered the Volscians' territory up to the coast (8.1.6).

deployed for an engagement in which the city of Rome would be the victor's prize. At that point, there was a heavy shower of rain, intermixed with hail, and this caused such havoc in both battle lines that the combatants retired to their camps barely able to hold their weapons, the enemy now the least of their fears. 3. The next day the lines were again drawn up in the same spot, and a storm of similar intensity separated them once more. And yet their return to camp was on both occasions followed by amazingly bright and tranquil weather. 4. On the Carthaginian side the phenomenon was given a religious significance, and it is said that Hannibal was heard to remark that on one occasion he had been denied the will, and on the other the opportunity, to take Rome.

Trans. J. C. Yardley

As Levene argues,[13] Livy stresses the supernatural connotations of the rain and hail that prevented the Carthaginians from bringing their attack on Rome, and which are not mentioned at all by Polybius.[14] The voice of the primary narrator does not make any explicit connection between the rainstorm and the divine protection accorded to Rome; however, such a connection is powerfully suggested both by the interpretation of Hannibal's soldiers and by the broader narrative context.[15]

In this case, the falling of rain and hail fulfils several of the functions that I have observed at work in the other passages examined in this section: it causes the failure of the Carthaginian attack on Rome; it prefigures Hannibal's eventual inability to defeat Rome; it adds drama to the events; and above all, it points to the mysterious workings of divine forces, whose protection of Rome is connected with the Romans' superior moral fibre vis-à-vis their treacherous enemy.

3 Focalization

Ancient rhetorical theory considered vividness (*enargeia*) to be one of the most important qualities of historical writing, and recent years have witnessed a growing scholarly interest in ancient historians' use of vision and visuality.[16] Feldherr's chapter in this volume discusses how *enargeia* could prompt ancient readers to choose among different perspectives on past events and to question the authority of a historical

---

[13] Levene (2010: 287–9); cf. also Levene (1993: 59–60).
[14] In Polyb. 9.6.5–6, the Romans happen to have enlisted new troops on that very day, and thus have a large number of soldiers ready to defend the city. When the Carthaginians see the Roman forces lined up against them, they give up attacking the city and draw back instead.
[15] As Gärtner (1975: 42) and Levene (2010: 287–8) point out, at 26.8.5, Quintus Fabius Maximus speaks against the idea of abandoning the siege of Capua to bring reinforcements to the city, stating: *Romam cum eo exercitu qui ad urbem esset Iovem foederum ruptorum ab Hannibale testem deosque alios defensuros esse.* See further Levene (1993: 58–60), (2010: 291).
[16] On ancient notions of ἐνάργεια (in Latin *evidentia*, *demonstratio* or *inlustratio*), see e.g. Demetr. *Eloc.* 209–20; *Rhet. Her.* 4.68.55; [Longinus], *Subl.* 15; Quint. *Inst.* 6.2.29–33, 8.3.61–71; Otto (2009: esp. 31–4), Webb (2009: 87–130), Plett (2012: 7–21, 37–50), on vision in Livy, see e.g. Feldherr (1998), Jaeger (2007).

narrative, as well as how historians could use it to express ideas about the aims of their accounts. Among his examples are Polybius's and Livy's narratives of the battle of Lake Trasimene (217 BCE), where thick fog prevented the combatants (and especially the Romans) from perceiving their surroundings.[17]

I shall not focus on the metahistorical value of vision and blindness in the *Ab Urbe Condita*, but will rather examine Livy's use of the narrative technique by which atmospheric phenomena direct the reader's gaze towards specific places or events, usually by way of internal focalization. This, I argue, is an important means for creating vivid narratives of military events.

I discussed a striking example of such a technique in a previous article, where I analysed the role played by the mist, the wind, and the sun in the account of Scipio's sea-crossing from Sicily to Africa in Book 29.[18] Here, the alternating moments of vision and blindness involve the reader in the perspective of the Roman men on their ships and build to the moment when the whole of the African coast appears before the Romans' eyes. In this case, the vision opening up in an almost cinematic manner is not just a physical vista but also an ideal one: what appears before the soldiers – and the readers – is the view of Africa as the next object of Roman rule, with the Roman gaze symbolizing their power over Hannibal's land. With reference to Feldherr's chapter in this volume, one can say that, in this case, the characters' and the reader's vision come together to provide a vivid representation not just of one event, but of broader historical processes.

In battle accounts, the same technique can work effectively to put the outcome of combat before the reader's eye, in all its significance. A famous example is provided by the above-mentioned battle of Lake Trasimene. Towards the end of the narrative, Livy reports that 6,000 soldiers from the Romans' advance line managed to escape the slaughter by way of a sortie and reached the top of a nearby hill (22.6.8–9):

> 8. sex milia ferme primi agminis per adversos hostes eruptione impigre facta, ignari omnium quae post se agerentur, ex saltu evasere, et cum in tumulo quodam constitissent, clamorem modo ac sonum armorum audientes, quae fortuna pugnae esset neque scire nec perspicere prae caligine poterant. 9. inclinata denique re, cum incalescente sole dispulsa nebula aperuisset diem, tum liquida iam luce montes campique perditas res stratamque ostendere foede Romanam aciem.

> 8. About 6,000 at the head of the column had made a spirited charge through the enemy facing them, and thus managed to exit from the defile, unaware of what was happening behind them. They halted on a knoll, but heard only the shouting and clash of arms, and because of the mist they could not see, or know, how the battle was going. 9. It was only when the issue was decided that the sun's heat dispersed the mist, and brought on the light of day. Then, in the now clear sunlight, the hills

---

[17] On the importance of the theme of perceptual failure in this narrative see also Levene (2010: 267–70), Clark (2014: 80–1) (who underlines the agency of the fog).
[18] Fabrizi (2016).

and plains revealed to them that the battle was lost, and the Roman army hideously slaughtered.

Trans. J. C. Yardley

This scene develops, of course, the central theme of perceptual failure, which runs throughout the account of this battle; at the same time, it also highly effectively brings the narrative of the fighting to a close by condensing the entirety of the Roman defeat into one vivid, impressive scene.

A similar technique is at work in Livy's account of the battle of Cynoscephalae (33.6–10), where the Romans fought in 197 BCE against Philip V of Macedon. On the day of the battle, thick fog fell on the area around the range of hills called Cynoscephalae ('Dogs' Heads'),[19] so that, at the beginning, Romans and Macedonians were not even able to see each other (33.6.12–7.4). The combat started when a Roman reconnoitring party suddenly came into view of a Macedonian garrison stationed on the hilltops (33.7.5). Only while the fighting between those two groups of soldiers (to which the reinforcements sent by Flamininus were soon added) was already raging (33.7.6–8) did the fog start to clear.

At this point, readers are granted a comprehensive view of the battlefield focalized through Philip (33.7.8–11):

> 8. ... rex, ut qui nihil minus illo die propter effusam caliginem quam proelium expectasset, magna parte hominum omnis generis pabulatum missa, aliquamdiu inops consilii trepidavit; 9. deinde, postquam nuntii instabant, et iam iuga montium detexerat nebula, et in conspectu erant Macedones in tumulum maxime editum inter alios compulsi loco se magis quam armis tutantes, 10. committendam rerum summam in discrimen utcumque ratus, ne partis indefensae iactura fieret, 11. Athenagoram ducem mercede militantium cum omnibus praeter Thracas auxiliis et equitatu Macedonum ac Thessalorum mittit.

> 8. ... After the widespread darkness that had fallen, however, the last thing the king expected on that day was a battle, and he had sent out a large section of his forces of every category on a foraging expedition. For a time he dithered, at a loss what to do. 9. The messages, however, then became insistent; the cloud had now lifted to reveal the hilltops; and the Macedonians came into view massed together on a prominence higher than the others and defending themselves more by virtue of their position than their weapons. 10. Concluding that, come what may, he had to throw everything into the fight so as not to sacrifice part of his army by leaving it unsupported, 11. Philip sent out the leader of his mercenary troops, Athenagoras, with all the auxiliaries (apart from the Thracians) along with the Macedonian and Thessalian cavalry.

Trans. J. C. Yardley

---

[19] For the localization of the battle, see Walbank (1967: 577–9) (with further bibliography), Hammond (1988).

Livy here departs from his main source, Polybius, whom he otherwise follows closely.[20] Polybius (18.22.2) has the king receive news from the messengers coming from the battlefield and mentions the clearing of the fog only as a factor that causes Philip to send reinforcements (since one of the main reasons for not fighting is no longer extant). Livy, on the other hand, uses the clearing of the fog to present the events directly through Philip's eyes and guide the reader's gaze toward the hill. While Polybius speaks of 'hilltops' in general, Livy sets the action on the highest hilltop of all. As a result, the prominence upon which Romans and Macedonians fight stands out as the main landmark within the battlefield and thus works as a sort of spotlight for the combat raging on its top. Scholars have generally interpreted the strong visual quality of Livy's narrative of Cynoscephalae as a means for involving the reader in the events and for stressing the importance of the battle.[21] I suggest that another effect is at work here – namely, that the fog contributes to characterizing the two opposing forces and their commanders.[22] This will be discussed in the next section.

4 Characterization: Philip V, the Romans and the fog at Cynoscephalae

While relating the arrival of the mist on the day of the battle, Livy elaborates on its effect on each of the two armies. First, the Romans (33.6.12):

> tertio die primo nimbus effusus, dein caligo nocti simillima Romanos metu insidiarum tenuit.
>
> On the third day there was a downpour followed by a fog dark as night, and this pinned down the Romans, who were afraid of being ambushed.
>
> *Trans. J. C. Yardley*

The detail concerning the Romans' fear of ambush is completely absent in the corresponding passage from Polybius (ἐπιγενομένου δ'ὄμβρου καὶ βροντῶν ἐξαισίων, πάντα συνέβη τὸν ἀέρα τὸν ἐκ τῶν νεφῶν κατὰ τὴν ἐπιοῦσαν ἡμέραν ὑπὸ τὴν ἑωθινὴν πεσεῖν ἐπὶ τὴν γῆν, ὥστε διὰ τὸν ἐφεστῶτα ζόφον μηδὲ τοὺς ἐν ποσὶ δύνασθαι βλέπειν, 18.20.7).[23] Instead, it resonates with a recurring theme of the *Ab Urbe Condita*, that of Roman armies falling prey to foreigners' ambushes (on which see below, §6). Most

---

[20] The narrative of Cynoscephalae in Livy 33.6–10 corresponds to Polyb., 18.19–27; cf. Briscoe (1973: 1), Tränkle (1977: 27), Hammond (1988: 60). Livy abridges Polybius at several points (cf. Tränkle (1977: 84–5)), and reworks some passages, for example – as I show in what follows – by concentrating more on Philip's emotions. For comparison of specific points, see Briscoe (1973: 256–66). For a recent comparison of Polybius and Livy see Eckstein (2015), which I discuss below (50–1).
[21] Cf. e.g. Walsh (1961: 186), Luce (1977: 41), Tränkle (1977: 101).
[22] For a similar role played by landscape in characterizing historical actors cf. Laporte (in this volume). For the 'characterizing function' that space in narratives can fulfil see De Jong (2012: 15).
[23] Polybius is quoted from the edition Buettner-Wobst (1962). Translations are from Paton (1926).

interestingly, it is recalled later, when, at 33.7.4, Livy reports that Flamininus sent out scouts to find where the enemy was encamped:

> Romanus ... exploratum tamen ubi hostis esset decem turmas equitum et mille pedites misit, monitos ut ab insidiis, quas dies obscurus apertis quoque locis tecturus esset, praecaverent.

> The Roman commander ... did send out a scouting detachment of ten squadrons of cavalry and a thousand infantry to locate the enemy, warning them to beware of an ambush, which the poor daylight would hide even in the open.
> *Trans. J. C. Yardley*

Again, nothing of the sort is in Polybius, who merely writes at 18.21.1 that Flamininus 'pushed forward ten squadrons of horse and about a thousand light-armed infantry, sending them out with orders to go over the ground reconnoitring cautiously' (trans. W. R. Paton).

When the focus shifts to Philip, the text presents the difficulty of the Macedonian army on the march rather differently (33.7.1–2):

> 1. Philippus maturandi itineris causa, post imbrem nubibus in terram demissis nihil deterritus, signa ferri iussit; 2. sed tam densa caligo occaecaverat diem ut neque signiferi viam nec signa milites cernerent, agmen ad incertos clamores vagum velut errore nocturno turbaretur.

> 1. To speed up his progress Philip, undaunted by the clouds that had come down to ground level after the rainstorm, ordered an advance. 2. But the fog that had darkened the daylight was so thick that the standard-bearers could not see the road or the soldiers the standards; and the column, wandering about toward indistinct shouts as if lost in the night, was thrown into disarray.
> *Trans. J. C. Yardley*

This corresponds to Polybius 18.20.8–9:

> 8. οὐ μὴν ἀλλ' ὅ γε Φίλιππος κατανύσαι σπεύδων ἐπὶ τὸ προκείμενον, ἀναζεύξας προῄει μετὰ πάσης τῆς στρατιᾶς. 9. δυσχρηστούμενος δὲ κατὰ τὴν πορείαν διὰ τὴν ὁμίχλην, βραχὺν τόπον διανύσας ...

> 8. Philip, however, who was in a hurry to effect his purpose, broke up his camp and advanced with his whole army, 9. but finding it difficult to march owing to the mist, after having made but little progress ...
> *Trans. W. R. Paton*

Livy develops Polybius's rather sober remark into a graphic scene. He elaborates on the soldiers' sensory failure and their desperate attempt to orient themselves by the shouts of their comrades-in-arms.[24] Scholars have singled out this passage as a typical example of Livian *enargeia*.[25]

The disorientation experienced by the Macedonian soldiers prefigures a theme which will be central in the account of the battle, namely Philip's lack of control over events.[26] Scholars generally agree that both Polybius and Livy present Philip at Cynoscephalae as irresolute, driven by his emotions, and ultimately incapable of reacting to unexpected circumstances. In order to fully understand such a representation, a preliminary summary of the events appears necessary.

The battle started almost by chance when the Roman scouts stumbled into a Macedonian garrison. Fighting on the ridge ensued and gradually intensified as both Philip and Flamininus, who were encamped, respectively, to the north and the south of the range of Cynoscephalae, sent reinforcements.[27] Then Philip, deceived by the overoptimistic reports coming from the field, decided to lead his entire army up the ridge and against the enemy. Flamininus, too, leaving his right wing and the elephants in reserve, moved against the Macedonians with his left wing and lightly armed soldiers and joined the part of his men who had by then been pursued down to the level ground; the Romans thus started making their way up the hills once more. Philip came up the ridge with only the right section of his phalanx – the left, which had been out to forage, following, still half in disarray. The Macedonian right initially had the upper hand against the Roman left, but then Flamininus moved from the left to the right of his line and launched his right wing against the disorganized Macedonian left. The latter made virtually no resistance and fled. The final blow was struck when twenty Roman maniples executed an encircling manoeuvre and attacked Philip's right from behind; the phalanx, which was incapable of turning, was then cut to pieces.

In the accounts of both Polybius and Livy, all the main turning points of the battle are marked by Philip's rash choices, but Livy seems to underline the king's emotionality even more than his Greek model does. Upon receiving his men's requests for help, Philip 'dithered, at a loss what to do' (*inops consilii trepidavit*, 33.7.8) – a comment which is absent in Polybius – and it was only when the fog cleared to reveal the Macedonians under pressure that he resolved to send reinforcements. To be sure, Livy provides a rational explanation for this choice ('he had to throw everything into the fight so as not to sacrifice part of his army to leave it unsupported', 33.7.10), but he omits the further

---

[24] For auditory details as a means to involve the reader in the narrated events, cf. Feldherr (in this volume).
[25] Walsh (1961: 186–7), Tränkle (1977: 100–1).
[26] For lack of control as a central theme in Livy's account of Cynoscephalae, cf. recently Clark (2014: 162–4). As she points out, neither side at first appears fully in control of the landscape, but the Romans eventually succeed in imposing their own control over it.
[27] This is what one learns from Polyb. 18.20.9, according to whom Philip, 'finding it difficult to march owing to the mist, after having made but little progress, . . . entrenched his army and sent off his covering force with orders to occupy the summits of the hills which lay between him and the enemy' (transl. W. R. Paton). Since Philip was marching from north-east (cf. Walbank (1967: 576–9)), this means that he remained north of the hills. Livy 33.7.3, on the other hand, writes that the king crossed the range of hills. This would mean that Philip was on the same side of the range as the Romans – which does not make sense in terms of what follows. Livy's subsequent narrative, however, is consistent with Polybius's topography.

reason constituted by the disappearance of the fog (cf. above: 46), which in his account serves as a scenic effect presenting the Macedonians' desperate situation. All in all, Livy seems to place a heavier emphasis on the king's emotions than on his rational considerations in this passage.

Later, both historians present Philip's decision to recall his army from foraging and lead it against the enemy as conflicting with the king's own dislike for the terrain, and as caused by his ill-founded reliance on the news brought by messengers. Once more, Livy appears to enhance Polybius's motif of irrational choice. The Greek historian explains why the terrain was not suitable for battle: the Cynoscephalae 'are very rough and broken and attain a considerable height' (33.22.9; trans. W. R. Paton). Philip thus foresaw the difficulties that the rough landscape would cause in battle but was persuaded by the messengers, whose words the historian reports in direct speech, to lead his army out of the camp. Livy's version is at the same time more concise and more vivid (33.8.1–2):

> 1. laetior res quam pro successu pugnae nuntiata, cum alii super alios recurrentes ex proelio clamarent fugere pavidos Romanos, 2. invitum et cunctabundum et dicentem <...> temere fieri, non locum sibi placere non tempus, perpulit ut educeret omnes copias in aciem.

> 1. The engagement was reported more positively than the Macedonian success warranted since men running back from the battle in waves called out that the Romans were fleeing in terror, 2. and this made Philip bring all his troops into action, reluctant and hesitant though he was – it was a reckless manoeuvre, he declared, and he liked neither the locale nor the timing.
>
> *Trans. J. C. Yardley*

As Briscoe notes, 'L[ivy] chang[es] the direct speech of the Macedonians to indirect, but verbaliz[es] Philip's thoughts.'[28] In this way, the focus lies on the king's own feelings rather than on the circumstance that led him to act in a certain way. The way those feelings are presented – with the polysyndetic tricolon *invitum et cunctabundum et dicentem*, followed by the asyndetic and anaphoric series *temere fieri, non locum sibi placere non tempus* (without any further explanation of why Philip disliked the terrain and the timing) – conveys the image of a man in utter panic. In the end, one almost gets the impression that Philip went to battle against his own will, being pushed, rather than persuaded, to take that course of action.[29]

When Philip reaches the top of the ridge with his phalanx, Livy describes the sequence of feelings the king went through as he saw the action develop: first great joy (*ingenti gaudio est elatus*, 33.8.9), as he saw the weapons and bodies of the fallen Romans on the hilltop and the combat raging close to the enemy camp; then fear and uncertainty

---

[28] Briscoe (1973: 260).
[29] Eckstein (2015: 414) interprets this as an instance of Livy's dramatization of the Polybian material: 'the king reluctantly commits his phalanx to battle, which will end in catastrophe'.

(*paulisper incertus an in castra reciperet copias trepidavit*, 33.8.10), as he realized that the tide had turned and his men were being pursued by the enemy; at last, pressed by circumstances, he resolved to deploy his men for battle despite the fact that part of his army was still on its way (33.8.11–12). Apart from adding the visual detail of the Roman weapons scattered on the hill,[30] Livy also complicates Polybius's description of Philip's psychological reactions – first joy, then the realization of the necessity to fight (18.24.6-7) – by adding an intermediate phase of fear and uncertainty. Thus, Philip emerges once more as not only a rash and emotional character, but also a cowardly one.

Assessing Livy's characterization of Flamininus in the account of Cynoscephalae is considerably more difficult.[31] Scholars have noted that, while Polybius describes him as a competent and rational general, who acts based on the careful assessment of circumstances, the *Ab Urbe Condita* represents him as driven by necessity and chance almost as much as Philip is. Recently, Eckstein (2015, 411–16) has interpreted the dissimilarity in terms of the different historical and literary aims of the two historians: whereas Polybius develops a lesson in generalship for an audience of statesmen, Livy is principally interested in providing a highly moving account that celebrates a great victory of Rome. The 'desperation and desperate improvisation' which, in Eckstein's reading, characterize the actions of *both* commanders during the battle (412–13) are thus part and parcel of the drama that Livy puts before his reader's eye.[32]

While I agree that the kind of contrast which is at work in the *Histories* is not found in the *Ab Urbe Condita*, I suggest that the emphasis should be shifted. It is true that Livy eliminates Polybius's detailed descriptions of the rationale underlying Flamininus's choices, but it is hard to recognize any sign of desperation in the consul's reactions to the shifting circumstances of the battle, which are swift and logical.[33] The fact is, rather, that the narrative does not show any particular interest in Flamininus's thoughts and feelings,[34]

---

[30] Walsh (1961: 186) quotes this as one further example of Livy's *enargeia*. Clark (2014: 165) interprets this view as a vivid representation of Roman control over the countryside.

[31] On Flamininus's overall representation in the *AUC*, see (with contrasting interpretations) Walsh (1961: 101), Briscoe (1973: 22–47), Tränkle (1977: 144–54), Carawan (1988).

[32] Cf. also Carawan (1988), who suggests that this less positive assessment of Flamininus's strategic qualities might go back to annalistic sources that were hostile to him.

[33] As Eckstein (2015: 415) himself admits, Flamininus proves 'a quick opportunist who certainly does not panic'. See e.g. the contrast between Flamininus's quick sending of reinforcements at 33.7.7 (*quingenti equites et duo milia peditum ... propere missa*) and Philip's panic in the same situation (33.7.8).

[34] The reader gets to know Flamininus's thoughts only at three points (and, in each case, very briefly). The first is 33.8.3, where the commander is said to have 'done the same' (*idem et Romanus*) as Philip (i.e. deploying his troops) because he was 'prompted by necessity rather than because circumstances favoured combat' (*magis necessitate quam occasione pugnae inductus*, trans. J. C. Yardley). Contrary to suggestions by Eckstein (2015: 414) and, to a lesser degree, Carawan (1988: 222–3), no analogy between the two commanders seems to be implied here: Livy is just saying that Flamininus, like Philip, deployed the whole of his forces, not that his motives were the same as Philip's. The second passage is 33.9.6, where Flamininus launches the decisive charge against the left flank of the Macedonian phalanx because '[h]e thought that if some of the enemy's forces were overwhelmed they would drag the rest along with them' (*ratus partem profligatam cetera tracturam*, 33.9.6). The latter is a gross simplification of Polyb. 18.25.4–5 but is neither an emotional nor a desperate choice. The third passage is 33.10.3–4 where, after the rout of the Macedonian phalanx, Flamininus sees the survivors raising their spears and is at first uncertain what that might mean.

while it privileges Philip's mental processes. The focus of attention, throughout the narrative, seems to be the moral and military failure of the king, who throughout proves himself incapable of living up to the glorious fame of the Macedonian kingdom.[35]

The fact that the character of Flamininus emerges from Livy's account as a less impressive strategist than he does from Polybius should not detract from the awareness of the fundamental difference existing between the two opponents. While the consul, though pressed by circumstances, reacts promptly to them, the king is swayed by his own fears and emotions. In a way, the less emphatic focus on Flamininus as a strategist has the effect of reducing the contrast between two individual generals and increasing the contrast between Macedon and Rome.

The fog appears functional to such a distinction. By creating an atmosphere of uncertainty in the hours preceding the battle, it brings out the different moral outlooks of the two sides. The Romans *are* scared, but it is fear of ambush – that is, the recurrent uneasiness felt by Romans in the *Ab Urbe Condita* in the face of their enemies' deceit.[36] Flamininus proves, in this respect at least, a cautious commander, who sends out scouts with specific instructions to beware of ambush. Philip's soldiers, on the other hand, seem lost from the very beginning, as they stumble in the mist. Later, the clearing fog works to involve the reader in the king's perspective: the reader sees the battlefield with Philip's eyes, realizes his inability to grasp what is going on until the very end and participates in his ever-shifting emotions.

5 Symbolism: the mist at Magnesia and the vacuity of Eastern display

The mist plays a conspicuous role in another battle account from the *Ab Urbe Condita*: that of the battle of Magnesia, which the Romans fought against king Antiochus III of Syria in 190 BCE, at 37.39–44. It is my aim in this section to show that such a role is essentially symbolic: rather than concretely affecting the course of events, the mist here lays bare the fundamental weakness of Antiochus's army and thus both prefigures and explains the outcome of the fighting.

The narrative – like so many battle accounts in ancient historiography – begins with the description of the two opposing forces.[37] This section appears particularly interesting, not only because it is exceptionally long and rich in exotic detail, but also for the clear

---

[35] The emptiness of the *fama* of Macedon is explicitly stated by Flamininus in his speech to his troops (*Fama stetisse non viribus Macedoniae regnum; eam quoque famam tandem evanuisse*, 33.8.5–6; cf. Clark (2014: 164)), which appears to be, in several respects, a reply to Philip's speech at 33.3.11–4.3 (cf. e.g. *multa iam saepe memorata de maiorum virtutibus simul de militari laude Macedonum*, 33.3.12).

[36] Fear (on both sides) also accompanies the encounter between the Roman scouts and the Macedonian garrison in Livy 33.7.5: *ubi ventum ad insessos tumulos est, pavore mutuo iniecto velut torpentes quieverunt; dein nuntiis retro in castra ad duces missis, ubi primus terror ab necopinato visu consedit, non diutius certamine abstinuere*. Tränkle (1977: 102) notes that Livy here turns a brief Polybian account into a dramatic sequence of psychological states. For Romans' anxieties about enemy treachery, as deployed through the use of terrain and weather, cf. Östenberg (2018).

[37] For array as a standard element in ancient battle narratives see Lendon (2017: esp. 58–62).

opposition between the two armies that it sets from the very beginning. The Roman array is introduced with the words *Romana acies unius prope formae fuit et hominum et armorum genere* ('The Roman battle line was more or less uniform in terms both of men and weaponry', 37.39.7, trans. J. C. Yardley). Emphasis is placed on the uniformity of the army, whose bulk is constituted by the two Roman legions in the centre and the two legions of Latin allies on their sides (37.39.7–8). On the right side, Livy goes on to explain, the consul also deployed Eumenes' auxiliaries and the Achaean peltasts (*caetrati*) – some 3,000 foot-soldiers in total – but he stresses that these constituted a sort of external addition to the '"regular" battle formation' (*extra hanc velut iustam aciem*, 37.39.9, trans. J. C. Yardley).[38] Further still to the right – and thus all the more 'external' – were a squadron of 3,000 horsemen (of whom, however, the text specifies that they were mostly Roman) and corps of Cretans and Trallians (37.39.9–10). On the left side, four squadrons of Roman cavalry were stationed.[39]

In the description of Antiochus's deployment, on the other hand, Livy heavily stresses its diversity, as the introducing remark at 37.40.1 makes clear: *regia acies varia magis multis gentibus, dissimilitudine armorum auxiliorumque erat* ('The king's line of battle was more diverse, composed as it was of many races with different weaponry and different supporting troops', trans. J. C. Yardley). Subsequently, the text lists no fewer than twenty-five different corps of various ethnic origins (some of them composed, in their turn, of different peoples).[40] In some cases, it reports the foreign names of such squadrons (e.g. *phalangitae, agema, cataphracti, argyraspides*); attention is also devoted to their weaponry and fighting techniques, especially if they are exotic (as in the case of the Arab archers mounted on dromedaries at 37.40.12), or if they exercise a particular visual impact (as with the elephants placed on the front of the phalanx, which, as Livy tells at 37.40.4, were made more impressive by their ornaments).

This is a fine example of how a historian can creatively use a standard element of ancient historical writing – namely, the array section that typically precedes the account of the fighting – in order to give a battle narrative a certain slant. The text sets the compact

---

[38] It should be noted that, in fact, these foot soldiers *were* part of the 'regular battle formation'; cf. Weissenborn and Mueller (1907: 68), Briscoe (1981: 347). Livy's remark should be understood as part of a rhetorical strategy that opposes the diversity of Antiochus's army to the ethnic homogeneity of the Roman force.

[39] 2,000 Macedonians and Thracians, who had voluntarily joined the Roman force, were left to guard the camp (37.39.12).

[40] These are, in the order in which Livy mentions them, as follows: At the centre: *phalangitae* (16,000), divided into ten sections on the front, separated by pairs of elephants (each carrying four armed men plus the driver). On the right side: 1,500 Galatian infantry; 3,000 *cataphracti* (mail-clad cavalry); the *agema* (1,000 cavalry, composed of Medes and 'an admixture of cavalry from many races in the same region'); a herd of sixteen elephants; the 'royal company' (*regia cohors*), or *argyraspides*; 1,200 Dahae (mounted archers); 3,000 light infantry, made up of Cretans and Trallians; 2,500 Mysian archers; a corps of Cretan slingers and Elymean archers, totalling 4,000. On the left side: 1,500 Galatian infantry and 2,000 Cappadocians, armed in similar fashion; 'a mixture of all kind of auxiliary troops', totaling 2,700; 3,000 *cataphracti* plus 1,000 other horsemen forming the 'royal squadron' (*regia ala*: Syrians, Phrygians, and Lydians); before the latter, scythe-bearing chariots and dromedaries mounted by Arab archers; Tarentines, 2,500 Galatian horsemen; 1,000 Neocretans; Carians and Cilicians, 1,500 in total; 4,000 *caetrati* (Pisidian, Pamphilian and Lycian); Cyrtian and Elymean auxiliaries; sixteen more elephants.

Roman force against the huge and diverse army of the Eastern king. That Livy tended to think of ethnic diversity as a weakness for an army has been recently stressed in Levene's analysis of the battle of Zama in Book 30.[41] While the accent there lay, above all, on the incommunicability among the peoples composing Hannibal's army – each of them speaking a different language – at Magnesia the enumeration of contingents joins the idea of diversity to that of a vacuous display of size.

In fact, it is precisely the exorbitant length of Antiochus's battle-line that proves fatal to the king (37.41.2–4):

2. nebula matutina, crescente die levata in nubes, caliginem dedit; 3. umor inde velut ab austro perfudit omnia; quae nihil admodum Romanis, eadem perincommoda regiis erant: nam et obscuritas lucis in acie modica Romanis non adimebat in omnes partes conspectum, et umor toto fere gravi armatu nihil gladius aut pila hebetabat; 4. regii tam lata acie ne ex medio quidem cornua sua conspicere poterant, nedum extremi inter se conspicerentur, et umor arcus fundasque et iaculorum amenta emollierat.

2. There was a morning mist that rose to form clouds as the day advanced and produced overcast conditions. 3. Then a drizzle, like that brought by the south wind, dampened everything. While these factors had no adverse [e]ffects[42] on the Romans, they were particularly disadvantageous for the king's troops. Their line being relatively short, the faintness of the light did not hamper the Romans' view in any direction and, their troops being almost all heavy-armed, the drizzle did not take the edge off swords or spears. 4. With such a wide line of battle, the king's men were unable to see from the centre to their wings, and much less could the flanks keep each other in sight, while the drizzle had taken the tautness out of bows, slings, and spear thongs.

Trans. J. C. Yardley

This passage is remarkable in how it turns a meteorological phenomenon into both a graphic representation of the strengths and weaknesses of each army, and a prefiguration of the outcome of the combat.

The corresponding section of Polybius's *Histories* is unfortunately lost, but comparison with other historical accounts of the same battle can help to appreciate the textual strategy of the *Ab Urbe Condita*. Appian (*Syr.* 33.171), who was drawing on either Polybius or an annalistic source that depended, in turn, on Polybius,[43] has the mist take away the sight of

---

[41] Levene (2010: 239–44). He interprets Livy's portrayal of the battle as a 'pessimistic warning' (244), since by Livy's time the Roman army had itself started to become a multiethnic force.
[42] 'Affects' in Yardley's translation is probably a printing mistake.
[43] For the idea that Appian was following Polybius see e.g. Brodersen (1991); Rich (2015) with a history of the problem and further bibliography. For the idea that he was following a later annalistic source: Goukowsky (2007: CXIII–CXXV), with further bibliography. For a treatment of the main issues concerning Appian's account of the battle see e.g. Goukowsky (2007: LXXXIX–CXIII), Rich (2015: 97–9).

the battlefield for both armies without distinction. Zonaras (9.20, p. 289, ll. 8–13 Boissevain), the Byzantine epitomist of Cassius Dio, reports the occurrence of both rain and mist.[44] According to Zonaras, rain fell first, making bows and slings useless.[45] Then came the mist, which proved a more serious hindrance to Antiochus's army than to the Romans. One reason for this was that the Romans already had the upper hand and thus did not panic; another was that Antiochus's army included more archers and cavalry, for whom visibility was more vital than for infantry troops fighting at close quarters.[46]

Livy alone describes the effect of the mist in terms of the inability of Antiochus's troops to see one another because of the disproportionate size of the army. It is even more interesting to observe that, despite being so emphatically mentioned at the outset of the narrative, the mist does not, in fact, play any crucial role in what follows. What proves decisive is the panic of the horses attached to Antiochus's scythe-bearing chariots, which start running here and there and throw the king's army into disarray (37.41.5–12);[47] as a consequence, the left wing and then the phalanx come apart as the Romans advance (37.42.1–6). A later attempt to attack the Roman camp is frustrated by the energetic reaction of the military tribune Marcus Aemilius Lepidus and by Attalus's intervention (37.42.7–43.5).

In other words, the text introduces an element at the outset which is not strictly functional to the development of the action, but which plays a fundamental role in laying bare one of the main weaknesses of the king's army. The very length of the battle-line, far from corresponding to real strength, results from the addition of unamalgamated peoples, each maintaining their own particular features and weaponry. This is not just a further example of the problems posed to armies by the presence of different ethnic components; it is also a graphic depiction of the vacuity of Eastern power and riches. The inability of the centre to see the extremities, let alone of the extremities to glimpse each other, symbolically suggests the disjointed nature of the army and the inability of its commanders to control the variety of realities it includes, no matter how impressive a spectacle they might provide. Paradoxically, then, the mist here seems to have the function of making something evident to the reader – precisely by hiding something else from characters' view.

6 Fog and the landscape of ambush

My observations in sections 3–4 suggest that atmospheric phenomena can work symbolically in military narratives to bring out the moral strength or weakness of

---

[44] Rain also features in Frontin. *Str.* 4.30; Flor. 1.24.17.
[45] Zonaras probably means that the dampness slackened the strings of bows and slings.
[46] Cassius Dio's sources have been an object of scholarly debate. If he used Livy in the narrative of Magnesia (which belonged to Book 19), it is clear that the *AUC* was not the only source. Whether he drew on Polybius is uncertain. For a summary of the debate with further bibliography see Simons (2009: 7–8).
[47] The use of these elaborate chariots, which ultimately proved to be completely ineffectual (indeed, counterproductive), appears as one more sign of Antiochus's empty display of forces (cf. *inani ludibrio*, 12). The irony of the situation is emphasized at 37.42.1: *Ceterum vana illa res verae mox cladis causa fuit* ('Nevertheless, that futile episode soon proved to be the cause of a real calamity').

commanders and peoples (as at Cynoscephalae), or the character and identity of the community that constitutes an army (as at Magnesia). I would like to conclude my examination by turning my attention to a specific type of account in which the narrated occurrence of mist or rain can participate in the development of a moral theme, viz. narratives of ambush.

Romans' falling prey to foreigners' ambushes is a recurrent motif in the *Ab Urbe Condita*, where it often serves to explain Roman defeats.[48] While Romans themselves can occasionally resort to ambush, this occurs much more rarely; moreover, ambushes set by Romans are usually problematized or motivated by specific circumstances.[49] In general, Livy tends to present the use of ambush as ethically problematic and opposed to a 'Roman' open way of fighting. This is why, as in the above-mentioned account of Cynoscephalae, the danger of falling into an ambush provides a constant source of worry for Roman soldiers and generals.[50]

Cynoscephalae is not the only instance in which atmospheric phenomena reinforce the pattern of visual manipulation and deceit inherent in ambushes. At 10.32.5–8, for example, the Samnites take advantage of the fog to attack a Roman camp (294 BCE):

5. cum castra castris conlata essent, quod vix Romanus totiens victor auderet, ausi Samnites sunt – tantum desperatio ultima temeritatis facit – castra Romana oppugnare, et quamquam non venit ad finem tam audax inceptum, tamen haud omnino vanum fuit. 6. nebula erat ad multum diei densa adeo ut lucis usum eriperet non prospectu modo extra vallum adempto sed propinquo etiam congredientium inter se conspectu. 7. hac velut latebra insidiarum freti Samnites vixdum satis certa luce et eam ipsam premente caligine ad stationem Romanam in porta segniter agentem vigilias perveniunt. 8. improviso oppressis nec animi satis ad resistendum nec virium fuit.

5. The two camps lay close to each other, and the Samnites ventured to take a gamble that the Roman, though so often the victor, would hardly have ventured to take – such is the recklessness that sheer desperation produces – and that was to attack the Roman camp. Such a foolhardy undertaking did not achieve its end, but it was not entirely ineffective. 6. There was a fog that remained thick for most of the day, so thick as to remove visibility, not only cutting off from view that which lay beyond the rampart but even preventing people from recognizing each other at close quarters when they met. 7. The Samnites used this as cover for a surprise

---

[48] Cf. e.g. 7.34.1–2, 9.2.6–9 (the Caudine Forks, on which see e.g. Horsfall (1982; 1985: 203–4), Morello (2003), Oakley (2005: 52–60)), 9.31.6–16, 22.4.2–4, 22.28.3–8, 25.16, 27.26.1–28.2, 38.40–1, 39.20.6–8. On Hannibal's use of ambush in Livy see Pausch (2019); on the use of the motif for characterizing the Ligurians, see Fabrizi (2017b).

[49] Livy's account of the Hannibalic war, for example, features some ambushes set by Romans, but it is stressed that adoption of this strategy is due to the need to oppose a particularly deceitful enemy; on the problems connected with the Roman appropriation of the 'Hannibalic model', see Levene (2010: 228–36); and cf. my own observations in Fabrizi (2017a).

[50] Roth (2007: 390) connects this with Romans' ineffectiveness in scouting in the mid-Republican period.

attack. When it was barely dawn and the fog obscured such light as there was, they came forward to a carelessly guarded Roman outpost at one of the camp gates. 8. The guards, taken by surprise, had neither the spirit nor the strength to resist.

Trans. J. C. Yardley

The fog becomes an integral part of the war landscape – or, better, reshapes it. As scholars have shown, Livy's ambush narratives usually involve the presence of stereotyped landscapes: very often a gorge or valley, traversed by a narrow path and surrounded by steep wooded mountain flanks, or in some cases hills in which the assailers lay hidden.[51] The common implication is precisely that the use of landscape as a weapon plays a major role in explaining Roman defeats against enemies whom the Romans would conquer in regular battle.[52]

In the present passage, there is no landscape of this sort, since what is being narrated is not an ambush in the proper sense of the word, but rather an assault on a camp. However, the fog takes the place of the usual landscape of ambush (*Hoc velut latebra insidiarum freti*, 7); it is interesting that, as Oakley (2005: 352–3) remarks, the expression *nebula erat* in section 6 seems to recall the '*est locus* formula', which is a frequent way to introduce scenic descriptions in Latin literature.[53] As a result, the attack can be represented as an ambush, which confirms the *topos* according to which the Samnites are only able to defeat the Romans by means of treachery.

A special kind of visual deceit is produced by the mist at 41.2.4–7, where another foreign people, the Histri, fall upon two garrisons that are guarding a Roman camp by a lagoon of the river Timavus (178 BCE).[54] The text creates the expectation of an ambush by sketching some typical scenic elements: the Histri are said to lurk in a hidden place behind a hill (*post collem occulto loco consederunt*, 41.2.1), from which they follow the Roman column on the march *obliquis itineribus*, waiting for any suitable occasions to attack them (41.2.2).

Not only is their eventual assault on the camp accompanied by the mist, but also the very disappearance of the mist deceives the Romans further:

4. nebula matutina[55] texerat inceptum; qua dilabente ad primum teporem solis, perlucens iam aliquid, incerta tamen ut solet, lux speciem omnium multiplicem intuenti reddens, tum quoque frustrata Romanos, multo maiorem iis quam erat hostium aciem ostendit. 5. qua territi utriusque stationis milites ingenti tumultu cum in castra confugissent, haud paulo ibi plus quam quod secum ipsi attulerant terroris fecerunt. 6. nam neque dicere quod fugissent, nec percunctantibus reddere

---

[51] On the landscape of ambush cf. the studies quoted above, n. 48; moreover Oakley (1997: 7–10).
[52] Cf. Reitz-Joosse (in this volume).
[53] Cf. e.g. Enn. *Ann.* 20 Sk.; Sall. *Cat.* 55; Verg. *Aen.* 1.159, 1.441, 1.530, 3.163, 7.563. For this formula in Livy, see e.g. 6.24.2, 10.9.8, 21.25.9, 22.28.3; and Oakley (1998: 239–40), with further examples. For some instances from Greek literature, cf. van Rookhuijzen (in this volume).
[54] For a discussion of the topography see Briscoe (2012: 37–8).
[55] Note that the beginning of this sentence is the same as in 37.41.2 (quoted above: 53).

responsum poterant; et clamor in portis, ut ubi nulla esset statio quae sustineret impetum, audiebatur; et concursatio in obscuro incidentium aliorum in alios incertum fecerat an hostis intra vallum esset. 7. una vox audiebatur ad mare vocantium; id forte temere ab uno exclamatum totis passim personabat castris.

4. An early morning mist had concealed the beginning of the Istrians' enterprise. This lifted with the first warmth of the sun, but even as the light grew somewhat brighter, it was still murky (as is often the case) and magnified the size of everything. The Romans were deceived into thinking that the enemy force was much larger than it actually was. 5. The soldiers of both detachments were terrified. They fled to the camp in a great panic and compounded the fear their initial stampede had provoked 6. when they were unable to explain their flight or indeed to answer any question at all. Then an outcry was heard from the camp's entrances since there was no detachment to fend off an attack. Rushing about in the darkness had caused the Romans to bump into one another so much that it was unclear whether or not the enemy was within the rampart. 7. Amidst the shouting, a single voice was heard: 'To the sea!' This chance, ill-considered outburst from one man reached every corner of the camp.

Trans. J. D. Chaplin

This passage is remarkable both for the density of expressions that relate to the themes of perceptual failure and deceit (*texerat*; *incerta*; *speciem omnium multiplicem*; *frustrata*, 4; *nam neque dicere... poterant*; *obscuro*; *incertum*, 6), and for the way in which it seems consciously to vary a set of motifs which recur elsewhere. While usually – as in the cases of Trasimene and Cynoscephalae – the disappearance of the mist leads to vision, in this case a second type of visual deceit follows the first: the still-feeble sunlight makes the enemy army seem larger than it is (4). It is not clear whether such an effect is produced by the fact that the sunlight penetrates though still-lingering mist, or simply by the feebleness of the morning sun; regardless, the text insists on the Romans' increasing bafflement.

Visual deceit gives way – just as at Trasimene – to auditory deceit. Amidst the shouts running through the Roman camp, nobody seems to know where the enemies are (6). In the end, the shout sent out by one man is propagated through the camp and causes almost the entire Roman force to rush to the sea (7). Despite the heroic resistance of the military tribune M. Licinius Strabo and his legion (10), the Histri conquer the camp (11–13). Only later will the Romans put their forces back together and eventually take the camp back from the Histri (41.4.3–4).

This narrative is arranged according to a typical pattern: the Romans suffer a defeat at the hands of enemies who resort to treachery; later, they recover from the blow, react, and eventually take revenge on their foes. Here, the mist stresses the theme of treachery; the utter disorientation it provokes in the Romans helps to account for their momentary defeat. The weather is thus part of that uncontrollable physical world that enemies can use to their advantage and whose threat, as shown by Östenberg (2018: esp. 254–9), constantly lurks behind the surface of Roman conquest.

7 Conclusions: historiography, war and landscape

This chapter has investigated how Livy's narrative of Roman history represents landscapes of war as 'realm[s] of experience', to use Elizabeth Minchin's definition again – that is, how the text prompts the reader to think about combatants' experience of landscapes which are, for them, inextricably tied with fighting and death. I have focused on weather conditions – above all on dramatic phenomena like rain, hail or fog – because of their potential to alter combatants' perception and experience of the terrain.

I hope to have shown that the *Ab Urbe Condita* construes the weather as an integral element of war landscapes, one which stands in a dynamic relationship to topography: in some cases, it can enhance the potential of some topographies for specific military tactics (as at Trasimene or Timavus), it can reshape them (as is the case with the Samnites' ambush), or it can deeply affect the way historical actors come to know the terrain (as with Philip at Cynoscephalae). In this way, landscapes emerge not as something static, but as living environments, which help or hinder human action[56] and reflect the psychological states and moral outlook of the main actors.

On the other hand, atmospheric phenomena can also play a crucial role in involving the reader in the characters' experience of a landscape, by means of suspense or internal focalization. In this way, human experience is made central to the interpretation of history. In some cases, the human experience of landscapes also involves the recognition of supernatural agency; while the latter is rarely explicitly stated in the *Ab Urbe Condita*, the almost mysterious occurrence of some atmospheric phenomena leaves the door open for the idea of divine support for Rome.

I would like to conclude my discussion by returning to the question from which I started, which I now formulate in a slightly different way: What *is* a landscape of war? In other words, how does such a widespread and destructive phenomenon as war affect the way human beings look at the physical world around them, perceive it, and make sense of it?

Compare Livy's approach to landscape with a particular strand of the ancient and modern discourse about war that several of the chapters in this volume (e.g. Brockliss; Minchin; Zientek) investigate: that of the violence that war inflicts on nature, or of the longing for idealized landscapes in contrast to landscapes of war and death. The approach to landscape that one observes in Livy's *Ab Urbe Condita* reveals a significant contrast to such discourses; and most of the following observations might likely be applied to other ancient historians as well.[57]

Livy's text does not, as a rule, represent the effects of war in terms of traumatic disruption. There are, to be sure, some isolated exceptions, such as the Carthaginians' ravaging of the lovely landscape of Campania in 22.14.[58] In general, however, the relationship of human beings with nature, as portrayed in the *Ab Urbe Condita*, turns on

---

[56] Cf. Östenberg (2018).
[57] Cf. e.g. Riggsby (2006: 21–45) on Caesar's *Bellum Gallicum*.
[58] See Biggs (2016) for a comparison with Roman pastoral poetry and my observations in Fabrizi (2017a).

issues of control vs. lack of control. When, for example, combatants perceive a landscape as frightening or horrifying, this has nothing to do with the kind of perversion of nature that William Brockliss (in this volume) shows at work in poetry of the First World War, or that Laura Zientek (also in this volume) discusses with regard to Lucan. Rather, it can be compared to what Bettina Reitz-Joosse (again in this volume) observes with reference to Parthian 'geographies of defeat', namely the perceived failure to control an environment which is felt to be alien or hostile (or both).[59]

Of course, control of the terrain is an essential aspect of strategy and, as such, it can be expected to constitute a major issue in any historical account of military operations. What is especially interesting, however, is how the *Ab Urbe Condita* moralizes such an issue, insisting on failures of control as the consequences of one's feebleness of character (as is the case with Philip V), of a strained relationship to the gods (as with Flaminius at Trasimene or Hannibal's attempt to attack Rome), of insufficient social cohesion (as at Magnesia), or of temporary lack of thoughtfulness and caution (as with ambushed Romans).

Thus, the reader of Livy's history is prompted to imagine the physical world primarily as a space of conquest, on which the spatial, political and ethical structures of Rome are gradually imposed – but which, due to its inherent instability (which the weather so aptly exemplifies), constantly threatens to escape such control.

Bibliography

Biggs, T. 2016. 'Contesting *cunctatio*: Livy 22.14, Fabius Maximus, and the Problem of Pastoral.' *Classical Journal* 111 (3): 281–301.
Briscoe, J. 1973. *A Commentary on Livy. Books XXXI–XXXIII*. Oxford: Clarendon Press.
Briscoe, J. 1981. *A Commentary on Livy. Books XXXIV–XXXVII*. Oxford: Clarendon Press.
Briscoe, J., ed. 1986. *Livius Ab urbe condita libri XLI–XLV*. Stuttgart: Teubner.
Briscoe, J., ed. 1991. *Titi Livi Ab urbe condita libri XXXI–XL*, 2 vols Stuttgart: Teubner.
Briscoe, J. 2012. *A Commentary on Livy. Books 41–45*. Oxford: Oxford University Press.
Briscoe, J., ed. 2016. *Titi Livi Ab urbe condita*, Vol. 3, *Libri XXI–XXV*. Oxford: Oxford University Press.
Brodersen, K. 1991. *Appians Antiochike (Syriake 1,1–44,232)*. Text *und Kommentar nebst einem Anhang: Plethons Syriake-Exzerpt*. Münchener Arbeiten zur alten Geschichte 3. Munich: Editio Maris.
Buettner-Wobst, Th., ed. [1893] 1962. *Polybii Historiae*, Vol. 3, *Libri IX–XIX*. Stuttgart: Teubner.
Carawan, E. M. 1988. '*Graecia liberata* and the Role of Flamininus in Livy's Fourth Decade.' *Transactions of the American Philological Association* 118: 209–52.
Carter, T. A. and D. J. Veale. 2013. 'Weather, Terrain and Warfare: Coalition Fatalities in Afghanistan.' *Conflict Management and Peace Science* 30 (3): 220–39.
Chaplin, J. D., trans. 2007. *Livy. Rome's Mediterranean Empire. Books 41–45 and the Periochae*. Oxford: Oxford University Press.

---

[59] For control over nature as a fundamental aspect of Roman imperialism, which is reflected in Roman discourses about defeat, see Östenberg (2018).

Clark, V. 2014. 'Landscapes of Conquest: Space, Place, and Environment in Livy's *Ab Urbe Condita*.' PhD diss., Princeton University.
De Jong, I. J. F., ed. 2012. *Space in Ancient Greek Literature*. Mnemosyne Supplements 339. Leiden: Brill.
Eckstein, A. M. 2015. 'Livy, Polybius, and the Greek East (Books 31–45).' In *A Companion to Livy*, edited by B. Mineo, 407–22. Malden, MA: Wiley-Blackwell.
Fabrizi, V. 2015. 'Hannibal's March and Roman Imperial Space in Livy, *Ab urbe condita*, Book 21.' *Philologus* 159 (1): 118–55.
Fabrizi, V. 2016. 'Space, Vision, and the Friendly Sea: Scipio's Crossing to Africa in Livy's Book 29.' In *Seemacht, Seeherrschaft und die Antike* (Historia - Einzelschrift 244), edited by E. Baltrusch, H. Kopp and C. Wendt, 279–89. Stuttgart: Steiner.
Fabrizi, V. 2017a. '"The Cloud that (...) sat on the Mountaintops": A Narratological Analysis of Space in Livy's Account of Quintus Fabius Maximus' Dictatorship.' *American Journal of Philology* 138 (4): 673–706.
Fabrizi, V. 2017b. 'La città e il mondo: insidie del paesaggio e identità romana in *Ab urbe condita* XXXVIII–XL.' In *Miscellanea graecolatina V*, edited by S. Costa and F. Gallo, 131–55. Milano: Biblioteca Ambrosiana.
Feldherr, A. 1998. *Spectacle and Society in Livy's History*. Berkeley, Los Angeles and London: University of California Press.
Gärtner, H. A. 1975. *Beobachtungen zu Bauelementen in der antiken Historiographie besonders bei Livius und Caesar*. Wiesbaden: Steiner.
Goukowsky, P., ed. 2007. *Appien, Histoire Romaine*, Vol. 6, *Livre XI, Le livre syriaque*. Paris: Les belles lettres.
Hammond, N. G. L. 1988. 'The Campaign and the Battle of Cynoscephalae in 197 BC.' *Journal of Hellenic Studies* 108: 60–82.
Horsfall, N. 1982. 'The Caudine Forks: Topography and Illusion.' *Papers of the British School at Rome* 50: 45–52.
Horsfall, N. 1985. 'Illusion and Reality in Latin Topographical Writing.' *Greece & Rome* 21: 197–208.
Jaeger, M. 2007. 'Fog on the Mountain: Philip and Mt. Haemus in Livy 40.21–22.' In *A Companion to Greek and Roman Historiography*, Vol. 2, edited by J. Marincola, 397–403. Malden, MA: Wiley-Blackwell.
Lendon, J. E. 2017. 'Battle Description in the Ancient Historians. Part I: Structure, Array, and Fighting.' *Greece & Rome* 64 (1): 38–64.
Levene, D. S. 1993. *Religion in Livy*. Leiden: Brill.
Levene, D. S. 2010. *Livy on the Hannibalic War*. Oxford: Oxford University Press.
Luce, T. J. 1977. *Livy. The Composition of His History*. Princeton, NJ: Princeton University Press.
McDonald, A. H. 1957. 'The Style of Livy.' *Journal of Roman Studies* 47 (1/2): 155–72.
Morello, R. 2003. 'Place and Road: Neglected Aspects of Livy 9.1–19.' In *Studies in Latin Literature and Roman History*, vol. 11, edited by C. Deroux, 290–307. Brussels: Latomus.
Oakley, S. P. 1997. *A Commentary on Livy. Books VI–X, Vol. 1, Introduction and Book VI*. Oxford: Clarendon Press.
Oakley, S. P. 1998. *A Commentary on Livy. Books VI–X*, Vol. 2, *Books VII–VIII*. Oxford: Clarendon Press.
Oakley, S. P. 2005. *A Commentary on Livy. Books VI–X*, Vol. 4, *Book X*. Oxford: Clarendon Press.
Ogilvie, R. M., ed. 1974. *Titi Livi Ab urbe condita*, Vol. 1, *Libri I–V*. Oxford: Oxford University Press.
Östenberg, I. 2018. 'Defeated by the Forest, the Pass, the Wind: Nature as an Enemy of Rome.' In *Brill's Companion to Military Defeat in Ancient Mediterranean Societies*, edited by J. K. Clark and B. Turner, 240–61. Leiden: Brill.

Otto, N. 2009. *Enargeia. Untersuchung zur Charakteristik alexandrinischer Dichtung.* Hermes Einzelschriften 102. Stuttgart: Steiner.
Paton, W. R., trans. 1926. *Polybius. The Histories*, Vol. 5. Loeb Classical Library 160. Cambridge, MA: Harvard University Press.
Pausch, D. 2019. 'Who Knows what Will Happen Next? Livy's *fraus Punica* from a Literary Point of View.' In *Textual Strategies in Ancient War Narrative: Thermopylae, Cannae and Beyond*, edited by L. van Gils, I. de Jong and C. Kroon. Leiden: Brill.
Plathner, H.-G. 1934. 'Die Schlachtschilderungen bei Livius.' PhD diss., Universität Breslau.
Plett, H. F. 2012. *Enargeia in Classical Antiquity and the Early Modern Age. The Aesthetics of Evidence.* Leiden: Brill.
Rich, J. 2015. 'Appian, Polybius and the Romans' War with Antiochus: A Study in Appian's Sources and Methods.' In *Appian's Roman History: Empire and Civil War*, edited by K. Welch, 65–124. Swansea: Classical Press of Wales.
Riggsby, A. 2006. *Caesar in Gaul and Rome. War in Words.* Austin: University of Texas Press.
Roth, J. P. 2007. 'War.' In *The Cambridge History of Greek and Roman Warfare*, Vol. 1, *Greece, the Hellenistic World and the Rise of Rome*, edited by P. Sabin, H. van Wees and M. Whitby, 368–98. Cambridge: Cambridge University Press.
Scheid, J. 'Livy and Religion.' In A Companion to Livy, edited by B. Mineo, 78–89. Malden, MA: Wiley-Blackwell.
Simons, B. 2009. *Cassius Dio und die römische Republik. Untersuchungen zum Bild des römischen Gemeinwesens in den Büchern 3–35 der Ῥωμαικά.* Berlin: De Gruyter.
Spencer, D. 2010. *Roman Landscape: Culture and Identity.* Cambridge: Cambridge University Press.
Tränkle, H. 1977. *Livius und Polybios.* Basel: Schwabe.
Walbank, F. W. 1967. *A Historical Commentary on Polybius*, Vol. 2, *Commentary on Books VII–XVIII.* Oxford: Clarendon Press.
Walsh, P. G. 1961. *Livy. His Historical Aims and Methods.* Cambridge: Cambridge University Press.
Walsh, P. G., ed. 1989. *Titus Livius Ab urbe condita libri XXVI–XXVII*, 2nd edn. Leipzig: Teubner.
Walters, C. F. and R. S. Conway, eds. 1919. *Titi Livi Ab urbe condita*, Vol. 2, *Libri VI–X.* Oxford: Oxford University Press.
Webb, R. 2009. *Ekphrasis, Imagination and Persuasion in Ancient Rhetorical Theory and Practice.* Farnham: Ashgate.
Weissenborn, W. and H. J. Müller, eds. 1907. *T. Livi Ab urbe condita libri.* Vol. 8.2, *Buch XXXVII–XXXVIII.* 3rd edn. Berlin: Weidmann.
Winters, H., G. E. Galloway, Jr., W. J. Reynolds and D. W. Rhyne, eds. 1998. *Battling the Elements. Weather and Terrain in the Conduct of War.* Baltimore: The John Hopkins University Press.
Yardley, J. C., trans. and D. Hoyos, intr. 2006. *Livy. Hannibal's War. Books Twenty-One to Thirty.* Oxford: Oxford University Press.
Yardley, J. C., trans. and D. Hoyos, intr. 2013. *Livy. Rome's Italian Wars. Books 6–10.* Oxford: Oxford University Press.
Yardley, J. C., trans. and D. Hoyos, intr. 2017. *Livy. History of Rome*, Vol. 9, *Books 31–34.* Loeb Classical Library 295. Cambridge, MA: Harvard University Press.
Yardley, J. C., trans. 2018. *Livy. History of Rome*, Vol. 10, *Books 35–37.* Loeb Classical Library 301. Cambridge, MA: Harvard University Press.

CHAPTER 3
THE CHALLENGE OF HISTORIOGRAPHIC *ENARGEIA* AND THE BATTLE OF LAKE TRASIMENE[1]

Andrew Feldherr

1 Introduction: the paradox of *enargeia*

'The best historian is the one who ... makes his narrative like a painting.'[2] Plutarch's precious account of one ancient reader's response to an historiographic text underpins an idea that *enargeia*, or *evidentia* – the quality of style whereby the audience seems directly to see what is being described in a narrative[3] – is the defining excellence of historiography. But what exactly this assertion reveals about Greek and Roman history writing has become much more controversial thanks to recent debates about the rhetorical nature of the genre. The connotations of *evidentia*'s English derivative, evidence, point in one direction. Ancient history practically begins with the assertion that the ears are less trustworthy than the eyes and frequently claims to attain to the truth of what happened by relying on autopsy or eyewitnesses rather than mere hearsay.[4] Thucydides famously claims to offer clarity (*to saphes*, 1.22.4)[5] in his account of events, and Polybius presents his history as a spectacle (*theorema*, 1.2.1). Putting audiences in the position of spectators who can 'see for themselves' what happened might naturally seem to complete a hermeneutic circuit from past to present by granting them the authenticating experience of vision. But as Ruth Webb (1997) has shown, *enargeia* as the rhetoricians describe it does not rely on approximating the actual visible properties of

---

[1] Earlier versions of this chapter were presented as papers at the Universities of São Paulo and Toronto and at Claremont College. I am grateful to the audiences on those occasions for their suggestions, and to John Marincola and the editors of this volume for their comments on a preliminary draft. Many improvements, but none of the remaining flaws, are due to their advice.

[2] 'καὶ τῶν ἱστορικῶν κράτιστος ὁ τὴν διήγησιν ὥσπερ γραφῇ πάθεσι καὶ προσώποις εἰδωλοποιήσας. ὁ γοῦν Θουκυδίδης ἀεὶ τῷ λόγῳ πρὸς ταύτην ἁμιλλᾶται τὴν ἐνάργειαν, οἷον θεατὴν ποιῆσαι τὸν ἀκροατὴν καὶ τὰ γινόμενα περὶ τοὺς ὁρῶντας ἐκπληκτικὰ καὶ ταρακτικὰ πάθη τοῖς ἀναγινώσκουσιν ἐνεργάσασθαι λιχνευόμενος' (Plut. *De glor. Ath.* 347A; 'And of historians the best is the one who fashions his narrative like a picture in respect to emotions and characters. Thucydides at any rate always strives in his account towards such *enargeia*, desiring to make the hearer a spectator and to render for the readers the emotions of astonishment and distress that befell eyewitnesses').

[3] Ancient definitions in Lausberg (1998: 359–60).

[4] Hdt. 1.8; on autopsy in ancient historiography, see most conveniently Marincola (1997: 72–95), and the fuller treatment by Schepens (1980).

[5] Walker (1993: 375), cites Woodman (1988: 23–8) (an essential discussion) arguing that this 'clarity' refers to the rhetorical effect of *enargeia*, against those who interpret the phrase as a claim to truth or historical accuracy. See also Moles (1993a).

the particular scenes and objects it represents. The images *enargeia* evokes reside in the minds of the readers, not in the world out there. Moreover Plutarch specifies that he praises the historian who makes an image of his text 'in respect to emotions and characters', and these emotions are said to enhance not the readers' apprehension of the way things really were but their own 'feelings of astonishment and distress'. Also, worryingly for any assumption that the device evokes the authenticating power of vision, it was a strategy for giving vividness to entirely fictional events as well. Thus, alongside the alignment of *enargeia* with the historian's attempt to help his audience see what really happened, those convinced of the fundamentally rhetorical basis of ancient historiography discuss *enargeia* in terms not of truth but a 'reality effect'.[6] The historian's goal was verisimilitude, whether to stimulate an audience's emotional response – a motive generally disclaimed even by those writers whose work best accomplishes it – or to enhance the authority and plausibility of the narrative.

Since *enargeia* offers a limiting case to either approach – the time when historiography comes the closest to objective representation or to rhetorical construct – what both perspectives generally share is an acceptance of Plutarch's claim that making a narrative like a painting was a technique especially at home in history writing. My aim in this chapter, by contrast, will be to highlight how *enargeia* constitutes a challenge for ancient readers, not least because it accommodates both of the contrasting understandings of historical representation polarized in the scholarly debate I have sketched. Through a close reading of Polybius's and Livy's accounts of the battle of Lake Trasimene I intend first to show the disruptive potential of visual mimesis in ancient historiography – its ability to make its audience aware of the difference between reading and seeing – and then to explore how historians use such awareness programmatically to sharpen an audience's understanding of their own aims in representing the past. I chose to focus on Trasimene because the circumstances of the battle give both historians scope for a detailed treatment of visual phenomena and because, in the case of Livy, a pattern of allusions to Polybius's narrative highlights the programmatic potential of this theme. But I also want to offer a methodological suggestion about why battle narratives in general provide both ancient historians and modern scholars with particularly useful contexts for interrogating the relationship between *enargeia* and historiography: On the one hand, battles are both sensory and sensational. They give access to a range of unusual and extraordinary sights and sounds and correlate those experiences with extreme emotional reactions on the part of the participants. But on the other hand, they are also moments of profound historical, and hence historiographic, significance. They both instantiate long-term transformations in the fortunes of states and for that reason demand the kind of causal explanations that were also defining features of historiography as a genre (Cic. *De or.* 2.63). Their combination of immediate impact on those present with the power to reveal larger historical patterns makes them almost inevitably occasions for reflection on

---

[6] Despite its somewhat overschematized accounts of ancient verisimilitude and historiography (1986: 147), Barthes' essay on 'The Reality Effect' provides a helpful discussion of alternative approaches to the kinds of details on which *enargeia* depends.

any narrative's aims and effects. The particular notion of landscape in this context can also helpfully reinforce the interpretative challenge created for readers of these scenes. As much recent work on the concept has stressed, landscape is not simply space, but space perceived and interpreted from the perspective of a particular subject.[7] This subjectivizing of space may on the one hand elicit an awareness on the part of the reader of an initial viewer. But at the same time landscapes are also powerfully modeled by cultural and literary codes: so, for example, it is enough to mention a few stereotypical features for the reader to recognize a pastoral landscape. As Horsfall has shown, Livy in his account of the battle of the Caudine Forks, added descriptive elements that conform precisely to this convention.[8] Thus, from the interpreter's perspective the setting Livy creates for the battle would potentially evoke these unreal landscapes while the very act of offering such description, composing space into a landscape, has an authenticating dimension in that it reproduces the experience of an actual viewer.

The subject of *enargeia* in Greek historiography was treated in 1993 by Andrew Walker in an article whose range and originality make it an essential point of reference. In keeping with the rhetorical turn in historiography, Walker had the general aim of shifting attention in studies of the Greek historians from the content to the form of their narratives. By using historians' deployments of *enargeia* as self-reflexive moments, *mises en abyme*, which modeled the responses of their own audiences to their representations of the past, Walker discovered an approach that revealed the variety of ways that historians conceptualized and constructed the rhetorical effects of their works. What had looked before like different attitudes towards history were treated as strategies for historical representation. Walker fully appreciates that readers can distance themselves from internal audiences as well as identifying with them and that as a result these scenes provide not only a script for the reception of historiography but also a way of dramatizing the 'problems of writing history'.[9] My aim here is to present not disagreement with Walker's analyses but rather a difference in perspective. I take my primary orientation not from the ways in which ancient rhetorical theory and practice made it easier for audiences to visualize the events they read about, but rather from the fundamentally paradoxical nature of *enargeia*: words do not make you see.[10] The presence of internal spectators raises a complementary narratological dilemma since, while they can focalize a reader's experience of narrated events as 'sight', their own presence as objects of representation equally makes it possible for the historian's audience to adopt a perspective that sees them from without.

From the other direction, the privileged relationship between historiography and vision also requires some qualification. As the work of Adriana Zangara has particularly

---

[7] Discussions of the concept and its relation to others like 'space' or 'environment' are of course numerous and varied, but Spencer (2010) and the introduction to Gilhuly and Worman (2014) offer helpful recent 'overviews' by and for classicists.
[8] Horsfall (1982); see also Oakley (2005: 34).
[9] Walker (1993: 375).
[10] See Mitchell (1994: 151–3) on the concept of 'ekphrastic hope'.

highlighted, historians use the imagery of vision in many contrasting ways, and making an audience seem to view events directly as witnesses stands in striking contrast to helping them see patterns and processes that are *not* visible in the world.[11] The historian's own narrative simultaneously re-structures the act of vision and intervenes between the present and the past to become the subject of an act of metaphorical seeing that is not at all like the real thing. Thus, before making my own syncrisis between Polybius and Livy, I will begin by stressing that the problems in the writing and reception of history to which episodes of *enargeia* draw attention allow for serious challenges to its coherence as a narrative form. The Thucydidean reader may not be able to reconcile the experiences of reading with those of viewing; indeed *enargeia* makes available viewpoints that challenge the historian's own control over his text rather than putting the reader in his shoes. So too it is not always the case that the historian necessarily achieves or even aims at a 'reality effect'. Both Polybius and Livy offer contrasting understandings precisely of how historiography aims at an effect of unreality, differentiating what it 'shows' from what can be seen.

Before entering the mists of battle, it will be helpful to illustrate my claim that the relationship between vision and historical knowledge was anything but straightforward with a brief discussion of the Herodotean episode that contains the famous claim about the 'ears being less trustworthy than the eyes' (ὦτα γὰρ τυγχάνει ἀνθρώποισι ἐόντα ἀπιστότερα ὀφθαλμῶν, 1.8), voiced not by the historian himself but by the character Candaules (and it already points to the challenge this claim poses to Herodotus's audience that this is also the first instance of reported speech in the work).[12] Herodotus had begun his narrative with an account of bouts of woman-snatching between Greeks and barbarians that would have been surprising not just for their rationalization of mythical stories but for the particularizing detail that makes it possible to imagine them happening. Thus, he specifies that Io and the Argive maidens were standing near the stern of the ship when the Phoenicians kidnapped them (1.1). But if we conclude that this ability to set events before the eyes of his audience will be an unproblematic aspect of his historiographic method, an even more fully described scene that follows very shortly after and treats a similar subject should make us reconsider: the scene in which the Lydian king Candaules persuades his bodyguard Gyges to watch concealed in the royal bedchamber as his wife undresses so that he will be believe his accounts of her beauty (1.8–10).

---

[11] The rich and complex discussion in Zangara (2007) is organized around a tension between two modes of vision constructed by ancient historians: *synopsis* and *enargeia*. In the former, the historian reveals history itself as something that possesses a form to be seen, while *enargeia* predominantly reproduces the pathos of direct experience of specific moments thanks to the rhetorical virtuosity of the historian. My arguments about the disruptive potential of *enargeia* owe much to her account of the aporia that results from these conflicting ways of seeing history while a possible distinction between our approaches has to do with my localization of such ambiguities even within in the phenomenon of *enargeia* itself thanks to the discrepancies between narrative focalizations it allows.

[12] For a contrasting reading of the programmatic value of the episode, see Benardete (1969: 12–13).

Here the historian not only adds a new level of representational presence to his account – again, Candaules is the first figure whose speech is reported directly – he also performs a sort of 'metaenargeia'. For the character Candaules both constructs Gyges as a viewer and lays out the arrangement of the room in a way that makes it available to our own visual imagination as Herodotus's readers.[13] It is in this context that the king gives voice to the claim about the trustworthiness of autopsy as opposed to hearing. But beyond the unreliability of the judgment of the source of this statement, the marvel Candaules shows Gyges is explicitly one that ought not to be seen. To a listener who remembers the boundaries drawn in Homer, where it belongs to the gods alone to see the past, while mortals can only hear the reports,[14] Candaules' rejection of hearing as insufficient for human beings (ἀνθρώποισι) may itself appear transgressive. Correspondingly, the plot that he concocts shows a shockingly un-Herodotean lack of awareness of both the past and the future.

To Candaules' gnome about the ears being less trustworthy than the eyes, Gyges responds with one of his own: 'A woman strips off her shame together with her clothes: this good advice was discovered long ago for men and it is necessary to learn from it' (πάλαι δὲ τὰ καλὰ ἀνθρώποισι ἐξεύρηται, ἐκ τῶν μανθάνειν δεῖ, ibid.). Gyges' capping of Candaules' word ἀνθρώποισι contrasts seeing not with hearing but with understanding and substitutes for a view of the present a wisdom enjoined by the past. Candaules' vivid imagination of exhibiting his wife's body to a stranger also blinds him to the consequences of the action. His despotic efforts to control Gyges' gaze contrast with his utter failure to predict that his wife too will see Gyges. Indeed she combines seeing with the understanding that Gyges had urged on his master in vain (καὶ ἡ γυνὴ ἐπορᾷ μιν ἐξιόντα. Μαθοῦσα δὲ . . ., 1.10). Candaules thus connects an assumption that only seeing is believing with an inability to contextualize the act of vision in the present in relation to the past or the future. Like Croesus, Candaules thinks of visual contact entirely in terms of showing, and the contribution to his own reputation that comes from another's seeing his blessings. But as Herodotus takes over the story, a different model of vision leads to a reversal of the king's plot when a thinking, responsive viewer interprets what she sees. The *apodexis* of Herodotus, by contrast to Candaules', comes to incorporate the reader.[15] Indeed to the extent that Herodotus allows his audience to perceive Gyges' presence, and to understand Candaules' motives, he has aligned their perspective not with the unwilling voyeur's but with the queen's. And this combination of moving his audience away from Candaules' imagined viewer and towards the unforeseen spectator, someone who was imagined as seen, not seeing, constructs the historian's use of vision to draw together past and present as already far more complex than the simple reproduction of what was on view at the moment described by the narrative.

---

[13] On Candaules' 'stage managing' of this scene, but also on the striking lexical differences between his account and Herodotus's, see Purves (2014: 99–102).

[14] Cf. *Il.* 2.486, ἡμεῖς δὲ κλέος οἶον ἀκούομεν οὐδέ τι ἴδμεν.

[15] On the relationship between Candaules' spectatorial 'fantasy' and Herodotus's narrative, see Travis (2000).

2 The limits of sight: Thucydides' naval battle at Syracuse

If Herodotus embeds the claim about the evidentiary value of vision in a context that invites his audience to step back from the scene and understand the distinctive perspective that history offers, then the most famous example of historiographic *enargeia*, Thucydides' description of the naval battle at Syracuse (7.70–1), seems to consolidate and sharpen that generic claim. For here the opposition between sight and comprehension is even more starkly demonstrated and expressed, in a scene in which both armies are shown as watching the sea battle from the shore (7.71.1–5):

> Ὅ τε ἐκ τῆς γῆς πεζὸς ἀμφοτέρων ἰσορρόπου τῆς ναυμαχίας καθεστηκυίας πολὺν τὸν ἀγῶνα καὶ ξύστασιν τῆς γνώμης εἶχε, φιλονικῶν μὲν ὁ αὐτόθεν περὶ τοῦ πλείονος ἤδη καλοῦ, δεδιότες δὲ οἱ ἐπελθόντες μὴ τῶν παρόντων ἔτι χείρω πράξωσιν. πάντων γὰρ δὴ ἀνακειμένων τοῖς Ἀθηναίοις ἐς τὰς ναῦς ὅ τε φόβος ἦν ὑπὲρ τοῦ μέλλοντος οὐδενὶ ἐοικὼς καὶ διὰ τὸ ἀνώμαλον τῆς τάξεως ἀνώμαλον καὶ τὴν ἔποψιν τῆς ναυμαχίας ἐκ τῆς γῆς ἠναγκάζοντο ἔχειν. δι' ὀλίγου γὰρ οὔσης τῆς θέας καὶ οὐ πάντων ἅμα ἐς τὸ αὐτὸ σκοπούντων, εἰ μέν τινες ἴδοιέν πῃ τοὺς σφετέρους ἐπικρατοῦντας, ἀνεθάρσησάν τε ἂν καὶ πρὸς ἀνάκλησιν θεῶν μὴ στερῆσαι σφᾶς τῆς σωτηρίας ἐτρέποντο· οἱ δ' ἐπί τι ἡσσώμενον βλέψαντες ὀλοφυρμῷ τε ἅμα μετὰ βοῆς ἐχρῶντο καὶ ἀπὸ τῶν δρωμένων τῆς ὄψεως καὶ τὴν γνώμην μᾶλλον τῶν ἐν τῷ ἔργῳ ἐδουλοῦντο· ἄλλοι δὲ καὶ πρὸς ἀντίπαλόν τι τῆς ναυμαχίας ἀπιδόντες, διὰ τὸ ἀκρίτως ξυνεχὲς τῆς ἁμίλλης καὶ τοῖς σώμασιν αὐτοῖς ἴσα τῇ δόξῃ περιδεῶς ξυναπονεύοντες ἐν τοῖς χαλεπώτατα διῆγον· αἰεὶ γὰρ παρ' ὀλίγον ἢ διέφευγον ἢ ἀπώλλυντο. ἦν τε ἐν τῷ αὐτῷ στρατεύματι τῶν Ἀθηναίων, ἕως ἀγχώμαλα ἐναυμάχουν, πάντα ὁμοῦ ἀκοῦσαι, ὀλοφυρμός, βοή, νικῶντες, κρατούμενοι, ἄλλα ὅσ' ἂν μεγάλῳ κινδύνῳ μέγα στρατόπεδον πολυειδῆ ἀναγκάζοιτο φθέγγεσθαι. παραπλήσια δὲ καὶ οἱ ἐπὶ τῶν νεῶν αὐτοῖς ἔπασχον, πρίν γε δὴ οἱ Συρακόσιοι καὶ οἱ ξύμμαχοι ἐπὶ πολὺ ἀντισχούσης τῆς ναυμαχίας ἔτρεψάν τε τοὺς Ἀθηναίους καὶ ἐπικείμενοι λαμπρῶς, πολλῇ κραυγῇ καὶ διακελευσμῷ χρώμενοι, κατεδίωκον ἐς τὴν γῆν.

And the armies on the shore on both sides, so long as the fighting at sea was evenly balanced, underwent a mighty conflict and tension of mind, the men of Sicily being ambitious to enhance the glory they had already won, while the invaders were afraid that they might fare even worse than at present. For the Athenians their all was staked upon their fleet, and their fear for the outcome like unto none they had ever felt before; and on account of the different positions which they occupied on the shore they necessarily had different views of the fighting. For since the spectacle they were witnessing was near at hand and not all were looking at the same point at the same time, if one group saw the Athenians prevailing anywhere, they would take heart and fall to invoking the gods not to rob them of their safe return; while those whose eyes fell upon a portion that was being defeated uttered shrieks of lamentation, and they were more enslaved in their understanding by the sight of what was being done than those engaged in the action. Others, again, whose gaze was fixed on some part of the field where the battle was evenly balanced, on account of the long-drawn uncertainty of the conflict were in a continual state of most distressing suspense, their very bodies swaying, in the extremity of their fear, in accord with their opinion of the battle; for always they were within a hair's breadth of escaping or of perishing. And in the same army of the Athenians, as long as the fighting was equal, it was possible to hear all things at once: lament and outcry, "winning" and "losing" and all the diverse kinds of cries that a great army in great danger would be constrained to utter. The men also on board the Athenian ships were affected in a similar way, until at last the Syracusans and their allies, after the fighting had been maintained a long time, routed the Athenians and pressing on triumphantly, with loud cries and exhortations, pursued them to the land.

Trans. C. F. Smith, adapted

The army watching the battle from the land not only fail to gain a comprehensive picture of what is happening, but their understanding is further compromised by the emotional effects of that partial vision. In Thucydides' striking phrase, when those spectators happened to see an Athenian ship defeated they were 'enslaved as to their reason' (τὴν γνώμην ... ἐδουλοῦντο, 7.71.3).

One strand in Walker's reading of this episode looks back to Thucydides' methodological preface in Book 1. The internally depicted spectators recall those witnesses from whom Thucydides constructs his narrative of events. This effort is there described as 'laborious, because those present at each action do not give the same account' (1.22.3). The spectators' view is therefore contrasted with the imagined presence of the historian as 'privileged spectator'[16] constructing a narrative that overcomes the limitations of his sources, and his own readers, their attention diverted to the plane of discourse, perceive 'the struggle to attain a "complete vision" of contemporary history'. But in addition to underlining that direct visual experience offers not so much a means as an obstacle to attaining this historical vision, I want to stress that the historian's victory in that metaphorical struggle remains very much uncertain, and the representational strategies he uses in this battle contribute to that interpretative openness. As Walker and others note, the crucial question of how Thucydides will reconcile these contrasting perspectives to attain a correct and comprehensive account of events is never explicitly answered in the work's preface.[17] And the resulting uncertainty is only amplified by another unusual aspect of the narrative itself. In the much-quoted words of W. S. Ferguson, 'Thucydides fails even to suggest the factors that determined the outcome. Instead he dwells on certain typical incidents in the confused fighting that followed, and then turns our attention to the spectators on the shore, and leaves us to infer the manifold vicissitudes of the protracted struggle from the agony of fear, joy, anxiety.'[18] While

---

[16] Walker (1993: 372).
[17] Walker (ibid.); cf. Marincola (1997: 69).
[18] Ferguson (1927: 308), quoted by Connor (1984: 196–7, n. 32) and then Walker (1993: 360, n. 14).

Ferguson's judgment may neglect the amount of coherence and explanation in Thucydides' preceding chapter, it remains striking that the decisive turning point in the battle not only lacks explanation, but appears in a subordinate temporal clause to mark a new phase in the response to events.

The staging of this decisive moment suggests a somewhat different way of thinking about the role of spectators in the episode. Rather than treating them either as a foil to the historian's perception or, concomitantly, as a screen that must be penetrated by both historian and reader in order to see history, we can instead recognize the spectators and their emotions *as* the focus of the narrative. This approach stresses another division that further complicates the historian's audience's choice between seeing the battle as a witness or through the eyes of history. In the very act of describing the spectator's fear, the historian creates what Mieke Bal calls a 'hinge' in the focalization of the scene: the reader can both share the responses of the spectators and keep those spectators themselves in view as the object of representation.[19] The challenge then is not only to see history through the spectators' gaze, but to see their responses historically. When Thucydides emphasizes their physical closeness to the action as the cause of their confusion (δι' ὀλίγου γὰρ οὔσης τῆς θέας, 7.71.3), such spatial proximity anticipates their lack of the kind of temporal distance a historian brings to the action. This emerges most clearly in the depiction of their responses as haphazard and ephemeral because they depend on where someone happens to be looking and last only as long as the battle. Even the unifying fear that comes with the full realization of defeat is located in a single temporal instant (ἐν τῷ παραυτίκα, 7.71.7). The transience of that emotional devastation is immediately contrasted with the long view of the historian, who can make a comparison across time to the experiences of the Spartans at Pylos (7.71.7).

A shift in the audience's attention here from the battle to the spectators themselves has other effects as well. Most strikingly, it adds a second problem to the question of whether an objective account of events can in fact be assembled from the responses of

---

[19] Bal (1985: 113–14). Mine is admittedly a very 'low tech' application of narratalogical theory. For more background on the term focalization and its development in the context of readings of Livy, see Tsitsiou-Chelidoni (2009). To be a little more explicit, I am assuming that an awareness of internal perspectives (that is of internal audiences responding to events) creates a potential ambiguity in focalization that goes beyond what is technically designated as such, viz. when it is left unclear whether the understanding of events related in the narrative belongs to the narrator or to a figure within it, e.g. 'Johnny looked at the cake: coconut glistened on its surface like sunlight on a tropical ocean.' The statement 'the Romans saw nothing' inevitably creates two levels of focalization, whether they are exploited by the narrator or not: reference to perception in any context opens the doors for imagining another 'story' to be told about what is happening, especially in a context where both the ability to narrate implies a pretended knowledge of events (which distinguishes history from fiction) and narration closely aligns itself with visual representation, as it does in *enargeia*, so that the reader too is encouraged to 'see'. Thus, I am not dissuaded by Rood (1998: 294–6). And though he too avoids the term 'focalization', Davidson (1991: 13) offers a helpful description of this way of reading: 'Polybius, then, can be seen writing through the eyes of others. He gives us sometimes several different viewpoints of the same event. We are told how Hannibal viewed the crossing of the Alps, as well as how other historians have presented it, and how Scipio the Elder saw it. These different views of the same episode are not primarily cited for *variatio*, I think, nor especially to characterize the observers, but take their own place as events within the history he is composing. They can be seen as little narratives, fragmentary versions of what was going on, overlaying one another and competing with each other.'

spectators: whether emotions themselves can be described historically. On the one hand, as Rutter observes,[20] there is a striking contrast between the disorder Thucydides depicts and the clearly articulated structure of the narrative itself. The logic of the narrative, however, conspicuously breaks down when the audience's perspective merges most closely with the participants. When Thucydides reproduces not sights but sounds, the result is onomatopoetic cacophony and a pushing to the limit of grammatical clarity, but again this lasts only an instant: 'in the same army of the Athenians, as long as the fighting was equal, it was possible to hear all things at once: lament and outcry, "winning" and "losing"' (ἤν τε ἐν τῷ αὐτῷ στρατεύματι τῶν Ἀθηναίων, ἕως ἀγχώμαλα ἐναυμάχουν, πάντα ὁμοῦ ἀκοῦσαι, ὀλοφυρμὸς βοή, νικῶντες κρατούμενοι, 7.71.4), a daringly constructed sentence even for Thucydides. The distance between response and representation appears also in the initial metaphor about the 'enslavement' of the spectators' judgment, especially in the context of the contrast drawn in that sentence between observers and participants. As a hyperbolic metaphor, the expression brings attention to the transient experience of the watchers. But the momentary absorption this allows the reader in the spectator's own absorption will be corrected by a reminder of the metaphor's literal appropriateness in this situation. For the conclusion of Thucydides' account of the entire Sicilian expedition comes when those very observers, at any rate those who survive, will indeed be enslaved. The word's connotations therefore can stimulate the readers' own awareness of their historical situatedness, their ability to look back on events as Thucydides does when he recalls the parallel of Pylos, which implicitly contrasts with his preceding claim that the spectators' terror was incomparably great (οὐδεμιᾶς ... ἐλάσσων). But such distance must work against the capacity of the emotion itself to break down boundaries among levels of audience and by doing so both to pull them from real historical time into the immediate present of the narrative, which makes them like the internal audience, who are in turn like the participants. The descriptions of temporality in the passage look back to Thucydides' methodological preface not only in evoking the 'present' witnesses to events (οἱ παρόντες, 1.22.3): the same immediacy of response is also implied for the audience of Thucydides' rival historians. These listeners are interested in the pleasure that comes from a 'contest piece' that is itself of the moment (ἀγώνισμα ἐς τὸ παραχρῆμα, 1.22.4), and this is contrasted with the profit gained by those who want 'to see the clarity of events' (τῶν τε γενομένων τὸ σαφὲς σκοπεῖν). The impressionability and partiality of witnesses folds into the pursuit of pleasure by audiences, as here the boundaries between audience levels collapse into a single instant of experience.

W. R. Connor answers Ferguson's criticism of Thucydides' deflecting his narrative from the battle to the spectators with the reminder that 'since morale is the crucial factor in the remaining chapters of the seventh book, Thucydides' description is well adapted to his narrative purpose.'[21] But while Connor's point that emotions themselves have historical consequences is well taken, the emphasis on the haphazardness of the

---

[20] Rutter (1998: 56), with discussion by Hornblower (2008: 695).
[21] Connor (1984: 197, n. 32).

spectators' experience suggest some ways in which representing those emotions within history tests the capacities of both the narrative and its readers. The depiction of emotions as both immediate and timeless can itself challenge Thucydides' conception of his history's distinctive value. For emotions appear not just as recurring factors in human events but as a challenge to the perception of historical difference. They do not just allow one to foresee future events through the study of past ones, they pull the reader into the past and obliterate the differences created by history. When Thucydides mentions the similarity between the Athenians' experiences at Syracuse and the Spartans' at Pylos, it is at once a vindication of his history and a challenge to its explanatory value. If the Athenians had had Thucydides' account of Pylos in their hands before the expedition, they might have known to expect the unexpected. But such learning may be more difficult than it seems. Notice that the similarity itself is tellingly partial (παραπλήσιά τε ἐπεπόνθεσαν, 7.71.7); to elide the difference between the two risks misrepresenting an experience that is significant for its uniqueness. As the war itself is the greatest of all, so the Athenians' terror (*ekplexis*) was less than none. And yet to remove the possibilities for comparison may also limit the possibilities for description and understanding. If this tragedy was the greatest of all, you cannot imagine what it was like. The focus on the emotions, as Connor suggests, looks forward to the total destruction of the Athenians at the climax of the narrative, the point when the tragic irony of their emotional 'enslavement' is detonated. And yet as Connor himself memorably shows, the focus there is on the indescribability of emotion, the inability of language to convey the extremity of suffering: 'conquered entirely and in every respect, suffering no little ill in nothing, with an utter destruction, as the saying is, on land and on sea, and there was nothing that was not destroyed'.[22] On the one hand, emotional experience appears harnessed to the unfolding of history as effect becomes cause, but if emotions can reveal history, history may not be able to show emotions: the foreshadowing of the Athenian expedition at Pylos, its turning point at Syracuse, and its denouement in the quarries all collapse into an immediate experience that the *logos* cannot express. It might be indicated through *enargeia*, but *enargeia* might also point most effectively to its absence.

The connection between the experiences of the spectators and the events at Pylos point to a final challenge that *enargeia* may realize for Thucydides' audience. For what would explain, or be explained by, the similarity? Francis Cornford describes how Thucydides traces the 'causes of the Sicilian expedition from Fortune at Pylos to Nemesis at the quarries of Syracuse',[23] and as his language makes clear, the 'causes' he has in mind

---

[22] κατὰ πάντα γὰρ πάντως νικηθέντες καὶ οὐδὲν ὀλίγον ἐς οὐδὲν κακοπαθήσαντες, πανωλεθρίᾳ δὴ τὸ λεγόμενον καὶ πεζὸς καὶ νῆες καὶ οὐδὲν ὅ τι οὐκ ἀπώλετο, καὶ ὀλίγοι ἀπὸ πολλῶν ἐπ᾽ οἴκου ἀπενόστησαν, 7.87.6. Notice that thanks to word play even those few from many who actually escape destruction are enmeshed by it, ἀπὸ πολλῶν~ἀπώλετο. See Connor (1986: 207–9), who concludes 'the possibilities [that the disaster has some divine cause] are awesome enough and converge in a common recognition, that the destruction of the expedition has reached – and surpassed – the limits of human experience and comprehension'.

[23] Cornford (1907: 244). As he elsewhere observes (ibid.: 88–9) the Pylos episode itself was one of the great demonstrations of the role of accident in history, since it is only by chance that the Athenian fleet puts in at Pylos at all; see Grethlein (2010: 253).

look less to modern historiography than to tragedy. Without reproducing arguments for a tragic Thucydides, we might briefly observe that if we see in the trajectory history here sketches a relation between events that hints at causes beyond the explanatory framework that shapes the historian's narrative, this too may be connected with the depiction of the spectators' experience. Indeed their own emotions have as causes the direction in which each happens to be looking (7.71.3). And perhaps the spectators' random and partial response to chance events should actually be taken seriously as an alternative to the historian's retrospective analysis of the connections between causes and effects. The Athenians did not have to lose the battle, and had they won, the story Thucydides would have to tell about the war would be very different. The attentions of the Athenian spectators, riveted by whatever their gaze happens to fix on, seem to thrust us into a world where nothing causes anything – where outcomes are determined in the moment. This use of counterfactuals to challenge teleological narratives forms a central claim of Jonas Grethlein's work on ancient historiography, and he uses this passage from Thucydides to demonstrate how *enargeia*, by introducing the perceptual experience of those to whom the future really is still the future, conveys 'the openness of our experiences'.[24] Some might resist the suggestion that Thucydides would so radically call into question the very premises of his work. But if such reflections do not follow from the author's intentions, this may offer an even stronger demonstration of how a glimpse of the reality of the past – a reminder that there were real spectators at this event – can imperil rather than enhance the authority of a historical narrative.

3 Between reality and representation

Walker's understanding of *enargeia* as a rhetorical device aiming at verisimilitude forms part of a 'post-modern' approach to Thucydides, who never aimed at the accurate adherence to truth claimed for him by post-Rankean historians. The attention given to the role of rhetorical adornment in historiography in the works especially of T. P. Wiseman and A. J. Woodman has made clear how historians turn to standard descriptive topoi and parallel stories to flesh out a scanty historical record into a fuller, realistic-seeming account of events. Such detail is, of course, one of the essential techniques of *enargeia*.[25] The impression that one could describe the particular qualities of a scene or place can contribute at once to the reader's ability to imagine such a scene as really happening and to the historian's authority by suggesting that he possesses the information to elaborate his account in this way. From such practices Woodman draws important

---

[24] Grethlein (2010: 248–52) (quotation from p. 249) borrows the term 'sideshadowing' from Morson (1994) to describe how this contemporary view of events in process suggests alternative realities to the way the historian knows the story will go. See also Grethlein (2013: 15–19).
[25] The Greek rhetorical term for such embellishment was *akribeia*. Walker (1993: 366–7) highlights its significance for both the historian's authority and for an approach to *enargeia*. His argument that *akribeia* in this context refers not to 'accuracy' but 'fullness of description' draws on Schultze (1986: 126).

conclusions about the fundamentally different expectations a Greek or Roman audience brought to their reading of history: they were aware that the rhetorical elements of history involved not only style but content.

And yet, according to Cicero in the prologue to the *De Legibus*, it was appropriate for readers of history to apply the criterion of truth, just as it was for readers of poetry to apply the criterion of pleasure (*cum in illa omnia ad veritatem, Quinte, referantur, in hoc ad delectationem pleraque, Leg.* 1.5). This does not mean that ancient readers believed everything they read, but that 'is it true?' is an appropriate question to ask of an historical text as it is not of a poetic one. The reality effect of a text in such a case cannot be isolated from a potential reference to reality itself. And if we take Cicero at his word here, the problem that emerges with *enargeia* is that the more detailed the description, and the more it has the potential to suggest reality, the more an educated reader will know that the details are not true. Again *enargeia* becomes the site where a focus on the text potentially interferes with perceiving the reality that text claims to represent. Maybe ancient readers did respond to what they read as Woodman suggests. Some almost certainly did. But the kind of conflicting responses I have tried to describe seem more likely to arise, and the conflicts themselves to matter more, in ancient historiography than in a modern Rankean narrative where a responsible historian will include details only if that's the way it really was.

Grethlein's presentation of the problems of narrative historiography[26] provides a valuable complement to Woodman's approach because he is not concerned to establish different expectations among Greek and Roman audiences but rather explores how even narratives that aim to represent the truth necessarily falsify the events they describe. Even eyewitness accounts can never truly match the experience of presence because they always involve hindsight if only in the recognition that the experience was worth describing. The more detail, even authentic detail, a narrative includes, the less likely that all of this information would have been noticed by any actual participant or spectator. Though narrators and audiences may not always acknowledge these difficulties, they are always available for exploration.[27] And certainly ancient historiography never lacks for polemic statements about where rivals' narratives fail. Every society must use narrative, like they must use language. And every act of narration is governed by conventions and expectations that make such communication possible in the face of its ontological difficulties. But to assume that these conventions solve the problem of narrative – that ancient readers just looked the other way when Herodotus specifies that Io was standing by the stern of the ships when the Phoenicians kidnapped her, while we want to ask how he could possibly have known that – places implausible limits on the variety and sophistication of ancient historians and their audiences and attempts to make simple what should be complicated.

---

[26] Grethlein (2013: esp. 1–26).
[27] Grethlein (2013) analyses how ancient historians negotiate between the poles of reproducing authentic experience and the teleology inevitably involved in narrating.

The model of historiography as rhetoric provides convincing explanations of how historians went about their work as authors. But when we consider how ancient audiences responded to those works, the generalizing tendencies of contemporary narratological theory offer an important corrective. In the case of scenes like the battle in the Syracusan harbor, this means highlighting the inevitable ambiguities of narratives that contain embedded audiences to explain the self-referential capacities of *enargeia*. The ability to see with those spectators or to see them seeing presents in concentrated form a tension of perspective inevitably present in all historical accounts between the conspicuousness or transparency of the representation itself in relation to what it claims to represent. The presence of an internal audience actualizes the choice between alternatives, both intellectually – providing an occasion for reflection on potential differences in perspective, a *mise en abyme* for the act of interpretation – and experientially, since the comprehension of the narrative allows for a flipping back and forth between distance and absorption present in any form of mimesis. The generic claims of history raise the stakes of this encounter with the assertion that what is represented has a status beyond the construction of the author, that it is real, and the spectators who offer access to the experience themselves really saw what really happened. Perhaps we have it the wrong way around in referring the special connection between historiography and *enargeia* to either the notion of autopsy as proof or to historians' debt to rhetorical precepts in constructing their narratives. It may be better instead to emphasize how the narratological alternatives of distance and absorption that *enargeia* as a formal device inevitably raises dramatize the central question historiography as a genre poses its readers – is what it depicts true? – while at the same time that generic claim to truth intensifies the reader's negotiation of *enargeia*'s own ambiguities in perspective.

4 Polybius and the spectacle of history

One historian who certainly does not acquiesce in renouncing strict fidelity to the truth for narrative effect is Polybius. Marincola's recent study of his attack on Phylarchus's methods of narrative (2.56, the passage at the centre of the debate about the existence of a school of Hellenistic historians who sought to incorporate the effects of tragedy into their writings),[28] shows that Polybius's polemic aimed neither at his rival's interest in making the past visible, nor even the emotional responses he aims to provoke. Rather, the very detail that makes it possible to visualize a scene like the fall of Mantinea requires the inclusion of falsehood. Thus, the primary distinction the historian wishes to draw in this passage is precisely between mere plausibility and truth: 'It is not a historian's business to startle his readers with sensational descriptions, nor should he try, as tragic poets do, to represent speeches which might have been delivered, or to enumerate all the possible consequences of events under consideration; it is his task first and

---

[28] Marincola (2013), with further bibliography on 'tragic history'. The emphasis on truth as a distinguishing feature of Polybian history in this polemic is also highlighted by Wiater (2017).

foremost to record with fidelity what actually happened and what was said, however commonplace this may be.'[29]

Polybius's criticisms of Phylarchus have seemed contradictory to scholars precisely because he himself programmatically emphasizes the visual aspects of his own work and presents it as something to be seen, a *synopsis* (1.4.2) or *theorema* (1.2.1). In linking his polemic about tragic history to the specific issue of truth, Marincola aims to resolve this contradiction and to prevent it from obscuring how much attention Polybius himself pays to creating visual images through narrative. Here I would like to draw a somewhat broader distinction between the kind of direct visual access to events Phylarchus's descriptions offer and Polybius's own use of vision. This parallels Davidson's observations on the competing viewpoints Polybius incorporates in his work, as well as the fundamental distinction Zangara makes between *synopsis* and *enargeia*.[30] Polybius's presentation of his history as a spectacle does not mean that he aims to make the events he describes immediately accessible to the sight of his audience as if they had been present. Rather he values history precisely because it can make visible what no actual human spectator could otherwise see.[31] This largely has to do with the question of scale; history makes it possible to subsume under one gaze events dispersed across space and time. Thus, he says in 1.4.1:

τὸ γὰρ τῆς ἡμετέρας πραγματείας ἴδιον καὶ τὸ θαυμάσιον τῶν καθ' ἡμᾶς καιρῶν τοῦτ' ἔστιν ὅτι, καθάπερ ἡ τύχη σχεδὸν ἅπαντα τὰ τῆς οἰκουμένης πράγματα πρὸς ἓν ἔκλινε μέρος καὶ πάντα νεύειν ἠνάγκασε πρὸς ἕνα καὶ τὸν αὐτὸν σκοπόν, οὕτως καὶ <δεῖ> διὰ τῆς ἱστορίας ὑπὸ μίαν σύνοψιν ἀγαγεῖν τοῖς ἐντυγχάνουσι τὸν χειρισμὸν τῆς τύχης, ᾧ κέχρηται πρὸς τὴν τῶν ὅλων πραγμάτων συντέλειαν,

What is distinctive to our work and wondrous about the events of our time is this: as fortune has turned nearly all the affairs of the *oikumene* in one direction and forced them to bend toward one and the same target, it is necessary through history to bring together under one comprehensive gaze for all who happen upon it the workings of fortune, which she has applied to the completion of all deeds.

The wondrous qualities may reside in events themselves, but they can only be perceived under the synoptic view of history. Indeed if we pay attention to the metaphors in this sentence, we may note that the physical actions described – bending, aiming at a target, etc. – can only be visualized through Polybius's language.

---

[29] δεῖ τοιγαροῦν οὐκ ἐκπλήττειν τὸν συγγραφέα τερατευόμενον διὰ τῆς ἱστορίας τοὺς ἐντυγχάνοντας οὐδὲ τοὺς ἐνδεχομένους λόγους ζητεῖν καὶ τὰ παρεπόμενα τοῖς ὑποκειμένοις ἐξαριθμεῖσθαι, καθάπερ οἱ τραγῳδιογράφοι, τῶν δὲ πραχθέντων καὶ ῥηθέντων κατ' ἀλήθειαν αὐτῶν μνημονεύειν πάμπαν, (κ)ἂν πάνυ μέτρια τυγχάνωσιν ὄντα, 2.56.10.

[30] Davidson (1991: esp. 18–20) and Zangara (2007) (see above, n. 11).

[31] This is, of course, to oversimplify a more complex array of perspectives, as described by Davidson (1991: 16): 'By using the simile [sc. of spectacle] Polybius himself provides for us, we can look at the *Histories* as a series of concentric circles of spectators, from the combatants in the centre to the remote reader in the twentieth century. These spectators located at various distances from the action, and at various levels of involvement, see through each other, one level mediating the gaze of the next.'

Polybius's connection between the scale of his history and the distinctive spectacle it offers also emerges in his critique of Phylarchus's method of visual narrative. Here it takes the form of a contrast, very relevant to our earlier discussion of Thucydides, between immediate impressions of a single event and the distinctive diachronic perspective of history (2.56.13–14):

> τὰς πλείστας ἡμῖν ἐξηγεῖται τῶν περιπετειῶν, οὐχ ὑποτιθεὶς αἰτίαν καὶ τρόπον τοῖς γινομένοις, ὧν χωρὶς οὔτ' ἐλεεῖν εὐλόγως οὔτ' ὀργίζεσθαι καθηκόντως δυνατὸν ἐπ' οὐδενὶ τῶν συμβαινόντων. ἐπεὶ τίς ἀνθρώπων οὐ δεινὸν ἡγεῖται τύπτεσθαι τοὺς ἐλευθέρους; ἀλλ' ὅμως, ἐὰν μὲν ἄρχων ἀδίκων χειρῶν πάθῃ τις τοῦτο, δικαίως κρίνεται πεπονθέναι...,

Phylarchus merely relates most of the catastrophes of his history without suggesting why things are done or to what end, apart from which it is impossible either to feel pity reasonably or anger appropriately at any of the events. Who for example does not regard it as an outrage for a free man to be beaten? But if anyone provokes this action because he was the first to use violence, he is considered rightly punished.

A knowledge of causes and effects – precisely the aspects of his own work highlighted in the preface – provides an understanding of events quite at odds with the sight of any particular vivid detail.

5 Approaching Lake Trasimene in Polybius and Livy

The battle of Lake Trasimene, where a Roman army was defeated by Hannibal and their commander, the consul C. Flaminius, slain, offers an especially valuable opportunity for analyzing the relationship between any larger 'vision' of history made available to the historian's reader and a direct view of events of the past. If, as I have been arguing, the structural features of *enargeia* invited attention to an historian's approach to the past through a potential tension between the perspectives of his audience and of imagined spectators within the narrative, at Trasimene such tension reaches an extreme since the most important internal audience for the battle, the Roman troops, are blinded by a thick mist.[32] The final section of this chapter will consider how the narratives of this battle by two different historians, Livy and Polybius, treat this moment of internal blindness and what it reveals about their own construction of the role of vision in understanding the

---

[32] Both here and in the analysis that follows, it is also important to recognize the contrasting point emphasized by Fabrizi, both in her 2016 article and in the chapter in this volume, that weather phenomena are also a powerful tool for making the experience of the battle immediately accessible to the reader. I do not argue that the sensory responses of the internal audience at Trasimene are not made available to readers, but rather that a concomitant awareness of the possibility of distance and separation from these responses also has a role in their comprehension of the scene and that both are accentuated in a case where, paradoxically, absorption equals blindness.

past. But the situation is a little more complicated and interesting because of the intertextual relationship between the two passages. Anyone reading Livy's treatment will be immediately struck by his obvious debt to Polybius. Rather than regard this as a problem of source criticism, I follow the lead of David Levene in interpreting it as an allusion.[33] Polybius integrates the account of Trasimene into a narrative that thematizes the role of vision to highlight how his history reveals a reality that transcends both particular perceptions and the writer's mere simulation of them. Livy's similar attention to visual perspectives allows him to differentiate the spectacular aspects of his history from his predecessor's *theorema*.

To set the stage for the battle, we must go back to the beginning of the campaigning season in the spring of 217, for throughout this larger episode the faculty of vision becomes an important motif in Polybius's narrative.[34] Already in the winter camp, there has been great dissension among the Gallic contingents, and Hannibal thwarts their attempts on his life by means of a series of disguises – wigs that render him unrecognizable not only to chance acquaintances but even to those who know him well (3.78). In order to remove the causes of Gallic unhappiness, he begins the campaigning season early. First, as Polybius tells it, he makes extensive enquiry from the natives about possible routes into Etruria. The longer paths are all well known to the enemy (προδήλους, 3.78.6), but the shorter one will seem unexpected to them (παράδοξον φανησομένην, 3.78.7). Hannibal, since he is naturally inclined to do the unexpected, chooses this option. However, he only proceeds after investigating the exact depth of the water and making sure that it will be fordable. He also reckons that the pack animals are expendable, since supplies will be abundant once they reach Etruria, and that the feckless Gauls will be a problem (3.79.1–5). The crossing, while harrowing, conforms to his expectations. The African and Spanish troops make it through the marshes – they are tough and the ground is firm. The Gauls, however, have a much harder time since the route has been made muddier and they are not able to deal with adversity. The pack animals mostly die, but their corpses provide little islands on which the men can pile the luggage and get some sleep. Polybius also notes that Hannibal catches an inflammation that eventually costs him the sight in one eye (3.79.6–12).

The passage as a whole highlights two consistent features of Polybius's Hannibal, both of which relate to the power of sight. First, he makes himself invisible to his enemies, both the subversive Gauls and his Roman opponents. But on the other hand he uses inquiry and investigation to gain foresight of the circumstances through which he will pass, and this strategic planning causes his success. This knowledge of the landscape contrasts with the apprehensions of the rest of his troops who learn of their commander's

---

[33] Levene (2010: 126–63).
[34] My comparison of Livy and Polybius's crossing of the marshes is deeply indebted to the reading offered by my student Virginia Clark (2014: 74–8). Though her argument more directly concerns Livy's distinctive portrayal of Hannibal's relation to the Italian landscape, she too stresses the difference between Polybius's emphasis on Hannibal's strategic planning and knowledge and the lack of such forethought in Livy. She also notes the parallels with issues treated in the crossing of the Alps. I have tried below to indicate specific observations drawn from her analysis.

plans by rumor (φήμη) but also generalize about the dangers they face, creating a mental image (ὑφορώμενος, 3.78.8) based on the assumption that since they will be crossing a marsh, they will be sucked down in bogs. Hannibal, however, has done his homework by carefully investigating the depth of the water, as he had previously learned about the routes into Etruria from local witnesses.

Such different approaches to landscape may well recall Polybius's account of the crossing of the Alps, some thirty chapters before (3.47–8), where again Hannibal had carefully investigated the topography before beginning the journey. Polybius's own stake in Hannibal's energetic research cannot be missed since the historian reports it in the midst of criticizing the false and careless accounts of the crossing concocted by Polybius's rivals (3.48.10–12). These rivals reveal their nefarious Phylarchan desire to astonish their readers through miraculous stories but are simultaneously refuted by Hannibal's own foresight and also by Polybius himself, who relies on a very Thucydidean combination of autopsy and the examination of witnesses to construct his own true version of events.[35] Hannibal's strategies in the present passage may again demonstrate the particular value of Polybian historiography, which provides not only a model of good strategy but the information about geography and landscape upon which it can be based. And this alliance is hinted at when what Hannibal foresees turns out to match closely the historian's account of what really happened. The Carthaginian rank and file, by contrast, construct an image of what they are to face following the procedure of those historians who add details based on rhetorical models and a sense of what is likely to happen in any siege of a city whether or not it actually happened in any particular instance.

Livy gives a very different picture of this campaign, though his account conforms to Polybius's quite closely in content. Thus, Hannibal's reliance on disguises does not testify to his ability to thwart Gallic plots on his life, but rather forms part of a description of the circumstances that inspire the fear motivating his early departure from winter quarters (22.1.4).[36] Whereas Polybius presents the longer route into Etruria as better known to the Romans and therefore the one they would expect him to take, Livy omits this fact, as he does Hannibal's care in ensuring that they would find shallow water and firm footing. Indeed Livy's description of even the first ranks of Hannibal's troops nearly swallowed up in deep water (22.2.5–6) seems pointedly to refute both Polybius and the Polybian Hannibal's expectations. In depicting the crossing itself, Livy resorts to a very visualized description both of the circumstances of the march and its effects on the troops (22.2.5–9):

---

[35] βουλόμενοι τοὺς ἀναγινώσκοντας ἐκπλήττειν τῇ περὶ τῶν προειρημένων τόπων παραδοξολογίᾳ, 3.47.6 vs. ἡμεῖς δὲ περὶ τούτων εὐθαρσῶς ἀποφαινόμεθα διὰ τὸ περὶ τῶν πράξεων παρ' αὐτῶν ἱστορηκέναι τῶν παρατετευχότων τοῖς καιροῖς, τοὺς δὲ τόπους κατωπτευκέναι καὶ τῇ διὰ τῶν Ἄλπεων αὐτοὶ κεχρῆσθαι πορείᾳ γνώσεως ἕνεκα καὶ θέας, 3.48.12. Livy, as Levene (2010: 150–2) describes and other scholars cited ad loc. had noted, translates these historiographic exaggerations to the anxieties experienced by the Carthaginian troops themselves. And perhaps he has a Polybian model for this transference in the passage under discussion, where the army's imaginary fears contrast with Hannibal's prudent investigation.

[36] Clark (2014: 75) interprets it as stressing Hannibal's duplicitous character, another divergence from Polybius's emphasis.

Primi, qua modo praeirent duces, per praealtas fluvii ac profundas voragines, hausti paene limo immergentesque se, tamen signa sequebantur. Galli neque sustinere se prolapsi neque adsurgere ex voraginibus poterant neque aut corpora animis aut animos spe sustinebant; alii fessa aegre trahentes membra, alii, ubi semel victis taedio animis procubuissent, inter iumenta et ipsa iacentia passim morientes; maximeque omnium vigiliae conficiebant per quadriduum iam et tres noctes toleratae. Cum omnia obtinentibus aquis nihil ubi in sicco fessa sternerent corpora inveniri posset, cumulatis in aqua sarcinis insuper incumbebant, aut iumentorum itinere toto prostratorum passim acervi, tantum quod exstaret aqua quaerentibus ad quietem parvi temporis, necessarium cubile dabant.

The troops in front, wherever their leaders showed the way, through the steep and bottomless whirlpools of the stream, almost sucked up by mud and plunging in, nevertheless followed the standards. But the Gauls were able neither to support themselves if they slipped nor to rise out of the pools; they sustained neither their bodies with their spirits nor their spirits with hope. Some could hardly drag their tired limbs along; others, their courage yielding once for all to their weariness, dropped down and died amongst the baggage animals, for these too were lying all about. What distressed them most of all was the want of sleep, which they had now endured for four days and three nights. And since everything was under water and they could find no dry spot on which to stretch their weary bodies, they would pile their packs in the flood and lie down on these, or the heaps of pack animals that were everywhere strewn about along the line of march would afford a makeshift bed – for all they asked was a place that stood out above the water, where they could snatch a little sleep.

Trans. B. O. Foster, adapted

The detail of the troops' sleeping on the corpses of pack animals suggests the extent of their suffering, rather than being part of its solution. Livian *enargeia* in this case seems to offer a view of reality that Hannibal either does not perceive or conceals, while Polybius's more abstract descriptions of what the troops suffered allies his reader's perceptions with Hannibal's strategic expectations. The culmination of both accounts – Hannibal's loss of sight, which results from hardships that are not presented as part of his calculations – therefore seems in Livy to symbolize a fundamental lack of awareness that contrasts with the Carthaginian's short-term reliance on deceptions (22.2.10–11). Clark notes a telling example of that blindness in a little detail Livy includes that is absent from Polybius.[37] Polybius's Hannibal learns about the specific marshes he is about to cross, it is true. But such foresight would do no good in Livy, since he specifies that this was an unusually heavy year of flooding (*qua fluvius Arnus per eos dies solito magis inundaverat*, 22.2.2). And by adding this fact, Livy does more than make the point that even Polybian foresight cannot predict the anomalous or fortuitous event. The unusual height of the Arno flood

---

[37] Clark (2014: 76).

connects it with a whole string of *prodigia* which Livy – again unlike Polybius – has just recounted (22.1.8–13).[38] There is a visual pattern in events after all, but one that Hannibal with his famous lack of *religio* (21.4.10) will be temperamentally unable to see.[39]

Anyone attempting to read such symbolic significance into Hannibal's blindness in Polybius's account would receive explicit correction from the historian himself. Polybius introduces an authorial digression to praise Hannibal's reasoning and strategy in language that contains a strong visualizing element reminiscent of his programmatic account of the spectacular elements of his history. The victor must adopt a comprehensive vision (συνθεωρεῖν, 3.81.2) of how to hit the mark (τοῦ σκοποῦ). Those in charge of affairs should observe (σκοπεῖν, 3.81.3) not the vulnerabilities of the body, but where some advantage appears in the soul of the enemy leader. Not only does Polybius reinforce the importance of metaphorical vision here in encouraging strategists to look beyond the physical to the (invisible) soul, but the language similarly shapes his readers' response to Hannibal himself. If they are inclined to look at the blindness that afflicts merely his body, they will miss the considerable advantages he owes to his capacity for strategic reasoning.

6 Trasimene and the battle of perceptions

In both narratives, therefore, by the time we reach Trasimene itself we have been prepared to interpret the representation of vision as a clue about how to read the text. And in both cases this effect demands not the assimilation of our viewpoint to that of the internal spectators, the sympathetic perspective opened out by the devices of *enargeia*, but an awareness of difference. The real experience of the Roman soldiers participating in the battle was an inability to see thanks to the mist that hung over the lake. A fully realistic description that 'made the reader' a spectator, in Plutarch's language, would be impossible. The narrative point of view, even in a simple statement like 'the Romans could not see', demands an external focalization. But the thematic use each historian makes of this discrepancy in viewpoints will be very much his own.

In Polybius's case, attention to the merely physical aspects of description contrasts with a strategic vision that takes in more than what meets the eye and 'sees' things that are hidden from sight. The fullest depiction of the site of the battle occurs in the account of Hannibal's preparations (3.83). As in the case of his arrival in Etruria, he seems to have a strategic conception of the landscape lacking to the Roman leadership. The accident of

---

[38] On the further significance of this placement, see Levene (1993: 38–40). Throughout Clark's argument she stresses as well how Livy attributes a kind of agency to the Italian landscape itself.

[39] At this point in Livy's narrative (22.3.1–2) Clark (2014: 77–8) notes a striking shift in the portrayal of Hannibal, who now suddenly manifests the Polybian attention to learning about the landscape absent in the account of the marshes. Thus Hannibal's blindness, which had previously been treated as a sign of his 'loss of authority and capacity for guidance', now lines up with the interpretation I have given of its significance in Polybius: 'Even as he loses an eye and his power of literal sight diminishes, Hannibal becomes much more authoritative, and gains a more practical and realistic approach to space and his movements through it.'

the morning mist, while certainly a factor in increasing the Romans' confusion, perhaps has a greater effect on the dynamics of Polybius's narrative by allowing him to dramatize the unexpected appearance (ἐπιφάνεια, 3.84.2) of Hannibal. The actual visible element, the mist, comes to symbolize Hannibal's opponents' lack of strategic cognition; it appears not only as a cause of confusion but also as a manifestation of it. In that way Polybius simultaneously depicts the mist's effects and penetrates it by redirecting the readers' attention away from the physical circumstances of the battle to abstract, psychological factors. Polybius describes the situation as taking away the commanders' power to recognize events. The Roman troops were delivered up to slaughter by the lack of judgment of their leaders (ἔτι γὰρ διαβουλευόμενοι τί δεῖ πράττειν ἀπώλλυντο παραδόξως, 3.84.5), something Hannibal had foreseen as much as he had made himself aware of the landscape. The delay of παραδόξως to the end of the sentence transfers to the level of discourse the surprise attack Hannibal launched in reality, even as it unites the failure of perception that occurs as a result of the physical conditions of the landscape with the strategic pattern of paradox throughout the campaign. In the first part of this encounter, Polybius seems less interested in describing the experience of battle than the perceptive and cognitive limits of the Romans. The paralysis of their reasoning is accentuated by the men's progressive assimilation to the position of animals. Herded together along the lakeshore, some men experience a complete breakdown of mental processes (διὰ τὴν παράστασιν τῆς διανοίας, 3.84.9) that leads them to attempt to swim away, until they are cut down with only their heads sticking out of the water. This much more vivid image of the troops slipping down to destruction in the lake, where increasing *akribeia* accompanies a description of the Romans' experience as 'pitiful' (ταλαιπώρως), recalls the fate the Carthaginian troops expected when they entered the marshes. In that case, however, the foresight of their commander kept them from perishing like the beasts in fact did. The Celts' own miseries, which Polybius had also described with the adverb ταλαιπώρως (3.79.6), add a new element of contrast. The Gauls are undisciplined and unaccustomed to labor, yet the forethought of their commander saves even them. The Romans are well habituated to discipline, yet even they perish because of the failure of leadership. Thus, even the most vividly described moment of the battle leads from *sympatheia* to *suntheoria*, to a comparison of similar scenes that ultimately directs the audience to the abstract causes of material effects. Just so the Romans literally disappear from the readers' field of vision as they sink under the lake.

Livy's description of the battle follows Polybius's closely in its general organization and emphases but constructs a different kind of contrast in perspectives and uses it to convey different historiographic aims. He too progressively isolates the Roman perspective from others within the narrative, using national adjectives to differentiate the Carthaginians, in a commanding position above the mist, from the Romans trapped within it (22.4.5–7).

Poenus ubi, id quod petierat, clausum lacu ac montibus et circumfusum suis copiis habuit hostem, signum omnibus dat simul invadendi. Qui ubi qua cuique proximum fuit decucurrerunt, eo magis Romanis subita atque improvisa res fuit,

> quod orta ex lacu nebula campo quam montibus densior sederat agminaque hostium ex pluribus collibus ipsa inter se satis conspecta eoque magis pariter decucurrerant. Romanus clamore prius undique orto quam satis cerneret, se circumventum esse sensit, et ante in frontem lateraque pugnari coeptum est quam satis instrueretur acies aut expediri arma stringique gladii possent.

> The Carthaginian, once he had accomplished his aim of shutting the enemy in between the lake and mountains and surrounding them with his troops, gave the signal for all his forces to attack at once. As they charged down, each at the nearest point, their onset was all the more sudden and unforeseen inasmuch as the mist from the lake lay more thickly on the plain than the mountain, and the attacking columns had been clearly visible to one another from the various hills and had therefore delivered their charge at more nearly the same instant. From the shouting that arose on every side the Romans perceived, before they could clearly see, that they were surrounded; and they were already engaged on their front and flank before they could properly form up or get out their arms and draw their swords.
>
> Trans. B. O. Foster, adapted

As Levene notes, such stratification by nationality that puts the Carthaginians above the mist does not occur in Polybius.[40] If this distinction encourages a kind of assimilation between the reader and the blinded viewer – both *Romani* – we will find that Livy has at once extended the possibility for such a blurring of perspectives and continually emphasizes what his own reader can see. Where the Polybian narrative provides an externally focalized view of the Romans' loss of perception, Livy recreates this experience much more emphatically (in the ancient sense) through a kind of rhetorical particularization of effects recalling the narrative strategies of *enargeia*. This can be illustrated by the following passage (22.5.4):

> et erat in tanta caligine maior usus aurium quam oculorum. ad gemitus uolnerum ictusque corporum aut armorum et mixtos strepentium pauentiumque clamores circumferebant ora oculosque.

> And in such heavy mist, the ears were of greater use than the eyes. They were turning face and eyes in the direction of groans arising from wounds and the clash of bodies or arms and the combined shouts of those crying out and of the terrified.

This extension of sensory confusion from the visual to the auditory forms a distinctive theme in Livy's treatment of the scene.[41] By describing the experience of the troops present at the battle not only in terms of what they saw but what they heard, perhaps Livy simulates their experience even more directly for an audience that is also apprehending

---

[40] Levene (2010: 269).
[41] Levene (2010: 269).

events not by seeing them but by hearing them. If it seems fanciful to suggest that *gemitus*, *ictus* and *clamores* reproduce the groans and clashes of the battlefield through onomatopoeia, the account of men attempting to see sounds has the potential to draw together the confusion of the soldiers present on the battlefield and the historical audience's isolation from visible reality. Livy thus goes pointedly further than Polybius in making the sensory experience of the past available to his readers, while at the same time using this alignment of perceptions to figure the limits and frustrations of *enargeia*. As the soldiers' reliance on their senses puts them at the mercy of Hannibal, so too great an attention to the immediately perceptible experiences of the past, without the perspective of historical distance, diminishes his audience's awareness and leads them into a dead end where the goal of seeing the past as present must always elude them.

A final demonstration of how Livy intensifies and interprets the soldier's sensory deprivation comes with a detail he has interpolated into this generally Polybian description from the Roman historian Coelius Antipater. 'So great was the ardor of their courage, so intent was the mind of each on the battle, that no one of those fighting even perceived that earthquake which laid low great parts of many cities of Italy and turned swift streams from their course' (*tantusque fuit ardor animorum, adeo intentus pugnae animus, ut eum motum terrae qui multarum urbium Italiae magnas partes prostrauit auertitque cursu rapidos amnes, . . ., nemo pugnantium senserit,* 22.5.8).[42] This conclusion helps mark a crescendo of blindness. Hannibal had concealed his troops, and the mist had rendered the soldiers blind to their landscape, but they could still hear. Now they seem to have lost that sense as well and are further unable even to feel. What is more, what they fail to notice is not only a general phenomenon but also a religious one as well, another in the series of *prodigia* that begin the book. The phrase Livy uses to describe their absorption in their confusion, *intentus . . . animus,* may also help alert the reader to the larger significance of the episode. In his preface, when Livy prescribes how his history should be read, Livy had used the same expression to instruct his reader, who, rather than sorting out the truth of claims to divine origins in the distant past, should direct his mind (*intendat animum, praef.* 9) to the customs and patterns of life through which *imperium* was gained and lost.[43] To remember that phrase here prompts a recognition of the act of reading itself and of the difference between what the reader sees and what the soldiers see. The soldiers' *ardor animorum* may be exemplary, just the thing Livy wants his readers to notice, but it is perceptible when they are looked at rather than focalizing the perceptions of the audience.

---

[42] Fr. 14b *FRHist* (= 20P). See Levene (2010: 268, n. 16). But if Livy is using Coelius as a source here, he intensifies this indication of the Romans' lack of perception as well. At least in the sentence attributed to him in Cic. *Div.* 1.78, Coelius merely indicated that there were frequent earthquakes throughout northwest Italy at the time of the battle. There is no mention of their being felt at Trasimene itself (unless Livy is playfully commenting on the very incompatibility between his two alternative sources, a veristic one that has no room for the supernatural and one with a strong divine presence but logical inconsistencies: On the one hand if the earthquake in Coelius was so strong why didn't anybody notice it at the time/why isn't it in Polybius? On the other, there may be more things in heaven and earth than appear even in Polybius's synopsis of 'universal history').

[43] The phrase *animos intendunt* (restored by Mueller) also appears in another programmatic moment of spectatorship in Livy's early books to describe the audience for the duel between the Horatii and the Curiatii at 1.25.2.

7 The clearing: the death of Flaminius

This moment when the Romans within the narrative seem to attain complete sensory isolation marks a striking transition in Livy's account of the battle. The historian's attention shifts from the generalized experience of individual Roman soldiers to the death of the consul Flaminius, killed in single combat by a Gaul named Ducarius. For a reader with the Polybian version in mind, this striking intrusion signals a more general change of direction in the narrative. Far from making Flaminius's death the centre of his battle description, Polybius simply notes, as an element in the breakdown of the Roman command structure, that he is cut down at the hands of a band of Celts (3.84.6). In Livy's case not only are we obviously following a different account of the battle, but the whole scene takes place in a completely different visual environment and exemplifies a quite different approach to *enargeia*.[44] As opposed to soldiers who do not even notice an earthquake, Flaminius himself seems to possess the ability to perceive his situation in detail, and to respond wherever he notices his troops are struggling (22.6.2). The verb *senserat* used to describe his ability to see was precisely the one used to designate what the soldiers could not feel. And Flaminius is as conspicuous as he is clear-sighted. Since his arms are so distinctive, enemies target him, and his own troops gaze upon them. Ducarius not only recognizes him by his armour but even by the details of his facial appearance, perhaps a reversal of the disguises Hannibal had used to conceal himself from his own Gallic allies. The inconsistency between the necessity for clear vision to explain the events described here and the murky mist in which the rest of the battle takes place signals further historiographic transformations. If Polybius was recognizable as the leading source for Livy's general presentation of the battle, that very loss of perception perhaps becomes a figure for a historiography grounded in experiential truth. That's the way the battle really was, but in what follows we leave the mist of reality behind. If that is so, then Livy's use of the techniques of rhetorical narrative to create a vividly detailed account of Flaminius's death comes to signal its own motion away from the truth. Not only does he record details not in Polybius, such as the name of the Gallic challenger,[45] but he even puts in a bit of direct speech: "'Behold", he exclaims to his fellow Gauls, "here is the one who cut down our legions and devastated our fields and city. This victim will I now offer to the ghosts of our citizens so foully killed'" (*'<en>' inquit 'hic est' popularibus suis, 'qui legiones nostras cecidit agrosque et urbem est depopulatus; iam ego hanc uictimam manibus peremptorum foede ciuium dabo'*, 22.6.3). Just what a Gaul would say, and that is the point. If pursuing the real truth of what the soldiers saw leads the audience itself towards a recognition of blindness, the much more visible account of Flaminius's duel was particularly vulnerable to being read as the product of rhetorical *inventio*. And

---

[44] Fabrizi's essay in this collection analyses another example of a sudden shift from mist to clarity, at the Romans' decisive defeat of Philip V at Cynoscephalae (33.7.8–11). There the effect is very different: thanks to Livy's including mention of the fog lifting, Philip's perception of his defeat appears veristically integrated with Livy's presentation of the battle as a whole.

[45] Though Levene (2010: 268) suggests again Coelius Antipater as a source.

correspondingly, while Ducarius's recognition of Flaminius may provide a moment of internal focalization, Livy's account of the climax of the duel seems not to be seen through the eyes of any of the participants. Livy remarks that this was the beginning of the Roman retreat, but there is no attempt to capture the pathos of the Romans' watching their consul fall. None of the bodies swaying in terror or buoyed up by success that Plutarch admired in Thucydides or that Livy himself adds to his account of the duel between the Horatii and Curiatii. Indeed Livy has been echoing precisely that kind of emotionalized description in his earlier account of the battle. In the death of Flaminius, then, Livy has distinguished the construction of a spectacle for his viewers from his effort to reproduce the experiences of those present at the time.

The recognition of this duel not just as an un-Polybian detail but as a distinct anomaly in Livy's account of the battle was made by David Levene.[46] For him, a pattern of slight inconsistencies in several of Livy's battle narratives, signaled by divergence from a Polybian intertext, helps move the Roman historian away from Polybius's sense that history's utility derives ultimately from its direct observance of reality. The breaks in sequences of cause and effects serve not so much to undermine confidence in Livy's historiographic authority as to leave space for elements of the uncanny. Ultimately, such discrepancies direct the audience's attention to those aspects of events that mere human reason cannot explain, especially towards Rome's maintenance of good relations with the gods, which emerges as crucial at key moments of Livy's text, and to which Flaminius himself is conspicuously blind here. To Levene's persuasive reading, we may add a consideration of how Livy's applications of *enargeia* form part of this pattern. Polybius contrasts the big picture his history can present of the strategic realities of the battle, a perspective that aligns his account of the battle with Hannibal's planning for it, with the lack of perception experienced by the shepherdless flock of Roman victims. Livy constructs a divergence between two kinds of realism, what the Romans really saw and a verisimilar episode exposed primarily to the gaze of his audience, to contrast the perspective of those looking on events from those who look on his representation of events.

Livy had famously compared his work to an *inlustre monumentum* (*praef.* 10), that is, as something visually available to be seen by his audience. But a visible monument is not necessarily the same thing as a monument that makes the past visible, and it is precisely the total view of the work as a whole that enables the historian's audience to see events differently from the participants – participants who in this case have lost the ability not just to contextualize the defeat at Trasimene but to perceive the larger picture of the importance of Rome's relationship with the gods which a broader historical view encourages. Livy's readers can make many illuminating connections between Flaminius's duel and other events they have encountered in their reading. They can measure it against the duels undertaken with Gauls in Book 7 by Manlius Torquatus (7.10) and Valerius Corvus (7.26). They can also set it against the *devotiones* of the Decii (8.9–10, 10.28–9), other examples of the conspicuous death of a Roman general in battle. In both

---

[46] Levene (2010: 268–70).

cases the comparison will point out significant differences in this episode as well as the clues to their interpretation. Flaminius loses the duel, and his death leads not to victory, as should be the case in a *devotio*, but to a rout. Why? *Devotio* is a religious ritual; it only works when the participant has subordinated himself to the power of the gods. So too the duels in Book 7 not only highlight the value of history and exemplarity, they also depend on the combatants' following orders. Flaminius neglects rituals and omens, antagonizes rivals, and despises any collective authority that attempts to constrain him. No wonder he fails, and the manner of his failing conveys the fundamental subject Livy memorializes, the customs and personal characteristics that lead to the growth or collapse of *imperium*. Flaminius's actions can be understood when they are compared and contrasted to similar gestures and type scenes from earlier and later history, just as Hannibal's apparent victory must be set in the much larger historical pattern, to which he himself is blind, that leads to his own defeat. This is not simply a question of perceiving a narrative whole or of setting individual incidents in a larger historical pattern, as was suggested by the references to Pylos in Thucydides' account of the battle at Syracuse. Rather Livy enables his readers to recognize likenesses and differences between similar scenes separated by vast distances in his narrative, and by doing so to gain a new understanding of the connections between elements of the narrative on a smaller scale (the connection between Flaminius's death and his insubordination or his neglect of omens), neither of which are directly apprehensible to the internal audience. And in conclusion I want to suggest that the patterning of narrative on actual Roman sculptural monuments can indeed illustrate the effect Livy achieves here. Consider for instance the column of Marcus Aurelius, where the viewer can pick out similar or analogous figures unifying disparate events, and where there is the possibility for a vertical narrative – like the rain miracle – that cannot be seen by any of the participants within the 'horizontal' flow of events.[47] An example from Livy's own time would be the typological similarity between figures on the *Ara Pacis*, like Aeneas and Augustus who are brought together over vast temporal distances by similarities of gestures and function. This aspect of Livy's monumentality does not follow from the vividness of its description of the specific scene, but only from making the reader a viewer of the entire monument.

Bibliography

Bal, M. 1985. *Narratology: Introduction to the Theory of Narrative*. Toronto: University of Toronto Press.

---

[47] In the 'rain miracle' an epiphany of a divine figure dripping rain from his wings signifies a flood that resulted in a Roman victory. The vertical division in this individual tableau, with the divine cause represented above and in visual isolation from its effect on the perceptible world (one Roman seems to be trying to see through the god's wings) continues in the composition of the column as a whole. For the scene below depicts a river aligned precisely with the flow from the rain divinity; though none of the soldiers crossing that river could of course be expected to see the miraculous source of the river. The way the medium of the column allows at once for the viewer to connect thematically related tableaux within the impression of a continuous representation of history forms one strand of Brilliant's analysis of 'The Column of Trajan and its Heirs' (1984: esp. 104–16).

Barthes, R. 1989. *The Rustle of Language*, translated by R. Howard. Berkeley, CA: University of California Press.
Benardete, S. 1969. *Herodotean Inquiries*. The Hague: Martinus Nijhoff.
Brilliant, R. 1984. *Visual Narratives: Storytelling in Etruscan and Roman Art*. Ithaca: Cornell University Press.
Chaplin, J. 2000. *Livy's Exemplary History*. Oxford: Oxford University Press.
Clark, V. 2014. *Landscapes of Conquest: Space, Place, and Environment in Livy's Ab Urbe Condita*. PhD diss., Princeton University.
Connor, W. R. 1984. *Thucydides*. Princeton: Princeton University Press.
Davidson, J. 1991. 'The Gaze in Polybius' Histories.' *Journal of Roman Studies* 81: 10–24.
Fabrizi, V. 2016. 'Space, Vision, and the Friendly Sea: Scipio's Crossing to Africa in Livy's Book 29.' In *Seemacht, Seeherrschaft und die Antike*, edited by E. Barltrusch, H. Kopp and C. Wendt, 279–89. Stuttgart: Franz Steiner Verlag.
Ferguson, W. S. 1927. 'The Athenian Expedition to Sicily.' In *The Cambridge Ancient History*, Vol. 5, edited by J. B. Bury, S. A. Cook and F. E. Adcock, 282–311. Cambridge: Cambridge University Press.
Gilhuly, K. and N. Worman, eds. 2014. *Space, Place, and Landscape in Ancient Greek Literature and Culture*. Cambridge: Cambridge University Press.
Grethlein, J. 2010. *The Greeks and their Past: Poetry, Oratory, and History in the Fifth Century* BCE. Cambridge: Cambridge University Press.
Grethlein, J. 2013. *Experience and Teleology in Ancient Historiography: Futures Past from Herodotus to Augustine*. Cambridge: Cambridge University Press.
Hornblower, S. 2008. *A Commentary on Thucydides*. Vol. 3. Oxford: Oxford University Press.
Horsfall, N. 1982. 'The Caudine Forks: Topography and Illusion.' *Papers of the British School at Rome* 50: 45–82.
Lausberg, H. 1998. *Handbook of Literary Rhetoric*, translated by M. T. Bliss, A. Jansen and D. E. Orton. Leiden: Brill.
Levene, D. 1993. *Religion in Livy*. Leiden: Brill.
Levene, D. 2012. *Livy on the Hannibalic War*. Oxford: Oxford University Press.
Marincola, J. 1997. *Authority and Tradition in Ancient Historiography*. Cambridge: Cambridge University Press.
Marincola, J. 2013. 'Polybius, Phylarchus, and Tragic History.' In *Polybius and His World: Essays in Memory of F. W. Walbank*, edited by B. Gibson and T. Harrison, 73–90. Oxford: Oxford University Press.
Mitchell, W. J. T. 1994. *Picture Theory*. Chicago: University of Chicago Press.
Moles, J. 1993a. 'Truth and Untruth in Herodotus and Thucydides.' In *Lies and Fiction in the Ancient World*, edited by C. Gill and T. P. Wiseman, 88–121. Liverpool: Liverpool University Press.
Morson, G. S. 1994. *Narrative and Freedom. The Shadows of Time*. New Haven: Yale University Press.
Oakley, S. P. 2005. *A Commentary on Livy Books VI–X. Vol. 3, Book IX*. Oxford: Clarendon Press.
Purves, A. 2014. 'In the Bedroom.' In *Space, Place, and Landscape in Ancient Greek Literature and Culture*, edited by K. Gilhuly and N. Worman, 94–129. Cambridge: Cambridge University Press.
Rood, T. 1998. *Thucydides: Narrative and Explanation*. Oxford: Oxford University Press.
Rutter, N. K. 1998. *Thucydides: History of the Peloponnesian War Books VI and VII: A Companion to the Penguin Translation*. Bristol: Bristol Classical Press.
Schepens, G. 1975. '"Ἔμφασις und ἐνάργεια in Polybios' Geschichtstheorie.' *Rivista storica dell'Antichità* 5: 185–200.
Schepens, G. 1980. *L'autopsie' dans la méthode des historiens grecs du Ve siècle avant J.-C.* Brussels: Paleis der Academiën.

Schultze, C. 1986. 'Dionysius of Halicarnassus and his Audience.' In *Past Perspectives: Studies in Greek and Roman Historical Writing*, edited by I. Moxon, J. Smart and A. Woodman, 123–43. Cambridge: Cambridge University Press.

Spencer, D. 2010. *Roman Landscape: Culture and Identity*. Cambridge: Cambridge University Press.

Travis, R. 2000. 'The Spectation of Gyges in P. Oxy. 2382 and Herodotus Book 1.' *Classical Antiquity* 19: 330–59.

Tsitsiou-Chelidoni, C. 2009. 'History beyond Literature: Interpreting the 'Internally Focalized' Narrative in Livy's *Ab urbe condita*.' In *Narratology and Interpretation. The Content of Narrative Form in Ancient Literature*, edited by J. Grethlein and A. Rengakos, 527–54. Berlin: De Gruyter.

Walbank, F. W. 1990. 'Profit or Amusement: Some Thoughts on the Motives of Hellenistic Historians.' In *Purposes of History: Studies in Greek Historiography from the 4th to the 2nd Century BC (Studia Hellenistica 30)*, edited by H. Verdin, G. Schepens and E. de Keyser, 253–66. Leuven: Leuven University Press. [= F. W. Walbank (2002) *Polybius, Rome and the Hellenistic World*, Cambridge: 231–41.]

Walker, A. 1993. 'Enargeia and the Spectator in Greek Historiography.' *Transactions of the American Philological Association* 123: 353–77.

Webb, R. 1997. 'Mémoire et imagination: les limites de l'enargeia dans la théorie rhétorique grecque.' In *Dire l'évidence*, edited by C. Lévy and L. Pernot, 229–48. Paris: Editions L'Harmattan.

Wiater, N. 2017. 'The Aesthetics of Truth: Narrative and Historical Hermeneutics in Polybius' Histories.' In *Truth and History in the Ancient World: Pluralising the Past*, edited by I. Ruffell and L. Hau, 202–25. London: Routledge.

Wiseman, T. P. 1979. *Clio's Cosmetics*. Leicester: Leicester University Press.

Woodman, A. J. 1988. *Rhetoric in Classical Historiography*. London and Sydney: Croom Helm.

Zangara, A. 2007. *Voir l'histoire: Théories anciennes du récit historique*. Paris: Vrin.

PART II
LANDSCAPES OF RUIN AND RECOVERY

CHAPTER 4
THE PROBLEMS WITH AGRICULTURAL RECOVERY IN LUCAN'S CIVIL WAR NARRATIVE

Laura Zientek

1 Introduction

When Lucan writes about a battlefield, the human experience of the place – that is, the landscape itself[1] – is woven into his interpretation of the battle fought there, from preparations to aftermath. Lucan focalizes an anthropocentric view of the environment through the actions and processes of war, including the construction of siege-works and other large-scale landscape engineering, the movement and encampment of armies, the alteration of land during the course of battle preparation and fighting, and the use of natural resources. Several studies of Lucan's poem have focused already on how war changes the landscape,[2] and this study builds on the idea of war's transformative effects on the natural world and their ramifications for human life. In particular, this chapter examines how Lucan represents battlefields as transformed agricultural landscapes, distant temporally but not spatially. Moreover, just as the actions and processes of war reshape the landscape, so too do agricultural processes such as ploughing, planting and water management. Lucan's environmental poetics of war derive their poignancy from the representation of war and agriculture as overlapping anthropogenic processes with distinct moral implications in this narrative of civil conflict.

Vergil's *Georgics* is the *locus classicus* for agricultural recovery on a former battlefield, where a cycle of war and peace resolves, at least temporarily. Other literary and historical predecessors provide the necessary context to inform how Lucan's poetic programme adopts and adapts the trope of post-war agricultural recovery. Within Lucan's poem, reading battlefields in terms of their recovery from the damages wrought by war is a troubled endeavour for several reasons, not least of which is the chronology of poetic narrative and poetic composition: the battlefields in the *Bellum Civile* were active only slightly longer than a century before Lucan wrote about them. While Vergil's *Georgics* also addresses the civil war battles of the mid-first century BCE – and does so more contemporaneously than Lucan – Vergil's poetic narrator looks back on the battlefields

---

[1] Cosgrove (1984), Layton and Ucko (1999: 3), Spencer (2010: 1).
[2] On the transformative consequences of war on the landscape, see Ambühl (2016), Hardie (2008), Hughes (2014: 152–5), Leigh (2010), Makins (2013), Masters (1992), McCutcheon (2013), McIntyre (2008), O'Gorman (1995), Reitz-Joosse (2016).

from some imagined point in the far future.³ Lucan's repeated use of agricultural language and imagery in the context of war has several intranarratorial effects: it destabilizes the process of agricultural recovery, leading instead to emptiness or a reclaiming of the land by wilderness; it re-contextualizes the use of a battle's organic matter (blood and corpses) as harmful rather than helpful, leading not to bumper crops but rather to lasting mutations; it abandons the resolution of the war/peace cycle entirely, with war simply producing yet more war; and it co-opts agricultural images for war narratives. Not only do Lucan's battlefield landscapes clearly demonstrate how Lucan reshapes the literary trope of the war/recovery cycle in which battlefields become productive agricultural land again, but in doing so he imbues his battlefields with a sense of permanence. And though the medium of epic intrinsically recalls the idea of immortality through memory, Lucan's battlefields – and the war that produced them – live on as physical realities of place separate from monument or memorial and resistant to the return of agriculture as a peacetime activity. The image of lasting ruin (*etiam periere ruinae*, BC 9.969) has its roots in the abandoned fields of the prologue (1.28–9).

2 Literary and historical antecedents

At the end of the first book of the *Georgics*, Vergil describes a farmer who discovers the remnants of past battles while ploughing his fields and presents 'one of the great pathetic topoi of Roman writing on the civil wars' (G. 1.491–7):⁴

> nec fuit indignum superis bis sanguine nostro
> Emathiam et latos Haemi pinguescere campos.
> scilicet et tempus veniet, cum finibus illis
> agricola incurvo terram molitus aratro
> exesa inveniet scabra robigine pila,
> aut gravibus rastris galeas pulsabit inanis
> grandiaque effossis mirabitur ossa sepulcris.

> It was not unbecoming for the gods to enrich with our blood Emathia and the broad fields of Haemus twice. Surely a time will come when in those lands a farmer working the land with curved plough will discover a spear corroded with rough rust, or will strike with heavy hoes empty helmets, and he will wonder at the huge bones from excavated graves.

The simplest dichotomy in these verses seems to pair the distinction between war and peace with that of battle and agriculture,⁵ though in reality this division cannot be made

---

³ Verg. G. 1.491–7, esp. 1.493: *scilicet et tempus veniet*.
⁴ Leigh (1997): 293.
⁵ Makins (2013: 169): the discovery of bones and armour 'trigger[s] the recognition of the field as *battlefield*'.

so cleanly. War imagery is threaded throughout the *Georgics*. The farmer and his tools are compared to a soldier and his weapons.[6] The plough defines the farmer as a hero within his own literary context in a way comparable to the *heros* of epic with his *arma*.[7] Agriculture works because the farmer brings order to the natural environment by 'conquering' it.[8] Throughout, there is a deep-rooted ambiguity in the *Georgics* about using the landscape for agriculture, war, or even agriculture *as* war.[9] And yet, despite this ambiguity and shared imagery, war and agriculture are two distinct forces acting upon the land in the *Georgics*.[10] Moreover, because the plough is connected to the literary construction of Roman identity and because it is connected to stories of Rome's foundation, the tradition of agriculture is likewise connected to this civilizing process which itself would be fundamentally disrupted by civil war.[11] Agriculture in the *Georgics*, then, represents two distinct but equally important ideas: first, the modification and mastery of the natural landscape by human beings for their benefit; and second, the establishment of 'law, order and peace'.[12]

The idea of blood-enriched battlefields is not unique to the *Georgics*. It recurs throughout the Augustan literary corpus but looks back further to models in earlier Greek poetry as well as a historical event which is preserved in Plutarch's later account. In Aeschylus's *Seven Against Thebes*, a messenger relays the words of the seer Amphiaraus, who claims: ἔγωγε μὲν δὴ τήνδε πιανῶ χθόνα, | μάντις κεκευθὼς πολεμίας ὑπὸ χθονός ('I, then, will enrich the earth, a seer concealed beneath enemy ground', *Sept.* 587–8). Vergil's verses seem to echo Aeschylus's, from the similarity of verbs (*pinguescere*/πιαίνειν) to the focus on the earth itself (*latos Haemi . . . campos*/πολεμίας ὑπὸ χθονός).[13] Moreover, in Thebes, a place where the citizens were thought to be autochthonous, it makes a visceral kind of sense that civil conflict would affect not just the citizens, but their land as well. Aeschylus is an early source for the trope of the bodies of the battle dead producing agricultural fertility; earlier Homeric poetry does connect the earth, as a

---

[6] Betensky (1979: 110) cites *ferro* (1.50), *exercet* and *imperat* (1.99), *comminus* (1.104), *vicit* (1.145) and *arma* (1.160). Wilhelm (1982) 221 interprets 1.493–7 as a refashioning of order from chaos by the farmer following the (mis)use of *ferrum* for weapons rather than ploughing. Putnam (1979: 71) notes the irony that 'the artistry used against the earth is a stepping-stone toward the martial artifacts man produces against himself'.
[7] Simons (2001: 534).
[8] Betensky (1979: 110). Cf. Low (1985: 8): 'Farming is a heroic activity, a kind of constructive warfare in which farmer and ox must labor together as fellow-soldiers.' However, note Thomas (2001: 126): 'the death of the ox (3.515–30) problematizes the constructiveness of the warfare'.
[9] Thomas (2001: 124): 'for Virgil [the countryside] was the site of war, between man and man, nature and man, with victory by either side deeply problematic'.
[10] Ambühl (2016: 311–12) notes that the 'perverted cycle of nature, where fertile fields are deserted by their farmers and turned into battlefields, only to become even more fertile for the benefit of future farmers thanks to the blood and the decomposing bodies of the fallen soldiers' in the *Georgics* also looks back to Catullus 64.
[11] Wilhelm (1982: 214) cites Ov. *Fast.* 4.825–6; Varro, *Ling.* 5.143; and Verg. *Aen.* 5.755 and 7.157–9. He also quotes Cic. *Rep.* 2.5, *rem publicam serere*, of Romulus 'sowing' the state (cf. *Tusc.* 14.31). See also Lucr. 5.1289–91, McCutcheon (2013: 262) and Spencer (2010: 14 and 45).
[12] Wilhelm (1982: 215); cf. Sayre (2017).
[13] Probably not a reference to the Amphiareion at Oropos; *Seven Against Thebes* was performed in 467 BCE, but the Amphiareion was probably not dedicated until the late fifth century. See Ustinova (2009: 96–8) on Amphiaraus and the underground.

primordial cosmic idea, with both life and death,[14] but the causal connection between battlefields and fertile farmland is absent. And although fertile fields are a mainstay of bucolic literature (e.g. Theoc. 10.47, πιαίνεται ὁ στάχυς οὕτως), this fertility is not based in the battlefield. Aeschylus is quite notable in this connection of war to agriculture and, in particular, of civil war's bloodshed to the fertility of the earth.

In the literature of the Augustan period, this trope becomes quite common and Vergil's verses resonate with those of Ovid, Propertius, and Horace. Horace writes in the first poem of his second book of *Odes* (*Carm.* 2.1.29–36):

> quis non Latino sanguine pinguior
> campus sepulcris inpia proelia
>   testatur auditumque Medis
>   Hesperiae sonitum ruinae?
> qui gurges aut quae flumina lugubris
> ignara belli? quod mare Dauniae
>   non decoloravere caedes?
>   quae caret ora cruore nostro?

What field is not richer by Latin blood, what field does not witness with graves impious battles and the sound of Hesperia's ruin heard by the Medes? What currents or rivers are unfamiliar with mournful war? What sea have Apulian slaughters not discoloured? What coast is lacking our blood?

Horace joins Vergil in his focus on blood – especially Roman blood (*Latino . . . sanguine*, 29; *cruore nostro*, 36) – enriching battlefields-turned-farmland (*pinguior. . . campus*, 29–30). The poem as a whole critiques Asinius Pollio's turn from tragedy to history, and seeks to prove Horace's own capability to address historical topics without abandoning his genre of choice. In doing so, Horace enters into a moment of intertextuality with Vergil's verses (*sanguine nostro | ... pinguescere campos*, G. 1.491–2) and thus continues to build a particularly Roman and Augustan way of writing poetry about civil war battles and their consequences.[15]

Propertius also addresses the aftermath of civil war battles fought on Italian soil in the first book of his *Elegiae* (1.22.3–10):

> si Perusina tibi patriae sunt nota sepulcra,
>   Italiae duris funera temporibus,
> cum Romana suos egit discordia civis,
>   (sic mihi praecipue, pulvis Etrusca, dolor,
> tu proiecta mei perpessa es membra propinqui,
>   tu nullo miseri contegis ossa solo),

---

[14] Floyd (1989); Kitts (2005).
[15] Henderson (1996: 109–14).

proxima supposito contingens Umbria campo
  me genuit terris fertilis uberibus.

If the Perusinian graves of the fatherland are known to you, the funerals of Italy in harsh times, when Roman discord led its own citizens, (Etruscan dust, especial grief to me, you suffered the scattered limbs of my kinsman, you did not cover the bones of him, wretched, with any soil), nearby fertile Umbria, bordering with its neighbouring plain, bore me from rich lands.

Here, the fertility of the Italian landscape (*Umbria ... | terris fertilis uberibus*) is juxtaposed with the bones of a fallen soldier, but in this case the connection seems to be less causal. Battlefield and farmlands share a border, but do not necessarily overlap, except in the verses of this *Elegy*.[16] Nonetheless, Propertius's personal experiences with Octavian's land confiscations inform his composition of this image,[17] and increase the resonance of Augustan poetic images of bloody civil war battles. Propertius's *sepulcra* (1.22.3) and *ossa* (1.22.8) allude to Vergil's *ossa sepulcris* (G. 1.497), while *terris fertilis uberibus* (1.22.10) recalls enriched fields (*pinguescere campos*, G. 1.492) more broadly.

Ovid also contributes to the development and nuance of this trope in the first of his *Heroides*, an imagined verse epistle from Penelope to Odysseus after the Trojan War (*Her.* 1.51–6):

diruta sunt aliis, uni mihi Pergama restant,
  incola captivo quae bove victor arat.
iam seges est, ubi Troia fuit, resecandaque falce
  luxuriat Phrygio sanguine pinguis humus;
semisepulta virum curvis feriuntur aratris
  ossa, ruinosas occulit herba domos.

For others Pergamum has been demolished, but for me alone it still stands, although its inhabitant, a victor, ploughs with a captured ox. Now there is grain where Troy used to be, and the earth, ready to be harvested by the sickle, enriched by Phrygian blood, abounds; the half-buried bones of men are struck by the curved plough, grasses hide the ruined palaces.

Note the similarity of language between Vergil's post-war arable field and Ovid's: *pinguis*/*pinguescere* made possible by *sanguinis* (an image with resonance in the poems of Horace and Propertius as well); *curvis ... aratris*/*incurvo ... aratro*; and the juxtaposition of *ossa* with *semisepulta*/*sepulcris*. In Ovid's depiction of the fields of Troy, battlefield and arable land occupy the same place and are separated not by space, but by

---

[16] See Makins (in this volume) for further discussion of this poem and the different types of landscape depicted within it.
[17] Parker (1992: 89). Enk (1946) identifies the parallel between these verses and *Georgics* 2.184–7.

time. In fact, Ovid's chronology seems accelerated here; this poem is meant to be understood as a letter from Penelope to Odysseus, not yet returned to Ithaca after the Trojan War. Within less than ten years, then, not only has agriculture taken over land that previously hosted Iliadic battles, it has completely replaced even the city of Troy itself, perhaps due to the fertility of the land from *Phrygio sanguine*. Even the implements of agriculture – the ox and plough – become symbolic both of conquest and of the finality of the victor's reinstitution of agricultural practice.

Outside of poetry, Plutarch's record of events from the *Life of Caius Marius* describes the people of Massilia surrounding their vineyards with the bodies of fallen soldiers. In combination with rainfall and the change of seasons, the fertility provided by the organic matter of the bodies produced years of great harvests after the battle of Aquae Sextiae in 102 BCE (*Mar.* 21.3):

> Μασσαλιήτας μέντοι λέγουσι τοῖς ὀστέοις περιθριγκῶσαι τοὺς ἀμπελῶνας, τὴν δὲ γῆν, τῶν νεκρῶν καταναλωθέντων ἐν αὐτῇ καὶ διὰ χειμῶνος ὄμβρων ἐπιπεσόντων, οὕτως ἐκλιπανθῆναι καὶ γενέσθαι διὰ βάθους περίπλεω τῆς σηπεδόνος ἐνδύσης ὥστε καρπῶν ὑπερβάλλον εἰς ὥρας πλῆθος ἐξενεγκεῖν καὶ μαρτυρῆσαι τῷ Ἀρχιλόχῳ λέγοντι πιαίνεσθαι πρὸς τοῦ τοιούτου τὰς ἀρούρας.

> Nevertheless they say that the Massiliotes bordered their vineyards with bones, and that the earth, after the bodies were consumed into it and after rains fell upon it through the winter, grew so rich and became through its depths so full of decay sinking in that it produced an exceedingly great harvest in the following seasons and testified to Archilochus saying that fields are fattened by this kind of event.

While Plutarch himself cannot be an antecedent to either Lucan or the Augustan poets, the historical events he describes were. Likewise, the adage that fields could be fattened (πιαίνεσθαι. . . τὰς ἀρούρας) by the fallen bodies of the war dead which Plutarch attributes to the seventh-century BCE poet Archilochus speaks to the antiquity of such stories and observations.

In general, these texts portray violent battles and grisly deaths, but also that this is not the eternal state of things. Eventually, war ends and battles are in the past, affecting the present only through memory and the physical changes they enact in the landscape. To this point, then, the return to agriculture and the use of former battlefields as productive farmland is the ultimate sign of recovery. The trope survives to the modern period as well and something similar appears in accounts from the American Civil War. Thomas S. Hopkins, who served in the Sixteenth Regiment of Maine Infantry,[18] narrated the battle of Fredericksburg and its aftermath:

> Between us and the Confederates, a distance of nearly a mile, lay an open, level field, where corn had been planted the preceding summer. The ground, frozen the

---

[18] Small (1886).

night before, and thawed again at midday, was miry and treacherous, and we often sank half-way to our knees....

Some years ago I revisited the battle-field. The bodies of the fallen had been gathered into the soldier's cemetery just back of the city, and near the deadly stone wall where the right of our army was engaged. I walked down the turnpike to where we fought. Nature had obliterated nearly every sign of the conflict, and the miry field across which we charged on that eventful December day was covered with waving corn. The sun shone as clearly, the birds sang as sweetly, and the flowers bloomed as brightly, as if that field had never been ploughed with shot and shell, and fertilized with the blood of brave men.[19]

In this later account of a battlefield during and after its battle, just as among the Augustan authors, agriculture indicates peace and agricultural virtue implies something idyllic.[20] Even the horrors of war enable some later productive influence in their ability to help crops grow. In both Roman and American texts, however, the environmental erasure of signs of war and the cycle of forgetting distance later observers of fields from the true horror of the *battle*field. Lucan's text, being focused on the civil war quite narrowly, does not allow a similar distance. American civil war texts such as Hopkins' narrative cannot be determinative in our understanding of Lucan's influences, but they can inform us about the range of literary responses a culture has to war landscapes.[21]

In Lucan's case, however, writing about civil war poses a whole slew of problems in representing the cycle of war and agricultural recovery in the landscape, including whether a world ruined by civil conflict *can* recover. In Lucan's treatment of these particular landscapes – battlefields and farmlands – we can see how the poet undermines the literary trope of fields enriched by war's remains. While peace and agriculture are closely linked in the Augustan literary world, Lucan's subversion picks up on their implied opposite, that the absence or destruction of agriculture and its landscapes is symptomatic of war.[22] Lucan alludes to his poetic predecessors both in their depictions of battlefield gore existing then enriching the fertility of fields, and in the use of specific words and phrases as part of his own *un*resolving cycle of battle/agriculture landscapes.

3 Destabilization

Lucan disrupts the war-recovery cycle by highlighting the absence of farmers and negating the value of the agricultural landscape by excising it from the narrative. This is

---

[19] Blaisdell (1893: 77 and 81).
[20] Johnston and Papioannou (2013: 138–9).
[21] Cf. the chapters by Brockliss and Makins in this volume.
[22] Compare Aratus, *Phaen.* 129–32: ἀλλ' ὅτε δὴ κἀκεῖνοι ἐτέθνασαν, οἱ δ' ἐγένοντο, | χαλκείη γενεή, προτέρων ὀλοώτεροι ἄνδρες, | οἳ πρῶτοι δὲ βοῶν ἐπάσαντ' ἀροτήρων (But when those also were dead, and the race of bronze, men more ruinous than their predecessors, were born, who first ate the ploughing-oxen ...).

part of his poetic programme from the very beginning, as he surveys the causes and damages of war: *horrida quod dumis multosque inarata per annos | Hesperia est desuntque manus poscentibus arvis* (Hesperia is bristling with thorn bushes and has been unploughed for many years, and hands are missing from the fields that ask for them, *BC* 1.28-9). Already, the landscape of Italy lies in ruin, with unploughed (*inarata*) fields overgrown by wild brambles. This is a landscape that has experienced some calamity with no prospects of recovery. The Italian countryside reads like a post-apocalyptic landscape or a ghost town in the American Old West, and evokes the kinds of questions asked in thought experiments on post-human environments.[23] Lucan seems to represent an alternate history, in which the civil war's destruction is ultimate and where landscape reverts to nature in the absence of people. Although arable farmland demands cultivators (*manus poscentibus arvis*), there are no farmers and hence no recovery. This image occurs at the beginning of the poem and is thus removed from any specific geographical or chronological context. We may perhaps consider it programmatic and allow it to colour our interpretation of other empty fields in the poem, especially because warfare directly impacted the ancient environment and the practice of agriculture. Historically, we know that 'campaigns devastated the countryside, slaughtered farmers and their families, and requisitioned or destroyed crops and buildings'.[24]

Later in Lucan's poem, other empty fields and inactive farmers provide what may as well be the backstory to the programmatic image of abandoned farmland in the proem. That is, they address how the fields could come to be abandoned and what particular aspect of the civil war was the catalyst to the cessation of agriculture. As Caesar marches his troops southward through Italy towards Rome in Book 2, the image of empty fields is relayed *ex negativo* to emphasize Caesar's role as invader (*BC* 2.439–45):

Caesar in arma furens nullas nisi sanguine fuso
gaudet habere vias, quod non terat hoste vacantis
Hesperiae fines vacuosque irrumpat in agros
atque ipsum non perdat iter consertaque bellis
bella gerat. non tam portas intrare patentis
quam fregisse iuvat, nec tam patiente colono
arva premi quam si ferro populetur et igni.

Caesar, raging in arms, rejoices that he holds no roads except by blood shed, that he does not wear down the borders of Hesperia empty of enemy and burst into empty fields and he does not squander the journey itself, and he wages one war after another. He is happy that he does not enter through open gates so much as

---

[23] Weisman (2007: 184); cf. Weiner (in this volume) on this same passage in the context of questionably successful monuments.
[24] Hughes (2014: 152). Consider also the concept of *deserti agri*, deserted lands, an agro-economic topic addressed by Roman authors from the third century CE onward; cf. Hughes (2014: 126), Soricelli (2012) and Grey (2007). Also Cic. *Verr.* 2.3.120–9.

break through them, and that he does not tread on fields with farmer permitting so much as plunder with iron and fire.

Lucan portrays a monstrous Caesar who prefers to set fire to farmland, rather than passing through with a farmer's permission. Behind this characterization is the implication that these very actions lead to the empty fields (the *vacui agri*)[25] and unmanned land of the initial post-cataclysm picture of Italy. The regular concerns of a farmer (drought, flood, disease) are absent; instead, war and those who wage it are the sole danger. The same idea is levelled as a threat by Gnaeus Pompey when he learns of his father's death: *has mihi poenas | terra dabit: linquam vacuos cultoribus agros, | nec, Nilus cui crescat, erit*; ('the land will pay these penalties to me: I will leave fields empty of farmers, nor will there be anyone for whom the Nile rises', *BC* 9.161–3). Gn. Pompey promises to make the land itself pay the penalty, by leaving previously fertile fields unworked, making agriculture untenable, and thus creating a landscape empty of inhabitants. Though this threat is unfulfilled in both history and Lucan's narrative, our poet has already provided an image of the hypothetical results in the post-apocalyptic landscape of Italy at the beginning of Book 1.

The destabilization of the agricultural process emerges again as part of the narrative of the siege of Massilia. In this case, the implements of successful agriculture are repurposed, taken from farmers and used to move lumber obtained through the destruction of the Massilian grove (*BC* 3.450–2):[26]

utque satis caesi nemoris, quaesita per agros
plaustra ferunt, curvoque soli cessantis aratro
agricolae raptis annum flevere iuvencis.

When enough of the grove had been cut, wagons procured from the fields carried it, and farmers, with oxen stolen, wept for the harvest of their soil left fallow by the curved plough.

Wagons (*plaustra*) are seized from the fields (*per agros*), with two direct results: the wood from the grove can be moved and any further agricultural action in these fields is rendered impossible, due to the seizure of the oxen which would otherwise pull the plough. Poetically, the removal of oxen from an agricultural context has precedents, as in Aratus's *Phaenomena*, translated by Cicero into Latin at *De Natura Deorum* 2.159. For

---

[25] NB: Lucan uses *vacuos ... agros* again at 2.602 in a simile in which Pompey, compared to a bull, yields before Caesar's approach. In Lucan's poetic predecessors, the phrase *vacui ... agri* is somewhat rare: cf. Verg. *G.* 2.54 (the benefits of space in arboriculture); Ovid *Met.* 7.653 (birth of the Myrmidons), and 11.35 (death of Orpheus). Potter (1992) suggests that *vacui agri* was also a term used of non-settled spaces on Roman frontiers.

[26] Concerning deforestation and Roman conquest, compare *BC* 9.426–30. On the repurposing of agricultural tools for war, see Verg. *Aen.* 7.506–21. And, by comparison, *Anth. Pal.* 6.236 of Octavian's Actium memorial, in which the rostra of captured ships become home to beehives: ὅπλα γὰρ ἐχθρῶν | καρποὺς εἰρήνης ἀντεδίδαξε τρέφειν (For the enemies' weapons in turn instruct on nourishing the fruits of peace).

Aratus and Cicero, and perhaps for Lucan as well, the re-purposing of oxen away from agriculture signals societal decline from something closer to an idealized style of living to one disrupted by violence.

The siege of Massilia lasted from April through to September of 49 BCE. When Lucan condenses the timeline,[27] this puts his weeping farmers (*agricolae... flevere*) into greater focus. The distant future is not part of this image, but the foreseeable future – the harvest season – has been rewritten by the presence of war to the detriment of crops and cultivators. These lines should be read against Vergil's *agricola incurvo terram molitus aratro* (a farmer, working the land with a curved plough, *G.* 1.494), where Lucan's *curvo... aratro... agricolae* alludes to Vergil's *agricola incurvo... aratro*. Vergil's farmer works the fields of a landscape upon which war has left its mark, but which has returned to peaceful productivity; Lucan's farmers mourn the loss of this future. Moreover, it should be noted that Lucan uses the word *agricola* only twice;[28] the other instance occurs in Book 1 as one of a series of portents, in another moment of intertextuality with *Georgics* 1.493–7: ... *tollentemque caput gelidas Anienis ad undas* | *agricolae fracto Marium fugere sepulchro* (... and farmers fled Marius raising his head near the chilly waters of Anio with his tomb broken, *BC* 1.582–3). Rather than characterizing *agricolae* by their actions or technology, Lucan includes them as the immediate witnesses to the horror of Marius's reemergence from his chilly grave near the Anio. Aside from the *agricolae* themselves, the key to the Vergilian reference is the grave (*sepulchro*), which mirrors the *effossis... sepulcris* (*G.* 1.497) that contain the weapons, helmets and bones at which the Vergilian farmer marvels. For Lucan the horrors of war and their effects on the landscape are not artefacts of the past: the new civil war between Caesar and Pompey causes the same horrors that existed during the time of Marius and Sulla to spontaneously re-emerge. These things are part of the landscape and do not stay buried, and unlike the remnants of a past battlefield that exist alongside the current agricultural landscape for Vergil's farmer, Lucan's *agricolae* near Rome and Massilia lament and flee the battlefield reemerging and taking over their farmlands.

4 Fertility and mutation

Elsewhere, the disruption of agricultural promise following the destruction of a landscape by war is more direct and grotesque. Whereas Vergil's farmer is actively working the fields when he finds evidence of past battles, and Ovid and Horace both acknowledge the power of blood to fertilize the soil into which it soaks, Lucan's image of infected, mutated plants instead evokes concepts of toxicity.[29] This occurs most notably and clearly in the aftermath of the poem's climactic battle at Pharsalus (*BC* 7.844–6, 851–4):

---

[27] Masters (1992: 20–1).
[28] Compare McCutcheon (2013: 264–70) on Vergil's strategic placement of the *pastor*.
[29] On the lasting effect of the Pharsalus war-dead on the landscape, see Gardner (2019: 195) and Makins (2013: 192–3). More broadly on toxicity Buell (1998) and on pollution Bradley (2012), Parker (1983: 160–6); cf. Lennon (2010; 2013), Makins (2016).

>   Latiae pars maxima turbae
> fastidita iacet; quam sol nimbique diesque
> longior Emathiis resolutam miscuit arvis.
> ...
> quae seges infecta surget non decolor herba?
> quo non Romanos violabis vomere manes?
> ante novae venient acies, scelerique secundo
> praestabis nondum siccos hoc sanguine campos.
>
> The largest portion of the Latin crowd lay disdained; and sun and rains and longer days mixed them, dissolved, into Emathian fields ... Which crop will rise not discoloured by infected growth? by which plough will you not violate Roman shades? Before this, new battle lines will come, and you will offer fields not yet dry from this blood for a second crime.

The process of decomposition is more clearly stated here than in Lucan's Augustan predecessors.[30] The majority of the war dead at Pharsalus simply return to the earth – and not just any earth, but specifically tillable earth as indicated by *arva*, a noun that takes its etymology from the verb for ploughing, *arare*. The result of this mixing of bodies, blood, and soil, however, is in no way beneficial. Crops grow, but are infected (*infecta*) and sickly in appearance (*decolor*).[31] *Decolor*, moreover, alludes back to Horace's question at the end of *Ode* 2.1: what sea has Apulian slaughter not discoloured (*quod mare Dauniae | non decoloravere caedes*, 2.1.34–5)?[32] The enrichment of soil indicated by *pinguis* and its cognates in Vergil's *Georgics*, Ovid's *Heroides*, as well as this same Horatian *Ode* is totally absent from Lucan's image, exchanged for mutated crops and fields full of bones (*pluraque ruricolis feriuntur dentibus ossa*, BC 7.859). Lucan's turn of phrase echoes both Vergil's *rastris ... pulsabit ... ossa* (G. 1.496–7) and Ovid's *feriuntur ... ossa* (Her. 1.55–6), but the language here is that of toxicity. Rather than having the remains of the war dead – bones, bodies, armour and weapons – serve as a reminder of the horrors of war even in the midst of an agricultural recovery, Lucan implies that these remains infect the land in which they lie, like a poison.[33] As Martin Dinter puts it, 'the dead bodies succeed in conquering Thessaly: *sed tibi tabentes populi Pharsalica rura | eripiunt camposque tenent victore fugato* (But the rotting hordes rob you [Caesar] of Pharsalian fields; they rout the conquerer and

---

[30] Note also the use of *resolutam* of the decay of human bodies into the soil and compare to *compage soluta* at 1.72, in the programmatic simile about apocalyptic conflagration and the dissolution of the cosmos.

[31] Cf. Vergil's sole use of *decolor* at Aen. 8.326 of the inferior ages that followed the idealized paradise of the Golden Age, complete with *belli rabies*. Compare also Sen. *Oed.* 41–2, *deseruit amnes umor atque herbas color | aretque Dirce* (of miasma in the Theban landscape) and 49–51, *denegat fructum Ceres | adulta, et altis flava cum spicis tremat, | arente culmo sterilis emoritur seges* (of the failed harvest). On related images to these infected crops, Ambühl (2016: 313) notes the poisonous herbs used by the Thessalian witches.

[32] Henderson (1996: 111) notes the connection between Lucan and Horace 2.1 as well as a potential intertext with the lost history of Asinius Pollio.

[33] Cf. the poisonous herbs gathered by the Thessalian witches.

possess the plains, *BC* 7.823–4)'.³⁴ The landscape absorbs the destructive qualities of civil war (*rabies, discordia, impietas, ruina*) and these taint new crops that grow, causing fundamental changes to their appearance and substance.

Though war pollutes the landscape most obviously here, Lucan describes an example of mutation caused by or present in blood in the bull examined by Arruns the haruspex, which portends the coming disaster with grotesquely mutated organs. Blood flows black rather than red (*diffusum rutilo nigrum pro sanguine virus*, 1.615), discoloured, as are the viscera (*terruit ipse color vatem ...*, 1.618). The entrails are discoloured because they are infected by blood (*infecta cruore*, 1.619),³⁵ a prodigious key to understanding the later depiction of the crops that grow at Pharsalus: *seges infecta* (7.851). This early moment of ominously terrifying mutation portends the civil war narrative that will unfold in the poem: the *nefas* embodied in this moment of literary haruspexy also applies to both the universal effects of civil war geographically and between humans and landscape, and any possibility of a post-war recovery.

5 War perpetuates war

In Lucan's text, the recovery cycle in which battlefields become agricultural land again is disrupted in yet another way when the poet exchanges crops, indicative of the temporal distance of war, with signs of war and its violence. In this scenario, war co-opts even the agricultural metaphor itself: war and peace – battles and farming – are not cyclical, but war begets itself in a self-perpetuating process. This perpetuation of war's hazards in the landscape exists in Vergil's text, but Lucan takes it further with these monstrous 'crops' consisting not of bones and armour but new, mutated growth and ongoing civil violence.

Marius's re-emergence from his tomb near the Anio is an early example of this pattern: *farmers* witness this ominous event (*tollentemque caput gelidas Anienis ad undas* | *agricolae fracto Marium fugere sepulchro, BC* 1.582–3). Rather than tending fields – existing as the active agents relative to their crops – the *agricolae* here see something far worse than mutated or discoloured grasses emerging from the earth. Lucan does not make these farmers unusual in any way aside from what they see. We can reasonably infer that they maintain their fields appropriately to the season. Since this portent follows Caesar's crossing of the Rubicon in January of 49 BCE, the farmers are in the winter part of their agricultural year, and so seeing anything at all growing is unseasonable (cf. Verg. *G.* 1.299); to see a spectre of past civil wars sprouting from their fields is an ultimate horror.

Civil war antecedents of the events in the *Bellum Civile* also follow this pattern. A reference to the Theban cycle and the Argonautica also inextricably connects war and growth from the earth (*BC* 4.549–56):

---

³⁴ Dinter (2012: 35).
³⁵ Cf. Sen. *Clem.* 1.11.1: *nempe post mare Actiacum Romano cruore infectum.*

> sic semine Cadmi
> emicuit Dircaea cohors ceciditque suorum
> vulneribus, dirum Thebanis fratribus omen;
> Phasidos et campis insomni dente creati
> terrigenae <im>missa magicis e cantibus ira
> cognato tantos implerunt sanguine sulcos,
> ipsaque inexpertis quod primum fecerat herbis
> expavit Medea nefas.

> So from the seed of Cadmus the Dircaean cohort sprouted up, and it fell by its own wounds, a dire omen for Theban brothers; on the fields of Phasis, the Earthborn, created from a sleepless tooth, in anger sent from magic spells, filled such great furrows with the blood of kin, and Medea herself trembled at the crime which first she made with untested herbs.

Lucan compares the self-killing of Roman soldiers to two separate myths involving autochthonous mythological soldiers: those that grew from the teeth of the dragon killed by Cadmus at Thebes[36] and those that grew from the dragon's teeth sown at Colchis. Both groups of dragon-tooth-soldiers turn on themselves (though the soldiers at Colchis do so through Medea's intervention). In doing so, they provide mythical exempla for civil conflict, a *dirum ... omen* for Oedipus's sons. While earlier versions of this myth such as Aeschylus's represented the agricultural recovery trope of post-war narratives (ἔγωγε μὲν δὴ τήνδε πιανῶ χθόνα, Aesch. *Sept.* 587), Lucan's version breaks the pattern. The *dirum ... omen* for the Theban brothers may as well be a dire omen – like Marius's return – for a Roman father-in-law and son-in-law. The language co-opts that of agriculture, just as the image itself is co-opted. Soldiers grow from seeds (*semina*) as if they are crops,[37] the *dentes* belong not to farming implements like rakes or hoes (cf. 7.859) but are the substance of the 'seeds' themselves, and the soldiers' blood irrigates the furrows of the field (*cognato tantos impleruntsanguine sulcos*).

Thus in Lucan's narrative the regrowth of civil war is perennial in its own battlefields. In a lament to and about the land of Thessaly after the battle of Pharsalus, another civil war battle – this time at Philippi – will perpetuate the cycle of violence: *ante novae venient acies, scelerique secundo | praestabis nondum siccos hoc sanguine campos* (7.853–4). The agricultural metaphor is still valid, given the ongoing attention to the fertilizing power of blood shed on battlefields, but the 'regrowth', this time, is in spirit rather than confined to a single physical space. The seeds of one battle are watered by the blood of its fallen soldiers and grow up again into the next harvest of war dead.

Lucan maintains a more unified geographical approach when describing the subsequent battlefields in North Africa. At the end of Book 4, Curio's battle against Juba results in African dust drenched in Roman blood (*BC* 4.793–5):

---

[36] Cf. Ovid, *Met.* 3.101–26. On Thebes and Rome as comparable in terms of origin stories and civil war narratives, see Braund (2006: 267–9). On Lucan's intertextuality with Ovid in this simile, see Watkins (2012: 92–5).
[37] Cf. *BC* 1.158–9 (*belli | semina*), 3.150 (*diri mala semina belli*), and 6.395 (*semina Martis*).

> Curio, fusas
> ut vidit campis acies et cernere tantas
> permisit clades compressus sanguine pulvis,
>
> Curio, when he saw his battle lines poured out on the fields and the dust, clumped together by blood, permitted him to see such great slaughter ...

The agricultural component is not immediately apparent. Contrary to the historical reality, Lucan does not describe this region as farmland; in fact, because it is portrayed instead as arid desert, Lucan makes a point of emphasizing both the general lack of floral growth and the exceptions to this pattern (the oasis at Siwa, etc.). Any arable land is in the west and is irrigated by means of precipitation rather than a ground-water source (*BC* 9.420–3).[38] In Lucan's Libya, however, blood seems to have greater life-giving power to the region's dusty soil than water, as in the case of Medusa's blood as it drips from her severed head, flown over the desert by Perseus (*BC* 9.696–9):

> illa tamen sterilis tellus fecundaque nulli
> arva bono virus stillantis tabe Medusae
> concipiunt dirosque fero de sanguine rores,
> quos calor adiuvit putrique incoxit harenae.
>
> Still that barren land and the fields producing nothing good take in the poison of dripping Medusa's gore and the horrible dew from her wild blood, which heat supports and cooks in the crumbling sand.

The earth is sterile, but any growth than can occur is not beneficial (*fecunda ... nulli | arva bono*) in fields which are classified by their very name as potential tillable land (cf. *BC* 1.205–7). Because *arvum* derives from the verb for ploughing, Lucan brings the agricultural metaphor directly into the sowing of blood into the dust. Fields that were merely *rura* (9.423) in Lucan's broader geographical excursus on Libya are now conceptually in the same category as Italy's abandoned fields (1.29), Pharsalus's battlefield-turned-cropland (7.728, 846), and fields nourished by silt carried by floods of the Nile (8.477, 8.526, 10.219); only when Medusa's blood 'fertilizes' the fields do they become *fecunda ... arva*. While this turn of phrase does not directly reproduce Vergil's *pinguescere campos* (*G*. 1.492), it certainly stands as a grotesquely but recognizably mutated echo.

6 Agricultural imagery for war

This systematic absorption of agricultural images and language into the context of war landscapes is especially clear when Lucan describes active battlefields and military camps

---

[38] Thomas (1982: 109–10) compares Lucan's exaggeratedly negative portrayal of Libyan agricultural practices to Sallust's less dire account: *ager frugum fertilis, bonus pecori, arbori infecundus* (*Iug*. 17.5).

The Problems with Agricultural Recovery in Lucan

with the term *arvum*.[39] During the siege at Ilerda, Caesar and his troops cut off the Pompeians from potable water during the aftermath of the flood (*BC* 4.308–13):

> si mollius arvum
> prodidit umorem, pinguis manus utraque glaebas
> exprimit ora super; nigro si turbida limo
> colluvies immota iacet, cadit omnis in haustus
> certatim obscaenos miles moriensque recepit
> quas nollet victurus aquas;

> If softer earth produced moisture, both hands squeeze out rich clods over their mouths; if muddy filth lies unmoving in black slime, every soldier at once fell to the obscene drink and, dying, took in waters he would not if destined to live.

Certainly, no crops are being tended in these fields; instead, Lucan emphasizes the misfortune of the survivors of battle and flood by calling those who lie dead on the battlefield *fortunati* (*BC* 4.319). Despite this context, verbal elements of a preferred agricultural recovery shadow the scene as it stands. The material of the ruined landscape is *arvum* and any potential moisture for the soldiers to drink makes the soil *pinguis*. Lucan immediately subverts implications of enrichment, however, in his following verses. This is not a healthy or seasonal abundance of water, but rather an overabundance that brings its own destruction, complete with filth (*colluvies*) and slime (*limo*) that bring death (*moriens*) with obscenity (*haustus... obscaenos*). Both floral and faunal sources of agricultural gain are exhausted by war's effects.

War co-opts agricultural language twice more in *BC* 4. The pasture land in Antony's camps on the island of Curicta off the Illyrian coast is barren (4.410–14):

> non pabula tellus
> pascendis summittit equis, non proserit ullam
> flava Ceres segetem; spoliarat gramine campum
> miles et attonso miseris iam dentibus arvo
> castrorum siccas de caespite vulserat herbas.

> The earth does not produce food for grazing horses, nor does golden Ceres bring forth any crop; the soldier deprived the field of grass and now with the field cut by wretched teeth, he has torn the dry grasses from the earth of the camp.

Here Lucan's allegorical portrayal of war suggests agricultural overreach or mismanagement: the camps exhaust the resources of the land upon which they were built, even to the point that soldiers graze like horses. The next example occurs during Lucan's narration of Curio's arrival in Africa, where fierce warfare blazes up in Libya's

---

[39] While the *TLL* cites *arvum* as applicable to fields or lands generally, as well as to specifically arable land, there is no distinct category of use for *arvum* as battlefield. See Ausfeld (1900–1906).

fields (*non segnior illo* | *Marte fuit, qui tum Libycis exarsit in arvis*, BC 4.581–2). Again, the presence of warfare is located within *arva*, already an odd word for a landscape that Lucan describes as sandy and arid. Here, the river Bagrada is *siccae sulcator harenae* (4.588) rather than any farmer or team of oxen, and the local landscape is poetically defined by two things: the myth of Antaeus and his defeat by Hercules, and the memory of Scipio Africanus's past victory. Lucan shapes myth and history in a way that causes agricultural landscapes to emphasize the horrors of war. In Lucan's recounting of the myth, the region's farmers have died (*periere coloni* | *arvorum Libyae*, 4.605–6), presumably at the hand of Antaeus, a Gigantic monster known for drawing strength from the earth, feasting on lions (4.602), and decorating with human skulls.[40] Lucan's Antaeus draws nourishment from the earth as if he himself were a bizarre monstrous crop (*rapit arida tellus* | *sudorem; calido complentur sanguine venae*, 4.629–30). Even after the mythic digression is concluded, the memory of Scipio's presence in these lands solidifies the *arva* as battlefields (*Romana hos primum tenuit victoria campos*, 4.660). Lucan almost completely elides the historical reality of this landscape as fertile land known for its production of grain and other crops. The ethnographic influences on Lucan's descriptions of Africa may explain this exaggerated desert landscape,[41] but the interjection of battles – between Hercules and Antaeus, as a memory of Roman victory, and in the form of Curio's clash with Juba – transforms and co-opts the context of the oddly non-fertile *arva*.

The most notable re-purposing of arable land (*arvum*) for battlefield in Lucan's poem follows the battle of Pharsalus.[42] The post-battle landscape of Pharsalus provides evidence for the pattern of mutation rather than enrichment as well as the seeding of war with war, two other modes of disrupting the war/agriculture recovery cycle in poetic landscapes, but these verses also demonstrate the same transference of agricultural language to battlefield landscapes. Caesar observes a land swimming with blood (*Caesar, ut Hesperio vidit satis arva natare* | *sanguine*, BC 7.728–9)[43] which cannot be anything but a battlefield. And yet, Lucan again uses the term that specifically evokes agricultural land use. Already in the narrative of Pharsalus's aftermath, we as readers are primed to understand this landscape in light of its other transformative purpose: to interpret soldiers, corpses and weapons in terms of farmers, fertilizer and ploughs. Caesar's perspective again affords us this double-vision in his observation of the battlefield landscape (*BC* 7.786–91, 94–5):

tamen omnia passo,
postquam clara dies Pharsalica damna retexit,

---

[40] Asso (2010: 223) *ad* 4.590 notes that Lucan's *scelerum non ... tantum* | *vidit ... pendere ...* | *postibus Antaei Libye* (2.162–4) is testimony to Lucan's knowledge of Antaeus's father's (= Poseidon's) temple being decorated with skulls. Cf. Pindar *Isthmian* 4.52–4, in which Pindar represents Libya as fertile farmland (τὰν πυροφόρον Λιβύαν).
[41] Leigh (2000: 99n.37); Thomas (1982: 110).
[42] For *Emathia arva* see: 4.255, 7.191, 7.846, 8.266; cf. *Thessalicis ... arvis* at 9.1073.
[43] Cf. *BC* 7.292–4, of Caesar's paraceleusis: *videor fluvios spectare cruoris* | ... | ... *et inmensa populos in caede natantis*. See Leigh (1997: 292–303) for commentary.

> nulla loci facies revocat feralibus arvis
> haerentes oculos. cernit propulsa cruore
> flumina et excelsos cumulis aequantia colles
> corpora ...
> ... iuvat Emathiam non cernere terram
> et lustrare oculis campos sub clade latentes.

> Nevertheless, [Caesar] having endured all these things, afterward when bright day renewed Pharsalian losses, the appearance of the place does not recall his eyes, clinging to funereal fields. He sees rivers flowing with blood and corpses piled up as high as lofty hills ... He is happy that he does not see the Emathian land and that he (instead) sees fields hidden under slaughter.

Arva may be proleptic here: in the aftermath of battle, it looks ahead to the 'recovery' pattern that Latin literature of the Augustan age had established. This new landscape, however, is so fundamentally changed that it wholly disrupts the cycle of recovery. Instead of battlefield returning to farmland, the *arva* continue as battlefield. Caesar here also reminds us of his return to Italy earlier in the poem when he rejoices in destroying the Italian agricultural landscape on his way to Rome (*iuvat, nec tam patiente colono | arva premi quam si ferro populetur et igni*, BC 2.444–5). Lucan does not linger on the effects of Caesar's joyful destruction in *BC* 2, but later in Thessaly the effects of Caesar's war are perpetual and evidenced in mutated, discoloured plants instead of new crops and in a graveyard (*Romani bustum populi*, 7.862) rather than farmland (7.855–9):

> omnia maiorum vertamus busta licebit,
> et stantes tumulos et qui radice vetusta
> effudere suas victis compagibus urnas,
> plus cinerum Haemoniae sulcis telluris aratur
> pluraque ruricolis feriuntur dentibus ossa.

> Although we turn out all the graves of our ancestors, both the mounds still standing and those which poured out their own urns, with joints overcome by an ancient root, more ashes are ploughed into the furrows of the Haemonian earth and more bones are struck by rustic teeth.

This is a place where the immediate effects of war on the landscape will persist into the future, but, as we have come to see with Lucan, the land experiences ongoing damage rather than gaining some enrichment for the soil. In fact, Lucan dramatically laments, if Pharsalus had been alone as a landscape of civil war, its perpetual ruin would have been a monument of *nefas*: no ploughs would have turned the earth (*nec terram quisquam movisset arator*, 7.861), farmers would have fled (*fugerentque coloni | umbrarum campos*, 7.862-3), herds would not have grazed (*nullusque auderet pecori permittere pastor | vellere surgentem de nostris ossibus herbam*, 7.864–5), and the land itself would have been as uninhabitable as any place in the arctic or torrid zones (*velut impatiens hominum vel solis iniqui | limite vel glacie*, 7.866–7).[44] This scenario is counterfactual given the ongoing cataclysm of civil war, and in this limitation it clarifies the vision of the post-battle landscape of Pharsalus as ruined by war, but not totally. Instead the war poisons the landscape in a way that affects its ability to be repurposed for the benefit of human beings.

7 Conclusion

The intertext between Lucan and his Augustan predecessors and the similarities across millennia in descriptions of war's effect on the landscape and the landscape's ability to recover contextualize Lucan's vision of war landscapes as particularly pessimistic. Vergil, Horace, Propertius and Ovid all describe war landscapes that returned to agricultural use. While the memory of blood and its physical effects remain, the battlefield is overwritten by peacetime activity. Likewise, in Pvt. Hopkins' descriptions of the landscape near Fredericksburg, VA the former battlefield was replaced by a near-idyllic landscape, complete with sunshine, birdsong, and fields of corn. Lucan breaks the pattern we see in the Augustan poets; his war and imagined post-war landscapes are exaggerated and symbolic in the extent of their ongoing state of ruin. These landscapes are not familiar to Lucan's predecessors any more than they are for modern readers of Hopkins' narrative.

Instead, Lucan displays something like an anachronistic pseudo-modernism, where the landscapes produced by the new technologies of warfare in the twentieth and twenty-first centuries seem to make Lucan's hyperbole into reality. The scars left behind by the trench warfare of the First World War and the nuclear fallout and chemical poisoning of subsequent wars demonstrate the same interruption of the landscape-recovery process Lucan described. Within the poem, the multifaceted disruption of the landscape's recovery represents war's consequences, yet this is not instructive to subsequent battlefield experiences. There is, however, a certain resonance for current audiences and scholars that is connected to how Lucan's narrative of national ruin is described as an exaggerated, metaphorical apocalypse, and how in wars of the modern period, this seems to become history and reality. War affects the landscape in ways that make recovery impossible or at least delayed, often beyond the lifetime of the generation who witnessed its destruction in the first place. Battlefields become conspicuous, predominant and even at times permanent.

Bibliography

Ambühl, A. 2016. 'Thessaly as an Intertextual Landscape of Civil War in Latin Poetry.' In *Valuing Landscape in Classical Antiquity: Natural Environment and Cultural Imagination*, edited by J. McInerney and I. Sluiter, 297–322. Leiden: Brill.

---

[44] Ambühl (2016: 313) identifies the 'inhabitants mentioned *ex negativo*' as 'the ploughman, the farmers, and the shepherd'. Cf. Papaioannou (2012: 94).

Asso, P. 2010. *A Commentary on Lucan, De bello civili IV*. Berlin: De Gruyter.
Ausfeld, C. 1900-1906. 'Arvus.' *Thesaurus Linguae Latinae* Vol. II 0, 731, 28.
Betensky, A. 1979. 'The Farmer's Battles.' In *Virgil's Ascraean Song: Ramus Essays on the Georgics*, edited by A. J. Boyle, 108–19, Berwick: Aureal Publications.
Blaisdell, A. F. 1893. *Stories of the Civil War*. Boston: Lee and Shepard Publishers.
Bradley, M., ed. 2012. *Rome, Pollution, and Propriety: Dirt, Disease and Hygiene in the Eternal City from Antiquity to Modernity*. Cambridge: Cambridge University Press.
Braund, S. 2006. 'A Tale of Two Cities: Statius, Thebes, and Rome.' *Phoenix* 60 (3): 259–73.
Buell, L. 1998. 'Toxic Discourse.' *Critical Inquiry* 24 (3): 639–65.
Cosgrove, D. E. 1984. *Social Formation and Symbolic Landscape*. Madison: University of Wisconsin Press.
Dinter, M. 2012. *Anatomizing Civil War: Studies in Lucan's Epic Technique*. Ann Arbor: University of Michigan Press.
Enk, P. J. 1946. *Sex. Propertii Elegiarum Liber I (Monobiblos)*. Leiden: Brill.
Floyd, E. D. 1989. 'Homer and the Life-Giving Earth.' *Classical World* 82 (5): 337–49.
Frazel, T. D. 2009. *The Rhetoric of Cicero's 'In Verrem.'* Göttingen: Vandenhoeck & Ruprecht.
Gardner, H. H. 2019. *Pestilence and the Body Politic in Latin Literature*. Oxford: Oxford University Press.
Grey, C. 2007. 'Revisiting the "problem" of *agri deserti* in late Roman Empire.' *Journal of Roman Archaeology* 20: 362–76.
Hardie, P. 2008. 'Lucan's Song of the Earth.' In *Papers on Ancient Literatures: Greece, Rome, and the Near East*, edited by E. Cingano and L. Milano, 305–30. Padova: Sargon.
Henderson, J. 1996. 'Polishing off the Politics: Horace's Ode to Pollio, 2.1.' *Materiali e discussioni per l'analisi dei testi classici* 37: 59–136.
Hughes, J. D. 2013. 'Warfare and Environment in the Ancient World.' In *The Oxford Handbook of Warfare in the Classical World*, edited by B. Campbell and L. A. Tritle, 128–42. New York: Oxford University Press.
Hughes, J. D. 2014. *Environmental Problems of the Greek and Romans: Ecology in the Ancient Mediterranean*, 2nd edn. Baltimore: Johns Hopkins University Press.
Johnson, T. S. 2009. 'Lyric, History and Imagination: Horace as Historiographer (C. 2.1).' *Classical Journal* 104 (4): 311–20.
Johnston, P. A. and S. Papaioannou. 2013. 'Idyllic Landscapes in Antiquity: The Golden Age, Arcadia, and the *Locus Amoenus.*' *Acta Antiqua Academiae Scientiarum Hungaricae* 53: 133–44.
Kitts, M. 2005. *Sanctified Violence in Homeric Society: Oath-Making Rituals in the Iliad*. Cambridge: Cambridge University Press.
Layton, R. and P. J. Ucko. 1999. 'Introduction: Gazing on the Landscape and Encountering the Environment.' In *The Archaeology and Anthropology of Landscape: Shaping Your Landscape*, edited by P. J. Ucko and R. Layton, 1–20. London: Routledge.
Leigh, M. 1997. *Lucan: Spectacle and Engagement*. Oxford: Clarendon Press.
Leigh, M. 2000. 'Lucan and the Libyan Tale.' *Journal of Roman Studies* 90: 95–109.
Leigh, M. 2010. 'Lucan's Caesar and the Sacred Grove: Deforestation and Enlightenment in Antiquity.' In *Lucan*, edited by C. Tesoriero, 201–38. New York: Oxford University Press.
Lennon, J. 2010. 'Pollution and Ritual Impurity in Cicero's *De Domo Sua.*' *Classical Quarterly* 60 (2): 427–45.
Lennon, J. 2013. *Pollution and Religion in Ancient Rome*. Cambridge: Cambridge University Press.
Low, A. 1985. *The Georgic Revolution*. Princeton: Princeton University Press.
Makins, M.W. 2013. 'Monumental Losses: Confronting the Aftermath of Battle in Roman Literature.' PhD diss., University of Pennsylvania.
Makins, M. W. 2016. 'Battlefields of Dread: Lucan's *Bellum Civile* and the Discourse of Toxicity.' Paper presented at the 9th Celtic Conference in Classics, Dublin, 24 June 2016.

Masters, J. 1992. *Poetry and Civil War in Lucan's* Bellum Civile. Cambridge: Cambridge University Press.

McCutcheon, J. 2013. 'Landscapes of War.' *Acta Antiqua Academiae Scientiarium Hungaricae* 53: 261–74.

McIntyre, J. 2008. 'Written Into the Landscape: Latin Epic and the Landmarks of Literary Reception.' PhD diss., University of St Andrews.

Nappa, C. 2005. *Reading After Actium: Vergil's Georgics, Octavian, and Rome*. Ann Arbor: University of Michigan Press.

O'Gorman, E. 1995. 'Shifting Ground: Lucan, Tacitus and the Landscape of Civil War.' *Hermathena* 158: 117–31.

Papaioannou, S. 2012. 'Landscape Architecture on Pastoral Topography in Lucan's *Bellum Civile*.' *Trends in Classics* 4: 73–110.

Parker, H. N. 1992. 'The Fertile Fields of Umbria: Prop. 1.22.10.' *Mnemosyne* 45 (1): 88–92.

Parker, R. 1983. *Miasma: Pollution and Purification in Early Greek Religion*. Oxford: Clarendon Press.

Potter, D. 1992. 'Empty Areas and Roman Frontier Policy.' *American Journal of Philology* 113 (2): 269–74.

Putnam, M. C. J. 1979. *Virgil's Poem of the Earth: Studies in the Georgics*. Princeton: Princeton University Press.

Reitz-Joosse, B. 2016. 'Land at Peace and Sea at War: Landscape and the Memory of Actium in Greek Epigrams and Propertius' *Elegies*.' In *Valuing Landscape in Classical Antiquity: Natural Environment and Cultural Imagination*, edited by J. McInerney and I. Sluiter, 276–96, Leiden: Brill.

Sayre, L. 2017. '"*How*/to Make Fields Fertile": Ecocritical Lessons from the History of Virgil's *Georgics* in Translation.' In *Ecocriticism, Ecology, and the Cultures of Antiquity*, edited by C. Schliephake, 175–95. Lanham, MD: Lexington Books.

Simons, K. 2001. 'Re-making the Georgic Connection: Virgil and Willa Cather's "My Ántonia".' *International Journal of the Classical Tradition* 7 (4): 523–40.

Small, A. R. 1886. *The Sixteenth Maine Regiment in the War of the Rebellion, 1861–1865*. Portland, ME: B. Thurston & Company.

Soricelli, G. 2012. 'Deserti agri.' In *The Encyclopedia of Ancient History*, edited by R. S. Bagnall, K. Brodersen, C. B. Champion, A. Erskine and S. R. Huebner, 2049–51. Chichester: Blackwell Publishing.

Spencer, D. 2010. *Roman Landscape: Culture and Identity*. Cambridge: Cambridge University Press.

Thomas, R. F. 1982. *Lands and Peoples in Roman Poetry: The Ethnographic Tradition*. Cambridge: Cambridge Philological Society.

Thomas, R. F. 2001. 'The *Georgics* of Resistance: From Virgil to Heaney.' *Vergilius* 47: 117–47.

Ustinova, Y. 2009. *Caves and the Ancient Greek Mind: Descending Underground in the Search for Ultimate Truth*. New York: Oxford University Press.

Watkins, S. 2012. 'Lucan "Transforms" Ovid: Intertextual Studies in the *Bellum Civile* and the *Metamorphoses*.' PhD diss., Florida State University, Tallahassee.

Weisman, A. 2007. *The World Without Us*. New York: Picador.

Wilhelm, R. M. 1982. 'The Plough—Chariot: Symbol of Order in the *Georgics*.' *Classical Journal* 77 (3): 213–30.

CHAPTER 5
LANDSCAPES IN SOPHOCLES' *OEDIPUS AT COLONUS* AND THE POETRY OF THE FIRST WORLD WAR
William Brockliss

1 Introduction

Landscapes are a major concern of Sophocles' *Oedipus at Colonus* (hereafter *OC*).[1] And in contrast with the majority of surviving tragedies, Sophocles chose to situate those landscapes in the Attic countryside, and this very likely at a time when Attica was under threat from Peloponnesian forces stationed at Deceleia.[2] The landscapes of the *OC* are, then, fictional analogues of what was at once Sophocles' homeland and probably at the time of composition[3] also a landscape of war. Similarly, for the play's first audience, who witnessed its depictions of Colonus in 401 BCE, the Peloponnesian threat to this and other areas of Attica was a recent memory.

This chapter argues that we can improve our understanding of the play's treatments of landscape by considering British poems from the First World War. This body of poetry has often been the focus of studies of classical reception, as in Elizabeth Vandiver's *Stand in the Trench, Achilles*.[4] But we can also adopt a comparative approach to the two corpora, setting the British poetry of the First World War alongside texts from antiquity, such as the *OC*.[5] This kind of approach is particularly valid if, as in this chapter, we focus on First World War poems that are not obviously indebted to classical models: none of the poems studied below makes explicit allusions to classical sources.

Consideration of poems from the First World War draws our attention both to ways in which the *OC* manipulates landscape and to possible responses to the play on the part of ancient viewers. We see that the Attic countryside of the *OC* is an idealized space, rather than a literal description of places that would have been familiar to fifth-century Athenians. And we recognize that spectators in the immediate aftermath of the Deceleian

---

[1] See Taaffe (1986), Blundell (1993), Von Reden (1998), Markantonatos (2007: 75–9, 91–2). On the importance of space and place in the *OC* cf. Allison (1984), Dunn (1992: 1–9), Edmunds (1996), Wilson (1997: 91–130), Jebb (2004: xxx–xxxix), Rodighiero (2012), Saïd (2012), Van Nortwick (2015: 81–113).
[2] Euripides' *Bacchae*, performed during the Deceleian War (cf. schol. *Frogs* 67), shows a similar interest in idealized, green spaces (esp. 862–76), but its setting is Thebes and the surrounding countryside.
[3] See discussion below.
[4] Vandiver (2010).
[5] Cf. Minchin and Weiner in this volume. Minchin compares dioramas of First World War battlefields with Iliadic landscapes of war; Weiner discusses Lucan's representations of the Roman civil war alongside Yugoslav commemorations of the Second World War.

War would have been able to construe the play's landscapes in two different ways – either as reassuring images of permanence or as visions of a lost idyll.

2 Landscapes of war in Sophocles' *OC*

The *OC* embraces four locales, all of which were important to the Deceleian War: the cities of Athens and Thebes, and potential burial grounds for Oedipus near each of them.[6] The plot centres on the contest between the two cities over the placement of Oedipus's tomb, which will bring benefits to one of them, in the form of a future victory (e.g. *OC* 389–94). But despite Creon's best efforts on behalf of the Thebans, Oedipus goes to his death at Colonus, a rural deme a little way to the north of Athens; accordingly, his grave will benefit the Athenians.[7]

Colonus provides the setting for the onstage action. Unsurprisingly, then, depictions of landscape in the *OC* focus on the deme; but they also embrace other parts of Attica. Lines 14–18 stress the sanctity of the land surrounding the grove of the Eumenides at Colonus, its wealth of flora and fauna, and its relationship to the city of Athens:

> πάτερ ταλαίπωρ' Οἰδίπους, πύργοι μὲν οἳ
> πόλιν στέφουσιν, ὡς ἀπ' ὀμμάτων, πρόσω·
> χῶρος δ' ὅδ' ἱερός, ὡς σάφ' εἰκάσαι, βρύων
> δάφνης, ἐλαίας, ἀμπέλου· πυκνόπτεροι δ'
> εἴσω κατ' αὐτὸν εὐστομοῦσ' ἀηδόνες·

> Oedipus, wretched father, the towers that
> Wreathe the city are in the distance, as my eyes perceive.   15
> But this is a holy place, as one can clearly imagine, burgeoning
> With laurel, olive, and vine; within, throughout the place,
> Close-winged nightingales sing beautifully.[8]

With these phrases Antigone describes the grove and the city for her blind father and encourages theatregoers to imagine this fictional space.[9] Subsequently, the chorus of Athenian elders adds further details to the play's depiction of Colonus. In the Parodos, they situate the grove of the Eumenides in a fertile valley traversed by a pleasant stream: 'the unspoken grassy valley, where the watered mixing-bowl runs with a stream of gentle

---

[6] Additionally, Polynices arrives from Argos to request Oedipus's aid against Thebes (1326–48).
[7] For Oedipus's aid to Athens cf. Burian (1974), Reitzammer (2018).
[8] Greek quotations are taken from Jones and Powell (1902), Avezzù, Cerri and Guidorizzi (2011). All translations are mine.
[9] Cf. Haselswerdt (2019) on how allusions to sound in this and other passages contribute to Oedipus' and the audience's conceptions of the play's landscapes. Antigone's words would also have drawn the audience's attention to the architecture of contemporary Athens – the towers of the Acropolis behind the Theatre of Dionysus: this first description suggests, then, that the Colonus of the play is a space where the real and the imaginary, the mythic and the contemporary converge (Edmunds (1996: 41–2), Travis (1999: 196–7)).

draughts' (155–60). Colonus's waters are also the focus of lines 469–70, where the chorus bids Oedipus to 'first bring liquid offerings from the holy, ever-flowing spring'. But the play's most highly developed depiction of Colonus or indeed of any other landscape is found in the First Stasimon, which describes the attractions of the deme and of Attica more generally. As the chorus informs Oedipus in the first strophic pair and second strophe (Soph. *OC* 668–706):

εὐίππου, ξένε, τᾶσδε χώρας	str. 1
ἵκου τὰ κράτιστα γᾶς ἔπαυλα,	
τὸν ἀργῆτα Κολωνόν,	670
ἔνθ' ἁ λίγεια μινύρεται	
θαμίζουσα μάλιστ' ἀηδὼν	
χλωραῖς ὑπὸ βάσσαις,	
τὸν οἰνωπὸν ἔχουσα κισσὸν	
καὶ τὰν ἄβατον θεοῦ	675
φυλλάδα μυριόκαρπον ἀνήλιον	
ἀνήνεμόν τε πάντων	
χειμώνων· ἵν' ὁ βακχιώτας ἀεὶ	
Διόνυσος ἐμβατεύει	
θείαις ἀμφιπολῶν τιθήναις.	680
θάλλει δ' οὐρανίας ὑπ' ἄχνας	ant. 1
ὁ καλλίβοτρυς κατ' ἦμαρ αἰεὶ	
νάρκισσος, μεγάλαιν θεαῖν	
ἀρχαῖον στεφάνωμ', ὅ τε	
χρυσαυγὴς κρόκος· οὐδ' ἄυπνοι	685
κρῆναι μινύθουσιν	
Κηφισοῦ νομάδες ῥεέθρων,	
ἀλλ' αἰὲν ἐπ' ἤματι	
ὠκυτόκος πεδίων ἐπινίσεται	
ἀκηράτῳ ξὺν ὄμβρῳ	690
στερνούχου χθονός· οὐδὲ Μουσᾶν χοροί	
νιν ἀπεστύγησαν, οὐδ' ἁ	
χρυσάνιος Ἀφροδίτα.	
ἔστιν δ' οἷον ἐγὼ	str. 2
γᾶς Ἀσίας οὐκ ἐπακούω,	695
οὐδ' ἐν τᾷ μεγάλᾳ Δωρίδι νάσῳ	
Πέλοπος πώποτε βλαστὸν	
φύτευμ' ἀχείρωτον αὐτοποιόν,	
ἐγχέων φόβημα δαΐων,	
ὃ τᾷδε θάλλει μέγιστα χώρᾳ,	700
γλαυκᾶς παιδοτρόφου φύλλον ἐλαίας·	

τὸ μέν τις οὐ νεαρὸς οὐδὲ γήρᾳ
συνναίων ἁλιώσει χερὶ πέρσας·
    ὁ γὰρ αἰὲν ὁρῶν κύκλος
λεύσσει νιν Μορίου Διὸς   705
χἀ γλαυκῶπις Ἀθάνα.

You have come to the mightiest stalls	str. 1
Of this land of fine horses, stranger,	
Brilliant Colonus,	670
Where the shrill nightingale	
Trills constantly	
Under cover of green glens;	
These places hold the wine-red ivy	
And the god's untrodden grove,	675
Leafy, ten-thousand-fruited, safe from the sun,	
Unblown of all	
Storm-winds; where the bacchant	
Dionysus ever treads,	
Accompanying his divine nurses.	680
There blooms under heavenly dew,	ant. 1
Through the day and always, the fine-clustered	
Narcissus, the great goddesses'	
Ancient crown, and with it	
The gold-glancing crocus; the sleepless	685
Wandering springs	
Of the Cephisus's eddies do not decrease,	
But ever daily	
Swift-bearing, it passes over the plains,	
With unsullied showers,	690
Over the breasted earth; the Muses' choruses	
Do not spurn it, nor	
Golden-reined Aphrodite.	
I have not heard that there is such a thing	str. 2
In the land of Asia,	695
Nor in the great Doric island	
Of Pelops is there ever such a shoot,	
A plant unconquered, self-generating,	
The dread of enemy spears,	
Which blooms greatest in this land,	700
The leaf of the gray-green olive, nurse of children.	
No youth nor he that dwells with old age	
Will render it vain, ravaging it with his hand;	

> For the eye of Zeus Morius,
> Which sees forever, looks upon it,   705
> And with him gray-eyed Athena.

The chorus both echoes its earlier descriptions of Colonus's waterways and develops themes from Antigone's speech near the opening of the play – sanctity, burgeoning vegetation, nightingales. But it also celebrates the blessings of Attica as a whole, such as Athena's gift of the olive.[10] In these lines, then, descriptions of Colonus and Attica merge into one another.[11]

We need to pay attention to the play's historical background if we are to understand the treatment of space and place in the *OC*. It is likely that, at the time of composition, Colonus, Attica, and other places mentioned in the play were landscapes of war. We know that Sophocles completed the *OC* before his death, which very likely occurred in 406 BCE, with the Deceleian War still in progress.[12] The play was then produced by the playwright's grandson in 401, shortly after the war ended in 404;[13] as such, the threat of conflict in these spaces would have been a recent memory.

We do not know for certain when Sophocles began work on the *OC*, but internal indications point to the time of the Deceleian War, which started in 413 BCE.[14] Sophocles' decision to focus on Colonus and the play's interest in the cult of Poseidon Hippios (1157–9, 1492–5) suggest a date after 411. Colonus carried political associations, which would have been important both for Sophocles and for the play's first audience, and which help us to date the play. In 411, the cult site of Poseidon at Colonus hosted the assembly at which the oligarchic regime of the Four Hundred was inaugurated (Thuc. 8.67.2–3). Sophocles was among the ten *probouloi* appointed after the failure of the Sicilian expedition, who allowed the establishment of the regime (cf. Arist. *Rh.* 1419a26–30). Perhaps, then, the play's celebrations of Colonus and its cult of Poseidon are attempts to cast the Four Hundred, and by extension Sophocles' own actions, in a positive light.[15]

---

[10] The chorus's juxtaposition of the 'unconquered' olive with references to Asia and the Peloponnese (694–9) seems to evoke events earlier in the fifth century, when an olive survived the Persian sack of the Acropolis and the Spartan king Archidamus spared the sacred olives of Attica (Hdt. 8.55; schol. *OC* 698; Edmunds (1996: 57–8), Rodighiero (2012: 62–4)).

[11] Cf. Jebb (2004) *ad OC* 668–719. The Second Stasimon (1044–95) ranges more broadly. The chorus imagines routes that Creon's henchmen might take and places where they might engage with Theseus's troops. Having seized Oedipus's daughters, they will either head south to Eleusis (1044–58) or 'approach the west from the pasture of Oea's snowy rock' (1059–63): they will flee towards either Megara or Boeotia. The other two choral odes likewise show an interest in landscape. The Third Stasimon (1211–48) compares old age with a north-facing headland beaten by waves and storm-winds; the fourth (1556–78) explores the Underworld.

[12] Sophocles' death occurred after the Dionysia in February/March 406, at which the playwright commemorated the death of Euripides, and before the Lenaea of January/February 405, when Aristophanes' *Frogs* showed Dionysus visiting Sophocles in the Underworld: cf. Edmunds (1996: 87). 406 BCE is therefore the more likely date, unless Aristophanes revised *Frogs* very speedily, early in 405, to mark Sophocles' passing.

[13] Soph. test. 41 Radt.

[14] See Edmunds (1996: 87–8). Cf. Kelly (2009: 18): '[t]he events [of the late fifth century BCE] are part of the context in which the *OC* needs to be read …'

[15] Cf. Edmunds (1996: 87–148). The fact that Colonus was Sophocles' own deme (Soph. test. 18 Radt) might have provided an added incentive for him to associate Oedipus's final hours with that location; perhaps the aged poet saw a reflection of himself in the aged hero. For biographical readings of the play cf. Daly (1986), Kelly (2009: 9–14).

But whether or not this is the case, the *OC*'s interest in Colonus would certainly have been topical in the late fifth century, and Sophocles' decision to focus on the deme is probably indicative of the time of composition.

During the latter years of the Deceleian War – that is, the time when the play is likely to have been composed – Colonus and the rest of Attica were under constant threat from a Peloponnesian garrison stationed at Deceleia, near the border of Attica and Boeotia. In the Archidamian War – the first phase of the Peloponnesian War as defined by Thucydides – the Spartans and their allies carried out raids on Attica but did not establish a permanent presence there. Following the Sicilian debacle, however, the Peloponnesians set up a garrison in Attica itself: 'With a focus on the plain and the strongest parts of the Attic countryside, and with the purpose of causing mischief they began to build the wall [at Deceleia], which was visible up to the city of Athens' (ἐπὶ δὲ τῷ πεδίῳ καὶ τῆς χώρας τοῖς κρατίστοις ἐς τὸ κακουργεῖν ᾠκοδομεῖτο τὸ τεῖχος, ἐπιφανὲς μέχρι τῆς τῶν Ἀθηναίων πόλεως, Thuc. 7.19.2).

From this base the Peloponnesians were able to carry out more frequent raids on the Attic countryside. These raids, in combination with the Peloponnesian occupation of Deceleia, would have had both an economic and a psychological impact on the residents of Athens. The Peloponnesians may not have succeeded in devastating the land itself. As Victor Hanson points out, Thucydides' description of the impact of the war at 7.27.5 focuses on slaves and movable goods, rather than on the destruction of cereal crops and fruit trees: 'The Athenians were being harmed greatly. They had been deprived of the whole countryside; more than 20,000 slaves had deserted, and of these the greater part were craftsmen; all their flocks and draught-animals had been lost.'[16] Nonetheless, as Thucydides emphasizes, the Athenians were 'harmed greatly' by the loss of such possessions. Both these losses and the presence of the Peloponnesians and their allies in Attica would have weighed on the minds of those watching from the walls.[17] As Thucydides explains (7.19.2), Deceleia was visible from Athens. *A fortiori*, the territory threatened by the fortress would have been visible to those within the city.[18]

As mentioned above, all the localities embraced by the *OC* played important roles in the Deceleian War. Athens and Thebes were two of the principal antagonists in the war, and the proposed burial grounds for Oedipus – one at Colonus, the other near Thebes – map onto places involved in that conflict: the area around Deceleia itself and the regions of Attica threatened by Peloponnesian forces. The burial place favoured by the Thebans makes partial sense in terms of the plot but is fully explicable if we remember the play's historical context. Creon, who arrives at Colonus to win Oedipus for Thebes, plans to bury him just outside Theban territory – i.e. a little way into Attica. A concern for pollution offers a plausible reason for such exclusion (398–406): Oedipus is not only a parricide but also tainted by an incestuous marriage. Nonetheless, it is surprising that the

---

[16] Hanson (1998: 160–6). Cf. *Hell. Oxy.* 17.4 McKechnie-Kern.
[17] Cf. Thuc. 7.28.4 (the economic impact of the occupation of Deceleia); Thuc. 6.91; Hanson (1998: 154, 172) (the psychological impact).
[18] During the Deceleian War, moreover, the Athenians had to keep watch constantly for fear of attack: see Thuc. 7.28.2. On the importance of viewing to the Deceleian War cf. Hanson (1998: 153, n. 48).

Thebans expect Oedipus to benefit them despite being buried in Athenian territory. The focus on this location makes sense, however, if we map the play's topography onto that of the Deceleian War: Athens faces a Boeotian enemy, Thebes, which hopes to draw power from a location just across the border into Attica, like the Peloponnesians and their Boeotian allies at Deceleia.[19]

The significance of this potential burial site, then, goes beyond its role in the story of Oedipus's final hours. The same can be said of the burial site eventually chosen by Oedipus. Like the border territory of Attica, Colonus was involved in the Deceleian War: along with other parts of Attica, the deme was threatened by Peloponnesian forces based at Deceleia. And indeed, the First Stasimon of the *OC* describes Colonus in such a way that it can stand for all the areas that were threatened by the enemy: the chorus depicts it as not only the site of particular religious cults but also as representative of Attica as a whole.

The play may, moreover, refer to events in the Deceleian War involving the area around Colonus. Diodorus Siculus (13.72.3–73.2) describes a Peloponnesian incursion into Attica from Deceleia, during which the Athenian cavalry engaged with their Boeotian counterparts, and the Spartan king Agis set up camp near Colonus, in the Academy. A scholium to Aristides, alluding to a time when Oedipus appeared to the Athenians and encouraged them to repel Theban invaders, may recall these events.[20] Some scholars link these two pieces of evidence with the play's allusions to future conflict with Thebes in Attica and to Oedipus' promise of aid to Athens against Thebes (409–11, 616–23).[21]

3 Landscapes in the British poetry of the First World War

The places mentioned in the *OC* were, then, landscapes of war in the late fifth century, and viewers may have associated Colonus with a particular episode from the Deceleian War. Additionally, Colonus formed part of the homeland of the play's first audience. To help us understand how spectators might have interpreted the relationships between the play's fictional spaces and the equivalent spaces in the real world, we can turn to descriptions of homelands and battlefields in the British poetry of the First World War. The passages considered below present a range of responses to such landscapes: poets might draw attention to the grim realities of the battlefield, might evoke an

---

[19] The location of Oedipus's tomb outside Theban territory may reflect a tradition that Oedipus was buried at Eteonus, just inside the border of Attica: cf. schol. *OC* 91; Avezzù, Cerri and Guidorizzi (2011: *ad OC* 399). But if so, the problem remains that the Thebans in the play expect such a burial site to offer them protection.
[20] Schol. Aristid. Ὑπὲρ τῶν τεττάρων 172.1 Dindorf.
[21] Cf. Avezzù, Cerri and Guidorizzi (2011: *ad OC* 411). If theatregoers made such connections, they could have interpreted them in accordance with either of the readings outlined below. Spectators who derived a message of endurance in the face of adversity from the play might have been comforted by thoughts that Oedipus had helped Athens in the past. For pessimistic viewers, memories of Oedipus' aid during the Deceleian War would have come as cold comfort, given Athens's catastrophic defeat shortly afterwards.

idealized but unrecoverable homeland, or might re-imagine the battlefield itself in idealistic terms.[22]

Some of the best-known representations of First World War landscapes focus on the horrors of war. In Wilfred Owen's 'The Show', for example, the poet imagines a region so damaged that it no longer has the appearance of an earthly landscape:

> My soul looked down from a vague height, with Death,
> As unremembering how I rose or why,
> And saw a sad land, weak with sweats of dearth,
> Grey, cratered like the moon with hollow woe,
> And fitted with great pocks and scabs of plagues.   5
>
> Across its beard, that horror of harsh wire,
> There moved thin caterpillars, slowly uncoiled.
> It seemed they pushed themselves to be as plugs
> Of ditches, where they writhed and shriveled, killed.
>
> By them had slimy paths been trailed and scraped   10
> Round myriad warts that might be little hills.
>
> From gloom's last dregs these long-strung creatures crept,
> And vanished out of dawn down hidden holes.
> (And smell came up from those foul openings
> As out of mouths, or deep wounds deepening.)   15
>
> On dithering feet upgathered, more and more,
> Brown strings, towards strings of grey, with bristling spines,
> All migrants from green fields, intent on mire.
>
> Those that were grey, of more abundant spawns,
> Ramped on the rest and ate them and were eaten.   20
>
> I saw their bitten backs curve, loop, and straighten.
> I watched those agonies curl, lift, and flatten.
>
> Whereat, in terror what that sight might mean,
> I reeled and shivered earthward like a feather.
>
> And Death fell with me, like a deepening moan.   25
> And He, picking a manner of worm, which half had hid

---

[22] For the plurality of poetic responses to the First World War cf. Vandiver (2010).

Its bruises in the earth, but crawled no further,
Showed me its feet, the feet of many men,
And the fresh-severed head of it, my head.[23]

The landscape that Owen describes is 'cratered like the moon' and with its 'sweats', 'scabs', 'warts', 'mouths', and 'wounds' has come to resemble a violated body rather than a space in the natural world. In turn the warriors themselves, whose real-life equivalents endured such bodily suffering in battle, are more reminiscent of writhing caterpillars than human beings. But when Death shows Owen a worm with his own severed head and 'the feet of many men', the violated bodies of Owen and other soldiers are assimilated to the wounded landscape.

The harmed earth of the battlefield is not, however, the only landscape described in this poem. The poem creates a stark and indeed exaggerated contrast between this scarred land and spaces that the soldiers have left behind: they are 'migrants from green fields, intent on mire' (18). The men appear utterly to have forgotten their homelands; now their focus is only on the mud before them. And while those homelands were green with vegetal fertility – an unmistakably positive notion – the only fertility that Owen associates with the battlefield is of a perverse and disturbing kind, a pullulation of lives extinguished as soon as they are born: the men are like bugs that spawn merely to eat each other.[24]

Owen has in fact amplified the differences between these two landscapes. The men are 'migrants from green fields' rather than 'migrants from plantings of monocultures, overgrazed hillsides, and choked industrial cities', which might be a more accurate description of their homelands. Owen's imagery, moreover, places special emphasis on the horrors of the battlefield: for instance, his allusions to open wounds offer a more vivid impression of a harmed landscape and of its associations with human suffering than a straightforward description of bomb-craters.

Other poems of the First World War likewise offer idealized pictures of lost homelands, but focus on such spaces in preference to the horrors of the battlefield.[25] Ivor Gurney's 'Strange Service' evokes an English landscape of hills, meadows, orchards, and streams:

Little did I dream, England, that you bore me
Under the Cotswold hills beside the water meadows,
To do you dreadful service, here, beyond your borders
And your enfolding seas.

I was a dreamer ever, and bound to your dear service,   5
Meditating deep, I thought on your secret beauty,

---

[23] Stallworthy (1983: 155–6).
[24] Cf. Owen's 'Spring Offensive' (Stallworthy (1983: 192–3)): the battlefield contrasts with a spring landscape that the soldiers have left behind. For the natural world in Owen's poetry see Silkin (1998: 202–19).
[25] Cf. Fussell (2013: 251–92) and Stevenson (2013: 133–40) on the retreat to pastoral idylls by poets of the First World War.

> As through a child's face one may see the clear spirit
> Miraculously shining.
>
> Your hills not only hills, but friends of mine and kindly,
> Your tiny knolls and orchards hidden beside the river   10
> Muddy and strongly-flowing, with shy and tiny streamlets
> Safe in its bosom.
>
> Now these are memories only, and your skies and rushy sky-pools
> Fragile mirrors easily broken by moving airs . . .
> In my deep heart for ever goes on your daily being,   15
> And uses consecrate.
>
> Think on me too, O Mother, who wrest my soul to serve you
> In strange and fearful ways beyond your encircling waters;
> None but you can know my heart, its tears and sacrifice;
> None, but you, repay.[26]   20

While Owen's soldiers forget their homelands, Gurney remembers his in these lines. And yet the spaces that he describes are now no more than memories. Gurney's emotional ties to them remain – they will live 'In my deep heart for ever' – but his visions of these spaces resemble mirror images that could be broken up by the wind, like a landscape reflected in a pond (13–15). These places are consigned to the realm of childhood dreams, while the poet endures an adult reality he could never have dreamt.[27] At the same time, this is an idealized landscape. We hear only of the gentle beauties of spaces undisturbed by human activities or even by less pleasant natural phenomena: there is no mention of towns, farms, or rainstorms. The boy Gurney is alone with his friends the hills and the earth his mother. The landscape of the Cotswolds in southern England, which was familiar to many of Gurney's contemporaries, offers him a 'secret beauty' (6) – perhaps, a beauty that he alone knows and appreciates.

Still other poems ascribe such idyllic qualities to the battlefield itself. Readers in recent decades have tended to prefer the grim aesthetic of poems such as Owen's 'The Show', but as Vandiver emphasizes, poems of the First World War frequently adopt a celebratory tone. Julian Grenfell's 'Into Battle' is a classic example of such.[28] Owen's composition depicts a harmed landscape to which his own body is finally assimilated, but Grenfell describes a union between the fecund earth and the soldier as he marches into battle. I quote the first thirty lines of Grenfell's poem:

---

[26] Kavanagh (2004: 4).
[27] Gurney's 'De Profundis' (Kavanagh (2004: 27)) likewise associates Cotswold landscapes with dreaming, but the narrator expresses the hope that he may return to them after the war.
[28] Vandiver (2010: 184–96) observes that 'Into Battle' was highly rated during the war and in the following decades.

The naked earth is warm with spring,
And with green grass and bursting trees
Leans to the sun's kiss glorying,
And quivers in the loving breeze;
And Life is Colour and Warmth and Light   5
And a striving evermore for these;
And he is dead who will not fight;
And who dies fighting has increase.

The fighting man shall from the sun
Take warmth, and life from the glowing earth;   10
Speed with the light-foot winds to run,
And with the trees a newer birth;
And when his fighting shall be done,
Great rest, and fulness after dearth.

All the bright company of Heaven   15
Hold him in their high comradeship –
The Dog-star and the Sisters Seven,
Orion's belt and sworded hip.

The woodland trees that stand together,
They stand to him each one a friend;   20
They gently speak in the windy weather,
They guide to valley and ridge's end.

The kestrel hovering by day,
And the little owls that call by night,
Bid him be swift and keen as they –   25
As keen of sound, as swift of sight.

The blackbird sings to him 'Brother, brother,
If this be the last song you shall sing,
Sing well, for you will not sing another;
Brother, sing!'[29]   30

There are clear differences between Owen's and Grenfell's depictions of soldiers and of the landscape of war. Owen's battlefield is a gray moonscape, but Grenfell's is an idyll blessed with sunshine, warmth, and greenery. While Owen's landscape seems devoid of natural features, Grenfell imagines trees, fertile earth, gentle breezes and blackbirds. Owen associates death in battle with fertility, but it is the fertility of worms that spawn

---

[29] Mosley (1999: 383–4).

merely to eat each other. Grenfell also suggests that death in battle brings with it a kind of fertility, but here it is the welcome fertility of burgeoning vegetation. The phrase 'Life is Colour and Warmth and Light | And a striving evermore for these' (5–6), which forms the transition from the depiction of the landscape to the description of the soldier, suggest that both he and the earth will forever seek out these blessings. Their 'striving' will, moreover, bear fruit. According to Grenfell's poem death in battle will bring renewed life, and only the avoidance of battle is truly inert: 'he is dead who will not fight; | And who dies fighting has increase' (7–8).[30] Grenfell's soldier will thus find 'fulness after dearth' (14); by contrast Owen's battlefield, littered with corpses, is 'weak with sweats of dearth' (3).

In fact, Grenfell's landscape and its relationship with the human body are reminiscent not so much of Owen's battlefield as Gurney's lost English homeland. Both spaces are blessed with vegetal fertility – Gurney's 'water meadows', 'knolls and orchards'; Grenfell's 'green grass and bursting trees'. Both poets offer an image of nature untroubled by the intrusions of other humans. Surprisingly, given that the soldier is marching into battle, Grenfell's 'fighting man' appears to be alone. Much as Gurney describes the hills as 'friends of mine and kindly' (9), the soldier's only comrades are drawn from the natural environment. Trees 'stand to him each one a friend' (20); a blackbird addresses him as 'brother'.

Yet there is an important difference between the places described in these poems: while the Cotswold landscape depicted by Gurney is distant in time and space from the poet's experiences on foreign battlefields, Grenfell's soldier enjoys the blessings of his landscape *as he enters battle*. In this way, Grenfell's description of the soldier's environment represents a greater departure from the characteristics of real landscapes. Gurney's is an idealized depiction of the Cotswolds, which, though not the inviolate paradise he suggests, did not witness any fighting in the course of the war. Grenfell, however, associates the battlefield itself with such idyllic qualities. He makes no mention of the mud, monotony and damaged earth that were actual features of First World War battlefields and which are given particular emphasis in Owen's 'The Show'.[31] And while the idyll described by Gurney endures only in his memories, Grenfell's soldier will continue to enjoy his pleasant environs after death.

Lastly, in a section of his sonnet sequence '1914' ('V. The Soldier', lines 1–8), Rupert Brooke offers a similarly positive image of a First World War battlefield, but does so by transposing a rural English idyll to that foreign location:

If I should die, think only this of me:
    That there's some corner of a foreign field
That is forever England. There shall be
    In that rich earth a richer dust concealed;

---

[30] For associations of fertile landscapes with battlefields and soldiers cf. Wilson's (1920: 45–6) 'Magpies in Picardy'.
[31] Cf. Borden-Turner's (1917: 99–101) 'The Song of the Mud'.

> A dust whom England bore, shaped, made aware, 5
>   Gave, once, her flowers to love, her ways to roam,
> A body of England's, breathing English air,
>   Washed by the rivers, blest by suns of home.[32]

Like Gurney's and Grenfell's poems, Brooke's lines depict attractive landscapes and suggest that the narrator alone enjoys them. Gurney remembers his childhood amid the 'secret beauty' of the Cotswolds; Grenfell's soldier achieves a personal union with the fertile earth as he faces death. Similarly, Brooke describes an isolated body in an idealized landscape and makes no mention of friends or comrades. England's gift of 'flowers to love' and 'ways to roam' seems to have been imparted only to him. And if he dies, the presence of his body alone will transform a plot of foreign soil into a second England.

In other respects, Brooke's lines resemble Grenfell's 'Into Battle' but not Gurney's 'Strange Service'. The English idyll that Gurney remembers on the battlefields of France is irrevocably lost. But Brooke imagines that his body carries with it the English air it once breathed, the river water that once washed it, the suns that once warmed it. As in Grenfell's poem but unlike Gurney's, the idyll described by Brooke will endure forever. Grenfell's soldier experiences 'A striving evermore' for the joys of spring; Brooke's body renders 'some corner of a foreign field | forever England'. Both poets, moreover, associate battlefields with fertility. Grenfell connects death in battle with the pre-existing fertility of spring landscapes. Brooke imagines his own death as a gift of 'richer dust' to 'a foreign field': his death will render a fertile soil still more fertile.[33]

4 Landscapes of war: a comparison

Our four poems from the First World War, then, offer very different treatments of landscape: Owen's wounded battlefield is quite unlike Grenfell's idyll; Gurney's lost homeland contrasts with Brooke's second England in 'a foreign field'. I would now like to compare these poems with the *OC*, in order to draw attention to the ways in which landscape is being manipulated in Sophocles' play. Some scholars have interpreted passages such as the First Stasimon simply as advertisements of the sorts of advantages that Athenians of the time would have associated with their land.[34] But our comparanda from the poetry of the First World War alert us to the departure of such descriptions from the sorts of natural phenomena that would have been familiar to the play's first audience. While Gurney, Grenfell, and Brooke offer idealized depictions of English homelands or foreign battlefields, the play's depictions of Colonus and Attica are idealized portraits of spaces that were at once Athenian homelands and landscapes of

---

[32] Brooke (1927: 115).
[33] Some other First World War poems offer less positive depictions of the incorporation of soldiers' bodies into the fertile earth: cf. Silkin (1998: 225–6) on Owen's 'A Terre' (Stallworthy (1983: 178–9)).
[34] E.g. Kelly (2009: 93–6).

war.³⁵ Viewers might, then, have noted distinctions between the landscapes of the *OC* and the equivalent spaces in the real world.

A number of the characteristics that the play attributes to Attica resemble those with which our First World War poets associate their idealized landscapes. We find a similar emphasis on abundant flora and fauna, and on gentler aspects of the natural world. For Grenfell the soldier marching into battle enjoys 'green grass and bursting trees' (2). In Sophocles' play, Colonus is 'burgeoning | With laurel, olive, and vine' (16–17), and Poseidon's sanctuary is blessed with 'ten-thousand-fruited' vegetation (676). Both Grenfell and Sophocles associate their idylls with birdsong. Grenfell's soldier hears the cries of kestrels, owls and blackbirds; Antigone hears the song of nightingales in lines 17–18, and the chorus emphasizes this detail in lines 671–3.³⁶

Sophocles' play and the poems of Gurney, Grenfell and Brooke all stress the gentle, nurturing qualities of their landscapes. Such qualities are for instance apparent in descriptions of waterways. Gurney mentions a 'strongly-flowing' river but also 'shy and tiny streamlets' (11); Brooke's body was 'washed by the rivers' of England (8); Sophocles' chorus allude to the 'wandering springs | of the Cephisus's eddies' (686–7), thereby echoing their earlier descriptions of Colonus and its waters. And while Gurney depicts the earth as a mother's body, Sophocles' chorus mentions the 'breasted earth' (691): like Gurney's, this image is suggestive of nurturing, maternal qualities.³⁷

The landscapes described by Sophocles and by our British poets are also untroubled by harsh weather. Grenfell's 'earth is warm with spring' and enjoys 'the sun's kiss' and 'the loving breeze' (1–4); in turn, his soldier 'shall from the sun | Take warmth, and life from the glowing earth; | Speed with the light-foot winds to run' (9–11). Brooke's body 'breath[ed] English air' and was 'blest by suns of home' (7–8). Sophocles' First Stasimon likewise describes a gentle climate. In this Southern European context, though, the chorus is understandably less enthusiastic about sunny weather and happier about the prospect of rain. Poseidon's sanctuary is 'Un-sunned, | Unblown of all | Storm-winds' (676–8); Colonus enjoys 'unsullied showers' (690) that feed the waters of the Cephisus.

We might also compare treatments of time and change in Sophocles' First Stasimon and in Gurney's, Grenfell's, and Brooke's poems. No other humans disturb the quiet of these places. Grenfell's soldier marches alone into battle, conversing only with the birds; the young Gurney enjoys the Cotswolds with only the hills as company; Brooke's body delights in England's blessings and alone enriches a foreign soil. Similarly, in Sophocles' First Stasimon the chorus describes Colonus as if it were frequented only by birds, animals and gods – and this despite the fact that these Athenian elders are themselves demesmen of Colonus (78, 1348). The chorus describes the sanctuary of Poseidon as

---

³⁵ For the idealization of Athens and Attica in the *OC* cf. Whitman (1951: 210), Blundell (1993), Mulroy 2014: lviii).
³⁶ For the significance of these nightingales cf. McDevitt (1972), Suksi (2001).
³⁷ Such suggestions of nurture are echoed both before and after this image: Dionysus is depicted with his nurses (680); the Cephisus is 'swift-bearing' (689); the olive is a 'nurse of children' (701).

'untrodden' (675): as we might expect, casual visitors may not encroach on such holy ground (36–40).[38] But the chorus also depicts Colonus and Attica more generally as if they were devoid of human inhabitants. Lines 668–9 allude to 'the mightiest stalls / Of this land of fine horses'[39]: the focus, then, is placed on these animals rather than on the humans who own and ride them.[40] Beside horses and nightingales, Colonus is the haunt of the gods: the Muses, Aphrodite, Dionysus and his divine nurses (678–80, 691–3). Similarly, Zeus and Athena watch over Attica (704–6), but no human inhabitants are mentioned.[41]

The concept of a landscape free from disturbance or change is complemented in our poems by references to timelessness or eternity, notions apparently incompatible with the perils and swift disasters of war. Grenfell's poem suggests that the soldier's 'striving' will outlast his death. The mini-idyll created by Brooke's corpse will be 'forever England' (3). Sophocles, who was probably composing at a time when the Attic countryside was faced with the threat of Peloponnesian incursions, describes vegetation that endures 'daily and forever' (688). In this respect, Sophocles' description of a land threatened by war parallels Grenfell's depiction of his soldier's environs. While Grenfell's soldier enjoys an eternal springtime, in Sophocles' First Stasimon, Colonus and Attica burgeon unceasingly.[42]

In the *OC*, however, the departure from natural landscapes through allusions to timeless blessings is both more and less striking than in the examples of British poetry that we have studied. Grenfell's 'Into Battle' departs more markedly from landscapes of war than Sophocles' descriptions. His association of the soldier's environment with ever-burgeoning vegetation creates a stark contrast with the grim realities of First World War battlefields. But despite the threat of Peloponnesian incursions, Colonus at the time of

---

[38] See also 150–68: when the Athenian elders describe the grove's gentle streams (155–60), they are in the process of ordering Oedipus to leave the holy ground.

[39] My term 'stalls' translates the word ἔπαυλα (669). Although this lexeme may refer to animal or human habitations (*LSJ* s.v. ἔπαυλος), the former sense is more likely at *OC* 669, given the allusion to horses in the previous line. Cf. Reitzammer (2018: 115), who cites *Od.* 23.358 and Soph. *OT* 1138 (ἔπαυλα/ἐπαύλους = sheepfolds).

[40] Horses are mentioned once more in the second antistrophe of Sophocles' ode (Poseidon 'established the healing bridle for horses', 714), but the only possible allusion to humans is with the word χερσί (716–17). Cf. Jebb (2004) and Avezzù, Cerri and Guidorizzi (2011), who print χερ-/σὶ παραπτομένα πλάτα ('oar fitted [παράπτω] to the hands', or (Kamerbeek (1984: *ad OC* 716–19)) 'oar "<driven> by the hands", "fastened along" a ship'). Some editors, however, emend these lines, removing the reference to hands: χέρσον | παραπτομένα ('flying past [παραπέτομαι] the dry land' – Dawe); χοροῖ̈ιν | παραπετομένα ('flying past, [following] choruses [of Nymphs]' – Lloyd-Jones and Wilson).

[41] The second antistrophe refers to Poseidon, the other major divine benefactor of Attica (707–15). The Second Stasimon, similarly, associates Attica with Zeus, Athena and Poseidon (1070–95), but also includes prayers to Apollo and Artemis. For associations of Colonus with divinities cf. *OC* 38–44 (the Eumenides), 53–6 (Poseidon, Prometheus), 1600–1 (Demeter). On the divine in the *OC* cf. Kamerbeek (1984: 15–20). The poets of the First World War, by contrast, do not usually include the divine in their descriptions of landscapes: cf. Borden-Turner (1917: 97–9), 'Where is Jehovah?'

[42] For other references to eternity in the First Stasimon cf. 682 (the narcissus blooms 'Through the day and always'); 685–6 (the 'sleepless ... springs' of the Cephisus 'do not diminish'); 688 (the river flows over the earth 'ever daily'); 698, 704 (the chorus has never heard the like of the 'unconquered' Attic olive, over which the ever-seeing eye of Zeus keeps watch).

the Deceleian War would not have been reduced to anything like the state of those landscapes.

Nevertheless, as a depiction of a homeland in wartime, Sophocles' description of burgeoning vegetation is more striking than Gurney's and Brooke's representations of England. Unlike the homelands remembered by those poets, the landscape of Attica was and still is characterized by aridity and poor soil.[43] The Cephisus, the major river of Attica, runs through Colonus (cf. *OC* 685–8). Owing to the presence of this waterway, Colonus would have boasted more fertile land than much of the rest of Attica. Yet the descriptions of the deme in our passages depart from the natural phenomena that would have been familiar to audiences from their own experience of the region. Colonus in the play is a paradise of gorgeous vegetation, as opposed to the somewhat more fertile territory that the region in fact possessed.

Likewise, the chorus's descriptions of Colonus's blessings as eternal and unchanging mark a clearer departure from the sorts of landscapes that Athenian audiences would have known than Gurney's or Brooke's poems from the landscapes of England. Gurney and Brooke exaggerate the natural blessings of English landscapes; nonetheless, the gentle, untroubled weather described in their poems is somewhat reminiscent of conditions in southern England, given the region's temperate climate. The climate familiar to Sophocles' audience was, by contrast, more changeable, but the chorus's words do not reflect this. Nor does the play acknowledge the impact of such a climate on the region's flora and waterways. In reality the narcissus is a flower of the brief Greek spring, but in lines 681–4 it blooms ceaselessly at Colonus.[44] Similarly, the river Cephisus seems immune to the arid Greek summer (685–91).

5 Possible reactions to the landscapes of Sophocles' *OC*

Our comparanda from the poetry of the First World War have alerted us to ways in which Sophocles' play manipulates landscapes in its depictions of Attica. Like Grenfell, Sophocles attributes unchanging, peaceful qualities to landscapes threatened by war – though Grenfell's descriptions depart more starkly from the characteristics of First World War battlefields. The *OC* also exaggerates the blessings of a homeland in a time of war, and that to a greater extent than Gurney's or Brooke's poems. Comparison with the poetry of the First World War can also give a sense of the ways in which viewers might have reacted to the representations of landscape in the *OC*. In what follows I explore two possible reactions that were available to ancient theatregoers: they could interpret Sophocles' descriptions of Colonus and Attica as either images of permanence and endurance, or evocations of a lost idyll.

According to some scholars, the play asserts that the boons with which it associates Attica in the fictional past will persist into the present and future. Adrian Kelly, for

---

[43] Cf. Thuc. 1.2.5, Hughes (2014: 62).
[44] For the brief blooming period of the Greek spring cf. Polunin (1980: 30–1).

example, identifies a message of continuity in the play as a whole and in the First Stasimon. He argues that such a message would have resonated with Athenians both at the time of the play's probable composition and at the time of its performance, when they were faced with the hardships of the Deceleian War and its aftermath.[45]

The evidence provided by our comparanda from the poetry of the First World War suggests that the *OC* could have provided just such an optimistic message: viewers might have concluded that the play's descriptions of landscapes reflected the enduring blessings of what were both Attic homelands and, from 413 to 404 BCE, landscapes of war. Grenfell's and Brooke's poems offer support for readings of this kind. Grenfell's 'Into Battle' unites the soldier's body with a burgeoning landscape and suggests that both will continue to enjoy vitality in the future: the dead soldier will 'striv[e] evermore' for the 'green grass and bursting trees'. Brooke's poem likewise suggests the endurance of the natural blessings that he describes. With the phrase 'forever England', Brooke seems to imply that England itself – with its 'rich earth', 'flowers', 'ways to roam', and clean rivers – will somehow endure, if only in the bodies of her sons.

Those watching the *OC* in 401 BCE might have understood in a similar fashion the play's allusions to the narcissus that 'blooms... | Through the day and always', to the Cephisus that 'ever by day | ... passes over the plains', or to the eternal stock of the olive: they might have inferred that these blessings had always been present and would always endure. On this reading, Kelly would be right to assert that the First Stasimon celebrates 'vitality and permanence',[46] continuing from the distant past to the present time of the audience and into an anticipated future.

Such interpretations would not dwell on the idealization of landscapes in our poems. A patriotic – or indeed jingoistic – reader of Brooke's lines might pass over the fact that they mention only the more pleasant features of English landscapes.[47] Similarly, patriotic readers of Grenfell might not consider implications of the departures of his descriptions from the actual characteristics of First World War battlefields. Such readers might focus instead on Grenfell's use of landscape to celebrate soldiers who gladly faced their deaths. Likewise, on the sort of reading proposed by Kelly, audience members would not focus on the hyperbolic aspects of Sophocles' First Stasimon but rather on its apparent optimism.

But there is another way to construe our passages from the *OC*, which takes into account the play's idealization of landscape. This is revealed when we reconsider Grenfell's and Brooke's compositions in the light of Gurney's poem. For Gurney on a

---

[45] Kelly (2009), with 68–9, 93–6 on the First Stasimon. Cf. Whitman (1951: 209–10), Burton (1980: 274–80). For Blundell (1993) and Markantonatos (2007), the *OC* suggests not the permanence of blessings for Athens but their possible renewal in the future.

[46] Kelly (2009: 94).

[47] Other readings are possible. Silkin (1998: 67–9) traces the jingoistic associations of Brooke's lines to propagandistic appropriations of his poetry: they are not, then, intrinsic to his poem. For Vandiver (2010: 325–8), Brooke's depiction of an eternal England might be construed as an 'attempt at (self-)consolation': Brooke is aware that his body might be lost on his death and thus be separated from his beloved homeland. His poem addresses such concerns with the assertion that his relationship with England will endure forever.

French battlefield, the idealized Cotswold landscape portrayed in 'Strange Service' lives only in his memories, and the constituents of this landscape might break up like 'rushy sky-pools ... easily broken by moving airs' (13–14). And while Grenfell and Brooke suggest that the idylls described in their poems will always endure, readers might resist such claims. Bearing in mind the horrors of the First World War battlefield, readers might baulk at the apparent celebrations of wartime landscapes in these poems. They might conclude that the blessings that Grenfell and Brooke attribute to foreign battlefields are no more substantial than the fragile landscapes of Gurney's memories.

Viewers were able to construe the chorus's descriptions of Colonus and Attica in a similar fashion. They had experienced the harsh realities of the Deceleian War, together with Peloponnesian threats to the landscapes of Attica. For such theatregoers the chorus's joyful celebration of unchanging idylls would have clashed with memories of Peloponnesian incursions into Attica and of the sufferings associated with them. For this reason, they might have resisted the play's idealization of Attic landscapes and might have inferred that the evocations of eternity in the First Stasimon were merely assertions on the part of the speakers. They were not obliged to accept the chorus's claim that Attica and Colonus would always possess the sorts of consummate blessings celebrated in the play: perhaps those spaces were untroubled idylls in the time of Oedipus, but the perfect qualities described by the chorus had not endured into the audience's own time. As with the readings of Grenfell's and Brooke's poems outlined above, then, the idealization of landscapes of war might have represented too great a departure from viewers' actual experiences. Just as Gurney's pleasant landscape is consigned to memory, spectators might have concluded that the flawless blessings ascribed to Colonus or Attica in the *OC* were consigned to the past.[48]

Comparison with poems of the First World War, then, has helped us to understand the ways in which Sophocles' play engages with the landscapes of the Deceleian War and also to explore possible reactions to such descriptions on the part of fifth-century Athenians. Like Gurney's depiction of an English homeland or Grenfell's description of a soldier's surroundings, the *OC* offers idealized responses to spaces that in the late fifth century were both Athenian homelands and landscapes of war. Viewers might have reacted to these landscapes as images of endurance in spite of Peloponnesian depredations. But they could also have resisted such suggestions and inferred that the blessings described in Sophocles' play were now no longer theirs.

Bibliography

Allison, R. H. 1984. '"This is the Place": Why is Oidipous at Kolonos?' *Prudentia* 16: 67–91.
Avezzù, G., G. Cerri and G. Guidorizzi, eds. [2008] 2011. *Sofocle: Edipo a Colono*. 2nd edn. Rome: Arnoldo Mondadori.

---

[48] A still more pessimistic reading suggests itself: given the departure of the play's landscapes from the actual characteristics of Colonus and Attica, viewers might have questioned whether these places ever enjoyed the sorts of blessings with which they are associated in the *OC*.

Blundell, M. W. 1993. 'The Ideal of Athens in *Oedipus at Colonus*.' In *Tragedy, Comedy and the Polis: Papers from the Greek Drama Conference, Nottingham, 18–20 July 1990*, edited by A. H. Sommerstein, S. Halliwell, J. Henderson and B. Zimmerman, 287–306. Bari: Levante Editori.
Borden-Turner, M. 1917. 'At the Somme.' *English Review* Aug.: 97–102.
Brooke, R. [1915] 1927. *The Collected Poems of Rupert Brooke*. New York: Dodd, Mead, and Company.
Burian, P. 1974. 'Suppliant and Saviour: Oedipus at Colonus.' *Phoenix* 28: 408–29.
Burton, R. W. B. 1980. *The Chorus in Sophocles' Tragedies*. Oxford: Oxford University Press.
Daly, J. 1986. '*Oedipus Coloneus*: Sophocles' *Threpteria* to Athens.' *Quaderni Urbinati di cultura classica* 22 (1): 75–93; 23 (2): 65–84.
Dawe, R. D., ed. [1979] 1996. *Oedipus Coloneus*. 3rd edn. Stuttgart: Teubner.
Dindorf, W., ed. 1829. *Aristides*, Vol. 3. Leipzig: G. Reimer.
Dunn, F. M. 1992. 'Introduction: Beginning at Colonus.' In *Beginnings in Classical Literature*, edited by F. M. Dunn and T. Cole, 1–12. Yale Classical Studies 29. Cambridge: Cambridge University Press.
Edmunds, L. 1996. *Theatrical Space and Historical Place in Sophocles' Oedipus at Colonus*. Lanham: Rowman & Littlefield.
Fussell, P. [1975] 2013. *The Great War and Modern Memory*. Oxford: Oxford University Press.
Hanson, V. D. [1983] 1998. *Warfare and Agriculture in Classical Greece*. Rev. edn. Berkeley: University of California Press.
Haselswerdt, E. 2019. 'Sound and the Sublime in Sophocles' *Oedipus at Colonus*: The Limits of Representation.' *American Journal of Philology* 140 (4): 613–42.
Hughes, J. D. 2014. *Environmental Problems of the Greeks and Romans*. Baltimore: Johns Hopkins University Press.
Jebb, R. C., ed. [1900] 2004. *Sophocles: Oedipus Coloneus*. 3rd edn, edited by P. E. Easterling. London: Bristol Classical Press.
Jones, H. S. and J. E. Powell, eds. 1902. *Thucydidis Historiae*. Oxford: Oxford University Press.
Kamerbeek, J. C. 1984. *The Plays of Sophocles: Commentaries, Vol. 7: The* Oedipus Coloneus. Leiden: Brill.
Kavanagh, P. J., ed. [1982] 2004. *Ivor Gurney: Collected Poems*. Rev. edn. Manchester: Carcanet.
Kelly, A. 2009. *Sophocles: Oedipus at Colonus*. London: Duckworth.
Lloyd-Jones, H. and N. G. Wilson, eds. 1990. *Sophoclis Fabulae*. Oxford: Oxford University Press.
Markantonatos, A. 2007. *Oedipus at Colonus: Sophocles, Athens, and the World*. Berlin: De Gruyter.
McDevitt, A. S. 1972. 'The Nightingale and the Olive: Remarks on the First Stasimon of *Oedipus Coloneus*.' In *Antidosis: Festschrift für Walther Kraus zum 70. Geburtstag*, edited by R. Hanslik, A. Lesky and H. Schwabl, 227–37. Vienna: Böhlau.
McKechnie, P. R. and S. J. Kern, eds. 1988. *Hellenica Oxyrhynchia*. Warminster: Aris & Phillips.
Mosley, N. [1976] 1999. *Julian Grenfell: His Life and the Times of His Death, 1888–1915*. 2nd edn. London: Persephone Books.
Mulroy, D. 2014. *Oedipus at Colonus*. Madison: University of Wisconsin Press.
Polunin, O. 1980. *Flowers of Greece and the Balkans: A Field Guide*. Oxford: Oxford University Press.
Radt, S., ed. 1977. *Tragicorum Graecorum Fragmenta*, Vol. 4: *Sophocles*. Göttingen: Vandenhoeck & Ruprecht.
Reitzammer, L. 2018. 'Sightseeing at Colonus: Oedipus, Ismene, and Antigone as Theôroi in Sophocles' *Oedipus at Colonus*.' *Classical Antiquity* 37 (1): 108–50.
Rodighiero, A. 2012. 'The Sense of Place: *Oedipus at Colonus*, "Political" Geography and the Defense of a Way of Life.' In *Crisis on Stage: Tragedy and Comedy in Late Fifth-Century Athens*, edited by A. Markantonatos and B. Zimmermann, 55–80. Berlin: De Gruyter.
Saïd, S. 2012. 'Athens and Athenian Space in *Oedipus at Colonus*.' In *Crisis on Stage: Tragedy and Comedy in Late Fifth-Century Athens*, edited by A. Markantonatos and B. Zimmermann, 81–100. Berlin: De Gruyter.

Silkin, J. [1972] 1998. *Out of Battle: The Poetry of the Great War*. 2nd edn. Houndmills: Macmillan.
Stallworthy, J. E., ed. 1983. *Wilfred Owen: The Complete Poems and Fragments, Vol. 1: The Poems*. New York: Norton.
Suksi, A. 2001. 'The Poet at Colonus: Nightingales in Sophocles.' *Mnemosyne* 54: 646–58.
Stevenson, R. 2013. *Literature and the Great War, 1914–1918*. Oxford: Oxford University Press.
Taaffe, L. K. 1986. 'Knowing his Place: Sophocles' *Oedipus at Colonus* 668–719.' In *Within the Dramatic Spectrum*, edited by K. Hartigan, 213–19. Lanham: University Press of America.
Travis, R. 1999. *Allegory and the Tragic Chorus in Sophocles' Oedipus at Colonus*. Lanham: Rowman & Littlefield.
Vandiver, E. 2010. *Stand in the Trench, Achilles: Classical Receptions in British Poetry of the Great War*. Oxford: Oxford University Press.
Van Nortwick, T. 2015. *Late Sophocles: The Hero's Evolution in Electra, Philoctetes and Oedipus at Colonus*. Ann Arbor: University of Michigan Press.
Von Reden, S. 1998. 'The Well-Ordered Polis: Topographies of Civic Space.' In *Kosmos: Essays in Order, Conflict and Community in Classical Athens*, edited by P. Cartledge, P. Millett and S. von Reden, 170–90. Cambridge: Cambridge University Press.
Whitman, C. H. 1951. 'Apocalypse: Oedipus at Colonus.' In *Sophocles: A Study in Heroic Humanism*, 190–218. Cambridge, MA: Harvard University Press.
Wilson, J. 1997. *The Hero and the City: An Interpretation of Sophocles' Oedipus at Colonus*. Ann Arbor: University of Michigan Press.
Wilson, T. P. C. 1920. *Waste Paper Philosophy, to which has been added Magpies in Picardy and Other Poems*. New York: George H. Doran.

CHAPTER 6
DISSENTING VOICES IN PROPERTIUS'S POST-WAR LANDSCAPES[1]

Marian W. Makins

1 Introduction

When waging war, human beings can alter the world around them in tangible, visible and long-lasting ways.[2] Many people can call to mind images of environmental devastation from battlegrounds like Vietnam, where the use of the herbicide 'Agent Orange' by the United States military caused incalculable harm both in the ecological sphere and to the long-term health of the population; or like the Western Front in northern France, where large tracts of land – once denuded of vegetation, now heavily forested – remain off-limits to all but the brave *démineurs* sent in by the government to locate and destroy 'dud' explosives left over from the First World War.[3] But when we approach the aftermath of war through the concept of landscape, we see that the natural environment – including environmental features like trees, fields, rivers and nonhuman animals – makes up only part of a complex picture; that landscape also encompasses human beings' experiences in and responses to the natural world. Just as ecology is a science of relationships, so too is landscape comprised of the dynamic relationships between human and nonhuman elements in the environment.[4] War can alter these relationships in long-lasting ways as well.

People may perceive a site or region as bearing the imprint of war long after all physical traces of combat have disappeared. In such cases, human effort may be required to prevent the place from losing its association with the conflict that, for some, transformed it into a different landscape altogether. Sometimes remembrancers intervene physically in the site itself, erecting monuments or leading interpretive tours to show the continuing relevance of past events. At other times, the enduring resonance of post-war

---

[1] This chapter is not the paper I presented at the 2017 Celtic Conference in Classics in Montréal, but both the chapter and I benefited greatly from the discussions we had there, and I remain grateful to everyone who participated. I would also like to thank those who heard and commented on earlier versions of this research presented at the 2014 annual meeting of the Classical Association of the Atlantic States in Washington, DC; the 2015 annual conference of the Classical Association (UK) at the University of Bristol; and the 2018 annual meeting of the Classical Association of the Middle West and South – Southern Section in Winston-Salem, NC, as part of a panel on 'Wounds and Wounded Bodies in Propertius' organized by T. H. M. Gellar-Goad.
[2] For an introduction to the environmental consequences of war in antiquity, see Hughes (2013). On the modern side, see Webster (1998), who emphasizes the impact of such transformations on communities.
[3] Webster (1998) offers compelling accounts of time spent in both places among people working to mitigate the long-lasting effects of past conflicts.
[4] Cf. Evernden (1978: 19–20).

landscapes takes shape primarily in the realm of artistic representation, where symbolism, not realism, holds sway. This chapter deals with just such a case: an ancient Roman poet who represents post-war landscapes in a fantastical way to highlight the real, if often intangible, effects of conflict on marginalized groups.

In what follows, I offer a reading of selected poems from the *Elegies* of Sextus Propertius, focusing on a number of passages in which the poet imagines civil war battle sites as uncanny spaces still dominated by the remains of the unburied dead. In each case, Propertius uses the rhetorical device of ecocentric personification to imply that elements of the natural environment have deliberately prevented the remains from disappearing. That is, he envisions nature contradicting its own laws to draw attention to losses suffered by the defeated.[5] I first discuss the representations of Umbria, the poet's native region, and neighbouring Etruria in *Elegies* 1.21–2 and 4.1. Propertius's imagery suggests that these closely connected areas have been transformed by the blood of those killed in the Perusine War of 41–40 BCE, such that the land now actively exposes evidence of Octavian's brutality and yields a particular type of poet to publicly mourn the losses suffered by his own and other families.[6] I then look at the apostrophe to Veii in poem 4.10, where Propertius conjures the unquiet grave of the once-great Etruscan city to put more recent events in perspective. I turn lastly to Propertius's representations of the Actian sea, primarily in poem 2.15, but also in 2.16 and 3.11. By continually tossing about the bones of Romans killed in the battle of Actium in 31 BCE, the 'battlefield' itself challenges the right of the victor to control it, visually and symbolically, with his own memorials. In a sense, then, these literary landscapes speak for the dead, and for survivors living under a regime that does not honour their losses.

This use of the word 'speak' requires clarification. Propertius does not attribute direct speech to the post-war landscapes he evokes. Rather, he shapes them with language and imagery such that they communicate certain sentiments which go beyond or even appear to contradict those offered by the poet-as-narrator. I am indebted in my approach to ecocritic Michael J. McDowell's 1996 article 'The Bakhtinian Road to Ecological Insight', in which he applies Mikhail Bakhtin's concept of dialogics to literary representations of landscapes. The plurality of voices that characterizes the dialogic form can arise from a proliferation of speakers with a text, including the author, narrators and individual characters. But distinct 'voices' do not emerge solely from literal speakers. In landscape writing, McDowell argues, the language used to describe landscape elements

---

[5] In ecocritical parlance, an ecocentric (as opposed to anthropocentric) perspective de-emphasizes human needs and claims on the natural world, recognizing that no one member of the biosphere is more important than another (Marland (2013: 850), Moore (2008: 5–6)). On the literary device of ecocentric personification in ancient literature (though without reference to Propertius), see Moore (2008: 44–55). I am not necessarily claiming an ecocentric agenda for Propertius, but rather observing that his poetry sometimes re-centres on the perspective of (an aspect of) the natural world, giving voice to the (imagined) feelings and demands of the non-human environment – even if, as one might well argue, he does so primarily to draw attention to perceived problems in human society.
[6] Gabba (1971) offers a concise overview of the conflict, its causes (including, crucially, Octavian's confiscation of land in the area for redistribution to veteran soldiers following the battle of Philippi in 42 BCE) and effects, with reference to the ancient sources. See also Dowling (2006: 48ff.).

may indicate something about how the author views the relationships between those elements or between them and human beings.[7] Moreover, by using certain kinds of language to describe (parts of) the landscape, an author can create 'speech zones' that permit literary landscapes to voice marginalized socio-ideological positions that dissent from their narrator's 'authoritative monologic voice'.[8] In a similar way, I argue, Propertius displaces onto personified war landscapes perspectives that might be risky to state outright, because they call into question the dominant narrative of the *pax Augusta* ('peace of Augustus').[9]

2 Perusia and around[10]

The ending of Propertius's first book of elegies – often called the *Monobiblos* – has garnered a great deal of scholarly attention, in part because of how sharply it diverges from the book's earlier material in both content and theme. Poems 1.1–19, all apparently set in Rome in the (poet's) present day, concern his love affair with Cynthia and, to a lesser extent, the loves of some of his friends.[11] The last three poems, however – to quote G. O. Hutchinson – 'break out of this sphere in opposite directions'.[12] The subject matter of 1.20 is mythological, and will not be discussed here. Poems 1.21–2 return to the realm of the personal, but take up new themes – family, origins, death, 'war and its effects on people and landscape'[13] – and, for the first time, connect the author and his poetic project to historical events that would have been not just familiar to his audience, but also politically sensitive at the time of publication in around 28 BCE.[14] Poems 1.21–2 are also the shortest in the book, at ten lines each; and both are geographically eccentric, in that they effect an imaginative translocation from Rome to Etruria (1.21) and Umbria (1.22). While some earlier critics dismissed these final poems as juvenilia or simply ignored them, more recent scholars have accepted the poet's challenge to reinterpret the foregoing work in their light.[15] My own reading in this section will focus specifically on the representation of war dead and landscape in these poems, concluding with a brief look at Umbria's dramatic reappearance in poem 4.1.

---

[7] McDowell (1996: 372).
[8] McDowell (1996: 374).
[9] See Cornwell (2017: ch. 5) for a thorough recent exploration of this concept. As is surely evident by now, I follow Gurval (1995), Heyworth (2007c), Stahl (1985), Welch (2005) and others who interpret Propertius's attitude toward Augustus and his achievements in the *Elegies* as ambivalent at best.
[10] This section contains some material condensed and reworked from my doctoral dissertation (Makins (2013: 171–89)).
[11] As the first word of the first poem, *Cynthia* may, in fact, have been the title under which the book initially circulated (Stahl (1985: 27)).
[12] Hutchinson (1984: 103).
[13] Putnam (1976: 93).
[14] Cairns (2006: 25) with discussion of the evidence for Propertius's early life.
[15] Important discussions of 1.21–2 in relation to the *Monobiblos* as a whole include Breed (2009), Clarke (2012), Davis (1971), Hutchinson (1984), Nethercut (1971), Nicholson (1999), and Stahl (1985).

Poems 1.21-2 work closely together, revealing a portrait of a landscape that unfolds bit by bit for the audience as they move through the couplets. The speaker in 1.21 is not Propertius *propria persona*, but a soldier named Gallus who has been involved in the fighting around Perusia (though the reader cannot deduce this right away). I will quote the poem in two sections to better appreciate the process by which Propertius helps the reader construct an image of the landscape in their mind's eye. The poem begins (1.21.1-4):

> Tu, qui consortem properas euadere casum,
>   miles ab Etruscis saucius aggeribus,
> quid nostro gemitu turgentia lumina torques?
>   pars ego sum uestrae proxima militiae.[16]

> You, who are hurrying to get away from our common disaster, wounded soldier from the Etruscan siege-works, why do you twist your popping eyes at my groaning?[17] I am a part of your army, the nearest part.[18]

The opening line strongly resembles a certain type of Latin funerary inscription in which the deceased reminds a passerby that death is the common fate of all humankind.[19] Indeed, I follow Heyworth and others who believe that the speaker of the poem is actually dead, a hovering spirit able to produce only a kind of disembodied groan (3; *nostro gemitu*).[20] Rather than the kind of generic appeal issued by a roadside epitaph, however, this recently deceased soldier is trying to communicate directly with a specific person, a comrade-in-arms who has been wounded and is attempting to flee the siege-works around an Etruscan city (2; *Etruscis ... aggeribus*). 'Common disaster' (1; *consortem ... casum*), then, refers to both death in general and the specific engagement in which both men were involved. The speaker appeals to the two men's relationship in line 4 in hopes of convincing the wounded soldier to stop and listen. At the same time, the appeal clues the audience in to the fact that speaker and addressee were fighting on the same side, and most likely the losing one.

At this point, the speaker reveals what he wants from the wounded soldier. He couches his request in a conditional prayer for the traveler's safety, which is a conventional element of the epitaph (1.21.5-10):[21]

---

[16] The text of Propertius has been taken from Heyworth (2007a). The text of 1.21 is particularly problematic, with almost every line subject to some debate. In general, I accept the explanations offered by Heyworth (2007b), which are well reasoned with textual parallels, except where noted. Fortunately, the details that establish the representation of landscape per se in the poem are not all that controversial.

[17] 'Why ... groaning': Heyworth (2007b).

[18] An attempt to preserve the ambiguity of *proxima*, which can mean 'nearest' in either a literal or a figurative sense, just as in English a friend can be 'close' (if they are right next to you) or '*close*' (if you trust them with your secrets).

[19] Du Quesnay (1992: 55); cf. Heyworth (2007b). See Reitz-Joosse (2016) for parallels with Hellenistic epigram elsewhere in the *Elegies*.

[20] So, Heyworth (2007b: 96) and Parker (1991: 328, n. 1), but *contra* Cairns (2006: 49), Du Quesnay (1992: 58) and others who understand the speaker as alive, but very near death.

[21] Davis (1971: 209-10), Du Quesnay (1992: 61-3).

> sic te seruato possint gaudere parentes: 5
> me soror Acca tuis sentiat e lacrimis
> Gallum per medios ereptum Caesaris enses
> effugere ignotas non potuisse manus;
> et, quaecumque super dispersa inuenerit ossa
> montibus Etruscis, haec sciat esse mea. 10

So may your parents be able to rejoice in your preservation: let my sister Acca feel from your tears that I, Gallus, after being snatched away through the midst of Caesar's swords, was not able to escape from unknown hands; and, whatever bones she might find scattered about on the Etruscan hills, let her know that these are mine.

The speaker prays that his wounded comrade might make it home alive, thus bringing joy to his parents, on condition that his sister Acca learn from the other man's tears what has become of her brother: that he, Gallus – for we now learn his name[22] – was 'snatched away through the midst of Caesar's swords' only to meet his death at 'unknown hands'. The reference to *Caesaris enses* all but confirms that the men were fleeing the siege of Perusia – as opposed to some other (formerly) Etruscan city, besieged at some other time – and that they were fighting in the army of Lucius Antonius. The precise meaning of *ignotas manus* is unclear; brigands, possibly, or Caesarian soldiers operating behind the lines.[23] It may be that Gallus himself does not know who killed him.[24] In any case, he does not dwell on the circumstances of his death, instead thinking ahead to a time when his sister Acca might find his unburied remains and recognize them as his.[25] She could then give him the funerary rites that would allow his spirit to find peace in the afterlife.

As to when and where she might be expected to make this discovery, however, Gallus is remarkably vague. Just about the only temporal inference the audience can make is that a fair amount of time will have elapsed, since he speaks of bones rather than a body.

---

[22] For a range of perspectives on the identity of Gallus and his possible relationship to the elegiac poet mentioned elsewhere in the *Monobiblos*, see Cairns (2006: 49–50), Du Quesnay (1992: 76–7) and Nicholson (1999: *passim*); Heyworth (2007b: 99) doubts the reliability of the text here, proposing that '*Gallum* has resulted from assimilation to the recurrent name . . . replac[ing] another name'.

[23] Brigands: Cairns (2006: 48–9), Du Quesnay (1992: 70–1, 82), Traill (1994: 93–5); Caesarians: Parker (1991: 330). Stahl (1985: 112) says only 'unknown assassins'. Massa-Pairault (2014: 151–2) makes the intriguing observation that the *ensis* is an instrument not only of war, but also of revenge, as in the proscriptions; these 'unknown hands' might represent stragglers from Octavian's army, emboldened by the knowledge that every fugitive was comparable to a man proscribed.

[24] Or perhaps this detail could be viewed as an authorial intrusion, since – as Heyworth (2007b: 100) points out – the family of the deceased can hardly know who killed him if they have never even found his body.

[25] This section of the poem contains some of the most hotly disputed readings, including the word Heyworth prints as *Acca* (2017a) following an emendation originally proposed by Scaliger (the transmitted text has *acta*). The name Acca may seem strange to modern readers, but the parallels adduced by Heyworth (2017b: 98–9) – including the close companion Camilla addresses as *Acca soror* at Verg. *Aen.* 11.823 – persuade me that such need not have been the case in antiquity.

And it is equally difficult to define the area where Acca should search. Gallus gives no indication of exactly where he fell relative to Perusia or how much ground he covered before being struck down. Nor does he actually *ask* the wounded comrade to tell Acca where he died, saying only that she will find bones 'scattered about on the Etruscan hills' (9–10; *dispersa ... ossa | montibus Etruscis*) – scant help to her, since Etruria is a hilly region and *dispersa ... ossa* must refer to the bones of many men, not just Gallus's own.[26]

It is possible to find reasons for Gallus's indeterminacy within the narrative context. Perhaps he takes it as a given that the other man will pass on information about the whereabouts of his body; perhaps he is simply not thinking clearly following the trauma of his death. In any event, his vagueness suggests to the reader an area of slaughter much larger than the patch of ground occupied by one dead soldier. What is more, the poem offers no guarantee that Gallus's comrade will be able to deliver his message, or that his sister will ever find his bones. Indeed, his imprecise instructions, coupled with the fact that he expects her to be gathering bones and not flesh, suggest that even Gallus has his doubts. And so we infer that his bones may still be lying exposed, along with countless others, more than a decade later. With the final lines of the poem, then, atop whatever associations the region previously held for his audience, Propertius has layered a new vision of the *montes Etrusci*, covered with the bones of those who died fighting Octavian in the Perusine War.

Poem 1.22 picks up on themes introduced in 1.21 – family relationships, identity and recognition, death in battle and the problem of unburied remains – and develops the new reading of the Etrurian landscape suggested by that poem's final couplet. Again, I will break the text into sections to better evaluate the layering of information and imagery as it unfolds. The first couplet appears to orient the reader more firmly than the previous poem did (1.22.1–2):

> Qualis et unde genus, qui sint mihi, Tulle, Penates,
> quaeris pro nostra semper amicitia.

> What sort of man I am and from what family, Tullus – what household gods are mine – you are always asking for the sake of our friendship.

The addressee, Tullus, should be familiar to readers of the *Monobiblos*, having been named already as the addressee of poem 1.1 and in several other places besides.[27] If Tullus is being addressed again here, then we can deduce that the speaker is Propertius (or at least his authorial persona). The set-up also marks poem 1.22 as a *sphragis*, or 'seal-poem', with which a poet 'signs' and authenticates their work. Such a poem typically

---

[26] Luisi (1984: 192).
[27] Most scholars identify Tullus as a nephew of L. Volcacius L. f. Tullus, *consul ordinarius* of 33 BCE. On this identification and its implications for the interpretation of Prop. 1.22, see esp. Cairns (2006: ch. 2), Heyworth (2007b: 101–2), Stahl (1985: 79–98). Cf. Heyworth (2007c: 95–7), who suggests that 'Tullus is intended to be read not as a real patron ... but as a poetic imitation of one'.

appears at the end of a book and supplies such details as the author chooses to include about their life.

Whatever comfort the audience might derive from recognizing the addressee – and thus the speaker – of 1.22 and from classifying it as a *sphragis*, however, the poem itself soon takes away again. It turns out this is not a typical *sphragis* at all. Most surprisingly, the author never names himself. In fact, the first word of the poem forecasts this omission: in place of the more usual interrogative *quis* ('who?'), here we have *qualis* ('what sort of man?'), suggesting that Propertius considers his actual name to be of secondary importance.[28]

So, it seems, we are to hear Propertius's answers to a friend's incessant questions about his family background. But the poem never really answers the questions it poses; at least not directly, and not in the way we might expect. Propertius waits until the final couplet to answer the question of his origins. In the intervening lines he simply hands Tullus – and the reader – pieces of the puzzle (1.22.3–5):

si Perusina tibi patriae sunt nota sepulcra,
    Italiae duris funera temporibus,
cum Romana suos egit Discordia[29] ciues, ...   5

If the fatherland's Perusine tombs are known to you, Italy's funerals during hard times, when Roman Discord attacked her own citizens, ...

The first puzzle piece is the mention of 'Perusine tombs' (3; *Perusina ... sepulcra*). This phrase does three things: it pins a definite location on the map, suggesting that Propertius comes from somewhere near Perusia;[30] it invites the audience to consider this poem alongside the previous one, which alluded to Perusia under siege; and it announces the continuation of that poem's martial and sepulchral themes. The area around Perusia might have any number of associations, particularly for someone whose family hails from there, but Propertius indicates that he will focus on the events and effects of the Perusine War.[31]

Even as the second couplet zeroes in on Perusia, however, it simultaneously suggests a much wider frame of reference. With the possessive *patriae*, Propertius makes Perusia's tombs the concern of all Romans; that is, he makes the region a metonym for every region of Italy affected by the civil wars.[32] This expanded focus is reinforced in the pentameter line, where the ambiguous modifier *Italiae* leaves open the question of whether the poet intends to characterize the Perusine *funera* as belonging to the whole

---

[28] Nicholson (1998: 155).
[29] *Discordia* is not capitalized in Heyworth (2007a).
[30] The Propertii were one of the most powerful families in nearby Asisium (modern Assisi). See discussion in Cairns (2006: 1–34).
[31] It is possible, though by no means certain, that the Volcacii Tulli came from Perusia, or at least from Etruria; see Heyworth (2007b: 101–2), with further bibliography.
[32] Putnam (1976: 100), Stahl (1985: 110).

of Italy ('Italy's funerals during hard times'), or simply fix the siege within the larger context of the civil wars ('the funerals during Italy's hard times').[33] The distinction is not trivial, because it relates to the larger question of whether Italy and Etruria are distinct as well – whether Rome is 'the *communis patria* of Italy' or just 'another city like Perusia' that 'happens to be omnipotent'.[34] Propertius thus imparts a fuzzy quality to the landscape of war, blurring its borders and suggesting that its relevance far exceeds its geographical area. In choosing to speak of the 'hard times' primarily in terms of tombs (*sepulcra*) and funerals/deaths (*funera*), rather than battles and the deeds of men therein, he also directs attention to the aftermath of the conflict rather than the conflict itself.

At this point, Propertius breaks off his train of thought to deliver an apparently incidental digression that in fact provides valuable information about Propertius's family and about 'what sort of man' he is (1.22.6–8):

> (sed mihi praecipue, puluis Etrusca, dolor:
> tu proiecta mei perpessa es membra propinqui,
>   tu nullo miseri contegis ossa solo):

(But to me especially, Etruscan dust, [you are] a source of pain: you have allowed the limbs of my kinsman to be thrown away, you cover the wretched man's bones with no soil):

It seems Propertius's references to the casualties suffered by Umbrian and Etrurian families during the civil wars have called to mind a kinsman whose body was never buried following his death in (one can only assume) the Perusine War. This tells us that Propertius's family was directly involved in that conflict, and likely not on the winning side. Many communities in Umbria and Etruria harbored resentment toward Octavian after he confiscated some of their land to distribute to his veteran troops following the battle of Philippi in 42 BCE.[35] This lingering sense of injustice led some families to make common cause with Lucius Antonius, brother of the triumvir, hailing him as their champion whether he liked it or not.[36] If the Propertii were among these families, it seems reasonable to infer that they had lost land in the confiscations, an inference later confirmed in Book 4.[37] The reference to bones (*ossa*) here also strongly suggests that this kinsman is to be identified with Gallus from the previous poem.[38] We now know, then, that Gallus' wish has not been granted; his sister has *not* been able to recover his remains.

---

[33] Nethercut (1971: 471): 'In the last elegy [of the *Monobiblos*], Propertius joins himself ... with the fate of a people, a country. Even if his response was determined at the start by a personal tragedy ..., Propertius, in I, 22, makes room for the misfortunes of others – the suffering of all Italy.'
[34] Putnam (1976: 100–1).
[35] Gabba (1971: 140).
[36] Gabba (1971: 148–9).
[37] Prop. 4.1B.127–8, discussed below. Heyworth (2007b: 101–2) raises the attractive, though highly speculative, possibility that Octavian had rewarded the Volcacii Tulli for their support with a grant of confiscated land in this region, imparting to Propertius's repeated addresses of Tullus 'a consistently sarcastic edge'.
[38] Such is the scholarly consensus; but cf. *contra* Du Quesnay (1992: 75–6).

This realization in turn cements the impression given in 1.21 that – at least in the poetic world constructed in the *Elegies* – the hills of Etruria have never resumed their peacetime character and can still be identified as a landscape of war.[39] Wanderers in these hills must be prepared at any moment to come upon the remains of soldiers killed fighting Octavian a decade ago.

This image of the landscape is improbable on several levels. First, the greatest number of casualties would presumably have been concentrated around the besieged city of Perusia, not spread out across the entire region. Second, even if Octavian made no arrangements for the disposal of the dead in Antonius's army, it seems likely that others – their own officers, comrades, or relatives – would have done so.[40] Third, things deposited on top of the earth tend not to remain there for such a long period, even absent human intervention. Natural factors such as wind, rain, subsidence, plant growth and the scavenging of animals might all contribute to the dispersal, dissolution and ultimate disappearance of human remains beneath a layer of earth.[41] For so many sets of bones to be still visible over a decade later, these natural processes must have been suspended in the post-war landscape. *Puluis* points in the same direction, implying that the burning of Perusia by Octavian's troops degraded the soil of the surrounding countryside until nothing but dust and ash remained.[42]

And yet, if enduring the Perusine War has in any sense weakened the landscape, it must have imparted certain powers to it as well, for Propertius blames the ground itself for preventing any soil from covering Gallus's bones.[43] He personifies the *puluis Etrusca* through a series of linguistic moves including direct address; the repetition of *tu*, which also conveys the speaker's extreme anguish; and the attribution of grammatical subjectivity (*puluis* being the subject of *perpessa es* and *contegis*). As Jacqueline Clarke has shown, the personification of the dust is also strongly gendered. Propertius departs from both the standard usage of the period and his own usage in earlier poems to adopt feminine modifiers for *puluis*, with the result that the Etruscan dust is linked to Cynthia – the only woman addressed directly in the *Monobiblos* except for a brief aside to some witches in poem 1.1 – and her callous treatment of Propertius, in which other landscapes have sometimes been implicated.[44] Feminizing *puluis* may also activate a secondary meaning of *proicere*, which can be used of exposing or casting out an infant. Thus to the

---

[39] Zientek (in this volume) reaches a similar conclusion regarding Lucan's depiction of post-war landscapes in the *Bellum Civile*. Cf. the related topos of battle sites covered with whitening bones in e.g. Verg. *Aen.* 12.36, Hor. *Sat.* 1.8.14–16, Ov. *Fast.* 3.707–8, Tac. *Ann.* 1.61, Stat. *Silv.* 2.7.65 and Amm. Marc. 31.7.16.
[40] On the treatment of the dead in Roman military units, see Hope (2018), with further bibliography.
[41] This is the process that has apparently taken place when Vergil (*G.* 1.493–7) imagines a Thessalian farmer marvelling at civil war-era bones and rusted weapons unearthed in his field; see discussion in Makins (2013: 160–71) and Zientek (in this volume), with further bibliography.
[42] On the burning of Perusia, see e.g. Cass. Dio 48.14.5; with Dowling (2006: 51).
[43] According to Roman religious law, 'the essential requirement was that a corpse should be covered with earth': Hope (2018: 39), citing Cic. *Leg.* 2.22.57.
[44] Clarke (2012: 371–2). The funerary context of these lines specifically recalls those poems (see e.g. 1.19.1–4) in which Propertius worries about how Cynthia might or might not care for his remains in the event of his death.

persona of the cruel mistress might be added that of a mother 'who has become so estranged and alienated from her Italian offspring that she lets them be abandoned, neglecting to cover and protect them'.[45]

The final couplet – in which Propertius at last answers one of Tullus's questions in an apparently straightforward manner – maintains the focus on landscape, but again disorients the reader by forcing them to redraw their mental map of the region around Perusia (1.22.9–10):

> proxima suppositos contingens Vmbria campos
>   me genuit terris fertilis uberibus.   10

The nearest part of Umbria, bordering on [*or*: polluting] the fields spread out below, bore me, [a place] rich in fertile lands.[46]

Up to this point Propertius has used the adjective *Etruscus* to modify (and thus identify) aspects of the Perusine War landscape: the siege-works around the city (1.21.2; *Etruscis... aggeribus*), a temporary, man-made landscape feature that helped locate Gallus's death in both time and place; the barren, bone-strewn hills (1.21.10; *montibus Etruscis*) where Acca should search for her brother's remains; and of course the unfeeling dust (1.22.6; *puluis Etrusca*) that denies Gallus its protection. At no point has Propertius suggested that the siege's influence on the landscape extended outward from Perusia in only one direction, or for a limited area; quite the opposite, as he has intimated that this funereal landscape could easily incorporate the rest of Italy (1.22.3–5). In the final couplet of 1.22, however, he makes a sharp cut across the imagined terrain, effectively dividing it into two landscapes: Etruria (which includes Perusia) and Umbria (in which lies Propertius's hometown of Asisium).

One could make the case that Perusia and Asisium belong in the same region, whatever we choose to call it. Both were originally settled by the Umbri; both were brought under Etruscan control by the fifth century BCE, with Perusia named as one of the twelve cities in the Etruscan League; and both fell to the Romans in the Third Samnite War (298–290 BCE). Both were impacted by Octavian's land confiscations and veteran-resettlement scheme.[47] And they lie only about 25 kilometres apart (Fig. 6.1). But dividing the territory in this way allows Propertius to present two distinct but complementary visions of war's long-term impact on landscape. We have already seen Propertius emphasize the emptiness and sterility of Etruria in 1.21–2. In contrast, he now characterizes Umbria, the land of his birth, as 'rich in fertile lands' (10; *terris fertilis uberibus*). Under other circumstances, this might sound like an almost trite way of hymning the agricultural productivity of his native region. But the words carry more

---

[45] Clarke (2012: 374).
[46] My translation of this couplet is informed by Hendry (1997: 602–3).
[47] Gabba (1971: 140): 'If one takes a close look at the literary and epigraphic evidence, one is forced to conclude that at least forty Italic cities, especially in Campania, Samnium, Umbria, Picenum, Etruria, and in northern Italy, were involved in the confiscations and the allotments of property.'

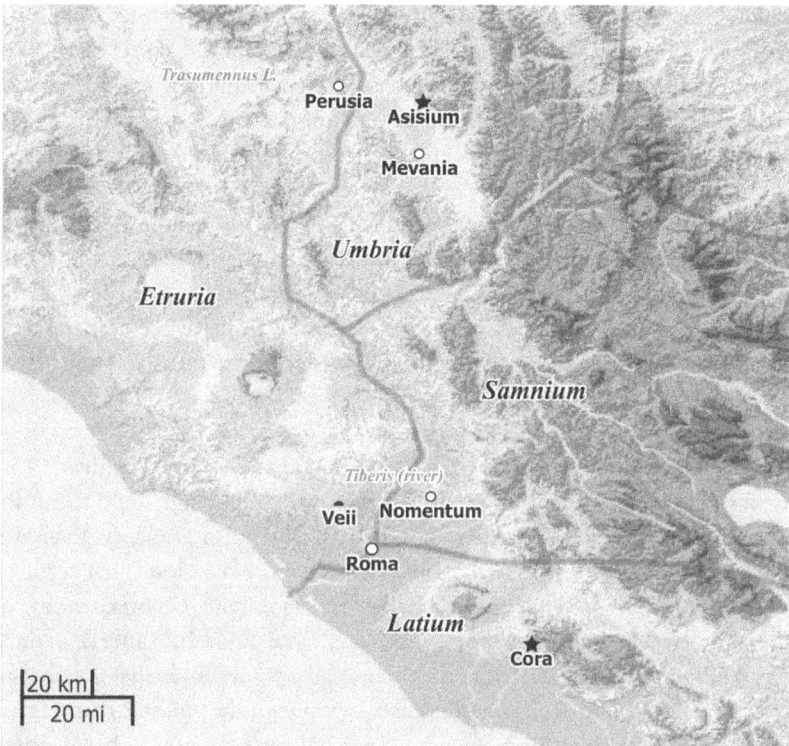

Figure 6.1 Map showing parts of ancient Etruria, Umbria and Latium. Created by Marian W. Makins with Antiquity À-la-carte (Ancient World Mapping Center). http://awmc.unc.edu/awmc/applications/alacarte/ [Accessed: 8 June 2020]. Licensed under the Creative Commons Attribution 4.0 International Licence (CC BY 4.0).

sombre shades of meaning. For the last eighteen lines, Propertius has been putting images of unburied bodies before the reader's eye; the sudden shift of emphasis to the agricultural fertility of the area can hardly fail to trigger a second interpretation: Umbria is fertile because of its proximity to the area where so many soldiers fell in battle and were never buried.[48] In other words, Propertius is activating a trope familiar from the work of other Augustan writers according to which human blood increases the agricultural fertility of a region.[49] Whereas Vergil (*G.* 1.491–2) famously applied this trope to a composite battlefield comprising both Philippi and Pharsalus, collapsing two civil war landscapes into one, Propertius seems to do the opposite in 1.22. It is as if Umbria has somehow absorbed and fattened upon the blood spilled in neighbouring Etruria, where the soldiers' bones remain frozen in place. Both have been affected by the war, but in different ways.

---

[48] Parker (1992), with Hendry (1997).
[49] E.g. Hor. *Carm.* 2.1.29–31: *quis non Latino sanguine pinguior | campus sepulcris inpia proelia | testatur?* ('What field made richer through Latin blood does not with its graves bear witness to impious battles?'). See discussion in Zientek (in this volume).

Wordplay further develops the already-gruesome picture. *Contingo*, often used to refer to 'touching' in a straightforwardly spatial or geographical sense, can also denote pollution or defilement through touch, such that here Umbria is contaminated by its contact with Etruria.[50] Furthermore, a pun on Umbria/*umbra* suggests that the poet's homeland has become a 'Land of Shades', in the sense of either 'a Hades on earth'[51] or a place where large numbers of the departed[52] are conspicuous in their absence. Even *suppositos* might carry the secondary meaning 'annexed' or 'made subject', alluding to Octavian's reconquest of the area.[53] These puns highlight the idea that the Umbrian landscape has been transformed through contact with Etruria and thus by the Perusine War. Whereas barren Etruria illustrates war's capacity to devastate or detract from a natural landscape, Umbria shows that the opposite effect is also possible – if in a decidedly ironic way.

What might it mean, then, for Propertius to have been 'borne' (10; *genuit*) by a place like Umbria, both polluted and enriched by the remains of Roman war dead? This verb also carries two relevant interpretations. On the one hand, *genuit* could mean that the fruitful region 'produced' or 'yielded' him, like an olive or a grape. In that case, one might wonder whether this human 'crop' bears traces of the blood that fertilized the soil.[54] On the other hand, *genuit* could be taken as personifying Umbria, making her the mother who 'gave birth to' the poet; just so, Clarke finds in Umbria a nurturing counterpart to the unfeeling Etruscan dust.[55] Instead, I would argue that the final couplet of 1.22 urges us to reconsider our earlier interpretation of the *puluis Etrusca*. Propertius does speak to her like she is uncaring and cruel, but her behaviour – her insistence on leaving Roman soldiers' bones exposed – has more in common with the poet's own project than he openly acknowledges. These uncovered bones function as *monumenta*, preserving a memory of the losses suffered by the region in terms of both human lives[56] and, metonymically, other sorts of costs as well. Were the bones to be covered up, as Propertius claims to want, his audience might more easily forget about this troubling

---

[50] Hendry (1997: 603), noting that Propertius's only other use of *contingere* in this 'pejorative and tactile sense' is in poem 1.1, frequently linked to 1.22 in both structure and theme.
[51] Hendry (1997: 603).
[52] In death alone, or perhaps also through emigration, like Propertius?
[53] *LSJ* s.v. *suppono* II.A–B. It is worth noting that Octavian in fact extended clemency to Lucius Antonius, his followers and the citizens (but not the leaders) of Perusia. Appian (*B Civ.* 5.5.46–7) says that Octavian was inclined to punish Lucius's veterans, but was prevented by the emotional pleas of his own troops – all the while suggesting that Octavian stage-managed this scene to make himself look both strong and merciful in the eyes of his supporters (Dowling (2006: 49)). In any case, Propertius implies that Octavian's treatment of the region was cruel and repressive; he may have known the story about Octavian's original desire to punish his adversaries or he may simply be exaggerating or embroidering, it is impossible to say which.
[54] Lucan makes this effect explicit with his reference at *BC* 7.851 to 'tainted crops' (*seges infecta*) and 'discolored grass' (*decolor herba*) growing on Roman civil war battlefields in Thessaly; see Zientek (in this volume).
[55] Clarke (2012: 376–8). Cf. DeBrohun (2003: 91 with n. 11).
[56] Poem 1.21 can be read as the words of a man dictating his own epitaph (Davis (1971: 210)); poem 1.22 confirms that Gallus' remains have not been found, meaning that the family would not have been able to provide him with an actual inscribed monument. Thus Propertius's double epilogue (1.21–2), which conjures the image of Gallus's uncovered (and seemingly uncoverable) bones and allows him to speak from beyond the grave, creates a kind of memorial artefact in words.

chapter in Rome's recent history: the confiscations, the siege and sack of Perusia, the executions of Perusine leaders subsequently ordered by Octavian as he sought to balance the virtues of *clementia* ('clemency') and *seueritas* ('strictness').[57]

Yet the *puluis* is a fictional construct, a fantasy. Despite lasting damage to the city of Perusia itself, the entire region did not become a barren boneyard. It is the *poet* who simultaneously raises the possibility of closure with his apostrophe (1.22.6–8), then shuts it down by investing the dust with the power to resist natural processes. He makes the dust complicit in a submerged challenge to the Augustan narrative, a challenge authored by both Propertius *and* the landscape that bore him. Rather than regarding these two female personifications as truly opposed to one another, then, I would emphasize what they have in common. Both landscapes, Etruria and Umbria, have been affected by the same conflict in perceptible and enduring ways. Both take on grammatical subjectivity, and with it a degree of agency, in Propertius's poetry. And both act to ensure that the memory of the conflict, the memory of the losses suffered by the people of the region, will live on: one by neglecting to care for (and thus conceal) the remains of a man like Gallus; the other, by producing a poet who will tell his story and emphasize the costs of the war that killed him.

A little over a decade later, Propertius revived and developed his portrayal of the Umbrian landscape in *Elegies* 4.1, the programmatic introduction to a book deeply invested in exploring topography and landscape.[58] Poem 4.1 comprises two distinct sections: in the first, Propertius lays out an ambitious plan to chart the development of Rome from its earliest beginnings; in the second, he is answered by a sceptical astrologer named Horos, whose name bespeaks his dual roles as Apollonian prophet and policer of (generic) boundaries.[59] At 4.1A.63–4, Propertius mentions his homeland by name for the first time since the end of Book 1, asking Bacchus to offer him ivy leaves:

ut nostris tumefacta superbiat Vmbria libris,
    Vmbria Romani patria Callimachi.

So that Umbria might swell with pride on account of my books – Umbria, fatherland of the Roman Callimachus!

Two lines later, however, Propertius asks Rome to favour his undertaking and tells her: 'this work rises for you' (67; *tibi surgit opus*). So where – with which *patria* – does Propertius's loyalty lie? Horos zeroes in on this ambiguity in his own quelling response, when he starts to recount the poet's life story (4.1B.121–8):

'Vmbria te notis antiqua Penatibus edit
    (mentior? an patriae tangitur ora tuae?)

---

[57] Dowling (2006: 51–2).
[58] On these aspects of Prop. 4.1 see esp. Welch (2005: ch. 1), with DeBrohun (2003: esp. 9–22, 102–13). *Elegies* 4 was published shortly after 16 BCE (Welch (2005: 1)).
[59] DeBrohun (2003: 20–1).

> qua nebulosa cauo rorat Meuania campo
>   et lacus aestiuis intepet Vmber aquis;
> ossaque legisti non illa aetate legenda   125
>   patris, et in tenuis cogeris ipse Lares:
> nam tua cum multi uersarent rura iuuenci,
>   abstulit excultas pertica tristis opes.'

'Ancient Umbria brings you forth [*or*: publishes/declares you] for a well-known family (do I speak falsely? or is the border of your fatherland touched upon?) where misty Mevania drips dew on the hollow plain and the Umbrian lake grows warm with the waters of summer. You have gathered your father's bones not at the age when they should be gathered, and you yourself are forced into an inferior abode: for while many bulls used to turn up your fields, the harsh surveying-rod has taken away the carefully cultivated wealth.'

The language and imagery in this passage recall 1.21–2 at several important points, including the references to Propertius's household gods in lines 121 and 126 (cf. 1.22.1); the touching/abutment of Umbria's border in line 122 (cf. 1.22.9); the gathering of bones in line 125 (cf. 1.21.9–10, 1.22.8); and the productivity of the Umbrian farmland in lines 127–8 (cf. 1.22.9–10).[60] *Patriae* in line 122 also recalls 1.22.3, though Horos clearly means Umbria alone – literally, the homeland of Propertius's deceased father – and not Italy as a whole. The personification of Umbria as the poet's begetter links the two passages as well. Whereas earlier Propertius said that Umbria 'yielded' or 'gave birth to' him (1.22.10; *genuit*), here Horos uses a form of *edere*, which can be used of literary publication and verbal utterance as well as biological reproduction.[61] Moreover, *edit* in line 121 is a present tense verb, implying that Umbria's authoring (authorization?) of Propertius is an ongoing process that did not end when he emigrated to Rome. In some sense, his native land is continuing to speak through him, even when he would seem to be pledging his primary allegiance to Rome.[62]

Propertius alludes to the Perusine War here as well, in subtle and less subtle ways. Jeri DeBrohun has persuasively argued that Horos's references to unusual Umbrian landscape features – Mevania's mistiness and the sun-warmed waters of the *lacus Vmber* – in lines 123–4 build on the Umbria/*umbra* pun and become 'reminders [to the reader] that Propertius' birthplace is a land intimately associated with mourning and death'.[63] (In fact, if S. J. Heyworth is correct in identifying the *lacus Vmber* with Lake Trasimene, Propertius is alluding to yet another landscape of war, one famous for the drowning of many Roman soldiers.[64]) A far less subtle hint arrives in lines 127–8 with the mention of the 'harsh

---

[60] Cf. DeBrohun (2003: 91–2).
[61] *LSJ* s.v. *edo* II.B–C.
[62] On Propertius and his two *patriae* in this poem, see DeBrohun (2003: 102–11), Welch (2005: 23–5, 154–5).
[63] DeBrohun (2003: 108–10), with Hendry (1997: 602–3).
[64] Heyworth (2007b: 430). On landscape in Livy's account of the battle of Lake Trasimene, see Fabrizi and Feldherr (in this volume).

surveying-rod' (*pertica tristis*) used in confiscating the land – and thus the wealth – belonging to Propertius's family. When studying this passage alongside *Elegies* 1.21-2, one might infer that the confiscation of his family's land actually strengthened the bond between poet and *Penates* instead of weakening it. Certainly his Umbrian background remains at the heart of his identity as a poet, and specifically an elegiac poet. Propertius first shows how much his identity is bound up in this multifaceted post-war landscape by spotlighting Gallus's fate and that of the region in his *sphragis*. Moreover, his focus on the sufferings of the local people, combined with the fact that he singles out Rome as the source of the discord that brought such grief to the rest of Italy, suggests a desire to advertise his loyalty to both his family and the region.[65] In 4.1B, then, Horos may be trying to show that Propertius's origins make him unfit to tackle the ambitious themes set out in 4.1A, but he inadvertently demonstrates that the exact opposite is true. The sorrows of his family in Umbria, so closely tied to the Perusine War and the injustices that precipitated it, make Propertius the ideal person to write about the rise of Rome, because Roman Italy is in fact a patchwork of landscapes of war, some very recent, others very old – as a passage in poem 4.10 makes clear.

3 Veii

In poem 4.10, Propertius recounts the three occasions on which Roman military commanders have dedicated *spolia opima* in the temple of Jupiter Feretrius in Rome.[66] The first was Romulus; next came Aulus Cornelius Cossus, who earned the right to dedicate *spolia opima* by killing Lar Tolumnius, the king of the Etruscan city of Veii, in 437 BCE. Propertius interrupts his account of Cossus's conquest to address Veii in an emotional apostrophe that recalls some of the imagery and themes we have seen associated with Etruria and Umbria elsewhere in the *Elegies*. Most significantly, he personifies the Veian landscape while highlighting the violence and sorrow involved in the Roman (re)conquest of Italy.

Before addressing Veii directly, Propertius sets the stage with two couplets that vividly illustrate how profoundly the political landscape of Italy has changed since the days of Cossus (4.10.23–6):

> Cossus at insequitur[67] Veientis caede Tolumni,
>   uincere cum Veios posse laboris erat.

---

[65] As Nethercut (1971: 466) points out, Propertius here makes the identification that Vergil carefully avoids at *Ecl.* 1.71–2.

[66] *Spolia opima* (lit. 'splendid spoils') were spoils taken when a Roman commander defeated an enemy commander in single combat (Welch (2005: 133)). Important recent discussions of *Elegies* 4.10 include Garani (2007), Ingleheart (2007), and Welch (2005: ch. 6); cf. Harrison (1989).

[67] Heyworth (2007a) prints *inficitur*, and it is tempting for the reasons outlined by him (Heyworth (2007b: 496)) and by Ingleheart (2007: 72), but I remain unpersuaded.

>   necdum ultra Tiberim belli sonus: ultima praeda 25
>   Nomentum et captae iugera terna Corae.

> But Cossus comes hot on the heels [of Romulus][68] with the slaughter of Veian Tolumnius, when it took some work to be able to conquer Veii.[69] War's sound had not yet gone beyond the Tiber; the most distant plunder [was] Nomentum and captured Cora's three *iugera*.

In just a few lines, Propertius sketches a map of the Roman Empire in its infancy from the perspective of someone stationed at its heart. The concentration of military language (e.g. *praeda, captae*) in lines 25–6 and an allusion to the sensory experience of battle (25; *belli sonus*) signal that Latium in this period should be viewed as a landscape of war. With Nomentum marking the edge of the conquered territory to the northeast and Cora, to the southeast (Fig. 6.1), Propertius identifies the river Tiber as the landscape feature orienting the Roman soldier's intuitive understanding of front and behind at the time of Cossus's campaign. In other words, the river is the boundary beyond which their current objectives lie, and crossing it means leaving a zone of comparative safety and entering one of danger.[70]

But Propertius explodes this mental model of the Latian landscape with his apostrophe to Veii, making clear that the Tiber, which embodied the limit of Rome's secure power when Cossus's army rode out, no longer held that significance when they returned (4.10.27–30):

> heu Veii ueteres, et uos tum regna fuistis
>   et uestro posita est aurea sella foro;
> nunc intra muros pastoris bucina lenti
>   cantat, et in uestris ossibus arua metunt. 30

> Alas, ancient Veii, you were then a kingdom, and in your forum was placed a gilded seat. Now inside the walls an unhurried shepherd's trumpet sounds, and they harvest the fields amidst your bones.[71]

Viewed from one angle, this is a peaceful, if fatalistic, image. Cities rise and fall, but this site of strife and slaughter has at least recovered such that it can nourish animals, crops and the human beings who depend on them. Ancient Veii has become a hybrid

---

[68] 'Comes hot on the heels' for *insequitur*: Ingleheart (2007: 72).
[69] 'When ... Veii': Welch (2005: 150).
[70] On the phenomenology of war landscapes, see Lewin (1917) and the introduction to this volume (1–3, 4–7, 14–15). Cf. Ambühl (2019) on touch and taste in Latin battle narrative; Minchin (in this volume) on sensory impressions of combat in the *Iliad*.
[71] Heyworth (2007b: 604) has 'amidst the bones of your men', which is one possible interpretation of *in uestris ossibus*, but conceals the productive ambiguity of the phrasing in Latin. It should be noted that Tolumnius died at least a generation before Veii was destroyed, so Propertius is compressing the timeline here (Cairns (2006: 291)).

pastoral-and-georgic realm wherein the *bucina* is blown not by a soldier in the heat of battle, but by a shepherd at ease in a peaceful (pacified?) landscape (29; *pastoris ... lenti*);[72] and the surrounding fields have been put into productive cultivation. It might even be seen as a tribute to Augustus, who settled veterans at Veii and invested in building projects there.[73]

At the same time, the vignette possesses much darker dimensions. In addition to the military resonance of *bucina*, the verb *metere* ('reap') can be used of killing in battle as well as of harvesting in an agricultural setting, not unlike the English 'mow (down)'.[74] *Vestris ossibus* is also ambiguous: are these bones Veii's because they belonged to men who once lived there, or because Veii was once a living organism – or both? Certainly, Propertius has personified the city to some extent merely by using direct address along with forms of *uos* and *uester*.[75] I would argue that despite the fantastical nature of such a conception, it is more intuitive to read *ossibus* as referring to Veii's own skeleton, at least initially. In that case, the line would imply that the people currently farming the Veian land are disturbing the mortal remains of an entity still capable of sensation. This would hardly be the only place in Roman literature where farming is associated with violence.[76] Agricultural activities can be interpreted as a form of violence against the earth in its natural state, for example. But another trope is also at work here, which Mario Labate has called 'the destroyer-plough' (*il aratro distruttore*).[77] As one of the implements used to mark out the dimensions of new settlements and return land to cultivation once old ones have been obliterated, the plough plays an important role in both the birth and death of cities – a dualism very much evident in this passage.[78]

At the end of the day, however, it is Propertius, not the people bringing in the harvest, who 'exposes' the bones of Veii and compels his audience to 'see' and to mourn the destruction of a once-great city. It is the poet, with his figurative and allusive language, who 'digs up' this episode in Rome's early history, dis-integrating the very heartland of Roman Italy and reminding the reader that it was not always one *patria*. Instead, Rome grew by pushing beyond one boundary after another and bringing other, older *patriae* under her control, sometimes by diplomacy and sometimes by destruction.[79] As illustrated by Propertius's sudden shift of perspective between lines 26 and 27 of the present poem, a victory for Rome has always meant defeat and loss – of life, autonomy,

---

[72] Fletcher (1989: 359).
[73] Cairns (2006: 292) reads ll. 27–8 as 'an implicit eulogy of Augustus'.
[74] *LSJ* s.v. *meto* II.A.2.
[75] Welch (2005: 153) notes that the repeated second-person pronouns and adjectives 'emphasiz[e] the connection between the poet and the fallen city' while drawing in the audience emotionally.
[76] See Zientek (in this volume), with further bibliography.
[77] Labate (1991: 174).
[78] Labate (1991: 173–4).
[79] Edwards (2011: 651) situates this episode in the Roman literary discourse surrounding ruined cities. Similar to how the landscapes described in this chapter undermine the narrative of Augustan peace, Edwards (2011: 646) shows that ruined cities 'often serve as traces of violent ruptures in the history of a city whose literary presences more usually work to emphasise continuity and durability.' Cf. Weiner (in this volume: 249).

heritage, home – for the conquered community.[80] The survivors or their descendants might eventually identify primarily as Romans, but older, regional alliances persisted, and memories of old losses inhered in the landscape. The apostrophe to Veii calls attention to this pattern and in so doing helps the reader to contextualize Propertius's earlier visions of Etruria and Umbria within the broader scheme of Roman history. Episodes of bitter civil conflict like the Perusine War can quickly reopen questions and unsettle allegiances that would seem to have been settled long before.[81]

4 The Actian sea

So far, I have looked at Propertius's treatment of post-war landscapes within Italy itself, with the poetic excavation of ruined Veii in 4.10 adding greater resonance to the representations of Etruria and Umbria in 1.21–2 and 4.1. But there is another major civil war battleground mentioned repeatedly in the *Elegies* that behaves similarly to those personified landscapes, namely the Actian sea.[82] Propertius mentions the battle of Actium for the first time in poem 2.1, while cataloguing the contexts in which he would have praised his patron Maecenas had he been formed for epic instead of elegy. Throughout this list of rejected topics Propertius consistently 'highlight[s] the defeated and their unsuccessful ambitions.'[83] At line 27 he turns from Greek subject matter to Roman (2.1.27–36):

> nam quotiens Mutinam aut ciuilia busta Philippos
>   aut canerem Siculae classica bella fugae,
> euersosque focos antiquae gentis Etruscae,
>   et Ptolomaei litora capta Phari,   30
> aut canerem Aegyptum et Nilum, cum attractus in urbem
>   septem captiuis debilis ibat aquis,
> aut regum auratis circumdata colla catenis,
>   Actiaque in Sacra currere rostra Via;
> te mea Musa illis semper contexerat armis   35
>   et sumpta et posita pace fidele caput.

For however often I was singing about Mutina or Philippi, the burial place of citizens, or the naval wars and a rout off Sicily, and the overturned hearths of the

---

[80] Cf. Ingleheart (2007: 73): 'Propertius' grief at the fate of Veii undermines any admiration at Rome's military success.'
[81] Hence, perhaps, Propertius's interest in bringing up the conquest of Etruria here; cp. Labate (1991: 173): 'Nella guerra di Perugia i lutti delle città etrusche avevano riacquistato tragica attualità.' Cf. Welch (2005: 155–7), who read the decapitation of Tolumnius at 4.10.37–8 as a deliberate reminder of the massacre known as the *arae Perusinae* ('Perusine altars'), in which Octavian allegedly had the senators from Perusia beheaded in a sacrifice to Julius Caesar.
[82] On Propertius's poetic response to Actium, see esp. Gurval (1995: chs 4 and 6), Reitz-Joosse (2016).
[83] Gurval (1995: 172), with discussion.

ancient Etruscan race, and the captured shores of the Ptolemaic Pharos; or if I was singing about Egypt and the Nile, when he was going weakly, dragged into the city with his seven waters held captive, or about the kings' necks encircled with gilded chains, and the Actian [ships'] beaks running along the Via Sacra; always my Muse would weave you into those arms, a mind firm in both the taking up and putting down of peace.

By this point, of course, the reader will have begun to suspect that Propertius is being at least somewhat disingenuous in disclaiming these topics, since he has already touched on 'the overturned hearths of the ancient Etruscan race' in 1.21–2.[84] He has simply approached the subject as befits an elegist: via individual subjective experience, emphasizing personal relationships and especially grief for the dead. Likewise he will soon treat the subject of Actium, but coming at the topic sideways and from an unexpected point of view – that of a lover considering how things would be different if everyone chose to live as he did (2.15.43–6):

non ferrum crudele neque esset bellica nauis
    nec nostra Actiacum uerteret ossa mare,
nec totiens propriis circum oppugnata triumphis   45
    lassa foret crines soluere Roma suos.

There would be no cruel weapons or ships of war, nor would the Actian sea be tossing our bones, and Rome – so many times assailed on every side by her own victories – would not be so weary of letting fall her hair [in grief].

This is a far cry from the kind of approach hinted at in poem 2.1, where the emphasis was to be placed on triumphal monuments like captured ships' beaks (34; *Actia ... rostra*) proudly displayed in the centre of Rome. Instead, Propertius casts his eye to the faraway battlefield itself, a seascape marked not by the spoils of a victor, but by the bones of Roman soldiers killed in the engagement.

Naval battles pose special challenges to those who would commemorate them. Because the 'ground' is perpetually shifting, it is generally not possible to mark the actual site of the battle with a trophy, burial tumulus or other physical monument. Indeed, the featurelessness of the water may make it difficult even to locate the battle site with any precision, still less to map its topography or recreate the movements of the battle.[85] The usual literary solution to this problem is to narrate events on the water with frequent reference to coastal vantage points.[86] The same principle applies to the building of real-

---

[84] And (though the reader may not know it yet) he will do so again in 4.10, just looking at a different Etruscan city at a more distant point in the past. Cf. Gurval (1995: 176), who finds in *euersos focos* a reference to the burning of Perusia by Octavian's troops. On the potential resonance of this phrase for Maecenas, the addressee of poem 2.1, see e.g. Massa-Pairault (2014: 153–4).
[85] van Rookhuijzen (in this volume).
[86] van Rookhuijzen (in this volume) calls this perspective the 'littoral gaze'.

life monuments. Following the battle of Actium, Octavian built victory markers at the sites of both his and Antony's camps; in addition, he founded a victory city, 'Nicopolis', below his own campsite and renovated a small sanctuary of Apollo near Antony's, on the opposite side of the Ambracian gulf.[87] Bettina Reitz-Joosse has convincingly argued in a recent article that Propertius's representation of the Actian seascape, constructed in a series of poems scattered throughout the collection, should be read as a response to Octavian's thorough reconfiguration of the coastlines around the gulf as a monument to his victory.[88] I do not wish to recapitulate her argument here, but will make just a few observations comparing the Actian sea in 2.15 to the depictions of Etruria and Umbria discussed above.

There are two personifications at work in *Elegies* 2.15.43–6 which combine to create an image of a dissident post-war landscape. The second, more developed of these figures Rome as a woman with her hair unbound in perpetual mourning. Whereas line 45 presents a paradox – as both conqueror and conquered, Rome might be considered either defeated or triumphant – the impression of grief-stricken exhaustion given in the following line shows that her frame of mind is anything but celebratory. Line 44 offers a proximate cause for her sorrow: the Actian sea (*Actiacum mare*), subtly personified as the subject of *uerteret*, is endlessly 'tossing' the bones of men killed in the battle of Actium. The first-person plural adjective *nostra* proves that, just as the bones scattered on the Etruscan hills in 1.21 did not all belong to Gallus, so too the sea is now filled with the bones of more than one soldier; and all of them are Roman.[89] In addition, like so many other verbs applied to war landscapes in the *Elegies*, *uerteret* has multiple shades of meaning. It could simply mean that the bones are being turned over and over, tumbled and tossed about on the surface of the waves; but it could also mean that the sea is 'overturning (= destroying)' the bones or 'turning' them in a perpetual rout.[90] Either way, the *Actiacum mare* seems to be deliberately defying the very natural properties that make naval battlefields so difficult to locate and monumentalize. Between wind, current and tide, there should be nothing left on the surface by this time by which to identify the site of the battle.[91] And yet, here are the bones, still visible. Once again, as with the *puluis*

---

[87] Reitz-Joosse (2016: 277–83) gives a detailed account of this process of memorialization along with helpful maps and illustrations. Cf. Gurval (1995: 65–81).
[88] Reitz-Joosse (2016); see also Gurval (1995: 259).
[89] Gurval (1995: 181). Cf. Reitz-Joosse (2016: 290): 'Rome fought Rome at Actium, and the sea now contains the bones of the anonymous Roman Everyman'.
[90] *LSJ* s.v. *uerto* I.A, B.2.e. Reitz-Joosse (2016: 293) discusses further resonances between this use of *uertere* and others at 2.16.39–40 (of Antony's warships turned to flight) and 3.11.69 (of the battle-lines commemorated by Leucadian Apollo). It is tempting to recall the compounded form *euertere* used at 2.1.29 (of the hearths of the Etruscan race).
[91] Indeed, these conditions made it exceedingly difficult to locate and recover the bodies of drowned sailors to give them funeral rites. Hence this impassioned statement from the normally matter-of-fact Vegetius (*Mil.* 4.44): *quid enim crudelius congressione nauali, ubi aquis homines perimuntur et flammis? . . . qui acerrimus casus est, absumenda piscibus insepulta sunt corpora.* ('What could be crueler than a naval engagement, when men are killed in the waves and by flames? . . . This is the bitterest misfortune, that their bodies are left unburied to be consumed by fish.')

Etrusca, Propertius decries the mistreatment of the Roman dead by an unfeeling landscape; but, again, he himself invested that landscape with the power to commit such cruelty in defiance of nature.

I think Propertius is sincere when he cedes the topic of the Actian shores (2.34.61; *Actia ... litora*) to Vergil and the epic genre. He, the elegist, has already in Book 2 begun to construct a 'shadow memorial' of the battle where no memorial can be built in truth: on the sea.[92] Nor will this memorial be limited to just the battle site itself. Like the Perusian battleground that dilated to encompass all Etruria and (albeit in a different way) Umbria, so Propertius will strongly suggest in a later poem that the *entire Ionian sea* will commemorate Caesar's victory/Rome's defeat.[93] And, as Robert Gurval has observed, the exhaustion of the personified Rome, 'assailed on every side by her own victories' (45; *propriis circum oppugnata triumphis*), 'puts the Actian victory firmly in the background of civil wars. It was not an isolated occasion. The dead in the Actian waters may thus be seen as representative of all Romans who died in the recent civil wars.'[94]

I would like finally to incorporate one other detail into this composite portrait of the rebellious Actian seascape, one found in a reference to the fatal consequences of Antony's enslavement by Cleopatra (2.16.37–8):

cerne ducem modo qui fremitu compleuit inani
    Actia damnatis aequora militibus:

Look at the leader who has just now, amidst useless [*or*: lifeless] shouting, filled up the Actian waters with doomed soldiers.

With *modo* ('just now') Propertius insists on the recentness and enduring relevance of the battle, but also implies that travellers in the Ionian might still be able to hear the cries of drowning Romans echoing over the waves.[95] Propertius's poetic shadow memorial thus offers readers a multisensory experience that engages the sense of hearing as well as that of sight.[96] Put another way, the sea lends its own voice – *fremitus* being after all most commonly used of inarticulate 'rushing, resounding, murmuring' sounds such as the ocean makes – to the restless but now-voiceless dead.

---

[92] '[Architectural historian J. M. Mayo], writing about WWI, uses the term to describe "environmental forms without monuments or periodic rituals to clarify their role in history", that are only intelligible as memorials to those who connect them with war events' (Reitz-Joosse (2016: 288, n. 25), the first to my knowledge to apply this term to Propertius's poetic construction of the Actian sea).
[93] Prop. 3.11.71–2: *at tu, siue petes portus seu, nauita, linques, | Caesaris in toto sis memor Ionio* ('But you, sailor, whether you are heading for port or leaving it behind, remember Caesar all over the Ionian'). Discussion in Reitz-Joosse (2016: 292–3).
[94] Gurval (1995: 181).
[95] Similarly, Pausanias (1.32.4) says that nocturnal visitors to the Marathon battlefield could hear horses neighing and men fighting.
[96] Reitz-Joosse (2016: 290–1) connects the drowning soldiers' 'useless shouting' (2.16.37; *fremitu ... inani*) to the lulling roar of the Ionian sea mentioned at 4.6.15–16. The fact that *inanis* can mean 'lifeless' in addition to 'vain, futile' may add additional poignancy here.

5 Conclusion

Most scholars agree that, to some extent, Propertius exhibits a divided allegiance between his home region and the Roman state. It is also generally agreed that Propertius dwells on the fate of both body and soul after death, and that he writes with particular poignancy about a soldier who died fighting against Octavian at Perusia. At no point, however, does Propertius openly criticize Augustus for his behaviour before, during, or after the Perusine War; or for his efforts as *princeps* to craft an official narrative or myth celebrating a 'peace brought about through victories on land and sea' (*RG* 13.1; *terra marique ... parta uictoriis pax*),[97] even when that meant Rome triumphing over herself, as at Perusia and Actium. Instead, as I have shown, he communicates these ideas to the audience via images of landscapes affected (or infected) by civil war. Chief among these images are Etruria, Umbria and the Actian sea, all of which appear in the *Elegies* to have been enduringly, perceptibly and (from a realistic perspective) improbably transformed by the deaths of Roman soldiers in civil war. The apostrophe to Veii in poem 4.10 recontextualizes the references to Actium and the Perusine War by showing how violent conquest of both the natural and the human elements in (especially Italian) landscapes has always undergirded Roman peace, progress and prosperity. In addition, Propertius endows his post-war landscapes with both the means and the desire to thwart the natural processes that would tend to disperse or conceal the remains of the Roman soldiers killed there, creating powerful testaments to the suffering of both the dead men and their families. From within these speech zones, landscapes voice positions that the poet himself can or will not.

Bibliography

Ambühl, A. 2019. 'The Touch and Taste of War in Latin Battle Narrative.' *Trends in Classics* 11 (1): 119–38.

Breed, B. W. 2009. 'Perugia and the Plots of the *Monobiblos*.' *Cambridge Classical Journal* 55: 24–48.

Cairns, F. 2006. *Sextus Propertius: The Augustan Elegist*. Cambridge: Cambridge University Press.

Clarke, J. 2012. 'Engendering Landscape: Propertius' Use of Place in 1.21 and 22.' *Phoenix* 66 (3/4): 364–80.

Cornwell, H. 2017. Pax *and the Politics of Peace: Republic to Principate*. Oxford: Oxford University Press.

Davis, J. T. 1971. 'Propertius 1.21–22.' *Classical Journal* 66 (3): 209–13.

DeBrohun, J. B. 2003. *Roman Propertius and the Invention of Elegy*. Ann Arbor: University of Michigan Press.

Dowling, M. B. 2006. *Clemency and Cruelty in the Roman World*. Ann Arbor: University of Michigan Press.

---

[97] On the concept of *terra marique parta pax* see Cornwell (2017: ch. 3), Reitz-Joosse (2016: 277, n. 2).

Du Quesnay, I. M. Le M. 1992. 'In memoriam Galli: Propertius 1.21.' In *Author and Audience in Latin Literature*, edited by T. Woodman and J. Powell, 52–83. Cambridge: Cambridge University Press.

Edwards, C. 2011. 'Imagining Ruins in Ancient Rome.' *European Review of History – Revue européenne d'histoire* 18 (5/6): 645–61.

Evernden, N. 1978. 'Beyond Ecology: Self, Place, and the Pathetic Fallacy.' *North American Review* 263: 16–20.

Fletcher, G. B. A. 1989. 'Further Propertiana.' *Latomus* 48 (2): 354–9.

Gabba, E. 1971. 'The Perusine War and Triumviral Italy.' *Harvard Studies in Classical Philology* 75: 139–60.

Garani, M. 2007. 'Propertius' Temple of Jupiter Feretrius and the *spolia opima* (4.10): A Poem Not to be Read?' *L'Antiquité classique* 76: 99–117.

Gurval, R. A. 1995. *Actium and Augustus: The Politics and Emotions of Civil War*. Ann Arbor: University of Michigan Press.

Harrison, S. J. 1989. 'Augustus, the Poets, and the *spolia opima*.' *Classical Quarterly* 39: 408–14.

Hendry, M. 1997. 'Three Propertian Puns.' *Classical Quarterly* 47 (2): 599–603.

Heyworth, S. J. 2007a. *Sexti Properti Elegi*. Oxford: Oxford University Press.

Heyworth, S. J. 2007b. *Cynthia: A Companion to the Text of Propertius*. Oxford: Oxford University Press.

Heyworth, S. J. 2007c. 'Propertius, Patronage, and Politics.' *Bulletin of the Institute of Classical Studies* 50: 92–128.

Hope, V. M. 2018. '"Dulce et decorum est pro patria mori": The Practical and Symbolic Treatment of the Roman War Dead.' *Mortality* 23 (1): 35–49.

Hutchinson, G. O. 1984. 'Propertius and the Unity of the Book.' *Journal of Roman Studies* 74: 99–106.

Ingleheart, J. 2007. 'Propertius 4.10 and the End of the *Aeneid*: Augustus, the *spolia opima* and the Right to Remain Silent.' *Greece & Rome* 54 (1): 61–81.

Labate, M. 1991. 'Città morte, città future: un tema della poesia augustea.' *Maia* 43: 167–84.

Luisi, A. 1990. 'Esempi di morte in combattimento nell'opera di Properzio.' In *'Dulce et decorum est': la morte in combattimento nell'antichità*, edited by M. Sordi, 187–96. Contributi dell'Istituto di storia antica 16. Milan: Vita e Pensiero.

Makins, M. 2013. 'Monumental Losses: Confronting the Aftermath of Battle in Roman Literature.' PhD diss., University of Pennsylvania.

Marland, P. 2013. 'Ecocriticism.' *Literature Compass* 10 (11): 846–68.

Massa-Pairault, F.-H. 2014. 'Properzio tra l'Etruria e Roma.' In *Properzio e l'età augustea. Cultura, storia, arte: Proceedings of the Nineteenth Conference on Propertius, Assisi-Perugia 25–27 May 2012*, edited by G. Bonamente, C. Santini and R. Cristofoli, 147–80. Turnhout: Brepols.

McDowell, M. J. 1996. 'The Bakhtinian Road to Ecological Insight.' In *The Ecocriticism Reader: Landmarks in Literary Ecology*, edited by C. Glotfelty and H. Fromm, 371–91. Athens, GA: University of Georgia Press.

Moore, B. L. 2008. *Ecology and Literature: Ecocentric Personification from Antiquity to the Twenty-first Century*. New York: Palgrave Macmillan.

Nethercut, W. R. 1971. 'The ΣΦΡΑΓΙΣ of the *Monobiblos*.' *American Journal of Philology* 92 (3): 464–72.

Nicholson, N. 1999. 'Bodies without Names, Names without Bodies: Propertius 1.21–22.' *Classical Journal* 94 (2): 143–61.

Parker, H. N. 1991. 'The Bones: Propertius 1. 21. 9–10.' *Classical Philology* 86 (4): 328–33.

Parker, H. N. 1992. 'The Fertile Fields of Umbria: Prop. 1.22.10.' *Mnemosyne* 45 (1): 88–92.

Putnam, M. C. J. 1976. 'Propertius 1. 22: A Poet's Self-Definition.' *Quaderni urbinati di cultura classica* 23: 93–123.

Reitz-Joosse, B. 2016. 'Land at Peace and Sea at War: Landscape and the Memory of Actium in Greek Epigram and Propertius' *Elegies*.' In *Valuing Landscape in Classical Antiquity: Natural Environment and Cultural Imagination*, edited by J. McInerney and I. Sluiter, 276–96. Leiden: Brill.

Stahl, H.-P. 1985. *Propertius: 'Love' and 'War.' Individual and State under Augustus*. Berkeley: University of California Press.

Traill, D. A. 1994. 'Propertius 1.21: The Sister, the Bones, and the Wayfarer.' *American Journal of Philology* 115 (1): 89–96.

Webster, D. 1998. *Aftermath: The Remnants of War*. New York: Vintage.

Welch, T. S. 2005. *The Elegiac Cityscape: Propertius and the Meaning of Roman Monuments*. Columbus: Ohio State University Press.

PART III
CONTROLLING LANDSCAPES AND
THE SYMBOLISM OF POWER

CHAPTER 7

JUSTIFYING CIVIL WAR: INTERACTIONS BETWEEN CAESAR AND THE ITALIAN LANDSCAPE IN LUCAN'S RUBICON PASSAGE (*BC* 1.183–235)

Esther Meijer

1 Introduction

Many of Lucan's landscapes show the effects of civil war, from the bloody red Massilian sea to Pharsalus, marked by Roman bloodshed in the decisive battle between Caesar and Pompey.[1] In this chapter, I consider the event that turns Italy itself into a landscape of war: Caesar's crossing of the Rubicon in Book 1. In this scene, the apparition of *Patria* begs Caesar not to proceed, and the Rubicon swells up in an attempt to hinder the general's passage.[2] I discuss how, in response to the protesting Italian landscape, Caesar attempts to justify his actions, and I suggest that he does so by evoking Roman rituals of war, including the fetial ritual of lawfully declaring war against a foreign enemy and fetial treaty solemnization.

We might wonder to what extent Caesar's engagement with these rituals justifies the civil war he is about to undertake, and how Caesar's actions compare to those of Pompey. By comparing the presentation of Roman rituals of war here with parallels in Pompey's proposed collaboration with the Parthians in Book 8 and the failed treaty between Aeneas and Latinus in *Aeneid* 12, I show how Caesar's interactions with the Italian landscape highlight the impossibility of constructing the civil war between Caesar and Pompey as a just war. Through this discussion, I explore what this impossibility might contribute to our understanding of Lucan's perception of the civil war that instigated the transition from Republic to Principate.

---

[1] For war and its transformative effects on landscapes, see e.g. Masters (1992), O'Gorman (1995), Leigh (2010), Hughes (2013), Zientek (2014), Ambühl (2016), Reitz-Joosse (2016), and many chapters in this volume.

[2] Swelling rivers are found in ancient literature from Homer onwards. See e.g. the introduction to this volume (3–14) on the Scamander in the *Iliad*. This is one of the few moments in Lucan's *Civil War* that forces the characteristically speedy general to slow down: after crossing the Rubicon, hardly anything forms an obstacle to Caesar's movement. Masters (1992: 1–10) has famously argued that the passage, as the work's proper opening, is programmatic for the entire *Civil War*, in the sense that it sets up contradictions between Caesar's urgency in crossing boundaries and Lucan's narrative obstructions to or compliances with Caesar's progress. Lucan's Caesar is generally characterized by great haste – perhaps a continuation of the general's rapid advance through Italy as it was represented in Caesar's *Civil War* and Cicero's letters. Cf. Roche (2009: 192–4, 204), Peer (2015: 59–61), Adema (2017: 237–9). Cf. also Caes. *BCiv.* 1.8; Cic. *Att.* 7.22.1, 8.13.1, 7.20.1.

2 Decentralizing Rome: landscape and identity

Lucan's landscapes often function as a medium through which civil conflict is articulated and political, civic and socio-cultural issues are explored.[3] Rivers and oceans in particular play an important role in this.[4] When the epic arrives at the Rubicon, we have already encountered such exploratory landscapes: the deserted and half-destroyed fields of Italy contrast with their fertile and cultivated counterparts in Virgil's *Georgics*, and, as Laura Zientek discusses in her chapter in this volume, hint at the impossibility of agricultural recovery and the sometimes permanent effects of this civil war. This uncultivated landscape contrasts poignantly with Rome's (self-)image as a community of farmer-citizens whose identity was rooted in working the land,[5] which can be seen in the context of Roman ethnocentrism, a model of Roman space that contrasts its centre, Rome, to its periphery in various expanding concentric circles: Italy, territory under Roman control, and the borders of the known world.[6] This Romanocentric approach, closely tied to Roman identity, generates a paradoxical dialectic between expansion and enclosure. How does one keep expanding the *imperium sine fine*, while maintaining supposedly impermeable boundaries and a fixed and solid Roman centre?[7] This anxiety underlies the decentralization of Rome and the Roman world that is recurrent throughout Lucan's *Civil War*.[8]

Crucially, this decentralization is prompted by Caesar's crossing of the Rubicon, which effectively collapses the legal boundary between two of these concentric circles, namely outside space (territory under Roman control) and inside space (Italy).[9] Accordingly, the Rubicon, a topographical referent that used to provide meaning within this spatial model of identity, loses its legal meaning. Caesar's crossing then does not only introduce us to some of the main themes of Lucan's epic and instigate the beginning of the civil war, but it also signals a conceptual shift in – or even an uprooting of – Roman identity.[10]

---

[3] My chapter complements groundwork laid especially by Gowing (2005), Spencer (2005, 2010), Thorne (2011), Dinter (2012), Zientek (2014 and her chapter in this volume).
[4] Bexley (2014: 374). Cf. e.g. the Tiber filled with blood and corpses of previous civil war victims (2.209–20); the sea battle at Massilia with water making corpses' features unrecognizable (3.509–672); the Araxes where Crassus died (8.431–9); Pompey's corpse buried at the edge of the land bordering on the sea (8.712–822); and, in contrast, Caesar claiming that he would not even mind being buried under the waves – as long as he is feared forever and by everyone (5.654–71).
[5] Cf. Leach (1974), Hardie (2006), Skoie (2006), Spencer (2010). See e.g. Cato *Agr. praef.*; Varro *Rust.* 2, *praef.* 1–2; Sall. *Cat.* 2, 10–13; Verg. *Ecl.* passim.
[6] Nicolet (1991: 29–33), Romm (1992: 46–8), Jaeger (1997: 9–10).
[7] Jaeger (1997), Rimell (2015).
[8] On decentralization in Lucan, see e.g. Ahl (1976: 170–3), Masters (1992: 93–9), Rossi (2000), Bexley (2014).
[9] Myers (2011) discusses how Lucan dismantles these traditional Roman notions of centre and periphery and creates a new concept of Roman space defined by the transgressions and violence of Caesar. I discuss the legal ramifications of the Rubicon crossing below (pp. 160–1).
[10] The Rubicon had probably not even been the legal boundary for that long: either for thirty years, if we believe that Sulla changed the boundary from the Aesis to the Rubicon around 80 BCE (see Mommsen (1863: 367–8), Hardy (1916: 66–8), Sumi (2002: 425–6)), or for eighty years, if we believe that Tiberius Gracchus moved the boundary to the Rubicon (for which, see Cuntz (1902: 28–34), Walbank (1957: 396–7) and (1972:

In what follows, I discuss how the Italian landscape protests its loss of meaning prompted by Caesar's advance on Rome visually, verbally and physically, and how Caesar then attempts to justify himself. He does so by evoking Roman rituals of war, including the fetial ritual of lawfully declaring war against a foreign enemy and fetial treaty solemnization. Soon, however, Caesar ends his diplomatic efforts and violates the landscape – and thereby Italy itself – by crossing the physically protesting river and deliberately seeking war. This illustrates the poem's conflation of *ius* and *scelus* (*ius datumque sceleri*, 1.2) and supports the general sense of disapproval, outrage and despair at civil war that permeates the epic.

3 Arriving at the riverbanks: *Patria* voices her concerns

After Caesar has crossed the Alps, he reaches the Rubicon (1.182–5). At the banks of the river, the *imago* of a visibly distressed *Patria* appears to him (1.186–9):

> ingens visa duci patriae trepidantis imago
> clara per obscuram vultu maestissima noctem
> turrigero canos effundens vertice crines
> caesarie lacera nudisque adstare lacertis, ...[11]

> Clearly to the leader through the murky night appeared
> a mighty image of his country in distress, grief in her face,
> her white hair streaming from her tower-crowned head;
> with tresses torn and shoulders bare she stood before him, ...

Several details of *Patria*'s portrayal correspond to common expressions of grief. Her loose hair, torn tresses and naked arms contribute to the image of a sorrowful, mourning *Patria*. She is also wearing a tower-crown (*turrigero*, 1.188). This image, I suggest, evokes the personifications of cities, peoples, and their lands as familiar from Roman iconography and triumphal processions.[12] Some of these representations feature conquered peoples wearing Greek dress, hairstyle and a mural crown, and adopting a friendly stance, indicating Roman construction of these peoples as adopted members of

---

24)). As such, the Rubicon losing its meaning represents only one step of a longer process in which Romans kept adapting their spatial identity. In fact, one could argue that continuous adaptation is inherent to Roman identity, as, from the early Kingdom onwards, Rome kept expanding its 'elastic' walls, and the integration of new citizens into an existing *patria* was an ever-existing issue (see Konstan (1986), Rimell (2015: 30–2)). Yet this particular instance of a topographic referent losing its meaning is especially relevant, as Rome's 'elastic' walls now move *inwards* rather than outwards, and as, from Lucan onwards, this moment was interpreted as related to a change of political institution.

[11] Citations of the Latin are from Shackleton Bailey (2009); translations are from Braund (2008).

[12] Gardner (1988), Ostrowski (1996), Östenberg (2009: 204–8). Roche (2009: 208) notes that, from the early second century CE, *Italia* is represented with a tower-crown on coins and (probably) on the Arch of Trajan at Beneventum.

the Roman community. But Lucan's *Patria* is more reminiscent of conquered peoples depicted as grieving and wearing unbridled hair, illustrating Rome's representation of them as conquered enemies and emphasizing Rome's (military) supremacy.[13] *Patria*'s mural crown underlines not only the fact that she represents the city of Rome, but – as mural crowns often emphasize the military siege of the places represented in Roman triumphs and reliefs[14] – it also anticipates Caesar's imminent conquest of the *urbs aeterna*. Perhaps, then, her image shows the transition and decentralization that Italy will go through as Caesar crosses the Rubicon: from the heart of the Roman community to one of Caesar's conquered enemies.[15] *Patria*'s evocation of triumphal iconography is particularly salient considering that Caesar's return to Italy from Gaul should have been accompanied by triumphs.[16] Instead, he is presented with a perverse and unjustified type of triumph: one acquired by the undertaking of civil war.[17] Next, *Patria*'s speech underlines the issues of justice and legality evoked by Caesar's actions (1.190-2):

'quo tenditis ultra?
quo fertis mea signa, viri? si iure venitis,
si cives, huc usque licet.'

'Where further do you march?
Where do you take my standards, warriors? If lawfully you come,
if as citizens, this far only is allowed.'

Patria's question about and appropriation of the Roman military standards (*mea signa*, 1.191) immediately calls attention to Caesar's belligerent and unlawful intentions.[18] She points out that the general and his army must stop here at the border of Italy if they have come as law-abiding citizens. After all, it was prohibited for generals or governors to guide their legions out of their assigned provinces since Sulla's establishment of the *lex Cornelia de maiestate*.[19] The anaphora *si iure venitis, si cives* (1.190-1) reminds us hereof and emphasizes the legal ramifications of *Patria*'s request. As such, *Patria*'s speech revisits

---

[13] Ostrowski (1996), Östenberg (2009: 205–8). The distinction was first made by Bienkowski (1900).
[14] Östenberg (2009: 204–5).
[15] *Patria*'s appearance has also been recognized to evoke Hector's apparition to Aeneas on the night of Troy's destruction at Verg. *Aen*. 2.268–97. Zientek (2014: 45–6) suggests that Lucan's *Patria* is a re-imagination of Roma's triumphant appearance in Anchises' speech about Rome's glorious future in *Aen*. 6.781–7. Mulhern (2017) points out *Patria*'s similarities to Roman *matronae* and widows, and interprets Caesar's rejection of her as indifference to Rome, as he 'embarks on his road away from his wife, Rome and Romanness to tyranny, luxury and a mistress'. Clearly, *Patria*'s appearance here is poignant and related to Rome's future.
[16] Cf. e.g. 1.286–9, 7.254–60.
[17] Cf. 1.12: *bella geri placuit nullos habitura triumphos*?: 'did you choose to wage wars which would bring no triumphs?'
[18] Throughout the epic, Pompey (2.592), Caesar (5.349) and Cato (9.281) all claim the *signa* for themselves. Cf. Roche (2009: 209).
[19] Cf. Cic. *Pis*. 50. Lintott (1981: 54–8) and Braga (2014: 89–91) discuss a potential precedent of this law, namely the *lex Porcia*. The precise date of this law is debated (possibly dating back to the second century BCE but definitely no later than 100 BCE), and it seems to have included prescriptions for governors, including a restriction of movement for governors with their armies.

the themes of transgression and *ius* as set out in the poem's introduction and marks their importance for the crossing.[20]

What is more, *Patria*'s speech sets up a negotiation between herself and Caesar. This negotiation is both spatial and legal: the river Rubicon is a physical element fixed onto terrestrial space, but it also has legal properties and differentiates Roman citizens on the inside from others, including potential enemies, on the outside. Therefore, Caesar's relation to *Patria* is currently defined by his position in space: if he decides to cross the boundary as a soldier, he becomes an enemy to the state, and Rome in turn becomes Caesar's enemy.[21] *Patria*'s appearance already shows the potential consequences of this action. It is now up to Caesar to respond to *Patria*'s concerns.

4 Caesar's response: rituals of war

Caesar's first reaction to *Patria*'s supernatural appearance is to tremble: perplexed, he halts on the edge of the riverbank (1.192–4). Soon, however, he picks himself up and responds with a speech that includes an invocation of several gods. These deities, characteristic of the Julio-Claudian emperors, are generally interpreted as a prefiguration of the Principate that Caesar's victory in this civil war helped to bring about.[22] Additionally, I suggest, they recall deities that are associated with Roman war rituals, especially fetial procedures of war declaration and treaty solemnization. Before discussing how Caesar's words and actions evoke these rituals, I will briefly contextualize the *fetiales* and their relevance to Caesar.

The *fetiales* are considered to be an old priesthood, dating back to the early Roman Kingdom.[23] The priests, the fetials, were traditionally involved with the Romans' relations with other peoples. They were responsible among other things for formal diplomatic action, including the performance of rituals by which a *bellum iustum*, a just war,[24] could be started, the solemnization of treaties, and the surrender of Romans who did not adhere to these procedures. As such, the fetials played an important role in Roman relations with other peoples, especially their enemies.

---

[20] Cf. 1.1: *bella ... plus quam civilia*, introducing the theme of transgression, and 1.2: *ius ... datum sceleri*, underlining the importance of *ius*.

[21] I owe my understanding of legal space in this passage to Willis (2011: 59–60).

[22] Grimal (1970: 56–9), Roche (2009: 210–2).

[23] A vast range of research on the fetials and related topics has been published. A selection includes Samter (1909), Wissowa (1912: 550–4), Ogilvie (1965), Ziegler (1972), Rich (1976), Saulnier (1980), Wiedemann (1986), Rüpke (1990: 97–124), Beard, North and Price (1998: 26–7), Santangelo (2008), Ager (2009: 17–25), Rich (2011: 187–90, 2013: 559–64). For a comprehensive overview of relevant scholarship, cf. Santangelo (2008: 63–4, nn. 1–2).

[24] The concept of 'just war' was likely well embedded in earlier Roman culture, but we only find developed views on it in the first century BCE. Cicero (*Off.* 1.11) discusses when it is just to commence a war, namely when others have harmed or threaten to harm the Romans, and emphasizes that no war is just or pious, unless a formal declaration of war has been made by the *fetiales* (see Ager (2009: 21–2), Cornwell (2015: 335–7)). For *bellum iustum* in association with the *fetiales*, see Cic. *Off.* 3.30.107–8, *Rep.* 2.17, 2.31; Livy 1.32.12, 42.47.8; Dion. Hal. 2.72.4.

While outlining the history of the fetial priesthood is quite complicated, as much of our evidence dates to the imperial period, the *fetiales* appear to have been active throughout the Republic.[25] Fetial ritual was certainly in the public eye during the imperial period,[26] when Augustus revived certain fetial rituals that were probably little known by then, although there must have been an established tradition for them, and incorporated them in the construction and justification of his autocratic regime. This includes Augustus's version of the fetial declaration of a just war by means of throwing a spear into the *ager quasi hostilis* near the Columna Bellica in an effort to officially declare war against Mark Antony and Cleopatra, as well as his closure of the so-called Gates of War.[27] Now most of our evidence regarding fetial rituals of war derives from antiquarian constructions of around this time.[28] In fact, sources on the fetial priesthood – mainly Livy (1.24.4–9, 32.6–10) and Dionysius of Halicarnassus (2.72.6–8) – mostly date from the early Principate onwards.[29] But fetial ritual procedures will probably not have been as clearly defined as these constructions may make us think. In fact, Livy's accounts appear to conflate fetial rituals,[30] and Virgil's rituals of war in the *Aeneid* evoke different aspects of fetial rituals too.[31] It is these recent and conflated fetial rituals of war that Lucan engages with in this passage.

Moreover, Caesar himself had a background in priesthood: as a young man he was nominated for the office of *flamen Dialis*. Later, he was elected to the pontificate and eventually he became *pontifex maximus*.[32] He also had personal experience with one of the fetials' practices: *deditio*, the surrender of Romans who had not adhered to fetial procedures or treaties, in order to deflect divine punishment from Rome.[33] In 55 BCE, Cato argued that Caesar should be surrendered to two German tribes, the Tencteri and Usipetes, since he had attacked them during a truce and massacred their diplomats.[34] Although Cato's motion was met with contempt and the *deditio* did not take place, Caesar can be seen to justify his actions in his *Gallic Wars*: he explains that he had to act swiftly to avoid a more serious war, as the Germans' supposedly violent behaviour constituted an increasing danger.[35] This is only one instance of diplomacy and rituals of

---

[25] See recently Santangelo (2008), Rich (2011: 190), Zollschan (2012: 119–44).

[26] Beard *et al.* (1998: 186), Rich (2011: 189): although it was probably one of the lesser priesthoods, the fetial college in the imperial period included members of the imperial family and some distinguished senators. See Rüpke (2008: 973–4) for a list of thirty-five *fetiales* in the imperial period, subsequently supplemented by Zollschan (2009).

[27] Rich (2013: 544, 561). As he explicitly mentions in his *Res Gestae* (*RG* 7), Augustus was a *fetialis* himself. On the closure of the Gates of War, cf. *RG* 13 and DeBrohun (2007: 258–60).

[28] Rich (2013: 595–64).

[29] See also e.g. Var. *Ling.* 5.86; Cic. *Leg.* 2.9, *Off.* 1.11; Livy 9.5, 10.45, 30.43; Plin. *HN* 22.2–3; Plut. *Num.* 12.3–5; Suet. *Claud.* 22, 25.5; Serv. 1.62, 9.52–3, 10.14.

[30] Rich (2013: 561–2).

[31] Cf. the opening of the Gates of War in Verg. *Aen.* 7.601–17 with Horsfall (2000: 391–2) and DeBrohun (2007: 263–9). I briefly discuss fetial treaty solemnization in the *Aeneid* below (pp. 169–70).

[32] It is generally agreed upon that Caesar was never inaugurated as *flamen Dialis*. Cf. Taylor (1941: 113–16) and Ridley (2000: 214–15).

[33] For *deditio*, see Rüpke (1990: 110–11), Ager (2009: 22), Rich (2011: 195–9).

[34] Cf. Plut. *Cat. Min.* 51.1-2, *Caes.* 22.4, *Comp. Nic. et Crass.* 4.3; Suet. *Iul.* 24.3.

[35] Caes. *BGal.* 4. Cf. Powell (2009), Morrell (2015).

war in Caesar's works. Notably, such diplomatic moments typically affect the pace of the narrative in strategic ways: Suzanne Adema discusses how, in Caesar's *Civil War*, long speeches that slow down the narrative tempo frequently occur in episodes in which diplomatic efforts are emphasized, but notes that the narrator focuses more on physical actions when negotiations are finished – or when they seem pointless from the start.[36] We will see that Caesar's strategic diplomacy contributes to the pace of Lucan's narrative too. Thus, Caesar's priesthood as *pontifex maximus* – undoubtedly still known to many people in Lucan's time due to his introduction of the Julian calendar – as well as his personal experience with diplomatic practices and rituals of war serve as a fertile background for Lucan's Rubicon passage.

5 Caesar's response: an invocation of ancient Roman gods

By travelling to the enemy's frontier and standing just outside it, Caesar has already fulfilled the first step of the fetial procedure of declaring war.[37] He then invokes a selection of gods to testify that his demands and actions are just, makes an implied demand – namely that he can cross the boundary as *Patria*'s *miles* rather than as citizen – and assigns blame to Pompey, his enemy. These actions are reminiscent of the three phases of fetial war declaration, namely *rerum repetitio* (stating one's complaints and demands at the enemy's frontier and swearing by a selection of gods that they are just), *testatio* (returning to the enemy's boundary and calling upon the gods to witness that people's injustice and the Romans' legitimate cause), and *indictio belli* (the official war declaration, a speech indicting the guilty party possibly accompanied by the throwing of a spear into the hostile territory).[38] Just as in Livy, these phases are conflated both with each other and with additional fetial rituals, including the solemnization of treaties. To start with, Caesar begins his speech with an invocation of several gods (1.195–200):

> mox ait 'o magnae qui moenia prospicis urbis
> Tarpeia de rupe Tonans Phrygiique penates
> gentis Iuleae et rapti secreta Quirini
> et residens celsa Latiaris Iuppiter Alba
> Vestalesque foci summique o numinis instar
> Roma, fave coeptis ...'

> At last he speaks: 'O Thunderer, surveying great Rome's
> walls from the Tarpeian Rock; O Phrygian house-gods of Iulus's clan

---

[36] Adema (2016: 225 and 2017: 237–9).
[37] Ogilvie (1965: 111), Rüpke (1990: 101–3). Cf. e.g. Livy 1.24.6, 8.14.5; Plin. *HN* 1.1.70; Serv. 9.52, 12.120.
[38] For a more elaborate discussion of the phases of fetial war declaration, see Holland (1961: 61–2), Ogilvie (1965: 127–8), Rüpke (1990: 99–109), Rich (2011). As discussed earlier, this is unlikely to be an accurate representation of the ritual as it was historically performed (Rich 2011 and 2013).

and mysteries of Quirinus, who was carried off to heaven;
O Jupiter of Latium, seated in lofty Alba,
and hearths of Vesta; O Rome, the equal of the highest
deity, favour my plans ...'

Firstly, in an act reminiscent of the oaths by Jupiter sworn in fetial ritual,[39] Caesar addresses Jupiter. The reference to the Tarpeian Rock recalls a historical paradigm of treachery,[40] since notorious criminals were hurled off the Rock to their deaths. Clearly, Caesar has understood *Patria*'s warning and is aware of what awaits him, should he transgress the law. Moreover, the temple of Jupiter Tonans was close to the Tarpeian Rock. This temple played an important role in the fetial ritual of solemnizing a *foedus*, a treaty.[41] The invocation of Jupiter Tonans, combined with the reference to the Tarpeian Rock and its associations of solemnizing and entering into treaties, makes it likely that Jupiter is called upon here as a witness to Caesar's speech in his capacity as the divine law-maker.[42] Caesar is here as Rome's *miles* (1.202), for the benefit of the state: may Jupiter strike him down with his thunderbolt, a common punishment for breaking a fetial treaty, if he is not.[43]

Caesar also calls upon Quirinus (1.197), which is usually interpreted as Caesar emphasizing his claim to Aeneas's heritage.[44] Quirinus was also called upon in the fetial *testatio* as an epithet of Janus,[45] and features in Polybius's account as one of the gods by whom the treaty between the Romans and Carthaginians was sworn in 279 BCE (Polyb. 3.25). The invocation might also have evoked memories of Janus Quirinus, whose temple doors – the so-called Gates of War presumably dating back to early Rome – were closed by Augustus to signal the pacification of the Empire through his victory in the civil war with Mark Antony and Cleopatra.[46] This aspect of Janus Quirinus, peace through victory, would have been particularly welcome to Augustan Rome after generations of (civil) wars. Lucan's Caesar here anticipates an idea that is specified later in his speech: the Republic needs to be pacified through Caesar's victory in this civil war, just as Augustus's victory paved the way for a pacified Principate. Thus, Quirinus's name with its connotations evokes a concern with the proper (ritual) beginnings and endings of wars that date back to early Roman times and that were particularly present in Roman society

---

[39] Livy 1.32.6–7, 1.32.10; Dion. Hal. 2.72.6, 2.72.8.

[40] Roche (2009: 212).

[41] Var. *Ling.* 5.41. See Springer (1954: 28).

[42] A similar invocation of Jupiter Tonans is found in Book 8, where Pompey refers to his seemingly fetial treaty with the Parthians (8.218–20). See below, pp. 165–6.

[43] The priest would swear that the Romans would not break the treaty, and if they would, Jupiter should smite them – much as the priest then struck a pig with a flint. Cf. Livy 1.24.7–9.

[44] Roche (2009: 212).

[45] Cf. Livy 1.32.10. Livy's manuscripts read *Iuno Quirine*, which has been emendated to *Iane Quirine*, as *et tu* indicates only one other god rather than two, and as the god Janus Quirinus is attested in several sources (cf. Aug. *RG.* 13; Hor. *Carm.* 4.15.9; Suet. *Aug.* 22; Macr. *Sat.* 1.9.16). For discussion, cf. e.g. Schilling (1960), Holland (1961: 60), Ogilvie (1965: 131–2).

[46] Quirinus as epithet for Janus was particularly favoured by Augustus (*RG* 13) and appears in Augustan literature onwards.

since Augustus's embracement and revival of them. As such, Lucan's Caesar anticipates and recalls Augustus's strategic employment of war rituals.

Next, Caesar invokes Jupiter *Latiaris*. This cult title belonged to Jupiter as he was worshipped on Mons Albanus, as the god of the Latin League. The League annually celebrated the *feriae Latinae* in his honour, when its members reinforced and honoured their ancient treaty through ritual sacrifice and a common meal.[47] In Republican times, the consuls were in charge of the festival: enacting the rituals properly bestowed them with authority and divine sanction and allowed them to leave Rome for provinces or military campaigns.[48] Caesar himself had a special relationship with the *feriae Latinae*, not in the least because the festival took place on Mons Albanus of which the *gens Iulia* was the custodian. Despite being in a hurry to chase Pompey to Greece in 49 BCE, Caesar took the time to celebrate the festival.[49] Following a passage about Caesar's acquisition and abuse of a range of powers and offices, Lucan describes Caesar's celebration of the *feriae Latinae*, that, the poet says, Jupiter Latiaris did not even deserve after Latium was conquered by the general (5.400–2). Caesar's invocation of Jupiter *Latiaris* therefore anticipates and evokes memories of his conquest of Italy and rise to power through civil war, which stands in stark contrast to the god's original association with the ancient treaty between the members of the Latin League.

Finally, Caesar calls upon Roma in what can be seen as the second important invocation of the fetials' *rerum repetitio* – in addition to Jupiter's invocation – namely that of the boundaries of the respective people.[50] Caesar emphasizes that Roma is equal to the other deities invoked (1.199: *summique o numinis instar*), one of several allusions to an episode in Book 8 that is connected to Caesar's Rubicon passage both intertextually and thematically.

Following Pompey's request to Deiotarus, king of Galatia, to deliver a request for assistance to the Parthian king (8.202–40), Pompey addresses an assembly of senators in an effort to legitimize his plan to enlist the Parthians' help against Caesar. In his speech, Pompey adapts the formula **numinis instar** and replaces *numinis* with *patriae* (8.262–3: *comites bellique fugaeque | atque* ***instar patriae***). He emphasizes that they still represent Italy despite having fled: essentially, the senate is having a meeting in exile.[51] Thus, Pompey's *instar patriae* calls attention to the decentralization of Rome and the Roman world prompted by Caesar's crossing of the Rubicon and his advance on Rome.[52]

Pompey's proposition to the Parthians also includes a reminder of the ancient treaties sworn between him and the Parthians (8.218–20):

---

[47] Cf. Fowler (1899: 95–7), Pasqualini (1996), Grandazzi (2008: 517–729), Simón (2011: 95–7). Cf. Var. *Ling.* 6.25; Livy 32.1; Dion. Hal. 4.49; Plin. *HN* 3.68; Macrob. *Sat.* 1.16.15.
[48] Simón (2011: 116–8, 124–6). If the consuls would not do so, they would be subject to failure, as befell C. Flaminius in 218 BCE and the consuls Aulus Hirtius and Vibius Pansa in 43 BCE (cf. respectively Livy 21.63.5–9, 22.1.4–7 and Cass. Dio 46.33–4).
[49] Caes. *BCiv.* 3.2. On Caesar and the *feriae Latinae*, see Pasqualini (1996: 251), Smith (2012: 275ff.), Luke (2014: 125ff.).
[50] Feeney (1991: 294) notes that the Republic's *Patria* speaks to Caesar, who invokes imperial Roma instead.
[51] Cf. 8.260–327. Cf. Roche (2009: 212–3).
[52] On this passage, and on geographic disorder in the *Civil War* more generally, see Ahl (1976: 170–3), Masters (1992: 93–9), Rossi (2000), Bexley (2014), as well as Reitz-Joosse (in this volume).

> si **foedera** nobis
> **prisca** manent mihi **per Latium** iurata **Tonantem**,
> per vestros astricta magos, ...

> If your former pact
> with me remains in force – the pact I swore by the Thunderer of Latium,
> the pact your holy men ratified – ...

Whether this treaty was historically sworn or not,[53] the reference to Jupiter *Tonans* suggests a fetial *foedus* and the additional reference to Latium evokes Caesar's invocation of both Jupiter *Tonans* and Jupiter *Latiaris*. Pompey's request also includes an appeal to Parthia to burst from her bounds and cross the Euphrates (9.235–6):

> tot meritis obstricta meis nunc Parthia ruptis
> excedat claustris **vetitam** per saecula **ripam** ...

> Now let Parthia, bound by all my services, break through
> her boundaries and cross the bank forbidden through the centuries ...

Pompey's words evoke Caesar's Rubicon crossing (1.223–5):

> Caesar, ut adversam superato gurgite **ripam**
> attigit, Hesperiae **vetitis** et constitit **arvis** ...

> When Caesar had crossed the flood and reached the opposite
> bank, on Hesperia's forbidden fields he took his stand ...

The intertext suggests a parallel between the Rubicon and the Euphrates, with both rivers representing the boundaries of the Roman Empire with respectively Gaul and Parthia.[54] The connection between the passages is established further by the words with which Pompey ends the speech to his troops, identical both in wording and position to Caesar's final invocation: *Roma, fave coeptis*; 'Rome, smile on my enterprise' (1.200 and 8.322).

Both rivals' enterprises cross multiple boundaries. Caesar's quest crosses moral, political and legal boundaries and allows civil war to enter the Roman Empire. Pompey, on the other hand, suggests resorting to barbarian troops to fight his war for him, thereby potentially enabling them to defeat the Romans. This is emphasized by Lentulus, who perceives Pompey's request to enlist the stereotypically barbarian Parthians as a danger

---

[53] Mayer (1981: 115) follows Lintott (1971: 501, n. 14) in concluding that there is no good evidence for an actual treaty and suggests that Lucan might have been thinking of the Parthian embassy to Pompey in 63 BCE in Syria (cf. App. *Mith.* 106; Plut. *Pomp.* 39.3).

[54] These words are only in such close vicinity to each other here and in 10.330: *modumque **vetat** crescendi ponere **ripas***, 'and [Memphis] forbids your banks to set a limit to your growth'; the final words of priest Acoreus's lengthy Nile-description. This intertext is less relevant to my discussion because grammar and context are different, but it is interesting that these similar words occur in a description of another river that fascinated the Romans.

not only to the Roman Empire itself, but also to what makes the Romans Roman.[55] Pompey's proposal is as dangerous for the Roman Empire and its values – if not more so – as Caesar's invasion of Italy. Thus, both generals are positioned on boundaries between outside and inside space and threaten to collapse them; Caesar by breaking the law and bringing in his army, and Pompey by bringing in the Parthians, thereby endangering the Empire and its values and habits. As such, Caesar's final invocation of Roma is heavily loaded: it represents the culmination of his invocations, aligns Rome with the other deities, but the connection with Pompey's dangerous request for Parthian assistance in Book 8 also underlines both the willingness of both generals to employ war and treaty rituals in ways that endanger the Roman state.

So Caesar, standing on the border of Italy, invokes a selection of gods that, in addition to prefiguring the Julio-Claudian dynasty, recalls early Roman times in which there was a great concern with (fetial) ritual war preparations, negotiations and treaty solemnizations. Caesar seems to be evoking these rituals in order to legitimize his 'enterprise' (*coeptis*, 1.200): his civil war against Pompey and the Roman Republic. Caesar then continues this diplomatic effort by stating his complaints and demands, an action typically part of the *rerum repetitio*.[56] The second part of his speech consists mostly of a justification for his imminent attack on Rome, an (implied) demand to continue as *miles* rather than as citizen, and an assignment of guilt to Pompey, who, Caesar complains, is the one who has made him into Rome's enemy (1.200–3):

> non te furialibus armis
> persequor: en, adsum **victor terraque marique**
> Caesar, **ubique tuus (liceat modo, nunc quoque) miles**.
> ille erit ille nocens, qui me tibi fecerit hostem.

> Not with impious weapons
> do I pursue you – here am I, Caesar, conqueror by land and sea,
> your own soldier everywhere, now too if I am permitted.
> The man who makes me your enemy, it is he will be the guilty one.

Caesar actively refrains from a belligerent attitude whilst justifying his war declaration. He emphasizes the defensive nature of his actions: he is not attacking his *patria* in frantic warfare (1.200), but Pompey is forcing him to declare war on Rome (*ille nocens*, 1.203).[57] Simultaneously, his language is militant and betrays his intentions: he describes himself as *victor* (1.201) and *miles* (1.202).

---

[55] Rossi (2000) discusses Pompey's journey from Italy to the East in the *Civil War* as an inverted parallel of Aeneas's journey from the East to Latium, one of several ways in which the poem shows geographical disorder (see n. 52).

[56] Cf. Livy 1.32.6–7; Dion. Hal. 2.72.6.

[57] In reaction to *Patria*'s emphasis on Caesar's transgression of the law (1.190–2), Caesar's speech contains legal language too. By calling Pompey *nocens*, a word strongly associated with crime and guilt (cf. *OLD*, s.v. *nocens* 2), he transforms himself from an active agent waging an unlawful war to a man forced to embark on this war justifiably. Cf. Willis (2011).

Yet Caesar is still concerned with fighting a just war. The words *victor terraque marique* (1.201) evoke the formula describing Augustus's practice of establishing peace through military victory.[58] This, in addition to Quirinus's invocation earlier, suggests that Lucan's Caesar seeks to justify his actions by aligning his advance on Rome with Augustus's later pacification of the Roman Empire. The essential difference is that Caesar's empire has not been pacified yet. Rather, Caesar is on a mission to achieve this goal, and now indirectly asks *Patria* for permission (*liceat modo*, 1.202) to continue his quest by marching on Rome as a soldier: a justifying demand that could be seen as the demands characteristic of the *rerum repetitio*.

In the second part of his speech, then, Caesar represents himself as serving the interests of Italy and his actions as necessary for the pacification of the Republic. Soon after, however, he abandons his diplomatic efforts. At first, he appears to cross the river hastily (1.204–5): he carries his military standards across the Rubicon, explicitly going against *Patria*'s request and signaling that he is going to war. Caesar does not allow *Patria* to reply anymore, either: rather, through his engagement with fetial war and treaty rituals, he has provided himself with the position of authority and justification typical of the Romans' (fetial) relations with other peoples:[59] *ille*, Pompey, is endangering the Republic, and therefore Caesar is authorized to wage his war.

As mentioned earlier, diplomacy affects the pace of the narrative in Caesar's own works in different ways: diplomatic efforts are often accompanied by long speeches, but there is more emphasis on physical actions when negotiations are finished, or when they seem pointless from the start.[60] Lucan's Caesar behaves rather similarly: his speeches dramatically slow down the rapid narrative tempo with which he passed over the Alps, and his behaviour at the Rubicon can be seen as a diplomatic effort. When his diplomatic 'negotiation' is finished – at least from Caesar's point of view – he undertakes action by physically crossing the Rubicon. Lucan's Caesar therefore corresponds to Caesar's Caesar in the sense that both are characterized by *celeritas* and a diplomatic approach to problems. This enables them to represent war as efficient and manageable, thereby selling war as a necessity.[61] In Caesar's *Civil War*, however, Caesar does describe further communication between him and Pompey through legates and emphasizes his willingness to settle the dispute and solemnize their potential agreement with an oath (*BCiv*. 1.8–9).[62] In this particular instance, then, Lucan rewrites Caesar-the-author. This minimizes and complicates Caesar's diplomatic efforts and underlines the closed nature of Caesar-the-protagonist's so-called negotiation with *Patria*, which in turn highlights the difficulties associated with the justification of this civil war.

---

[58] Aug. *RG* 13: *cum per totum imperium populi Romani* **terra marique** *esset parta* **victoriis** *pax*, 'whenever there was peace, secured by victory, throughout the whole domain of the Roman people on land and sea'. Cf. also Livy 1.19.3 (Augustus closing the 'Gates of War').

[59] A war would be considered just when a formal war declaration had been made by the *fetiales*, but the Romans generally allowed their enemies little or no opportunity to negotiate on this decision (Ager (2009: 21–2), Cornwell (2015: 335–7)).

[60] Adema (2016: 225 and 2017: 237–9). See above, p. 163.

[61] Adema (2017: 238).

[62] Cf. also Cass. Dio 41.5–6.

But Lucan's Caesar does not have the final say: the Italian landscape voices its concerns as well, as the Rubicon protests Caesar's crossing by swelling up (*tumidumque per amnem*, 1.204). So Italy protests Caesar's advance through the medium of landscape, rather than through legal or verbal means, as *Patria*'s apparition did.

The Rubicon's swelling does not hinder Caesar, and rivers will not form an obstacle for the general in the rest of the poem. As a result, at least from Caesar's point of view, spatial boundaries no longer make the legal distinction between Rome's *hostes* and *cives*: Rome has lost her power to organize space,[63] and incidentally, her spatial model of identity. Thus, Caesar's crossing of the Rubicon instigates the motif of geographic and political disorder as recurrent throughout the *Bellum Civile*.

6 Abandoning treaties and seeking war

After Caesar's speech, fetial war and treaty rituals are still implicitly present in the passage. Caesar's hurried crossing of the river is followed by a simile in which he is compared to a lion that, opposed by an enemy, gathers his rage and attacks his foe despite being wounded (1.205–12). This simile is part of a tradition of epic similes wherein a (wounded) lion opposes a foe and becomes angrier.[64] A wounded lion particularly relevant to my argument is found in Virgil's *Aeneid*.

Following his ally Camilla's death and the subsequent bloodbath between the Trojans and the Latins, Turnus approaches King Latinus with a request for single combat between himself and Aeneas. He is then compared to a wounded lion (Verg. *Aen.* 12.4–8). This request for single combat is followed up by the solemnization of a treaty between king Latinus and Aeneas, which contains several elements familiar from fetial ritual: a verbal formula required for striking (fetial) treaties and making vows,[65] preparations for the solemnization with priests wearing *verbena*, sacred boughs,[66] and invocations of fetial gods, mainly by Latinus.[67] However, these particular gods were typically not called upon

---

[63] Willis (2011: 58–78).
[64] Roche (2009: 216). Cf. Hom. *Il.* 5.136–43, 20.164–73; Verg. *Aen.* 9.792–6, 12.4–9; Lucan, *BC* 1.205–12; V. Fl. *Arg.* 3.587–9.
[65] Verg. *Aen.* 12.13: *concipe foedus*. Cf. *OLD*, s.v. *concipio* 12b. In his commentary, Tarrant (2012: 89) notes that *concipere foedus* as 'striking' a treaty only occurs here and in 12.158 (*conceptumque excute foedus*: 'Destroy the treaty that has been struck', referring to the same treaty). Tarrant argues that it could be a legitimate technical term, following the expression *concipere bellum*, but does not mention the *fetiales*. Instances of *concipere* suggesting a connection with the fetial priesthood include Var. *Ling.* 5.86 (*iustum conciperetur bellum* in a discussion of fetial war declaration); Livy 1.32.8 (*concipiendique iuris iurandi* when describing *rerum repetitio*), 5.25.7 (*conceptum votum* when describing a vow), 7.7.5 (*quae ipse concepisset verba iuraret*, again when describing a vow).
[66] Verg. *Aen.* 12.118–20. For *verbena* and the fetials, cf. Ogilvie (1965: 111), Rüpke (1990: 101–3), and Livy 1.24.6, 30.43.10; Plin. *HN* 22.3; Serv. 12.120.
[67] Verg. *Aen.* 12.197–202: Latinus invokes the earth, Janus, the gods of the Underworld, and Jupiter who punishes oath breakers with his thunderbolt. This corresponds to the invocations of celestial and infernal gods, Jupiter and Janus Quirinus (Livy 1.32.6–7; Dion. Hal. 2.72.6). The association with fetial ritual is strengthened further by the presence of *audiat* in Latinus's *audiat haec genitor qui foedera fulmine sancit* (12.200), as Livy uses *audire* in prayers exclusively pertaining to fetial ritual (Hickson (1993: 115–17)). Cf. Livy 1.24.7, 1.32.6, 32.10.

in treaty rituals, but in war declarations: Aeneas and Latinus appear to use a conflation of elements from both fetial rituals.[68] Additionally, Latinus swears by his infertile sceptre (Verg. *Aen.* 12.206-7). Perhaps this sceptre can be associated with the infertile spear that was hurled at the enemy after the war had been officially declared. After all, Livy (1.32.12) describes the fetial spear as *sanguineam*, an adjective derived from a species of cornel that is considered to be infertile by Macrobius (*Sat.* 3.20.3) and Pliny (*HN* 16.74, 176).[69] Maybe Latinus's oath already hints at the treaty's eventual failure: soon after the treaty's solemnization, war breaks loose when the Rutulian Tolumnius hurls a (fetial) spear towards the Trojans and there is an outbreak of fighting between both parties.[70]

Thus, this Virgilian treaty, leading to the eventual fusion of the Trojans and Latins into one Roman people – but only *after* the treaty is temporarily broken for a proto-civil war – comes across rather ambiguously. The conflation of elements of several fetial rituals reflects on the unjustifiable aspects of the proto-civil war between the Trojans and the Latins as opposed to a *bellum iustum* between Romans and an enemy. Lucan's simile, in which Caesar is likewise compared to an angered and injured lion, recalls this Virgilian lion simile and its associated narrative of war beginnings and broken treaties. Perhaps, then, Lucan's simile suggests that the civil war between Caesar and Pompey is like the proto-civil war between Trojans and Latins: necessary to unify the Roman people, but emblematic of the violence this unification is based on.[71]

Caesar's definite rejection of treaties becomes clear in his next speech, which takes place as soon as he reaches Italy's riverbanks. Following a description of the Rubicon that emphasizes its nature as a boundary,[72] Caesar announces that he is abandoning peace and seeking war instead (1.225-7):

'hic,' ait, 'hic pacem temerataque iura relinquo;
te, Fortuna, sequor. procul hinc iam foedera sunto;
credidimus satis <his>, utendum est iudice bello.'

And [he] said: 'Here I abandon peace and desecrated law;
Fortune, it is you I follow. Farewell to treaties from now on;
I have relied on them for long enough; now war must be our referee.'

---

[68] Tarrant (2012: 132) suggests that Virgil does not follow the fetial ritual for making a treaty too closely, 'perhaps wishing to avoid pedantry or blatant anachronism'.

[69] Scholars have interpreted the throwing of a spear into the hostile territory as symbolical (McDonald and Walbank (1937), Rüpke (1990: 107-8)) or magical (Ogilvie 1965: 135): made from infertile cornel and tipped with iron, the spear would attract and render infertile the enemy's potency.

[70] The hurling of the spear also recalls Pandarus's breaking of the treaty with the Greeks (Verg. *Aen.* 5.496-7; Hom. *Il.* 4.68-126), and Laocoon throwing a spear at the Trojan Horse's belly (Verg. *Aen.* 2.50-2 – not mentioned in the *Iliad*). Tarrant (2012: 156-7) notes that Tolumnius's spear is 'almost certainly' an allusion to the fetial practice of declaring war by casting a spear into the enemy's territory. Tolumnius's name also evokes Lars Tolumnius of Veii, who broke a treaty with the Romans by killing four of their legates and was consequently killed by Cornelius Cossus (Holland (1935: 211), Tarrant (2012: 155); cf. Livy 4.17-19).

[71] On the unifying role of violence in the Roman state in Lucan, see Connolly (2016).

[72] Cf. 1.213-22: *et Gallica certus | limes ab Ausoniis disterminat arva colonis* ('and [the Rubicon] separates the Gallic | fields from the farmers of Ausonia, a fixed boundary').

Caesar rejects treaties and officially declares war in a kind of *indictio belli*. He defends his hurried action by pointing out that legality has been scorned already anyway (*temerataque iura*, 1.225).[73] What does it matter, then, if Caesar himself does not play by the rules? Caesar specifically denounces *foedera* (1.226), with a phrase that recalls the doomed peace treaty between Aeneas and Latinus that I discussed earlier.[74] Caesar possibly refers to the disrupted triumvirate (*rupto foedere regni*, 1.4), or to a potential peace treaty with Italy – which, at this point, was not a real option anymore, as Caesar's speeches indicate. Only the war itself will decide who is on the right side of history.

The speech is followed by another simile, in which Caesar's swiftness is compared to a sling-bullet and an arrow (1.228–30):

sic fatus noctis tenebris rapit agmina ductor
impiger, et torto Balearis verbere fundae
ocior et missa Parthi post terga sagitta, ...

With these words, the leader pushed his army through night's darkness
tirelessly, swifter than the whirled thong of Balearic sling
or the Parthian's arrow shot over his shoulder, ...

Keeping in mind the recurring elements of fetial ritual and the concern with proper beginnings and endings of war in this passage, the reader might think of the ritual casting of the spear that completed the fetial war declaration and officially opened the war. Although Caesar is not compared to a spear directly, the bullet and arrow are comparable images that fulfil a similar purpose, especially since the simile accompanies the general's war opening and advance on Ariminum. Perhaps Caesar is likened specifically to a Balearic sling and a Parthian arrow rather than a spear because the *hasta* was a quintessentially Roman weapon.[75] Caesar's Roman identity is complicated throughout the passage anyway: he has just spent a decade in Gaul, and the inhabitants of Ariminum soon complain that they are always the first to witness the attacks of barbarians.[76] As such, Lucan's simile underlines Caesar's status as Rome's enemy – whereas Caesar himself has just characterized *Pompey* as Rome's enemy – and complicates his Roman identity.[77] Caesar claims to be fighting in the interest of *Patria*, but what does being Roman even mean anymore now that he has crossed the Rubicon and set in motion civil war and the decentralization of the Republic?

---

[73] Perhaps referring to the disintegration of the triumvirate, or the senate's manoeuvres, including the expulsion of Antony and Curio on 7 January in 49 BCE. See Roche (2009: 220–1) for a summary of interpretations.

[74] Roche (2009: 221) with Verg. *Aen.* 12.202–3: *nulla dies pacem hanc Italis nec foedera rumpet, | quo res cumque cadent*: 'No time shall break this peace and truce for Italy, however things befall.'

[75] Helbig (1908), Alföldi (1959), Rüpke (1990: 108).

[76] Cf. 1.248–57.

[77] For Caesar's attack on Rome as an attack by barbarian peoples, cf. also 1.483–4.

7 Conclusion

I have demonstrated that Lucan's Rubicon passage shows Caesar briefly slowing down to justify his crossing of the Rubicon and his undertaking of civil war by evoking Roman rituals of war and treaty solemnization. From the perspective of the Romans, these rituals typically justified their wars against others, but in this case, the rituals are applied to a war between Romans. The application of these Roman rituals of war to a civil war – both by Caesar in this passage, but also by Pompey in Book 8, as we have seen – therefore highlights a great problem. If both parties are Roman, which side is more justified in its actions?

The interactions between Caesar and the Italian landscape in this passage illustrate this issue. While Caesar evokes Roman rituals of war and thereby acts in the name of preserving the traditional Roman order and its laws, he does not give *Patria* an opportunity to respond. This is not an open negotiation, but an employment of rituals enacted by Caesar to provide himself with the authority to advance on Rome and to use military force against fellow Romans. Yet we have also seen that the Italian landscape vehemently protests Caesar's advance on Rome: firstly, verbally, as *Patria*'s apparition reminds the general of the legal consequences of his actions, and secondly, physically, as the Rubicon swells up in an attempt to hinder Caesar's progress. It is clear that the Italian landscape does not see this as a justified war, despite Caesar's employment of aforementioned rituals.

The interactions between Caesar and the Italian landscape in the Rubicon passage are therefore characteristic of the civil war between Caesar and Pompey, a war in which lawfulness has been conferred onto crime (*ius datumque sceleri*, 1.2), and in which it is impossible to know who took up weapons more justly (*quis iustius induit arma | scire nefas*, 1.126–7).[78] Only the outcome of the war will decide who is on the 'right' side of history. This is accomplished not only by the two generals, but by Romans themselves too: the greatness of Caesar is in their hands, as the general reminds his own troops before the battle of Pharsalus, and their fortunes are at stake here (7.253, 264–6). Just as the proto-civil war between the Trojans and Latins, and just as the civil conflict between Augustus and Mark Antony, then, this civil war between Caesar and Pompey is an undeniable part of the history of the Roman state, a history in which the reiterative violence of leaders and people repeatedly plays a unifying role.[79]

Bibliography

Adema, S. M. 2016. 'Encouraging Troops, Persuading Narratees: Pre-Battle Exhortations in Caesar's *Bellum Gallicum* as a Narrative Device.' In *The Art of History: Literary Perspectives on Greek and Roman Historiography*, edited by V. Liotsakis and S. Farrington, 219–39. Berlin: De Gruyter.

---

[78] Connolly (2016: 280), to whom I owe my understanding of reiterative violence in Lucan. On the powerlessness of law in wartime, cf. also 1.277, 1.348–9.

[79] Many thanks to Bettina Reitz-Joosse, Marian W. Makins and C. J. Mackie for organizing the Landscapes of War panel where the paper on which this chapter is based was originally presented, as well as for their feedback as volume editors. I am also thankful to my fellow panel participants for their helpful questions and comments.

Adema, S. M. 2017. *Speech and Thought in Latin War Narratives: Words of Warriors*. Leiden: Brill.
Ager, S. L. 2009. 'Roman Perspectives on Greek Diplomacy.' In *Diplomatics and Diplomacy in the Roman World*, edited by C. Eilers, 15–44. Leiden: Brill.
Ahl, F. 1976. *Lucan: An Introduction*. Ithaca: Cornell University Press.
Alföldi, A. 1959. 'Hasta – Summa Imperii: The Spear as Embodiment of Sovereignty in Rome.' *American Journal of Archaeology* 63 (1): 1–27.
Ambühl, A. 2016. 'Thessaly as an Intertextual Landscape of Civil War in Latin Poetry.' In *Valuing Landscape in Classical Antiquity: Natural Environment and Cultural Imagination*, edited by J. McInerney and I. Sluiter, 297–322. Leiden: Brill.
Asso, P., ed. 2011. *Brill's Companion to Lucan*. Leiden: Brill.
Beard, M., J. A. North and S. R. F. Price 1998. *Religions of Rome. Volume 1: A History*. Cambridge: Cambridge University Press.
Beck, H., A. Duplá, M. Jehne and F. P. Polo, eds. 2011. *Consuls and Res Publica: Holding High Office in the Roman Republic*. Cambridge: Cambridge University Press.
Bexley, E. 2014. 'Lucan's Catalogues and the Landscape of War.' In *Geography, Topography, Landscape: Configurations of Space in Greek and Roman Epic*, edited by M. Skempis and I. Ziogas, 373–403. Berlin: De Gruyter.
Bienkowski, P. 1900. *De simulacris barbarum gentium apud Romanos: Corporis barbarorum prodromus*. Krakow: Academia litterarum Cracoviensis.
Braga, R. 2014. *La lex de prouinciis praetoriis. Aspetti notevoli e questioni aperte*. Milan: EduCatt.
Braund, S. H., trans. 2009. *Lucan. Civil War*. Oxford: Clarendon Press.
Campbell, B. and L. A. Tritle, eds. 2013. *The Oxford Handbook of Warfare in the Classical World*. Oxford: Oxford University Press.
Connolly, J. 2016. 'A Theory of Violence in Lucan's *Bellum Ciuile*.' In *Wordplay and Powerplay in Latin Poetry*, edited by P. Mitsis and I. Ziogas, 273–98. Berlin: De Gruyter.
Cornwell, H. 2015. 'The Role of Peace-Makers (*caduceatores*) in Roman Attitudes to War and Peace.' In *Ancient Warfare: Introducing Current Research*, edited by G. Lee, H. Whittaker and G. Wrightson, 331–48. Newcastle upon Tyne: Cambridge Scholars Publishing.
Cuntz, O. 1902. *Polybius und sein Werk*. Leipzig: Teubner.
DeBrohun, J. 2007. 'The Gates of War (and Peace): Roman Literary Perspectives.' In *War and Peace in the Ancient World*, edited by K. A. Raaflaub, 256–78. Malden, MA: Blackwell.
Dinter, M. T. 2012. *Anatomizing Civil War: Studies in Lucan's Epic Technique*. Ann Arbor: The University of Michigan Press.
Durry, M., ed. 1970. *Lucain: Sept Exposés suivis de Discussions*. Genève: Fondation Hardt.
Eilers, C., ed. 2009. *Diplomatics and Diplomacy in the Roman World*. Leiden: Brill.
Fantuzzi, M. and T. D. Papanghelis, eds. 2006. *Brill's Companion to Greek and Latin Pastoral*. Brill: Leiden.
Feeney, D. C. 1991. *The Gods in Epic: Poets and Critics of the Classical Tradition*. Oxford: Clarendon Press.
Fowler, W. W. 1899. *The Roman Festivals of the Republic: An Introduction to the Study of the Religion of the Romans*. London: Macmillan.
Gardner, P. 1888. 'Countries and Cities in Ancient Art.' *Journal of Hellenistic Studies* 9: 47–81.
Gowing, A. M. 2005. *Empire and Memory: The Representation of the Roman Republic in Imperial Culture*. Cambridge: Cambridge University Press.
Grandazzi, A. 2008. *Alba Longa, histoire d'une légende: Recherches sur l'archéologie, la religion, les traditions de l'ancien Latium*. Rome: École française de Rome.
Grimal, P. 1970. 'Le Poète et l'Histoire.' In *Lucain: Sept Exposés suivis de Discussions*, edited by M. Durry, 51–118. Genève: Fondation Hardt.

Hardie, P. 2006. 'Cultural and Historical Narratives in Virgil's *Eclogues* and Lucretius.' In *Brill's Companion to Greek and Latin Pastoral*, edited by M. Fantuzzi and T. D. Papanghelis, 275–300. Brill: Leiden.

Hardy, E. G. 1916. 'The Transpadane Question and the Alien Act of 65 or 64 B.C.' *Journal of Roman Studies* 6: 63–82.

Helbig, W. 1908. *Zur Geschichte der* hasta donatica. Berlin: Weidmannsche Buchhandlung.

Hickson, F. V. 1993. *Roman Prayer Language: Livy and the* Aeneid *of Virgil*. Stuttgart: Teubner.

Holland, L. A. 1935. 'Place Names and Heroes in the *Aeneid*.' *American Journal of Philology* 56 (3): 202–15.

Holland, L. A. 1961. *Janus and the Bridge*. Rome: American Academy in Rome.

Horsfall, N. 2000. *Virgil, Aeneid 7*. Leiden: Brill.

Hughes, J. D. 2013. 'Warfare and Environment in the Ancient World.' In *The Oxford Handbook of Warfare in the Classical World*, edited by B. Campbell and L. A. Tritle, 128–42. Oxford: Oxford University Press.

Jaeger, M. 1997. *Livy's Written Rome*. Ann Arbor: University of Michigan Press.

Konstan, D. 1986. 'Narrative and Ideology in Livy: Book 1.' *Classical Antiquity* 5 (2): 198–215.

Leach, E. W. 1974. *Vergil's Eclogues: Landscapes of Experience*. Ithaca: Cornell University Press.

Lee, G., H. Whittaker and G. Wrightson, eds. 2015. *Ancient Warfare: Introducing Current Research*. Newcastle upon Tyne: Cambridge Scholars Publishing.

Leigh, M. 2010. 'Lucan's Caesar and the Sacred Grove: Deforestation and Enlightenment in Antiquity.' In *Lucan*, edited by C. Tesoriero, 201–38. Oxford: Oxford University Press.

Lintott, A. W. 1971. 'Lucan and the History of Civil War.' *Classical Quarterly* 21 (2): 488–505.

Lintott, A. W. 1981. 'What was the Imperium Romanum?' *Greece & Rome* 28 (1): 53–67.

Liotsakis, V. and S. Farrington, eds. 2016. *The Art of History: Literary Perspectives on Greek and Roman Historiography*. Berlin: De Gruyter.

Luke, T. S. 2014. *Ushering in a New Republic: Theologies of Arrival at Rome in the First Century BCE*. Ann Arbor: University of Michigan Press.

Masters, J. 1992. *Poetry and Civil War in Lucan's Bellum Civile*. Cambridge: Cambridge University Press.

Mayer, R. 1981. *Lucan. Civil War VIII*. Warminster: Aris & Phillips.

McDonald, A. H. and F. W. Walbank 1937. 'The Origins of the Second Macedonian War.' *Journal of Roman Studies* 27 (2): 180–207.

McInerney, J. and I. Sluiter, eds. 2016. *Valuing Landscape in Classical Antiquity: Natural Environment and Cultural Imagination*. Leiden: Brill.

Mitsis, P. and I. Ziogas, eds. 2016. *Wordplay and Powerplay in Latin Poetry*. Berlin: De Gruyter.

Mommsen, T. 1863. *The History of Rome*, trans. W. P. Dickson. London: Richard Bentley.

Morrell, K. 2015. 'Cato, Caesar, and the Germani.' *Antichthon* 49: 73–93.

Mulhern, E. V. 2017. 'Roma(na) Matrona.' *Classical Journal* 112 (4): 432–59.

Myers, M. Y. 2011. 'Lucan's Poetic Geographies: Center and Periphery in Civil War Epic.' In *Brill's Companion to Lucan*, edited by P. Asso, 399–415. Leiden: Brill.

Nicolet, C. 1991. *Space, Geography, and Politics in the Early Roman Empire*. Ann Arbor: University of Michigan Press.

Ogilvie, R. M. 1965. *A Commentary on Livy: Books 1–5*, Oxford: Clarendon Press.

O'Gorman, E. 1995. 'Shifting Ground: Lucan, Tacitus and the Landscape of Civil War.' *Hermathena* 158: 117–31.

Östenberg, I. 2009. *Staging the World: Spoils, Captives, and Representations in the Roman Triumphal Procession*. Oxford: Oxford University Press.

Ostrowski, J. A. 1996. 'Personifications of Countries and Cities as a Symbol of Victory in Greek and Roman Art.' In *Griechenland und Rom: Vergleichende Untersuchungen zu Entwicklungstendenzen und Höhepunkten der antiken Geschichte, Kunst und Literatur*, edited by E. G. Schmidt, 264–72. Erlangen: Universitätsverlag Tbilissi.

Pasqualini, A., ed. 1996. *Alba Longa: Mito, Storia, Archeologia: Atti dell'Incontro di Studio Roma Albano Laziale, 27–29 gennaio 1994*. Rome: Istituto Italiano per la Storia Antica.

Peer, A. 2015. *Julius Caesar's Bellum Civile and the Composition of a New Reality*. Farnham: Ashgate Publishing Company.

Powell, A. 2009. 'Julius Caesar and the Presentation of Massacre.' In *Julius Caesar as Artful Reporter: The War Commentaries as Political Instruments*, edited by K. Welch and A. Powell, 111–38. London: Duckworth.

Raaflaub, K. A., ed., 2007. *War and Peace in the Ancient World*. Malden, MA: Blackwell.

Rasmus Brandt, J. and J. W. Iddeng, eds. 2012. *Greek and Roman Festivals: Content, Meaning, and Practice*. Oxford: Oxford University Press.

Reitz-Joosse, B. 2016. 'Land at Peace and Sea at War: Landscape and the Memory of Actium in Greek Epigrams and Propertius' *Elegies*.' In *Valuing Landscape in Classical Antiquity: Natural Environment and Cultural Imagination*, edited by J. McInerney and I. Sluiter, 276–96. Leiden: Brill.

Rich, J. 1976. *Declaring War in the Roman Republic in the Period of Transmarine Expansion*. Brussels: Latomus.

Rich, J. 2011. 'The *Fetiales* and Roman International Relations.' In *Priests and State in the Roman World*, edited by J. H. Richardson and F. Santangelo, 187–242. Stuttgart: Franz Steiner Verlag.

Rich, J. 2013. 'Roman Rituals of War.' In *The Oxford Handbook of Warfare in the Classical World*, edited by B. Campbell and L. A. Tritle, 542–68. Oxford: Oxford University Press.

Richardson, J. H. and F. Santangelo, eds. 2011. *Priests and State in the Roman World*. Stuttgart: Franz Steiner Verlag.

Ridley, R. T. 2000. 'The Dictator's Mistake: Caesar's Escape from Sulla.' *Historia* 49 (2): 211–29.

Rimell, V. 2015. *The Closure of Space in Roman Poetics: Empire's Inward Turn*. Cambridge: Cambridge University Press.

Roche, P. A. 2009. *Lucan: De Bello Civili, Book 1*. Oxford: Oxford University Press.

Romm, J. S. 1992. *The Edges of the Earth in Ancient Thought: Geography, Exploration, and Fiction*. Princeton, N. J.: Princeton University Press.

Rosen, R. M. and I. Sluiter, eds. 2006. *City, Countryside, and the Spatial Organisation of Value in Classical Antiquity*. Leiden: Brill.

Rossi, A. 2000. 'The *Aeneid* Revisited: The Journey of Pompey in Lucan's *Pharsalia*.' *American Journal of Philology* 121 (4): 571–91.

Rüpke, J. 1990. *Domi Militiae: Die religiöse Konstruktion des Krieges in Rom*. Stuttgart: Franz Steiner Verlag.

Rüpke, J. 2008. *Fasti Sacerdotum: A Prosopography of Pagan, Jewish, and Christian Religious Officials in the City of Rome, 300 BC to AD 499*, trans. D. M. B. Richardson. Oxford: Oxford University Press.

Samter, E. 1909. 'Fetiales.' In *Pauly's Realencyclopädie der classischen Altertumswissenschaft*, edited by G. Wissowa 6 (2): 2259–65.

Santangelo, F. 2008. 'The Fetials and their "Ius".' *Bulletin of the Institute of Classical Studies* 51: 63–93.

Saulnier, C. 1980. 'Le role des prêtres fétiaux et l'application du *ius fetiale* à Rome.' *Revue historique de droit français et étranger* 58: 171–99.

Schilling, R. 1960. 'Janus. Le dieu introducteur. Le dieu des passages.' *Mélanges d'archéologie et d'histoire* 72: 89–131.

Schmidt, E. G., ed. 1996. *Griechenland und Rom: Vergleichende Untersuchungen zu Entwicklungstendenzen und Höhepunkten der antiken Geschichte, Kunst und Literatur*. Erlangen: Universitätsverlag Tbilissi.

Shackleton Bailey, D. R. 2009. *M. Annaei Lucani De bello civili libri X*. Berlin: De Gruyter.

Simón, F. M. 2011. 'The *Feriae Latinae* as Religious Legitimation of the Consuls' Imperium.' In *Consuls and Res Publica: Holding High Office in the Roman Republic*, edited by H. Beck, A. Duplá, M. Jehne and F. P. Polo, 116–32. Cambridge: Cambridge University Press.

Skempis, M. and I. Ziogas, eds. 2014. *Geography, Topography, Landscape: Configurations of Space in Greek and Roman Epic*. Berlin: De Gruyter.
Skoie, M. 2006. 'City and Countryside in Vergil's *Eclogues*.' In *City, Countryside, and the Spatial Organisation of Value in Classical Antiquity*, edited by R. M. Rosen and I. Sluiter, 297–325. Leiden: Brill.
Smith, C. J. 2012. 'The *Feriae Latinae*.' In *Greek and Roman Festivals: Content, Meaning, and Practice*, edited by J. Rasmus Brandt and J. W. Iddeng, 267–88. Oxford: Oxford University Press.
Spencer, D. 2005. 'Lucan's Follies: Memory and Ruin in a Civil-War Landscape.' *Greece & Rome* 52 (1): 46–69.
Spencer, D. 2010. *Roman Landscape: Culture and Identity*. Cambridge: Cambridge University Press.
Springer, L. A. 1954. 'The Cult and Temple of Jupiter Feretrius.' *Classical Journal* 50 (1): 27–32.
Sumi, G. S. 2002. 'Spectacles and Sulla's Public Image.' *Historia* 51 (4): 414–32.
Tarrant, R. J. 2012. *Virgil. Aeneid Book XII*. New York: Cambridge University Press.
Taylor, L. R. 1941. 'Caesar's Early Career.' *Classical Philology* 36 (2): 113–32.
Tellegen-Couperus, O., ed. 2012. *Law and Religion in the Roman Republic*. Leiden: Brill.
Thorne, M. 2011. '*Memoria Redux*: Memory in Lucan.' In *Brill's Companion to Lucan*, edited by P. Asso, 363–81. Leiden: Brill.
Walbank, F. W. 1957. *A Historical Commentary on Polybius*. Oxford: Clarendon Press.
Walbank, F. W. 1972. 'Nationality as a Factor in Roman History.' *Harvard Studies in Classical Philology* 76: 145–68.
Welch, K. and A. Powell, eds. 2009. *Julius Caesar as Artful Reporter: The War Commentaries as Political Instruments*. London: Duckworth.
Wiedemann, T. 1986. 'The *Fetiales*: A Reconsideration.' *Classical Quarterly* 36: 478–90.
Willis, I. 2011. *Now and Rome: Lucan and Vergil as Theorists of Politics and Space*. London: Continuum International Publishing Group.
Wissowa, G. 1912. *Religion und Kultus der Römer*. 2nd edn. Munich: C. H. Beck.
Ziegler, K.-H. 1972. 'Das Völkerrecht der römischen Republik.' *Aufstieg und Niedergang der Römischen Welt* 1 (2): 68–114.
Zientek, L. 2014. 'Lucan's Natural Questions: Landscape and Geography in the *Bellum Civile*.' PhD diss., University of Washington.
Zollschan, L. 2009. 'Review of: *Fasti Sacerdotum: A Prosopography of Pagan, Jewish, and Christian Religious Officials in the City of Rome, 300 BC to AD 499* by J. Rüpke.' *Bryn Mawr Classical Review* 2009.07.58 (available online: https://bmcr.brynmawr.edu/2009/2009.07.58, accessed 10 June 2020).
Zollschan, L. 2012. 'The Longevity of the Fetial College.' In *Law and Religion in the Roman Republic*, edited by O. Tellegen-Couperus, 119–44. Leiden: Brill.

CHAPTER 8
WRITING A LANDSCAPE OF DEFEAT: THE ROMANS IN PARTHIA
Bettina Reitz-Joosse

1 Introduction

This chapter deals with Roman literary representations of Parthia as a 'landscape of defeat' during the principate. I investigate how Roman authors' depictions of the spaces and landscape of Parthia relate to the traumatic military campaigns of the late republic (especially Crassus's disastrous defeat at Carrhae) and to the uneasy diplomatic accommodation between the two superpowers during the early empire. I argue that by writing Parthia as a 'landscape of defeat', Roman authors show how established modes of understanding, conquering and controlling landscapes failed in Parthia.

I focus on the literature of the principate, specifically on the period from Augustus's Parthian treaty up to the renewed (and, for a short time, successful) attempts at conquering Parthia under the emperor Trajan. In the first section of this chapter, I argue that Roman authors reflect on military setbacks in Parthia by questioning Roman understanding of Parthian terrain, geography and ethnography. I argue that they suggest, in different ways, that inadequacies of intellectual control over the area are directly related to the failure of Roman military control. In the second half of the chapter, I consider how Roman authors envisage the lasting effect of Roman defeat on the landscape of Parthia – in other words, Rome's failure to control the landscape in symbolic terms.

2 Geographies of victory and defeat

In ancient Rome, political power was closely tied to geographical knowledge, in a practical sense, since such knowledge facilitated military victory and conquest, but also intellectually, as a way of communicating and staking out territorial control and military might.[1] One of the best-known book openings of all time, the first sentence of Caesar's *De Bello Gallico*, is emblematic of this relationship. Starting with his famous opening sentence (*Gallia est omnis divisa in partes tres* ..., *BGall.* 1.1), Caesar ties geographical control to military conquest.[2] His very ability to describe Gaul in terms of 'geographic space' is presented as a result, and a symbol, of his own successful subjugation of the region.[3] The

---

[1] Dueck (2012: 16).
[2] For a detailed and sophisticated analysis of the stratagems of this opening section, see Riggsby (2006: 28–32).
[3] The categories of geographic, tactical and strategic space are adapted from Rambaud by Riggsby (2006: 24–8).

ethnographic chapters of his work fulfil a complementary function to this mapping of subjugated spaces: for example, Riggsby calls Caesar's 'aggressive naming' of the different Gallic and German tribes 'a gesture of possession'.[4] These literary strategies are emblematic of the perceived relationship between certain types of knowledge and military success in the Roman world. Geographical and ethnographical knowledge were required for gaining such success, but could also serve as an effective and powerful way of communicating them, by putting Rome at the centre of a mapped, controlled and comprehended empire. I argue that in literary depictions of Parthia in Roman texts, we see the reverse of this same coin. Frequently, Roman defeat in Parthia is conceptually tied to failures of understanding the geography of this vast territory and the nature of its unruly inhabitants.

Our assessment of actual Roman geographical understanding of Parthia in our period is hampered by the loss of a number of works which were read and consulted in imperial Rome.[5] We chiefly rely on sections of Strabo's *Geography* and of Pompeius Trogus's *Philippic Histories* (the latter only preserved in an epitome of Justin), and a few chapters in Pliny the Elder. On the basis of these and related accounts of Parthia, scholars of ancient geography have argued that the Roman contribution to the geographical understanding of the region was comparatively modest.[6] Roman military expeditions across the Euphrates had indeed provided a better idea of the very west of the Parthian territory, but for the remainder of the vast territory, topographical understanding was vague, and Roman knowledge about the extension and structure of the Parthian domain relied almost entirely on much older conceptions of the 'East' as the realm of the Achaemenids, Alexander or the Seleucids. Where more precise information seems to have been available, it usually relates to cities,[7] and tellingly, those cities about which geographic writers offer more than only their names are mostly Achaemenid or Hellenistic foundations (such as Ekbatana, Hekatompylos or Seleukia).[8] Information about what lay between those cities, and specifics of terrain and climate in the different regions of the vast empire, remain vague and often contradictory in Roman accounts.

The step from 'what geographers wrote' to 'what the Romans knew' is, of course, anything but straightforward:[9] if Strabo, for example, seems to underestimate the

---

[4] Riggsby (2006: 71). On Caesar's use of geography more generally Krebs (2006) and Riggsby (2017) with further bibliography (80); on ethnography see Dobesch (2001), Krebs (2010), Johnston (2017).

[5] For a detailed study of Roman geographical ideas about Parthia, see Lerouge (2007), esp. ch. 6 and Cameron (2019: *passim*). Lost are, for example, Hellenistic accounts based on Alexander's campaigns in the region (which took place long before the rise of the Arsacids, but would presumably have contained important information about scale and terrain of the region), or the 'Parthika' of Apollodorus of Artemita, a Greek in the Parthian empire, whose work Strabo appears to have consulted: Drijvers (1988: 281).

[6] Lerouge (2007: 238) concludes that Roman authors' accounts of Parthia, even where they are roughly contemporary, differ widely from each other, lacking both a developed tradition and real familiarity with the area. See also Traina (2011–12), Sonnabend (1986: esp. ch. 3.1) and Drijvers (1998) on Strabo.

[7] Sonnabend (1986: 270), and Lerouge (2007: 239–41), who suspects that some cities were known to the Romans as lying along trade routes, but remained 'nothing but names' (240).

[8] Sonnabend (1986: 270–1). About the 'genuinely Parthian' cities, the Romans seem to know much less. Other known cities are those in the far west, which the Romans had encountered during campaigns, such as Nicephorion, Carrhae or Anthemusia.

[9] Recently, Cameron (2019) has shown extensively how Roman geographical writings about Mesopotamia serve to articulate ideas about space and imperial power.

extension of the original territory of the Parthians, and depicts it, somewhat exaggeratedly, as a mountainous wilderness, does he know no better, or does he aim to sharpen the contrast between the humble beginnings of the Parthians and their present empire, and to offer an explanation for their harsh characteristics? And if Pliny describes Parthia as *undique desertis cincta*, is his point perhaps not geographic exactitude but the inaccessibility and inhospitality of both country and people? Nonetheless, the considerable factual differences between different late-republican and Augustan accounts of Parthia, their comparative brevity and vagueness all suggest that a well-defined, unified image of the geography of Parthia did not yet exist in Rome during the late republic and early empire. I suspect that it is an awareness of this insufficiency that a number of Roman literary authors, in the early empire and later, reflect on and narrativize in the texts I now turn to.

3 Lost in Parthia

In a passage in the fifth book of Ovid's *Fasti* dedicated to the twelfth of May and Mars Ultor, Ovid praises the return of the standards that the Romans had lost at Carrhae (a diplomatic feat achieved by Augustus in 20 BCE). The shame of their loss has apparently now been avenged. In this context, the Parthians are described as follows (Ov. *Fast.* 5.581–2):[10]

> gens fuit et campis et equis et tuta sagittis
> et circumfusis invia fluminibus
>
> There was a people, protected by its plains, its horses and arrows, and inaccessible because of rivers which flow around it.

Besides offering further support for the 'vague geographies' of Parthia current in the Roman empire (the only significant river border of the Parthian territory was the Euphrates in the West), this passage also contains a crucial trope of the Parthian 'landscape of defeat'. The *campi* presumably refer to the Mesopotamian plains, which are, like horses and arrows, weapons that the Parthians are imagined to possess and to be able to wield against the Romans. This idea of the 'landscape as a weapon', here expressed very concisely, pervades literary portrayals of Parthia and the Parthians ranging from brief mentions to extensive narratives.[11]

Such an extended narrative, in which this theme is developed at much greater length, is the Parthian section of Plutarch's *Life of Crassus*. Plutarch describes how in 53 BCE, Crassus

---

[10] On this passage see Weggen (2011: 148–9), Wissemann (1982: 120–1).
[11] Fabrizi (in this volume: 54–7) discusses the moral questions attached to making use of specific terrain in war. Östenberg (2018: 251–2) stresses that in Roman accounts the theme of the successful use of landscape as a weapon is especially prevalent when cunning barbarian enemies are fighting Romans on their own terrain, while 'in the areas closer to Rome, both armies are in principle on par when it comes to handling the terrain' (252).

crossed the Euphrates at Zeugma with an army of about 42,000 infantry and 4,000 cavalry, attended by a daunting array of bad omens. The treacherous Arab chieftain Ariamnes, in league with the Parthians, then leads the Romans away from the Euphrates valley and into the open plain (*Crass.* 22.1–2, discussed below). After this (according to Plutarch) disastrous decision, the Parthians continue to wield their native terrain as a weapon once the fatal engagement at Carrhae has begun: against the detachment of Crassus's son Publius, they use the very dust of the plain, enveloping the Romans in a cloud of sand, thereby robbing them of sight and speech, and thus making them an even easier target for the surrounding Parthian archers.[12] When Publius's troops, exhausted by heat and thirst, withdraw to a hill, they offer the Parthians another possibility for using the terrain to their advantage: ranged on elevated terrain, the soldiers make an even easier target for the Parthian archers.[13] Finally, the elder Crassus's attempted escape from the city of Carrhae by night is foiled by yet another deceiving guide, Andromachus, who leads the fugitives into an area full of treacherous marshes, where they lose their way and miss their opportunity of escape by night.[14]

The Parthian campaign in the *Life of Crassus* is characterized by a sequence of episodes which all show the Romans failing to understand – and thereby control – the Parthian terrain: they end up thirsty in the desert, blinded by the dust, lost in the marshes, or exposed on a hill. As Plutarch would have it, it is not the hostile terrain of the Parthian steppe *as such*, but rather the decisions the Romans make once they find themselves there, their insufficient strategic understanding of the terrain and spaces in which they operate, that leads to their defeat. Plutarch emphasizes this point by depicting several situations in which Crassus explicitly rejects an alternative strategy which is presented as geographically informed and therefore more advantageous.[15]

An entirely different and yet complementary reflection on the Roman understanding of Parthian spaces and their navigation can be found in Propertius's *Elegy* 4.3.35ff. Propertius's *Elegy* 4.3 takes the form of a letter sent by a young wife, Arethusa, to her husband Leucotas, who is far from home on military service. Arethusa is tortured by her husband's absence and jealously questions his faithfulness to her. In the opening lines of the poem, Arethusa provides a list of (exotic) locations where Leucotas has seen military service. Of these locations, 'Parthia' is the first (Prop. 4.3.7–10):

Te modo viderunt intentos Bactra per arcus,
 te modo munito Persicus[16] hostis equo,

---

[12] *Crass.* 25.4–5. On moments of obscured sight in battle and their significance in Roman historiography, see especially the chapters by Feldherr and Fabrizi in this volume.
[13] *Crass.* 25.9–10, also with emphasis on the devastating effects of the harsh climate on the battle-hardened Gauls.
[14] *Crass.* 29.1–5.
[15] E.g. Crassus's rejection of Artabazes' offer, who explicitly stresses the advantages of the landscape during a northern approach (19.2), and of Cassius's advice (20.2) of following the river so that the terrain might offer supplies and protect them from being surrounded by the enemy.
[16] For the MSS's *hericus*, Fedeli, Dimundo and Ciccarelli (2015) print *Sericus* (explaining their rationale on 526–7); Heyworth, *ferreus* (see also Heyworth (2007): *ad loc.*)); and Hutchinson (2006), *Persicus*, thus according the Parthian campaign two lines instead of one.

hibernique Getae, pictoque Britannia curru,
    ustus et Eoa decolor Indus aqua.   10

'Now you were seen by Bactra amid drawn bows, now by the Persian foe mounted on his mailed charger, by the northern Getans, by Britain with its painted chariots and the swarthy Indians burnt by orient waves.'[17]

It becomes clear in the course of the poem that Leucotas' current campaign is imagined to be the Parthian one – confirmed also by the final appeal of the poem (Prop. 4.3.63–72):

Ne, precor, ascensis tanti sit gloria Bactris,
    raptave odorato carbasa lina duci,
plumbea cum tortae sparguntur pondera fundae,   65
    subdolus et versis increpat arcus equis;
sed tua, sic domitis Parthae telluris alumnis,
    pura triumphantes hasta sequatur equos.
Incorrupta mei conserva foedera lecti!
    Hac ego te sola lege redisse velim;   70
armaque cum tulero portae votiva Capenae,
    subscribam salvo grata puella viro.

Let not the glory of scaling Bactra's walls, I pray, be worth too high a price, or the snatching of linen robes from some perfumed potentate, when leaden missiles are discharged from the whirling sling and the treacherous bow twangs from a horse that flees. Above all – so may the headless spear[18] follow your triumphal chariot when the sons of Parthia have been vanquished – keep inviolate the pledge of my marriage bed! Only on this condition should I desire you to return; and when I offer up your arms at the Capene Gate, I shall write below: from a grateful girl on her man's safe return.

The mention of Bactra and of the characteristic fighting techniques of the Parthians, who, in Roman texts, always shoot arrows backwards from horses over their shoulders, make it clear that Leucotas is now imagined to be fighting the Parthians.[19]

With this in mind, we turn to a central section of the poem, which depicts Arethusa's activities in the absence of her husband (4.3.33–40):

Noctibus hibernis castrensia pensa laboro
    et Tyria in chlamydas vellera secta suo;

---

[17] Translations of Propertius are taken from Goold (1999).
[18] The *hasta pura* was a distinguished military decoration. See Hutchinson (2006: *ad loc*).
[19] Roman authors regularly consider Bactra not only part of the Parthian empire, but even use it, as Propertius does here, as a stand-in for Parthia as a whole, demonstrating the extent to which Romans envisaged the Parthian empire in terms of Alexander's conquests hundreds of years earlier. See Hutchinson (2006: *ad loc.*) for examples.

et disco, qua parte fluat vincendus Araxes, 35
    quot sine aqua Parthus milia currat equus;
conor[20] et e tabula pictos ediscere mundos,
    qualis et haec docti sit positura dei,
quae tellus sit lenta gelu, quae putris ab aestu,
    ventus in Italiam qui bene vela ferat. 40

On winter nights I work at camp garb for you, and I sew together lengths of Tyrian wool to make a military cloak; I learn where flows the Araxes that you are to conquer, how many miles a Parthian horse can cover without water; and I try to find out from a map the worlds painted on it and the manner of this arrangement by the wise creator, what lands are sluggish with frost, what crumbling with heat, what wind will bring sails safely back to Italy.

Propertius depicts Arethusa creating a 'cognitive collage' of Parthia from the materials she studies.[21] She seems to be combining a variety of media which can offer her access to the kinds of information she desires. It is difficult to imagine quite what is meant by the *tabula* that contains *pictos mundos*. It is almost certainly not a scale map of the region.[22] Propertius may be thinking of a schematic representation of the entire world.[23] Arethusa also appears to be also consulting a written work on Parthian geography (telling her about the different climatic zones and winds, and even about local fauna) and possibly also an *itinerarium* – the most important means of navigation for military purposes, easily copied and consulted, and sure to feature landmarks such as the Araxes as well as distances.[24]

Arethusa is imagined by Propertius as a sophisticated and, entirely in character, slightly paranoid viewer-reader of this geographic material, who asks all the right (and uncomfortable) questions. While *itineraria*, if they were available, could easily tell one how many miles (*quot milia*) point A might be distant from point B, Arethusa is astute enough to realize that this information is not sufficient for the Romans: they also have to understand the terrain and the people and animals who live in it, in order to use

---

[20] For *cogor* in the MSS, Hutchinson (2006) prints *conor* (a conjecture of Broekhuyzen). Heyworth (1999) suggests *coner*, and in his 2007 edition, excises lines 37 and 38 entirely.
[21] On the 'cognitive collage' see further Minchin (in this volume). On this passage, cf. also Janan (2001: 65–8).
[22] On (the absence of) maps in the ancient Roman world, see Brodersen (1995). Others have assumed that Arethusa *is* actually looking at a map (Janan 2001: 65–6). See further Fedeli, Dimundo and Ciccarelli (2015: *ad loc.*). If *chlamydes* is an accurate conjecture, Arethusa's sewing may even be a sophisticated play on her mental 'creation' of a world at home, since geographers like Eratosthenes and Strabo described the world as chlamys-shaped (Zimmerman (2002)) – a suggestion which I owe to John Oksanish.
[23] Brodersen (1995: 101–2) on this particular scene ('Schemabild').
[24] One *itinerarium* of Parthia, Isidor of Charax's *Stathmoi Parthikoi*, survives from the Augustan period, but should almost certainly be dated well after the publication of Propertius' fourth book. On the *Stathmoi Parthikoi* (*FGrHist* 781 F 2, 1–19), see Hackl, Jacobs and Weber (2010: 2.190–8) and Kramer (2003). Since Arethusa explicitly mentions *pictos mundos*, she may be looking at an *itinerarium pictum* – in which different spaces and landmarks (such as the Araxes, or stations and fortified towns) were not drawn to scale, but connected by routes with information on the distance between different stations: Brodersen (2001: 16–19).

information about distances productively in interactions with the enemy. How long would it take not a Roman but a Parthian horse, not speeding along a Roman road but trekking through waterless terrain, to cover a particular distance?

Another emphasis of Arethusa's studies – different climates – is similarly astute. The shift from Parthian topography (37) to climatic zones (39) has seemed to some editors so incongruous that the couplet has sometimes been moved or even deleted altogether.[25] But as Plutarch's Crassus found to his cost, and as we shall see in more detail below, 'climate' is a crucial factor in properly understanding and navigating the challenges of Parthia – or in failing to do so. Arethusa, home alone with only a dog for company, is constructing the kind of intellectual control that the Roman armies 'on the ground' had signally failed to establish. The slightly paranoid personality with which Propertius endows her allows her to put her finger on the specific challenges facing the Romans on Parthian terrain, and her studies painfully contrast with the reality of Roman strategic management of these spaces in the recent past.

4 Failing ethnographies

Closely related to this sense of insufficient geographical understanding is a similar (perceived) failure to grasp the nature of the people who inhabited this unruly land. In Ovid's *Fasti* 5.581–2, cited on p. 179 above, Ovid suggests a fusion between people and land, by calling not Parthia but the *gens* inhabiting it *invia*, drawing on the basic ethnographic trope of the close connection between the characteristics of a particular terrain and the people who live there. In the case of the Parthians, I argue, this close relationship is conceived of as working to the Romans' disadvantage: fail to understand the land, and its people, too, may surprise you.

In Plutarch's *Life of Crassus*, we encounter an episode which questions Graeco-Roman ethnographic tools (and their applicability to Parthia) very effectively. As mentioned above, Plutarch has the double-crossing Arab chieftain Ariamnes lead the Romans away from the Euphrates and into the plains (Plut. *Crass.* 22.1–2):

Τότ' οὖν ὁ βάρβαρος, ὡς ἔπεισεν αὐτόν, ἀποσπάσας τοῦ ποταμοῦ διὰ μέσων ἦγε τῶν πεδίων ὁδὸν ἐπιεικῆ καὶ κούφην τὸ πρῶτον, εἶτα μοχθηράν, ἄμμου βαθείας ὑποδεχομένης καὶ πεδίων ἀδένδρων καὶ ἀνύδρων καὶ πρὸς οὐδὲν οὐδαμῇ πέρας ἐφικτὸν αἰσθήσει παυομένων, ὥστε μὴ μόνον δίψει καὶ χαλεπότητι τῆς πορείας ἀπαγορεύειν, ἀλλὰ καὶ τὸ τῆς ὄψεως ἀπαραμύθητον ἀθυμίαν παρέχειν οὐ φυτὸν ὁρῶσιν, οὐ ῥεῖθρον, οὐ προβολὴν ὄρους καθιέντος, οὐ πόαν διαβλαστάνουσαν, ἀλλ' ἀτεχνῶς πελάγιόν τι χεῦμα θινῶν τινων ἐρήμων περιεχόντων τὸν στρατόν.

---

[25] Lines 37 and 38 are moved by Fedeli, Dimundo and Ciccarelli (2015) to after 34. Heyworth (2007) excises 37–8 altogether (see Heyworth (1999: 74–5)).

At this time, accordingly, after the barbarian [i.e. Ariamnes] had persuaded Crassus, he drew him away from the river [Euphrates] and led him through the midst of the plains, by a way that was suitable and easy at first, but soon became troublesome when deep sand succeeded, and plains which had no trees, no water, and no limit anywhere which the eye could reach, so that not only did thirst and the difficulties of the march exhaust the men, but also whatever met their gaze filled them with an obstinate dejection. For they saw no plant, no stream, no projection of sloping hill, and no growing grass, but only sea-like billows of innumerable desert sand-heaps enveloping the army.[26]

In Plutarch's narrative, it is Ariamnes who persuades the Romans to leave the proximity of the river and thereby weakens the army because of the difficulty of the terrain and the lack of water.[27] The Parthian landscape, focalized through the eyes of the Roman legionaries, is marked entirely by the *absence* of what, to them, constitutes a 'normal' landscape: trees, water, a stream, grass, hills. The world in which the Romans find themselves is a strange 'otherworld', which frightens and disheartens them. Ariamnes recognizes the weakness that lies in the soldiers' response to their unfamiliar and harsh surroundings, and he taunts them as follows (Plut. *Crass.* 22.5):

ὁ δὲ βάρβαρος ἀνὴρ ὢν ποικίλος ἐκείνους μὲν ὑποπίπτων ἐθάρρυνε καὶ παρεκάλει μικρὸν ἔτι καρτερῆσαι, τοὺς δὲ στρατιώτας ἅμα συμπαραθέων καὶ παραβοηθῶν ἐπέσκωπτε μετὰ γέλωτος· 'Ὑμεῖς δὲ διὰ Καμπανίας ὁδεύειν οἴεσθε κρήνας καὶ νάματα καὶ σκιὰς καὶ λουτρὰ δηλαδὴ καὶ πανδοκεῖα ποθοῦντες; οὐ μέμνησθε δὲ τὴν Ἀράβων διεξιόντες καὶ Ἀσσυρίων μεθορίαν;'

But the Barbarian, who was a subtle fellow, tried to encourage them with all servility, and exhorted them to endure yet a little while, and as he ran along the side of the soldiers and gave them his help, he would laughingly banter them and say: 'Is it through Campania that you think you are marching, yearning for its fountains and streams and shades and baths (to be sure!) and taverns? But remember that you are traversing the border land between Assyria and Arabia.'

Ariamnes stresses the difference between the harshness of the Mesopotamian plain and the pleasant landscapes of Campania, which, in *his* version, feature not only all the characteristics of a *locus amoenus* (such as a stream and shade) but an additional layer of

---

[26] Translations of Plutarch are taken from Perrin (1916).
[27] Contrary to what Plutarch suggests, the route taken by Crassus and his army was in reality the most sensible one, and it also corresponds to the route set out in the late-Augustan *itinerarium* of Isidor of Charax (the *Stathmoi Parthikoi*): see Kramer (2003: 123) for the early stations of the *Stathmoi Parthikoi*, on which see also n. 24 above. The Euphrates valley itself is fertile, but the surrounding area is not, and the valley would not have been able to support so large an army. The chosen route led towards the Belikh river (a tributary of the Euphrates), rather than into an entirely waterless desert: Sampson (2008: 109–10).

culture: baths and even taverns. Through the figure of Ariamnes (both a βάρβαρος and ποικίλος), Plutarch challenges a well-worn ethnographic *topos*: the influence of the climate and terrain on a people's characteristics.[28]

In Graeco-Roman ethnographic discourse, the hot climate of the East was often related to the supposedly soft and degenerate nature of its inhabitants.[29] With relation to Parthia, this idea is, for example, expressed at some length in Book 8 of Lucan's *Bellum Civile*. After the battle of Pharsalus, Pompey considers fleeing to the Parthians to ask them for help against Caesar. This suggestion is rejected by his loyal advisors, and the senator Lentulus stresses the flaws of the plan in a chilling speech, in the course of which he dwells on the Eastern climate and the Parthians' resulting 'Oriental' characteristics at some length (Lucan, *BC* 8.363–76):

> omnis, in Arctois populus quicumque pruinis
> nascitur, indomitus bellis et mortis amator:
> quidquid ad Eoos tractus mundique teporem   365
> ibitur, emollit gentes clementia caeli.
> illic et laxas uestes et fluxa uirorum
> uelamenta uides. Parthus per Medica rura,
> Sarmaticos inter campos effusaque plano
> Tigridis arua solo, nulli superabilis hosti est   370
> libertate fugae; sed non, ubi terra tumebit,
> aspera conscendet montis iuga, nec per opacas
> bella geret tenebras incerto debilis arcu,
> nec franget nando uiolenti uerticis amnem,
> nec tota in pugna perfusus sanguine membra   375
> exiget aestiuum calido sub puluere solem.

Every native of the northern snows is vehement in war and courts death; but every step you go towards the East and the torrid zone, the people grow softer as the sky grows kinder. There one sees loose garments and flowing robes worn even by men. In the smiling land of Media, amid the plains of Sarmatia, and in the level lands that extend by the Tigris, the Parthian cannot be conquered because he has room for flight; but, where earth rises in hills, he will never climb the rough mountain ridges, nor fight on through thick darkness, when crippled by the failure of his bow, nor stem a river in fierce eddy by swimming; nor, when every limb is drenched in blood of battle, will he endure the long summer day beneath the stifling dust.[30]

---

[28] Hartmann (2008: 428) claims that Plutarch himself shows 'kein ethnographisches Interesse an den Parthern', but I would argue that his silence on the Parthians' characteristics is rather part of his portrayal of the Romans' ethnographic and geographic uncertainty.

[29] The 'scientific' rationale can already be found in the Hippocratic *Airs Waters Places*. See Sonnabend (105, with n. 69) with further background.

[30] Translations of Lucan are taken from Duff (1928).

Lentulus here applies the ethnographic principle that a warm climate has a direct effect on the nature of the people who inhabit it. The Parthians, not steeled by mountains, snows, rivers and rains, must therefore be soft and cowardly, and do not even count as a *gens virorum* (385).

The inadequacy of such a simplistic categorization of the Parthians was already apparent to Roman geographers and ethnographers. Lerouge points out that the portrayal of the Parthians in Rome is characterized by a certain 'doubleness', since they are often depicted as uniting or oscillating between the characteristics of 'degenerate Persians' and 'hardened Scythians'.[31]

Ariamnes doubly demonstrates the inadequacy of Roman ethnographic understanding of Parthia and its inhabitants.[32] First, he cruelly highlights the absurdity of the 'soft Easterners' *topos* by contrasting the harshness of the Parthian terrain with gentle, cultured Campania. By dwelling on Campania's manifold attractions, he implies that it is in fact the *Romans* who have been weakened by their native climate and surroundings. Second, the Romans' lack of knowledge of Parthia and its inhabitants contrasts painfully with the 'barbarian's' own superior understanding of the features of the Italo-Campanian landscape: he seems to have an uncanny understanding of what Campania is like (i.e. home to luxury villas and chic vacation resorts), what pleasures the Romans are yearning for, and how this affects their fighting spirit.[33] Through the figure of the Arab chieftain, Plutarch reflects on the inadequacy of the Romans' understanding of the people *and* their terrain.

5 Parthia as another world

So far, I have attempted to analyse the conceptual relationship that Roman authors construct between geography, ethnography and Roman military defeat in Parthia. This relationship closely relates to the rise of a particular image of Parthia during the early empire: Parthia as an *alter orbis*, a different world, divided from Rome by the Euphrates, and often endowed with its own *oceanus*, its own climate, skies, stars, etc.[34] Lucan explores

---

[31] See Lerouge (2007: 174–94) and Sonnabend (1986: 272–88). Ash (2018: 12) points out that this ethnographic doubleness is also touched on in the *Life of Crassus*: 'Plutarch, depicting one Parthian, Surena, tries to unite the two strands so that Surena's effete Persian appearance is said to mask formidable military talent (*Crass.* 24.1–2).'
[32] We are already prepared for this inadequacy in *Crass.* 18.4, where the Roman soldiers realize that what they have been led to believe about the nature of the Parthians is incorrect.
[33] His intellectual superiority is brought home by the word διεπαιδαγώγησε 'he guided them like children' which sums up the scene (*Crass.* 22.6). Campania was indeed seen as a moral 'weak spot' of the hardened Romans due to its beauty, pleasant climate and fertile terrain: see e.g. Sonnabend (1986: 105–6) on Cic. *Leg. Agr.* 2.95.
[34] See e.g. Manil. 4.674–5 (*Parthique vel orbis alter*) and 4.802–5, Sen. *Suas.* 2.7, Sen. *QNat.* 5.18.10, Tac. *Ann.* 2.2–3, (*petitum alio ex orbe regem*), and Lucan, *BC* 8, *passim* (Mayer (1981: 191–2)). This idea is related to, though subtly different from, the conception of a *divisio orbis* between the two powers, as expressed, for example, by Trogus: *Parthi, penes quos, velut divisione orbis cum Romanis facta, nunc Orientis imperium est* (Just. *Epit.* 41.1.1). See Sonnabend (1986: 202) on this and further passages and the conceptions behind them.

(and problematizes) this 'two worlds' concept in the greatest detail. When Pompey, after Pharsalus, dispatches King Deiotarus as an emissary to the Parthians, he tells him (Lucan, *BC* 8.211–14):

> 'quando' ait 'Emathiis amissus cladibus orbis,
> qua Romanus erat, superest, fidissime regum,
> Eoam temptare fidem populosque bibentis
> Euphraten et adhuc securum a Caesare Tigrim ...'

> 'Since', he said, 'the world, so far as it was Roman, has been lost by the disaster of Pharsalia, it remains, O most loyal of my kings, to test the allegiance of the East, of the nations who drink the Euphrates and the Tigris, as yet unmolested by Caesar.'

Pompey's rationale for sending Deiotarus *in devia mundi* (8.209) is unexpected: because of the battle at Pharsalus, the *Roman* world has been lost, which leaves only the option of flight to a different *orbis*: the East, the land of the Euphrates and the Tigris. Those rivers remain mercifully undisturbed (*securum*) by the world war's contamination, unlike the rivers of the *orbis Romanus*: only a few lines earlier, Pompey's ship had passed the mouth of the Peneus, dyed red by the Pharsalian slaughter, and now in turn infecting the sea: *litora contigerat, per quae Peneius amnis | Emathia iam clade rubens exibat in aequor* – 'He [Pompey] had reached the shore where the river Peneus, already red with the slaughter of Pharsalia, passed out into the sea' (8.33–4). For Pompey, Parthia is not a hostile landscape or a weapon in the hands of the Parthians, but a world untouched and uncontaminated by civil war and something like a safe haven.[35]

The 'other world' idea is spelled out even more clearly in Pompey's later speech to the senate in Cilicia (Lucan, *BC* 8.289–94):

> quare agite Eoum, comites, properemus in orbem.
> diuidit Euphrates ingentem gurgite mundum   290
> Caspiaque inmensos seducunt claustra recessus,
> et polus Assyrias alter noctesque diesque
> uertit, et abruptum est nostro mare discolor unda
> Oceanusque suus.

> Therefore, my companions, let us be up and hasten to the Eastern clime. The waters of the Euphrates shut off from us a mighty world, and the Caspian Gates hide boundless solitudes; in Assyria a different hemisphere makes the changes of night and day; they have an Ocean of their own, and a sea severed from ours and unlike in the colour of its water.

---

[35] Pompey's plans do not go down well with the senate. Lentulus, in his forceful reply, picks up on Pompey's depiction of Parthia as a different world, but uses it to illustrate the absurdity of seeking protection there (8.335–7): *quid transfuga mundi, | terrarum totos tractus caelumque perosus, | auersosque polos alienaque sidera quaeris* ... ('Why do you fly from our world, and shun whole regions of earth and sky? Why seek a heaven turned from ours, and foreign stars ...').

Pompey explicitly casts Parthia as a kind of 'Gegenwelt', an entire world explicitly 'other' (*alter*, 292), with its own *polus* and *Oceanus*,[36] and the Euphrates as the dividing line between the two worlds. In the early imperial period, depicting the Parthians as inhabiting a world of their own was a way of coming to terms with the fact that further extension of the empire towards the East had, at this point, proven impossible and impracticable.[37] While the logic of Roman expansionism encompasses the entire *orbis*, this logic is not compromised if the unconquerable Parthians do not actually inhabit *this* world, but a *different* one.[38] And imagining Parthia as fundamentally 'other' is a further means of rationalizing defeat: the crisis of confidence in the geographic and ethnographic grip on this part of the world can be resolved by conceiving of Parthia as a topsy-turvy otherworld, where normal rules do not apply. In *their* world, the Romans continue to be invincible, and their military supremacy remains beyond doubt. The image of Parthia as an *alter orbis* can be considered the ultimate rationalization of defeat in geographic terms.

6 Roman traces in the Parthian landscape

So far we have considered the Romans' narratives of their own failure to control Parthian territory intellectually, in terms of geography or ethnography. I now turn to another, complementary way in which Romans conceived of Parthia as a landscape of defeat. By focusing on lasting memorials of Roman defeat in the landscape of Parthia, Roman authors explore another way in which symbolic control of Parthian landscapes had failed.

The Romans were masters at expressing and communicating the conquest of landscape in symbolic terms – by erecting trophy monuments that visually dominated large areas, by founding cities and colonies, resettling inhabitants or renaming cities.[39] But in the case of defeat, the reverse was also possible. In Caesar's *Gallic War*, an emissary of the Helvetii warns Caesar to take care 'so that the place where they were standing should not acquire a name, from the disaster of the Roman people and the destruction of their army, or transmit the memory (thereof to posterity)'[40] – the exact fate of Carrhae,

---

[36] Mayer (1981: *ad* 290–4): 'Pompey argues that Parthia is in effect a world of its own, and to carry his point he lists its constituent elements ...'. See also his appendix on Parthia (pp. 191–2): '[A]ll four [lines 217, 292, 315, 337] allude to the fundamental otherness of Parthia and its fancied complete isolation from Mediterranean lands. The manner of the expression is linked by two common features: either the otherness is named outright with words of the al- root, or Lucan employs astronomical terminology.'

[37] Cf. Sonnabend (1986: 211): 'Wenn die Parther einer "anderen Welt" angehörten bzw. eine solche konstituierten, so involvierte dies, ganz im Sinne der augusteischen "Erneuerung", allemal eine stärkere Betonung des eigenen Lebensbereiches, des "orbis Romanus".'

[38] See Sonnabend (1986: 204) with further bibliography, and Nicolet (1988: 34–5) about Parthia inside and outside the empire/*orbis*.

[39] See e.g. Hölscher (2006).

[40] Caes. *BGall.* 1.13.5: *Quare ne committeret ut is locus ubi constitissent ex calamitate populi Romani et internecione exercitus nomen caperet aut memoriam proderet.* See also Clark (2014: 32, n. 60).

the site of Crassus's defeat. For example, Pliny the Elder's list of Arabian and Mesopotamian cities in Book 5 of the *Natural History* contains the following section (*NH* 5.86):

> Arabia supra dicta habet oppida Edessam, quae quondam Antiochia dicebatur, Callirrhoen, a fonte nominatam, Carrhas, Crassi clade nobile.

> Arabia above mentioned contains the towns Edessa, which was formerly called Antiochia, Calhirrhoe, named from its spring, and Carrhae, famous for the defeat of Crassus there.

Besides turning the name of Carrhae into a byword for defeat, the Romans also left 'monuments' on the plains of Mesopotamia, as, for example, Propertius points out. *Elegy* 4.6, the elegy for Actian Apollo, ends with a poets' symposium, during which the participants are imagined to sing the Roman deeds of war. After the Sygambri and Meroë, Parthia features, with Propertius suggesting as a suitable subject for a fellow-poet this double-edged praise for the recent diplomatic accommodation reached with the Parthians (Prop. 4.6.83–4):[41]

> Gaude, Crasse, nigras si quid sapis inter harenas:
>   ire per Euphraten ad tua busta licet.

> Rejoice, Crassus, if any consciousness be yours amid the grave's black sands: now we may cross the Euphrates to your tomb.

Ironically, as a sign of their great victory, the Romans are now free to visit the tomb of Crassus: a monument that recalls the murder of a Roman commander and one of the greatest defeats of Roman history.

This vision of Parthia as a landscape indelibly marked by Rome's ignominious defeat is explored most fully in Lucan's *Bellum Civile*. After Pompey has sketched his version of Parthia as a separate, alternative world, a safe haven as yet untainted by Caesar's crimes, Lentulus's reply conjures up quite a different vision of Parthia (Lucan, *BC* 8.431–41):

> non tibi, cum primum gelidum transibis Araxen,
> umbra senis maesti Scythicis confixa sagittis
> ingeret has uoces? 'tu, quem post funera nostra
> ultorem cinerum nudae sperauimus umbrae,
> ad foedus pacemque uenis?' tum plurima cladis   435
> occurrent monimenta tibi: quae moenia trunci
> lustrarunt ceruice duces, ubi nomina tanta

---

[41] The lines play on a motif from sepulchral epigrams, which often wonder whether there is consciousness in Hades. In Propertius's lines, Parthia takes the place of the Underworld: see Hutchinson (2006: *ad loc.*) with examples. For connections between these lines and Prop. 2.10 see Wissemann (1982: 102). Cf. Lucan, *BC* 8.822 and 851–8 for Roman travellers at Pompey's tomb in the (Egyptian) sand.

> obruit Euphrates et nostra cadauera Tigris
> detulit in terras ac reddidit. ire per ista
> si potes, in media socerum quoque, Magne, sedentem   440
> Thessalia placare potes.

As soon as you cross the cold Araxes, will not the ghost of that sorrowing old man, riddled with Scythian arrows [= Crassus], hurl this reproach upon you: 'We unburied ghosts hoped that you would come after our death to avenge our ashes: do you come to make a treaty and a peace?' Next, memorials of our defeat will crowd upon your sight – the walls, round which our beheaded generals were dragged; the place where the Euphrates closed over such famous men, and the Tigris carried the Roman dead underground and then restored them to sight again. If you can pass through these scenes, Magnus, you can also sue of Caesar enthroned on the field of Pharsalia.

In Lentulus' mind, everything about the Parthian landscape screams 'defeat' and therefore 'revenge'. In his speech, the Parthian landscape is the opposite of the 'blank slate' that Pompey imagined: the ghost of Crassus, which has haunted characters of the *BC* throughout, would welcome Pompey on the other side of the Araxes,[42] the very walls of a city recall that Roman leaders were apparently dragged around them,[43] and the rivers of Parthia *are* choked with dead after all – the mysterious underground channel from the Euphrates to the Tigris, described in Book 3, has transported the bodies of the fallen Roman soldiers of Carrhae.[44] Lentulus calls the walls and river *cladis monimenta*: the Roman defeat has turned the very cities and rivers of Parthia into the kinds of *monimenta* that no Roman ever wanted to leave behind.[45] The Romans have left their mark on Parthia, but in a cruel reversal of the usual Roman ways of claiming and controlling landscapes, Carrhae has become a byword for Roman defeat, a major sight of Mesopotamia is the tomb of the murdered Crassus, and the very fabric of the landscape has turned into *monumenta* of defeat.

---

[42] The unburied Crassus makes his first appearance already in line 11 of the poem (*umbra ... erraret Crassus inulta, BC* 1.11). See further Szelest (1979). In this scene, Pompey seems to be entering the Parthian territory not from the West (by crossing the Euphrates), but from Armenia in the north, by crossing the Araxes.
[43] On Lucan's use of *lustrare* here see Mayer (1981: *ad loc.*), who compares *Aen.* 11.190 and *BC* 5.416.
[44] In 3.261ff. the Tigris with its underground course features in a catalogue, on which see Bexley (2014: 362–7).
[45] This scene recalls the Allia episode in Livy's *AUC* 6.28.5, where the Allia is also called a *monumentum cladis* (these are the only two instances of the phrase in classical Latin). The Praenestini expect that the site of the Allia will terrify the Romans, but instead it encourages them to purge their earlier defeat. The scenario Lentulus sketches may be picking up on this scene, or in any case the situations can profitably be compared: like Livy's Romans, Pompey *should* be incited to war and revenge by the sight of the *monumenta cladis*, but instead, perversely, he wants to, in full view of these *monumenta*, enlist the Parthians' help and support against fellow Romans. On scenes of return to earlier battlefields in Roman literature, see Reitz-Joosse (2019). The Parthian *monumenta* also concentrate and refract other scenes from the past and the future of the epic and the epic tradition. Most notably, they foreshadow the death of Pompey, who will end up as a headless corpse (Mayer (1981: *ad loc.*)) and at the same time look back to the dragging of Hector around the walls of Troy. Through Hector, the scene also points forward to the visit of Caesar to the site of the 'real' Troy, another monument of defeat and tomb of his Trojan ancestors.

7 Conclusion

A number of themes and ideas about Parthia as a landscape of defeat in early imperial Rome have crystallized from this juxtaposition of texts from different genres and periods. Roman authors tend to depict the Parthian landscape as defying normal Roman modes of intellectual and symbolic control. Roman strategic and geographic understanding fails to comprehend Parthia, traditional ethnographic tools cannot reliably distil from the landscape the nature of its inhabitants, and as a result of failed physical and intellectual control, Roman monuments in Parthia communicate and commemorate not Roman conquest but ignominious defeat. Ultimately, the Parthian empire has to be consigned to an *alter orbis* in order to rationalize Rome's failure to establish control over this perplexing landscape of defeat.

Bibliography

Ash, R. 2018. *Tacitus: Annals Book XV*. Cambridge: Cambridge University Press.
Asso, P. 2011. *Brill's Companion to Lucan*. Leiden and Boston: Brill.
Bexley, E. 2014. 'Lucan's Catalogues and the Landscape of War.' In *Geography, Topography, Landscape: Configurations of Space in Greek and Roman Epic*, edited by M. Skempis and G. Ziogas, 373–403. Berlin and Boston: De Gruyter.
Brodersen, K. 1995. *Terra Cognita: Studien zur römischen Raumerfassung*. Hildesheim: Olms.
Brodersen, K. 2001. 'The Presentation of Geographical Knowledge for Travel and Transport in the Roman World: *itineraria non tantum adnotata sed etiam picta*.' In *Travel and Geography in the Roman Empire*, edited by C. Adams and R. Laurence, 7–21. London and New York: Routledge.
Cameron, H. 2019. *Making Mesopotamia: Geography and Empire in a Romano-Iranian Borderland*. Leiden and Boston: Brill.
Clark, J. 2014. *Triumph in Defeat: Military Loss and the Roman Republic*. Oxford and New York: Oxford University Press.
Dobesch, G. 2001. 'Caesar als Ethnograph.' In *Gerhard Dobesch. Ausgewählte Schriften. Band 1: Griechen und Römer*, edited by H. Heftner and K. Tomaschitz, 453–506. Köln and Weimar: Böhlau.
Drijvers, J. W. 1998. 'Strabo on Parthia and the Parthians.' In *Das Partherreich und seine Zeugnisse*, edited by J. Wiesehöfer, 279–93. Stuttgart: Steiner.
Dueck, D. and K. Brodersen. 2012. *Geography in Classical Antiquity*. Cambridge: Cambridge University Press.
Duff, J. D., ed./trans. 1928. *Lucan. The Civil War*. Cambridge, MA: Harvard University Press.
Fedeli, P., R. Dimundo and I. Ciccarelli. 2015. *Properzio: Elegie. Libro IV*. Nordhausen: Traugott Bautz.
Goold, G. P., ed./trans. *Propertius. Elegies*. Cambridge, MA: Harvard University Press.
Hackl, U., Jacobs, B., and Weber, D. 2010. *Quellen zur Geschichte des Partherreiches: Textsammlung mit Übersetzungen und Kommentaren*. Göttingen: Vandenhoeck & Ruprecht.
Hartmann, U. 2008. 'Das Bild der Parther bei Plutarch.' *Historia* 57 (4): 426–52.
Heyworth, S. J. 1999. 'Textual Notes on Propertius 4.3, 4.4, 4.5.' In *Amor: Roma. Love & Latin Literature*, edited by R. Mayer and S. Morton Braund, 71–93. Cambridge: Cambridge University Press.
Heyworth, S. J. 2007. *Cynthia: A Companion to the Text of Propertius*. Oxford: Oxford University Press.

Hölscher, T. 2006. 'The Transformation of Victory into Power: From Event to Structure.' In *Representations of War in Ancient Rome*, edited by S. Dillon and K. E. Welch, 27–48. Cambridge: Cambridge University Press.

Hutchinson, J. 2006. *Propertius: Elegies IV*. Cambridge: Cambridge University Press.

Janan, M. 2001. *The Politics of Desire: Propertius IV*. Berkeley: University of California Press.

Johnston, A. C. 2017. '*Nostri* and "The Other(s)."' In *The Cambridge Companion to the Writings of Julius Caesar*, edited by L. Grillo and C. B. Krebs, 81–94. Cambridge: Cambridge University Press.

Kramer, N. 2003. 'Das Itinerar Σταθμοί Παρθικοί des Isidor von Charax – Beschreibung eines Handelsweges?' *Klio* 85 (1): 120–30.

Krebs, C. 2010. 'Borealism: Caesar, Seneca, Tacitus, and the Roman discourse about the Germanic North.' In *Cultural Identity and the Peoples of the Ancient Mediterranean*, edited by E. S. Gruen, 202–21. Los Angeles: Getty Research Institute.

Krebs, C. 2006. 'Imaginary Geography in Caesar's *Bellum Gallicum*.' *American Journal of Philology* 127 (1): 111–36.

Lerouge, C. 2007. *L'image des Parthes dans le monde gréco-romain: du début du Ier siècle av. J.-C. jusqu'à la fin du Haut-Empire romain*. Stuttgart: Franz Steiner Verlag.

Mayer, R. 1981. *Lucan: Civil War VIII*. Warminster: Aris & Phillips.

Nicolet, C. 1988. *L'inventaire du monde: géographie et politique aux origines de l'Empire romain*. Paris: Fayard.

Östenberg, I. 2018. 'Defeated by the Forest, the Pass, the Wind: Nature as an Enemy of Rome.' In *Brill's Companion to Military Defeat in Ancient Mediterranean Society*, edited by J. Clark and B. Turner, 240–61. Leiden and Boston: Brill.

Perrin, B., ed./trans. *Plutarch. Lives, Volume III: Pericles and Fabius Maximus. Nicias and Crassus*. Cambridge, MA: Harvard University Press.

Reitz-Joosse, B. L. 2019. 'Lesen, schauen, spüren: Römische Schlachtfelder als literarische *monumenta*.' *Gymnasium* 126 (2): 127–46.

Riggsby, A. 2006. *Caesar in Gaul and Rome: War in Words*. Austin: University of Texas Press.

Riggsby, A. 2017. 'The Politics of Geography.' *The Cambridge Companion to the Writings of Julius Caesar*, edited by L. Grillo and C. B. Krebs, 68–80. Cambridge: Cambridge University Press.

Sampson, G. C. 2008. *The Defeat of Rome in the East: Crassus, the Parthians, and the Disastrous Battle of Carrhae, 53 BC*. Philadelphia: Casemate.

Sonnabend, H. 1986. *Fremdenbild und Politik: Vorstellungen der Römer von Ägypten und dem Partherreich in der späten Republik und frühen Kaiserzeit*. Frankfurt am Main: Peter Lang.

Szelest, H. 1979. 'Crassus in Lucans "Pharsalia."' *Eos* 67: 111–16.

Traina, G. 2011. 'Letteratura classica e spazio geografico Partico: alcune osservazioni.' *Geographia Antiqua* 20–21: 119–22.

Weggen, K. 2011. *Der lange Schatten von Carrhae: Studien zu M. Licinius Crassus*. Hamburg: Kovač.

Wissemann, M. 1982. *Die Parther in der augusteischen Dichtung*. Frankfurt am Main: Peter Lang.

Zimmerman, K. 2002. 'Eratosthenes' chlamys-shaped world: a misunderstood metaphor.' In *The Hellenistic World. New Perspectives*, edited by D. Ogden, 23–40. London: Classical Press of Wales.

CHAPTER 9
LANDSCAPE AND CHARACTER IN HERODIAN'S *HISTORY OF THE ROMAN EMPIRE*: THE WAR BETWEEN NIGER AND SEVERUS

Karine Laporte

1 Introduction

It was long thought that Herodian's method of composition came down to carelessness, theatrics and pervasive literary tropes. As such, the *History of the Roman Empire*, written in Greek in the third century CE, was viewed as a collection of inaccuracies and errors, be it about places, events, or people. Any knowledge of the years 180–238 CE in Roman history was instead drawn from other sources. Said to be more reliable, despite the similar charges they faced, these were namely the *Roman History* of Cassius Dio, a contemporary of Herodian, and the *Historia Augusta*, an anonymous compilation of imperial biographies published the following century.

Yet over the past decades, most scholars have lost interest in a strictly factual study of Herodian's work. It has indeed been recently shown that Herodian centres his historical interpretation on the representation of the emperor and of imperial power, which he showcases through various themes and motifs.[1] Consequently, modern views on Herodian's method of composition have also been renewed. For example, while Herodian's selective writing was noted early on, it was rather ascribed to his taste for dramatization and his overly rhetorical style. This peculiarity corresponded with a marked indifference for 'truth' and 'accuracy'.[2] According to this earlier consensus, Herodian not only engaged in a dubious factual selection, but also freely manipulated historical data for dramatic purposes. Through omission, transposition and invention, he was almost creating a work of fiction. By contrast, recent scholarship on Herodian tends to consider the choice, disposition and presentation of facts as literary strategies serving to organize the work around a certain narrative and thematic unity.[3]

Although Herodian begins the *History* with a somewhat conventional preface, the inner workings of his method of composition are explained at the end of

---

[1] E.g. Sidebottom (1998), Zimmermann (1999), Hidber (2006) and Kemezis (2014: 227–72).
[2] Among many others, Kolb (1972: 159–62).
[3] Drawing up a list of 'errors' in Herodian, Whittaker (1969–70: xxxix–xl, lviii) concludes that the historian makes fewer mistakes than it seems. Whittaker quite rightly proposes that Herodian carefully selects data for the sake of characterization. See also Sidebottom (1998: 2813–22) and Zimmermann (1999: 6–7).

Book 2.[4] Herodian first claims that Septimius Severus's reign has already been sufficiently dissected by numerous authors before him (i.e. itineraries, speeches, omens and portents, battlefield topography, military formations, losses suffered). Herodian insists that, unlike his predecessors, he has only included events he deemed 'the most important and conclusive' (2.15.6–7: τὰ κορυφαιότατα τοίνυν καὶ συντέλειαν ἔχοντα).[5] The author also commits to covering everything 'which merits attention and record' (2.15.7: λόγου καὶ μνήμης ἄξιον). While this methodological note may seem to concern the Severan episode alone, its effect can already be observed in the work's first two books. Reading these earlier episodes shows that Herodian's factual selection forms the basis of the literary techniques used throughout the *History*.[6]

Among these writing strategies is the use of space and landscape. As recently compiled by L. Pitcher, Herodian's spatial treatment mostly revolves around broad and vague tableaux, often composed of only a few lines.[7] Detailed representations of landscapes, whether natural or urban, are thus relatively rare. In general these are linked to the ongoing narrative, and follow the movements of the emperor or emperor-to-be. These descriptions mostly relate to the provinces, especially those at the borders. Italy is only occasionally depicted, while Rome emerges mainly in sporadic and incomplete sketches. When 'alien' lands are featured, Herodian frequently launches into ethnographical digressions, connecting space to mores, character and military tactics. At face value, some of these spatial descriptions seem to have been included simply out of historiographical convention, Herodian's personal interests, or a desire to show off stylistic skill. But on closer inspection, it becomes clear that these pictures go beyond intellectual curiosity or rhetorical practice.[8] Accordingly, many 'errors' or factual oddities found in landscape descriptions (as well as in the whole narrative) would be, to some extent, calculated.[9] Put otherwise, landscapes are not depicted for their own sake, but with a view to portraying characters.

As noted earlier, detailed topographical descriptions in the *History* are sparse. However, there is a significant concentration of such pictures in the work's numerous battle accounts. According to Herodian, one of the defining features of this period in

---

[4] The inclusion of a second preface partway through the story follows a tradition dating at least as far back as Herodotus and Thucydides.

[5] Unless stated otherwise, all translations are from the Loeb edition. Cf. this passage in Herodian with Luc. *Hist. conscr.* 27.

[6] Herodian points out that his work is addressed to a contemporary audience, for whom the recorded events were still fresh in memory (1.1.3). This may explain, in part, Herodian's pithiness, even if the author acknowledges that a later readership might also derive pleasure from his history. Cf. Luc. *Hist. conscr.* 57 on necessary brevity in topographical descriptions.

[7] See Pitcher (2012: 269–72), with Marasco (1998: 2868–70) and Kemezis (2014: 239–52) especially on the notions of centre and frontier in Herodian. On many aspects, Herodian's treatment of space seems not unlike that of Homer, see Minchin (in this volume).

[8] Pitcher (2012: 272–4): 'in Herodian, the thematic, symbolic, and characterizing functions of space are often linked at a fundamental level'. Bersanetti (1938) had argued that Herodian uses the contrasting themes of nonchalance and diligence to denigrate Niger and idealize Severus for dramatic purposes alone.

[9] Whittaker (1969–70: xliv–xlv) notes that Herodian erred mainly by omission. Citing Luc. *Hist. conscr.* 19, 57, Whittaker concludes: 'This was how Herodian was influenced by the standards of his age.'

Roman history was the rapid and often violent succession of a large number of emperors within a short stretch of time (1.1.4). As a result, the work's storyline is interspersed with constant power struggles. In these scenes, the landscape may hold various functions at the same time: backdrop, obstacle, helper, or even actor. To explore how Herodian uses landscapes of war to construct his narrative and, more specifically, to underline the distinctive traits of his characters, this article investigates the war between Pescennius Niger and Septimius Severus in 193-4.[10] Three episodes from this war are examined: the 'occupation' of Byzantium, the flood on Mount Taurus and the final battle near Issus. By carefully analysing these scenes, it will become clear that Herodian gives to landscapes of war an explanatory function linked directly to imperial figures.

2 Some formal characteristics

On 1 January 193 CE, only two months after succeeding Commodus, Pertinax was assassinated by the Praetorian Guard. With their crime going unpunished, the praetorians then decided to offer the empire to the highest bidder, who turned out to be Didius Julianus (2.6.4–14). Yet as soon as he was proclaimed emperor, Julianus surrendered to a life of leisure and luxury. Worst still, it was quickly revealed that he was unable to pay the enormous sums promised to the soldiers (2.7.1–2). Julianus wasted no time in earning the scorn of both people and army, pushing them to call on Pescennius Niger, then governor of Syria, for help (2.7.3). Niger was proclaimed emperor shortly after, at Antioch; there he casually established himself, instead of setting out for Rome (2.8.9–10). According to Herodian, this delay prompted Septimius Severus, at the time governor of Pannonia, to seek the emperorship (2.9.1ff). Proclaimed emperor by his troops, Severus immediately left for Rome, where he easily overthrew Julianus. With his new title confirmed by the senate, Severus temporarily appointed Clodius Albinus, governor of Britain, as Caesar. In doing so, Severus could concentrate his forces against Niger, whom he thought represented a greater threat to the east (2.15.1–5).

Our episode begins here. Alerted to Severus's imminent arrival in Syria, Niger posted guards at the ports and passes in the eastern provinces, appealed to the neighbouring kingdoms for aid, levied an army at Antioch, barricaded Mount Taurus and took Byzantium (3.1.1ff). Once Severus reached Asia, a first skirmish took place at Cyzicus (3.2.1ff).[11] After a first victory for Severus, the surrounding Greek cities took sides. Nicomedia, Laodicea and Tyre allied themselves with Severus, while Nicaea, Berytus and Antioch maintained their support for Niger (3.2.7ff; 3.3.3). Meanwhile, Severus's troops

---

[10] See Birley ([1971] 1999: chs 10–11) for a reconstruction of the events.

[11] In his account of the battle of Cyzicus, Herodian applies a different literary strategy, hence its absence from the present study. For this episode, he relies instead on the intervention of a third character, Aemilianus, to assume the military action and, especially, the blame of Niger's defeat. Herodian tries to explain the governor's betrayal as either a ploy on Severus's part, or as a case of personal jealousy. On a different note, Cyzicus probably did not amount to a total defeat for Niger; see Whittaker (1969–70: n. 4 *ad* 3.2.2) and Roques (1990: 242, n. 11).

were advancing through Bithynia, Galatia and Cappadocia. Arriving at Mount Taurus, they besieged Niger's army who had taken refuge there. Just when Severus's men were about to withdraw from the pass, a flood caught Niger's soldiers by surprise and forced them to concede a second victory. Severus was thus able to cross freely over into Cilicia (3.3.6–8). After a long and bloody battle at Issus, the Severan troops finally routed the opposing camp, who were quickly caught and massacred (3.4.1–5). Niger met a similar end (3.4.6–7).

Herodian provides a detailed story of the war between Niger and Severus, in spite of its temporal brevity and lesser political significance. Indeed, according to later accounts (and even Dio's contemporary version), only Julianus, among Severus's opponents, is said to have been emperor. Whenever Niger and Albinus are mentioned, they are generally regarded as usurpers and therefore receive minor coverage. Herodian, on the contrary, places Niger on the same level as Julianus and Severus. He achieves this largely by introducing Niger before Severus (as opposed to Dio), which makes Niger's character more relevant to the main plot. Indeed, following the *History*'s narrative flow, if Herodian had presented Severus first, he would have approached Niger more as a usurper, just as he does Albinus.[12] As is, Herodian's sequencing gives the impression of an equal-chance, three-way fight between Julianus, Niger and Severus. To assert Niger's importance, Herodian also uses similar narrative sequences to portray Niger's and Severus's accessions.[13]

More broadly, Herodian devotes considerable attention to Niger. Of the three civil wars in which Severus engaged, the strife against Niger takes up, proportionally speaking, the greatest amount of space in Herodian. Its importance can be understood, at least in part, by considering the place filled by Severus's civil wars in the *History*.[14] For one thing, Severus's reign is among the longest not only temporally, but also in terms of coverage. This symmetry may seem self-evident, were it not for the historian's tendency to freely condense or dilate the narrative. For instance, the thirteen years of Severus Alexander's reign take up some thirty Loeb pages, whereas Pertinax's two-month reign spreads out over some twenty pages.[15] Moreover, Herodian devotes more than two-thirds of his Severan account to the civil wars of 193–7, although those few years barely make up a quarter of Severus's entire reign. Expanding so the narrative enables Herodian to break up this Severan period into a greater number of smaller events. This technique also allows for more frequent and more detailed landscape descriptions, in line with Herodian's propensity to elaborate more on non-Italian space. For Herodian, Severus's reign is thus conducive to a concentration of such descriptions,

---

[12] In the *History*, Albinus only comes up once Severus has defeated Julianus, is marching out against Niger, and is already the legitimate emperor. Consequently, when Severus and Albinus finally face off, Albinus appears more as a usurper than a fully-fledged emperor.
[13] See Zimmermann (1999: 171ff.).
[14] Hidber (2006: 136–42) and (2007: 209–10).
[15] This discrepancy may also point to an unrevised work, especially for the later books. See Sidebottom (1998: 2813 and n. 183), for a summary of the arguments.

since it comprises several internal and external wars, as well as vast and frequent movements outside Rome and Italy.[16]

3 Byzantium

In the beginning of Book 3, Herodian describes at length the defensive measures that Niger undertook in preparation for Severus's imminent arrival. He inserts a rather detailed picture of Byzantium illustrating its wealth, prosperity and strategic position. Although Herodian's depiction is not strictly speaking a city encomium, it shares several of its themes, such as virtuous actions and topography.[17] Byzantium was (3.1.5–6):

> ... πόλιν τῶν ἐπὶ Θράκης μεγίστην τότε καὶ εὐδαίμονα, πλήθει τε ἀνδρῶν καὶ χρημάτων ἀκμάζουσαν·κειμένη γὰρ ἐπὶ τῷ στενοτάτῳ τῆς Προποντίδος πορθμῷ προσόδοις ταῖς ἀπὸ θαλάσσης τελῶν τε καὶ ἁλείας μεγάλως ὠφελεῖτο, γῆν τε πολλὴν καὶ εὐδαίμονα κεκτημένη ἐξ ἑκατέρου τῶν στοιχείων πλεῖστα ἐκέρδαινεν.

> ... the largest and most prosperous town of its day in Thrace, with a flourishing population and great wealth. Situated at the narrowest point of the straits of the Propontis, the city used to benefit enormously from shipping dues and fishing; it also possessed a lot of rich land and from these two elements made a great deal of profit.

In addition to its grandiose tone, Herodian's description includes qualities that are typical for city encomia, such as strength, size and beauty.[18] In a simple but expressive way, the historian piles up terms that evoke power and abundance (μεγίστην, εὐδαίμονα, πλήθει, μεγάλως, πολλήν, πλεῖστα – note the occasional superlative). Notably, Herodian does not mention the city's founding. This editorial decision can be related to the commonly established harmony between city encomia and personal encomia.[19] Accordingly, just as he frequently neglects the birth, childhood and education of his characters in order to focus on their own actions and merits, Herodian disregards the founding of Byzantium. Another reason for ignoring the event could be that it belonged to a past too far removed from his story both temporally and thematically.

---

[16] Other notable landscape descriptions in the *History*'s Severan passages: the city of Hatra (3.9.3–6), besieged by Severus *c.* 198–9, and the marshes of Britain (3.14.6–7), where the emperor led his final campaign in 208–11. See Pitcher (2012: 270–1). Interestingly, Herodian is thought to have drawn some elements of his work from pictorial material, and this may serve to explain, to an extent, the historian's particularly vivid style: see e.g. Whittaker (1969–70: n. 2 *ad* 1.7.5 and n. 1 *ad* 7.2.8), Roques (1990: 11 and 200, n. 63), Potter (2016: 331–5).
[17] For city encomia in general, see Pernot (1993: 178–216).
[18] Ibid., 191–2, on these attributes.
[19] E.g. Quint. *Inst.* 3.7.26: *laudantur autem urbes similiter atque homines*. In Men. Rhet. 1.346.27–31, city encomia combine the headings of praises of countries (position) and those of individuals (origins, accomplishments, conduct).

Herodian devotes the final third of his Byzantium picture to the city's fortifications (3.1.6–7):

περιτετείχιστό τε γενναίῳ τε καὶ μεγίστῳ ἡ πόλις τείχει, πεποιημένῳ μυλίτου λίθου ἐς τετράγωνον εἰργασμένου, τοσαύτῃ τε συναφείᾳ καὶ κολλήσει ὡς μηδένα οἴεσθαι τὸ ἔργον σύνθετον, ἑνὸς δὲ λίθου πᾶν πεποιῆσθαι. ἔτι γοῦν καὶ νῦν τὰ μένοντα αὐτοῦ ἐρείπια καὶ λείψανα ἰδόντι θαυμάζειν ἔστι καὶ τὴν τέχνην τῶν τὴν ἀρχὴν κατασκευασάντων καὶ τὴν ἀρετὴν τῶν ὕστερον καθῃρηκότων.

An enormous, strong wall surrounded the city, constructed out of mill-stone hewn into blocks and fitted together with such close mortises that one might think it was carved from a single block of stone rather than being jointed. Even when one sees the ruins of the wall as they are today, one has to admire the skill of the first builders and the power of those who later destroyed it.

In addition to praising their solidity, Herodian takes a marked interest in the history of the walls. This allows him to link certain moments of the storyline through the rampart's various iterations: construction, destruction, ruins.[20] More importantly, the initial stage, i.e. the construction, crowns the laudatory picture of Byzantium. It consolidates the city's power and serves to express approval (whether genuine or ironic, given the outcome) of Niger's measures.[21] By contrast, the second stage, i.e. the destruction, foreshadows Niger's defeat. The final stage, i.e. the ruins, is perhaps meant to emphasize Severus's harshness. By connecting these moments to his own time, Herodian can imply that the destruction was definitive, as if this was the only lasting trace of Severus's victory over Niger.[22]

There is no such depiction of Byzantium in Cassius Dio's story of Niger's occupation. Dio briefly reports that Niger had established himself at Byzantium, marched from there on Perinthus, but headed back upon receiving a bad omen (Cass. Dio 74.6.3). However, following Niger's defeat, Dio inserts a long and detailed description of Byzantium, where he recounts its sacking by Severus (Cass. Dio 74.10–14).[23] The themes are more or less the same as what we find in Herodian's representation, although Dio insists even more on the military aspect. Dio also talks at length about the fortifications, which he claims to have seen personally, both before and after their ruination (Cass. Dio 74.14.5). While Herodian remains vague on the wall's destruction, Dio attributes it by name to Severus. This would enable Dio to highlight the extent of the ravage and Severus's lack of

---

[20] Pitcher (2012: 270): 'The mode of narration here is mostly unsurprising, with Herodian deploying the scenic actorial standpoint of the anonymous focalizer…, whom he turns, however into a contemporary…, thus making the passage a variation of the "reference to the narrator's own time" motif. Even this limited effusiveness, however is strictly functional within its immediate narrative context.'
[21] Cf. 8.2.2–6, for a similar treatment of the Italian city Aquileia, soon to be besieged by Maximinus.
[22] On a possible reconstruction under Severus, see Platnauer (1918: 98).
[23] According to Millar (1964: 140), the story of Byzantium's siege in Dio, defined as a 'long set piece', was likely inserted, or at least modified, by Xiphilinus.

moderation.²⁴ As for the *Historia Augusta*, the *Vita Severi* records that Severus had managed to occupy Greece and Thrace, but that 'Niger already held Byzantium' (*Sev.* 8.12: *iam Byzantium Niger tenebat*). The anonymous author is similarly terse in describing the city's sacking by Severus: 'many communities, too, which had been on Niger's side, were punished with fines and degradation' (*Sev.* 9.7: *multas etiam civitates eiusdem partis iniuriis adfecit et damnis*). There is no mention of Byzantium in the *Vita Nigri*.

In Herodian, Byzantium belongs, as it were, to a 'non-event'. Following a long description of the city, the occupation itself is not depicted.²⁵ Herodian only mentions that Severus was aware of the situation at Byzantium, namely the city's capture and its defensive apparatus (3.2.1). At an impasse, Severus chose to cross more to the south, near Cyzicus, rather than to attempt an attack on Byzantium.²⁶ As such, Herodian's Byzantine picture may seem strictly decorative. Still this depiction, whose main themes are borrowed from city encomia, allows Herodian to explicate and approve the reasons that led Niger to seize the city first. To that end, Herodian's portrait of Byzantium shows a certain military direction, organized around the stronghold's defence potential, rather than a battle scene.

4 Mount Taurus

Arriving in Asia, Severus hurried to meet Niger. Throughout Severus's journey, several clashes would break out around the continent, like at Cyzicus.²⁷ These battles tend to follow the same pattern: Severus wins, Niger's troops flee towards the Taurus, and Severus continues his advance across the eastern provinces. Falling back to the Taurus, the

---

²⁴ Herodian uses a similar strategy in his story of Severus's sacking of Byzantium at 3.6.9. The author concentrates his description on the destruction of the city's marks of prosperity (καὶ θεάτρων τε καὶ λουτρῶν παντός τε κόσμου καὶ τιμῆς), and fails to mention the wall, or any other defensive device. Perhaps the 'civic' ravage of Byzantium is to be linked to Severus's many struggles in terms of internal politics, family relationships and dynastic continuity. It may also serve to underline Severus's tendency to apply military qualities and tactics in the civic domain, which Herodian deemed inappropriate.
²⁵ Kemezis (2014: 236) views this passage as a good example of 'streamlined content': by this time in the story, the Byzantine episode has lost its relevance for the main plot development, hence its compression by Herodian.
²⁶ Was there already an armed conflict at Byzantium? Herodian makes it seem like Severus launched a charge on the city only after defeating Niger, on his way to meet Albinus in Gaul (3.6.9). However, scholars tend to agree that Severus would never have left such a stronghold to the enemy and, albeit with questionable success, must have sent an army (no doubt under the command of Marius Maximus) immediately upon his proclamation at Rome. See Whittaker (1969–70: n. 2 *ad loc.*), Birley ([1971] 1999: 174–5), Rubin (1980: 97, nn. 57–8).
²⁷ Cf. 3.2.2–6 (Cyzicus); 3.2.7–10 (Nicaea-Nicomedia); 3.3.3–5 (Laodicea-Antioch and Tyre-Berytus). In *SHA*, *Pesc. Nig.* 5.8, there are two battles at Cyzicus, the second acting as the final battle at Issus. Whether the emperors were present or not on the battlefields (see Bersanetti (1938: 361), Rubin (1980: 101), Ward (2011: 158–65)), Herodian seems to distinguish the battle between Nicaea and Nicomedia from the other main clashes, on the basis that it resulted from a decision by the cities, taken independently from Niger or his generals. Herodian ascribes this development to the Greeks' natural propensity for civil war, which renders their particular allegiances mostly incidental (3.2.6–7). Significantly, the motif of fratricidal conflicts among Greek cities comes up several times in Herodian, but only within the context of this war (besides the aforementioned passages, 3.3.9; 3.6.9). Bekker-Nielsen (2014: 230–3), noting the 'staged' aspect of this passage in the *History*, comments: 'Unfortunately, his scenography is incompatible with geographical reality' (quote at 231).

fugitives were counting on the pass's presumed impregnability (3.1.4).[28] Like Byzantium, the Taurus held a key position: separating north and east, the site was likely to check Severus's progression (3.3.2: πανταχόθεν κωλύεσθαι).

In Herodian, the Taurus episode is the longest standoff between Niger and Severus, in terms not only of represented duration, but also of textual space.[29] Besides stretching over the majority of the war, it is not presented in a continuous narrative, but is interspersed with the story of other battles.[30] Furthermore, Herodian routes the intermediate battles of Cyzicus and Nicaea-Nicomedia towards the retreat of Niger's troops towards the Taurus, constantly characterized as secure and impenetrable. The author draws out the main action along the whole length of Severus's march across Asia, by breaking it up into a number of smaller scenes which slowly progress towards a shared outcome. In addition, the repeated appearance of Mount Taurus, always accompanied by a reminder of its strategic location, intimates that the site will come up again later on and more decisively. Indeed, the Taurus emerges as the final destination of all these micro-sequences, in terms of both action and story.

Bolstered by their earlier victories, Severus's troops reached Cappadocia and quickly besieged the stronghold where the enemy had fallen back. In this section, Herodian interweaves landscape description and narration. The site's defensive assets, so far hypothetical, now become actual obstacles (3.3.1–2):

πράγματά τε εἶχεν οὐ μικρὰ δυσβάτου διὰ στενότητα καὶ τραχύτητα οὔσης τῆς ὁδοῦ, βαλλόντων τε αὐτοὺς ἄνωθεν λίθοις καὶ γενναίως ἀπομαχομένων τῶν ἐφεστώτων ταῖς ἐπάλξεσι τοῦ τείχους. ῥᾳδίως δὲ ὀλίγοι πολλοὺς ἐκώλυον· τῆς γὰρ ὁδοῦ στενῆς οὔσης τὸ μὲν ἕτερον μέρος ὕψιστον ὄρος σκέπει, ἐπὶ θάτερα δὲ κρημνὸς βαθὺς τοῖς ἐκ τῶν ὀρῶν συρρέουσιν ὕδασι πόρος γίνεται.

There they took up their positions and besieged the defences, no easy task in view of the extremely difficult route along narrow, rough paths. In addition, the defenders fought bravely standing on top of the defences and throwing down rocks on to those below. A few men were easily able to keep a large force back since at a narrow point in the pass on the one side was a high overhanging mountain and on the other a steep precipice which provided a channel for mountain streams.

Here the impracticable nature of the terrain is at the heart of the action. Either the troops can exploit the landscape's natural advantages or they suffer from its hazards, leaving

---

[28] Rubin (1980: 119–20) argues that Niger, given the small number of soldiers he left at the pass, did not see the Taurus as an important defensive site. Rather, Niger would have expected a direct confrontation in Syria.
[29] Herodian may be describing the Cilician Gates, that is the main passage of the Taurus, although there were also other, lesser-known but similarly difficult passes. See Whittaker (1969–70: n. 2 *ad* 3.3.7) and Roques (1990: 243, n. 21).
[30] This narrative interlacing, affecting both chronology and space, is a technique that Herodian frequently uses whenever he is faced with multi-emperor years, such as 193 or 235–8. For these periods, there is an exceptional variety of protagonists, which alters the story's usual single-focus and narrative linearity and results in an intrication of events. See Sidebottom (1998: 2814–15), Hidber (2006: 199–208), Kemezis (2014: 237).

them wide open to enemy onslaught. To highlight the site's presumed safety, Herodian sets Niger's few soldiers (ὀλίγοι) against Severus's many troops (πολλοὺς). Similarly, the pass's easy defensibility marks a strong contrast with the hardships faced by Severus's forces while manoeuvring through the narrow ways. As such, Niger's foresight is strongly implied to have prevailed over the larger and more potent army of Severus, in spite of his upcoming defeat.

Since it has at last been integrated to the main action, it would be easy to imagine that the site has reached its narrative purpose. Yet it soon becomes clear that the Taurus is still another stage to pass on the way to the story's final outcome. After a last narrative break about the rebellions of the surrounding cities (3.3.3–5), Herodian resumes his story of the Taurus's siege.[31] Although it appeared that Niger's troops would prevail (3.3.7):

… νύκτωρ αἰφνιδίως ὄμβρων μεγίστων καταρραγέντων χιόνος τε πολλῆς (δυσχείμερος γὰρ πᾶσα ἡ Καππαδοκία, ἐξαιρέτως δὲ ὁ Ταῦρος) μέγας καὶ σφοδρὸς χειμάρρους καταραχθείς, ἐμποδισθέντος αὐτῷ τοῦ συνήθους δρόμου καὶ τοῦ ἐρύματος ἐπισχόντος τὸ ῥεῖθρον πολὺς καὶ βίαιος γενόμενος, τῆς τε φύσεως νικώσης τὴν τέχνην μὴ δυναμένου τοῦ τείχους ἀντέχειν τῷ ῥεύματι, διέστησε τῷ ὕδατι κατ᾽ ὀλίγον αὐτοῦ τὰς ἁρμογάς, ὑποχωρούντων δὲ τῶν θεμελίων τῷ ῥείθρῳ ἅτε διὰ σπουδῆς καὶ οὐ μετ᾽ ἐπιμελείας κατασκευασθέντων πᾶν ὤφθη, τὸν δὲ τόπον ὁ χειμάρρους ἀνοίξας ὡδοποίησεν.

… Then suddenly one night there were a series of enormous cloudbursts accompanied by heavy snow. (It must be remembered that the whole of Cappadocia has hard winters, particularly in the Taurus mountains.) As a result, a large, rushing mountain stream came pouring down and built up into an enormously powerful torrent because the normal channel was dammed up and was holding back the flow of water. In the end nature proved stronger than man's invention; the dam wall could no longer hold back the pressure, and the torrent gradually broke up the jointed masonry by the action of the water. When the foundations, which had been hastily and carelessly constructed, collapsed under the force of the torrent, the whole fortification was exposed and the raging torrent burst through it, clearing a channel for itself.

The full, overflowing style of this long description reflects the stream's unstoppable rush.[32] Herodian also encourages the idea of an incident both unavoidable and uncontrollable by insisting on the region's harsh climate and the storm's suddenness.

More importantly, Herodian stages nature as a main character. By contrast, both troops are momentarily removed from the action, even forgotten. This latest confrontation plays off the elements against a natural bastion reinforced by human construction. The

---

[31] Citing Niger's proven kindness (ἄλλως μὲν τὸ ἦθος πρότερον χρηστὸς ὤν) and validating (εἰκότως) his wrath against the rebellious cities, Herodian can instead blame the massacre's severity on the boldness of the Moorish soldiers, said to be 'extremely bloodthirsty' (φονικώτατοι) (3.3.4–5).

[32] See Worman (2015: 141–5) more generally on using water imagery to characterize literary style.

dramatic story of the torrent's push against the wall evokes the battles Herodian has already described: two roughly matched powers, an outcome long undecided, a turnaround, and, finally, a crushing victory.[33] Herodian even depicts the torrent with warriorlike attributes. For instance, the torrent is strong and violent (μέγας καὶ σφοδρὸς); it strikes with force (καταραχθείς); it intensifies in volume and forcibleness (πολὺς καὶ βίαιος). There are other episodes in Herodian where bad weather and other natural phenomena represent obstacles for the characters to overcome, bypass or cross. In those cases, they become an occasion for leaders to show competence or incompetence.[34] Here, however, nature dons a marked agency. As both armies were holding their ground, it was impossible to say whether tempest or fortress would emerge victorious. For a time, the rampart even managed to fetter (ἐμποδισθέντος) the mountain streams. Still, just like an army's fortuitous break, the torrent likewise 'broke up' (διέστησε) the bulwark's formation and forged ahead through the newly cleared path. Under this torrential pressure, the presumedly unbreakable fortifications proved to have been built in haste and finally gave way (3.3.7: διὰ σπουδῆς καὶ οὐ μετ' ἐπιμελείας).[35] Herodian sums up the outcome of this 'battle' in a sententious phrase: τῆς τε φύσεως νικώσης τὴν τέχνην. Beyond any human intervention, whether negligence or perseverance, nature established itself as the predominant force.[36]

When this final line of defence was crushed, Severus could continue easily into Cilicia. As seen, his progression was not made possible by the action of his army, but by the unexpected interference of a third party. With this strategy, Herodian can partially relieve Niger of his defeat, while largely imputing Severus's victory to a stroke of luck. Admittedly, Herodian describes the storm as an intervention of 'divine providence' (3.3.8: προνοία θεία), which is a common virtue in imperial rhetoric.[37] However, it seems to be more a case of internal interpretation, that of the Severan troops, rather than the expression of Herodian's own convictions. Indeed, whenever Herodian mentions 'divine providence', he pairs it with verbs of perception that tend to confine this supernatural belief to certain characters and, as such, to lessen its impact.[38] Even if Severus was able to make the most of it, Herodian describes the storm in its own right, its effect on human activity seeming to be merely collateral.

---

[33] See n. 44 on formulaic battles in Herodian.
[34] E.g. 3.14.5–10 (marshes of Britain); 6.7.6–8 (Severus's campaign into Germania); 8.4 (crossing of Maximinus's army to Aquileia). Fabrizi, in this volume, offers various weather-related examples of these functions in Livy.
[35] Compare 3.1.4 (Niger's orders) with 3.3.7 (their execution).
[36] According to Whittaker (1969–70, n. 1 *ad* 3.3.7), the battle may have taken place in autumn, on the basis that the surprise flood seems at odds with the harsh winter climate described by Herodian.
[37] There may here be traces of Severan 'propaganda', since the expression is generally related to a member of the Severan dynasty (2.9.7; 2.15.2; 4.3.6); see e.g. Manders (2012: 162–5). Cf. 3.9.12, where Herodian similarly credits Severus's victory over the Parthians to the emperor's good luck more than his good judgement.
[38] Cf. 2.9.7 (Severus convinced by omens and dreams to seize the emperorship); 2.15.6 (other signs and omens sufficiently discussed elsewhere for Herodian to exclude); 4.3.6 (Caracalla and Geta inspired by gods to divide the empire in two). This devaluation of portents is consistent with Herodian's relative scepticism seen throughout the *History*. See Whittaker (1969–70: n. 2 *ad* 3.3.8), Kuhn-Chen (2002: 308–13).

Notably, the siege of the Taurus does not appear as such in other sources. Many explanations have been proposed: e.g. Herodian has fabricated the episode; he alone gives a correct account; he has divided a single event (the battle of Issus) in two autonomous episodes.[39] Based on the limited coverage in other accounts, it seems that Herodian is exploiting a pre-existing but poorly defined situation.[40] In Dio, the final stage of the battle of Issus resembles the Taurus scene in Herodian's *History*, in which an unexpected storm breaks out, tipping the scales in favour of Severus (Cass. Dio 74.7.6–8). In Herodian, the storm only appears during the Taurus siege, not at Issus. That said, it is not unusual to find a similar motif in these two works, albeit shifted or even inserted in an entirely different context.[41] In these two manifestations of the storm, the themes are comparable: situation reversal, sudden and destructive flood, belief in divine providence. It is significant that Herodian, whether drawing on Dio or making use of a rhetorical motif, chooses this particular moment to exploit this powerful and determining image. For instance, this placement of the storm creates an analogy between the rush of both armies towards the Taurus and the surge of the torrent. It also allows Herodian to focus on the staging of nature, instead of combining several strategies at once.

Although this last leg concludes the Taurus sequence in the *History*, its main narrative elements interestingly mirror those of the previous micro-sequences: defeat of Niger's army, its flight and retreat to a new location, and Severus's advance. This subchapter's resolution becomes itself the start of the final sequence of this whole episode, namely the battle at Issus.

5 Issus

After an unexpected victory at Mount Taurus, Severus marched on eastwards. In the *History*, the decisive battle between Niger and Severus took place near Issus (3.4.2–3):

> συνέρχεται δὴ ἑκατέρωθεν ὁ στρατὸς ἐς τὸ κατὰ τὸν Ἰσσικὸν καλούμενον κόλπον πεδίον πλατύτατόν τε καὶ ἐπιμηκέστατον, ᾧ περίκειται μὲν λόφος ἐς θεάτρου σχῆμα, αἰγιαλὸς δὲ ἐπὶ θαλάσσης μέγιστος ἐκτείνεται, ὥσπερ τῆς φύσεως εἰργασμένης στάδιον μάχης. 3. ἐκεῖ φασὶ καὶ Δαρεῖον Ἀλεξάνδρῳ τὴν ὑστάτην καὶ μεγίστην μάχην συμβαλόντα ἡττηθῆναί τε καὶ ἁλῶναι, τῶν ἀπὸ τῶν ἀρκτῴων μερῶν καὶ τότε τοὺς ἀνατολικοὺς νενικηκότων.

The two forces converged on a very broad, long plain at the bay named Issus. Nature might have constructed a course for battle, with the ridge of hills that ran around the bay in the shape of an amphitheatre and the extensive beach that ran

---

[39] See Kolb (1972: 70–7). For Rubin (1980: 118) the storm initially belonged to the battle of Issus. Herodian, or his pro-Severan source, has edited it out from that narrative and instead transposed to it the Taurus's siege.
[40] See below on the main variants.
[41] E.g. the Byzantine picture seen above, or a similar description of the imperial apotheosis placed either at the death of Pertinax (Cass. Dio 74.4), or that of Severus (Hdn. 4.2).

down to the sea. This is the site, we are told, where Darius too, having fought his last and greatest battle with Alexander, was defeated and captured, and where the people of the northern regions on that occasion, too, defeated the Easterners.

In addition to a topographical description, this presentation of Issus also includes a long account of the battle between Alexander and Darius, which Herodian claims to have happened on the same site. It may seem that this allusion to a famous past event has been inserted in the story out of literary convention or the author's antiquarianism. If so, the earlier combat would then remain at the margins of the main plot and have no impact on the new battle. However, the comparison proves central to Herodian's narrative. Beyond embellishment or curiosity, Herodian seeks instead to create a strong and productive link between the two stories, both formally and thematically.

From the outset, Herodian presents the past episode as Darius's 'last and greatest battle' (τὴν ὑστάτην καὶ μεγίστην μάχην), which resulted in his defeat and capture. Although Alexander and Darius indeed fought at Issus, their final clash took place, contrary to Herodian's indication, at Gaugamela some two years later. Herodian's 'confusion' between these two famous battles has often been perceived as a case of typical negligence. On the basis of many errors and imprecisions with reference to Alexander, Z. Rubin posits that the comparison between the two events derives from Herodian's (still) unknown source. Additionally, given his ignorance or indifference for the Alexandrine motif, Herodian would have mixed up Gaugamela and Issus on his own.[42] There may be, beyond Herodian's use or abuse of his sources, a more fruitful interpretation.

By framing the first battle at Issus as critical, Herodian can first grant a certain weight to this new episode. But, more than dramatization or symbolical allusion, its story serves as model for the representation of the coming narrative. Through the outcome of the first battle, Herodian can already evoke that of the second: τῶν ἀπὸ τῶν ἀρκτῴων μερῶν καὶ τότε τοὺς ἀνατολικοὺς νενικηκότων. The combination of the adverb τότε and the perfect participle νενικηκότων also seems to suggest that this conclusion does not apply to the past battle alone. With this formulation and a certain onomastic ambiguity ('north' and 'east' are the only qualifiers), Herodian is able to gather in the same phrase the result of both battles. These are indeed soon confirmed to share a similar end (3.4.4: τὴν τύχην ὁμοίαν τῆς μάχης). Moreover, Herodian does not explicitly say in which role, that of Alexander or Darius, he casts Niger and Severus. He relies instead on their troops' provenance to assign them their respective parts and fates: the north corresponds to Alexander and Severus, the east to Darius and Niger.

According to Herodian, Alexander marked his victory with grand gestures: 'Today there is a city called Alexandria up on the ridge, which is a triumphal monument to commemorate this battle; also there is a bronze statue of the man who has given his name to the site' (3.4.3: μένει δὲ ἔτι νῦν τρόπαιον καὶ δεῖγμα τῆς νίκης ἐκείνης, πόλις ἐπὶ

---

[42] Rubin (1980: 217–18) sees this as a pure fabrication of Herodian. Whittaker (1969–70: n. 1 *ad* 3.4.3) suspects traces of a local tradition.

τοῦ λόφου Ἀλεξάνδρεια καλουμένη, ἄγαλμά τε χαλκοῦν οὗ τὴν προσηγορίαν ὁ τόπος φέρει). By pointing out that both city and statue were still standing (μένει δὲ ἔτι νῦν), Herodian is able to bind together a distant past (Alexander-Darius), a recent past (Niger-Severus), and his own present (time of writing and reading). Whereas the first battle 'lives' through the second, its physical traces are still visible in Herodian's time, half a century after the Niger-Severus war. Herodian makes use of a spatio-temporal connection similar to that seen in the case of Byzantium's walls, but takes it a step further: evoking the famous battle between Alexander and Darius becomes, as it were, a performative act, since it foists its main elements onto the new narrative. By recalling the earlier fight, Herodian is already composing the storyline of the second battle: location, players, stakes and outcome. In addition, the narrative influence is to some extent reciprocal: the new battle of Issus generates the memory of the older, or rather its 'reminiscence', but the older also dictates the structure of the new. Some of the narrative 'gaps' in the one can also be filled by adding, or inventing, details from the other, and vice versa. Ultimately, the lines of both episodes end up melting into each other, creating a sort of hybrid story, such that it becomes difficult to distinguish the features particular to one or the other.

Navigating between time and space, Herodian then proceeds to describe how the battle between Niger and Severus unfolded (3.4.4–5):

ἀντιστρατοπεδευσάμενοι γὰρ ἑκατέρωθεν περὶ ἑσπέραν, πάσης τῆς νυκτὸς ἐν φροντίσιν ἑκάτεροι καὶ δέει διαγρηγορήσαντες, ἅμα ἡλίῳ ἀνίσχοντι ἐπ' ἀλλήλους ἠπείγοντο, παρορμώντων ἑκατέρωθεν τῶν στρατηγῶν. προθυμίᾳ δὴ πάσῃ ἐνέπιπτον ὡς ὑπὲρ λοιπῆς καὶ τελευταίας ἐκείνης μάχης, κἀκεῖ τῆς τύχης διακρινούσης τὸν βασιλέα. ἐπὶ πολὺ δὲ αὐτῶν διαγωνισαμένων πολλοῦ τε ἐργασθέντος φόνου, ὡς καὶ τὰ ῥεῖθρα τῶν διὰ τοῦ πεδίου ποταμῶν ῥεόντων αἵματος πλεῖον ἢ ὕδατος κατάγειν ἐς θάλασσαν, τροπὴ τῶν ἀνατολικῶν γίνεται.

The two forces pitched camp about nightfall facing each other, and spent the entire night awake in anxious foreboding. At sunrise the armies advanced to meet each other, urged on by their respective commanders. With fierce energy they fell upon each other, as though this was the contest to end all battles and fate was then and there making its choice of emperors. For a long time the contest raged with heavy loss of life. The rivers of the plain carried more blood than water down to the sea. And then the rout of the eastern forces began.

By homogenizing contexts, outcomes and narrative sequences, Herodian can exaggerate the resemblance between the two battles. Many similarities can therefore be noted with the famous episode, recorded variously by the Alexander historians. For Rubin, Herodian has created this 'anemic summary' by deleting many details specific to the Niger-Severus battle and filling in the blanks with data taken from the Alexander motif.[43]

---

[43] Rubin (1980: 103–5).

However, as noted by Sidebottom, battle scenes in Herodian are often rather generic and formulaic.[44] The battle between Niger and Severus at Issus seems to be no exception: both armies set up camp in the evening, spend a restless night and launch a fierce battle at sunrise, which ends in a general carnage. Significantly, there are no clear identifiers for most of the sequence, up until 'the Illyrian troops' (οἱ Ἰλλυριοί) are said to chase after the vanquished army. Upon further consideration, the comparison is perhaps targeted more at the outcome of the new battle than its proceedings. Whereas Herodian evokes Alexander's triumphal acts, he only briefly cites Darius's defeat and capture.[45] However, following the events' uncanny resemblance, Herodian can use Darius's abridged end to plot out Niger's defeat. He can then colour this new outcome with its particular function and circumstances. By contrast with the more extravagant stories of Darius's flight, which should be somewhat familiar to his audience, Herodian keeps his account of Niger's end fairly short and simple (3.4.5–6).[46] He thus allows Niger to retain some measure of dignity: Niger was after all 'not a bad man, either as emperor or as an ordinary person' (3.4.7: μὴ φαῦλος ἄνθρωπος, μήτε ἄρχων μήτε ἰδιώτης).

If, as proposed, these two narratives can function as a whole, then it may be argued that Herodian ascribes the one victory to Alexander. Alexander is said to have fought and defeated Darius, while Severus seems somewhat detached from his own success. Alexander is also given more positive acts following his victory. Conversely, Severus is said to have imposed severe reprisals on his opponent's allies and to have issued pardons merely out of self-preservation (3.4.7–9).[47] The context of a civil war may have precluded Severus from fully celebrating his victory, a stance then reproduced in the *History*. Yet Herodian mentions that, after beating Albinus, Severus had two triumphal monuments erected to mark his recent victories (3.7.7). While it could have created another connection between the past and recent battles, Herodian defers the construction of such a trophy. Beyond accuracy, narrative streamlining, or fact amplification, postponing the first monument's erection allows Herodian to confine Severus's post-war approach to perpetuating citizen massacre.

---

[44] Sidebottom (1998: 2816, n. 195): 'In essence Herodian's historical battles are not constructed differently from the mythical combat of Ilus and Tantalus.' Perhaps this episode is to some extent programmatic: 'a long battle was fought in which both sides were evenly matched, and, since quite a number of men fell on either side ...' (1.11.2: ἰσορρόπου δὲ ἐπὶ πολὺ τῆς μάχης γενομένης ἑκατέρωθεν πεσεῖν ἱκανούς ...).

[45] For Darius's flight, see Arrian *Anab.* 2.11; Diod Sic. 17.34, 17.37; Curt. 3.11. Cf. also Plut. *Artax.* 9.1 for the death and flight of Cyrus the Younger following a battle with his brother Artaxerxes II.

[46] Herodian strives to nuance Niger's failure by inserting certain details that might otherwise seem trivial. Cf. Cass. Dio 74.8.3 and *SHA, Pesc. Nig.* 5.8, which are similarly schematic, but lacking the positive indicators found in Herodian (e.g. a fast horse, a small escort). By contrast, Macrinus's flight in the *History* (5.4.7ff.) is drawn out, complicated and farcical, similar to that of Nero (Cass. Dio 63.27.3; Suet. *Ner.* 48.1).

[47] Severus only ended up offering amnesty upon realizing that some of Niger's troops had managed to cross the Tigris River. He was indeed worried that the fugitives would seek vengeance through an alliance with the Persians (3.4.7–9). According to Cass. Dio 74.8.4, Severus spared all the senators in Rome, but imposed heavy reparations. In spite of their similarities, these passages highlight their authors' different interpretations of Severus's badness: for Herodian, cruelty, for Dio, greed.

Such a comparison between the two battles of Issus is not made explicit by Dio, although this passage is admittedly only extant in Xiphilinus's abridged version.[48] Dio places the battle near Issus, at a pass called the 'Cilician Gates' (Cass. Dio 74.7.2–3: αἱ Κιλίκειοι πύλαι). However, these seem to be not the 'Cilician Gates' at Mount Taurus, but rather the so-called 'Cilician-Syrian Gates', in the Amanus (Nur) Mountains, closer to Issus. This may explain why Dio comments on the site's etymology, but does not refer to Alexander.[49] Dio's only Alexandrine allusion in this episode comes up shortly before his account of Issus: apparently some of Niger's supporters were calling him a 'new Alexander' (Cass. Dio 74.6.2a: Ἀλέξανδρον νέον). However, unlike Herodian's treatment, it does not seem to have any particular effect on the story or the characters. The *Historia Augusta*, Victor, Eutropius and Orosius all identify Cyzicus as the site of Niger's defeat, ruling out any comparison with the famous past battle.[50]

In Herodian, the site of Issus is at the centre of the narrative: 'nature might have constructed a course for battle, with the ridge of hills that ran around the bay in the shape of an amphitheatre and the extensive beach that ran down to the sea' (3.4.2: ᾧ περίκειται μὲν λόφος ἐς θεάτρου σχῆμα, αἰγιαλὸς δὲ ἐπὶ θαλάσσης μέγιστος ἐκτείνεται, ὥσπερ τῆς φύσεως εἰργασμένης στάδιον μάχης).[51] This 'natural' theatre is not merely a literary device aimed at Herodian's external audience. When the battle was set to begin, the inhabitants of the neighbouring regions are indeed said to have gathered on the surrounding hills to watch (3.4.5: θεάσοιντο) the unfolding events at a safe distance. This description can therefore enable a 'live' re-staging of the first battle. Furthermore, although it functions as a narrative framework, landscape is not a barren device. More than a backdrop of limited evocative potential, Herodian's Issus is the place from which the whole account(s) emerges. By making the site into the story's focus, Herodian can draw from Issus's ancient history a notable event, similar to the upcoming story. The re-enactment of the battle between Alexander and Darius at Issus thus activates a productive analogy between a past and an ongoing event.[52]

6 Conclusion

Herodian's story of the war between Niger and Severus makes use of several literary devices to describe, shape and exploit the landscape. Some of these are rare, others even unique within the *History*, but all result from a careful composition. There also seems to

---

[48] Cf. Cass. Dio 74.7.1ff. See Rubin (1980: 230–1), with Potter (2016: 329–30, 332).
[49] Cf. Xen. *An.* 1.4.4.
[50] See *SHA*, *Sev.* 9.1, *Pesc. Nig.* 5.8; also Aur. Vict. *Caes.* 20.8; Eutr. 8.18.4; Oros. 7.17.
[51] Citing this episode, Molinier Arbo (2019: 193–4) comments: 'En somme, l'*oikoumène* d'Hérodien n'est rien d'autre qu'une immense scène de théâtre, un décor se prêtant merveilleusement aux drames humains' (quote at 194).
[52] For Potter (2016: 335) this 'appeal to stock scenes and themes', in both Dio's and Herodian's works, leads to 'the domestication of the distant', through which the historians are able to illustrate their understanding of past events for their readers.

be an underlying concern on Herodian's part to make the landscape visible, not only in these specific moments, but through various periods in time. Playing with different temporal layers, Herodian is able to re-enact or foreshadow events. In these visualizations, landscape acts both as object and anchor, around which is sketched a narrative. With these dynamic pictures, Herodian can then establish a close correspondence between landscapes of war and fighting emperors. Indeed, the depictions examined here are all directed towards the protagonists' character. In this episode, landscape helps generate a parallel characterization of the contenders. Whereas Herodian first defines Niger through procrastination and nonchalance, he constantly seeks to temper Niger's defeats against Severus. Conversely, Severus has certain of his victories downplayed or attributed to other factors than his command. In the *History*, the relation between Severus and Niger is therefore not black and white, where one would be strictly good and the other strictly bad. Herodian relies instead on a balance between vice and virtue, which exceeds personalities and tends towards the more universal idea of the good emperor.[53]

Bibliography

Bekker-Nelsen, T. 2014. 'Herodian on Greek and Roman Failings.' In *Roman Rule in Greek and Latin Writing: Double Vision*, edited by J. Majbom Madsen and R. Rees, 224–45. Leiden: Brill.
Bersanetti, G. M. 1938. 'Sulla guerra fra Settimio Severo e Pescennio Nigro in Erodiano.' *Rivista di filologia e di istruzione classica* 66: 357–63.
Birley, A. [1971] 1999. *Septimius Severus: The African Emperor*. London: Routledge.
Hidber, T. 2006. *Herodians Darstellung der Kaisergeschichte nach Marc Aurel*. Basel: Schwabe.
Hidber, T. 2007. 'Herodian.' In *Time in Ancient Greek Literature. Studies in Ancient Greek Narrative, volume two*, edited by I. J. F. De Jong and R. Nünlist, 193–212. Leiden: Brill.
Kemezis, A. 2014. *Greek Narratives of the Roman Empire under the Severans: Cassius Dio, Philostratus and Herodian*. Cambridge: Cambridge University Press.
Kolb, F. 1972. *Literarische Beziehungen zwischen Cassius Dio, Herodian und der Historia Augusta*. Bonn: Habelt.
Kuhn-Chen, B. 2002. *Geschichtskonzeptionen griechischer Historiker im 2. und 3. Jahrhundert n. Chr.: Untersuchungen zu den Werken von Appian, Cassius Dio und Herodian*. Frankfurt am Main: Peter Lang.
Manders, E. 2012. *Coining Images of Power. Patterns in the Representation of Roman Emperors on Imperial Coinage, A.D. 193–284. Impact of Empire, Vol. 15*. Leiden and Boston: Brill.
Millar, F. 1964. *A Study of Cassius Dio*. Oxford: Clarendon Press.
Molinier Arbo, A. 2019. 'L'Empire romain, citadelle assiégée? Recherches sur Hérodien et la géographie.' In *Histoire et géographie chez les auteurs grecs d'époque romaine*, edited by M. Coltelloni-Trannoy and S. Morlet, 185–207. Paris: Éditions de Boccard.
Pernot, L. 1993. *La rhétorique de l'éloge dans le monde gréco-romain*, 2 vols. Paris: Institut d'Études Augustiniennes.
Platnauer, M. 1918. *The Life and Reign of the Emperor Septimius Severus*. Oxford: Oxford University Press.

---

[53] This research was supported by a doctoral fellowship from the Social Sciences and Humanities Research Council of Canada (SSHRC). I would like to thank Albert Gootjes for his help in translating a first draft of this chapter and the organizers of the Landscapes of War conference for their generous award of a travel bursary.

Pitcher, L. 2012. 'Herodian.' In *Space in Ancient Greek Literature. Studies in Ancient Greek Narrative, Vol. 3*, edited by I. J. F. De Jong, 269–82. Leiden and Boston: Brill.
Potter, D. 2016. 'War as Theater, from Tacitus to Dexippus.' In *The Topography of Violence in the Greco-Roman World*, edited by W. Riess and G. G. Fagan, 325–48. Ann Arbor: University of Michigan Press.
Roques, D., trans. 1990. *Hérodien. Histoire des empereurs romains: de Marc-Aurèle à Gordien III (180 ap. J.-C.- 238 ap. J.-C.)*. Paris: Les Belles Lettres.
Rubin, Z. 1980. *Civil-War Propaganda and Historiography*. Brussels: Latomus.
Sidebottom, H. 1998. 'Herodian's Historical Methods and Understanding of History.' *Aufstieg und Niedergang der römischen Welt II* 34 (4): 2775–836.
Ward, J. S. 2011. 'Watching History Unfold: The Uses of Viewing in Cassius Dio, Herodian and the *Historia Augusta*.' PhD diss., New York University.
Whittaker, C. R., trans. 1969–70. *Herodianus*, 2 vols. Cambridge, MA: Harvard University Press.
Worman, N. 2015. *Landscape and the Spaces of Metaphor in Ancient Literary Theory and Criticism*. Cambridge: Cambridge University Press.
Zimmermann, M. 1999. *Kaiser und Ereignis: Studien zum Geschichtswerk Herodians*. Munich: Beck.

PART IV
MEMORY IN WAR LANDSCAPES

CHAPTER 10
SEASCAPES OF WAR: HERODOTUS'S LITTORAL GAZE ON THE BATTLE OF SALAMIS[1]

J. Z. van Rookhuijzen

1 Introduction

The term 'landscapes of war' easily conjures up images of classic battles fought on the land, and it can be forgotten that the sea is also part of the landscape. Sea battles have, of course, been a reality of wars throughout history. But how do ancient societies reflect upon such maritime encounters? Even more than the fields where war once raged, the surface of the sea is silent as to what precisely transpired there. Did, and could, the ancients reconstruct and commemorate such fights, and in what way(s) did they proceed?

This chapter seeks to formulate some answers to these questions by way of studying the 'seascape' of the battle of Salamis. After a preliminary note on the phenomenon of seascapes, I will mainly discuss the topography of that battlefield as it appears in, chiefly, Herodotus's account. I will make use of the term 'mnemotope' as coined by Jan Assmann in the sense of physical places to which stories have been attached.[2] As I have explored this topic in previous publications,[3] this term can be used to understand the topography in Herodotus's account: the places given by Herodotus do not in all cases allow us to reconstruct the topography of the battle, but only to localize the places where various anecdotes were believed to have taken place. This fits the observation by many scholars that some parts of the account are dramatized, and therefore fabricated. It will become clear that this perspective helps us in explaining why Herodotus made recourse to a few landmarks on the coasts of Attica and Salamis, as well as to various landmarks in the strait dividing them.

2 Reconstructing seascapes of war

As is observable in battle narratives discussed in other chapters in this volume, military confrontations are often transformed into a much simplified narrative with a large focus

---

[1] This chapter is a reworking of some parts of the author's dissertation published as *Herodotus and the Topography of Xerxes' Invasion. Place and Memory in Greece and Anatolia*. A fuller discussion can be found there: van Rookhuijzen (2018: 244) (on the battle of Salamis), (2018: 303) (on sea battles). I am grateful to the editorial team at De Gruyter for their kind permission to reuse some text and the map of the battle of Salamis, and to my supervisors and the editors of the present volume for invaluable comments on the manuscript. The text of Herodotus follows Wilson (2015).
[2] Assmann (1992: 59–60).
[3] van Rookhuijzen (2017; 2018: 5–38).

on anecdotes.[4] In such topographical narratives, chains of landmarks loosely indicate the position of armies and other agents of war. Maoz Azaryahu and Kenneth Foote argue that what they call 'historical spaces' (and which I would name *mnemotopes*) are arranged into three broad categories based on the scale of the area: (1) single points and places, (2) routes and paths, and (3) large areas.[5] In category 2, narratives are simplified into a collection of particular anecdotes, while the narratives are often enhanced using pre-existing dominant buildings and landmarks.[6] In category 3, which applies to large battles and military campaigns, even more simplification is required: 'time or space is shortened, concatenated, compressed, lengthened, embellished, straightened, or smoothed', often by selecting individual locations and claiming that actions took place nearby.[7] Azaryahu and Foote also argue that 'some historical events, especially those that conflate linear progression in both space and time, can easily be configured as a spatial narrative of history that dramatizes successive events'.[8] When complex historical events are traced in or projected onto the landscape, it is likely that they crystallize around individual landmarks, which may be 'concatenated' into spatial narratives. This insight is bound to have consequences for our thinking about such ancient authors as Herodotus. Indeed, scholars sometimes note problems in Herodotus's battle topography, but usually explain them as unproblematic and continue to use the topography to reconstruct the battle.[9] However, the observation that the narratives are fundamentally schematized makes it increasingly difficult to use them for the exact historicity of this topography. It is not only problematic whether the movements between the points are correct, but the landmarks themselves may be identified incorrectly, and the stories told at them historically inauthentic.

We may hypothesize that sea battles are even more liable to yield 'distorted' topographies than land battles: movements and stories are difficult to project on the featureless surface of the water, and landmarks of nearby coastal areas are required to identify the place of the battle. Therefore, stories which take place on the water are commonly told from nearby vantage points on the coasts: Azaryahu and Foote mention the modern example of the sinking of the *Empress of Ireland* in Canada's St Lawrence river in 1914, which is marked at Pointe-au-Père.[10] Like their terrestrial sisters, seascapes may then, ironically, also be *land*scapes of war, requiring *land*marks and battle*fields*. Taking Herodotus's account of the battle of Salamis (480 BCE) as a case in point, I would like to show various aspects of the dynamics of this 'littoral gaze': the process by which the coast receives a (frequently disproportionately) great amount of attention by commentators of events that took place on the water.

---

[4] Ferrill (1966: 102); Meyer (1954: 230); Whatley (1964).
[5] Azaryahu and Foote (2008: 183).
[6] Azaryahu and Foote (2008: 185–87).
[7] Azaryahu and Foote (2008: 187). Cf. Vansina (1985: 167–76) on the ways in which narratives are structured in memory.
[8] Azaryahu and Foote (2008: 193). Cf. Fentress and Wickham (1992: 49–51); Schudson (1995: 355–8).
[9] Optimistic notes in this regard can be found in Hignett (1963: 38), Pritchett (1985: 94; 1993: 298).
[10] Azaryahu and Foote (2008: 184).

3 Commemorating the battle of Salamis

After the devastation inflicted upon Athens and other places in Greece, the battle of Salamis was a turning point in the Persian wars. As the first true victory for the Greeks it was naturally subject to elaborate commemorative traditions. Dedications commemorating the battle are reported in Delphi, Athens and other places,[11] and Simonides is said to have written a lost poem celebrating the victory.[12] As we will see, commemorative engagement with the actual battlefield itself occurred too: trophies were erected on conspicuous points near the waters where the battle was believed to have been fought, and the Aianteia festival included boat races in which the youth of Athens interacted with the battlefield.

In Herodotus's account of the battle we may also recognize an attempt to engage with the battlefield. Many scholars have 'complained' that Herodotus gives mainly incidents of the battle, not a full strategical appraisal, nor an explanation of why the Persians were defeated.[13] I will argue that it is precisely his apparent difficulty in reconstructing the battle, and his reliance in that process on a coastal topography, which have caused this

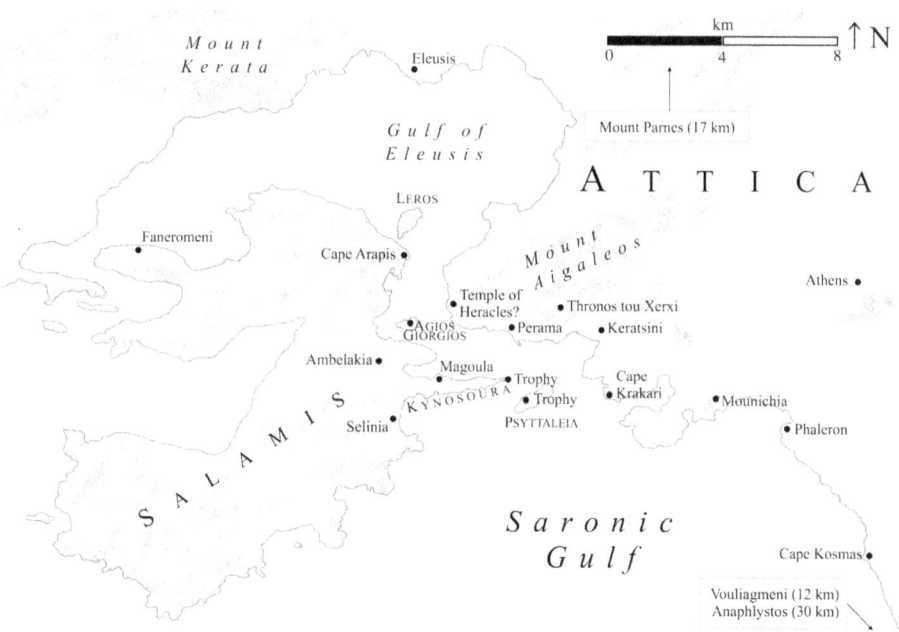

Figure 10.1 Map of Salamis and a part of Attica showing locations in the battle of Salamis. Drawn by René Reijnen and J. Z. van Rookhuijzen.

---

[11] Simon. *FGE* 12; Hdt. 8.121–2; Paus. 2.31.7, 5.11.5, 10.14.5; Plut. *Them.* 15.3.
[12] *Vita Pindari* 2.21; *Suda* s.v. Σιμωνίδης.
[13] Grundy (1897: 230), Hignett (1963: 231), Hammond (1988: 579), Cawkwell (2005: 99), Wallinga (2005: 58–60).

fragmented perspective on the battle. I will here limit myself to the discussion of three famous landmarks in the account: the islet Psyttaleia, the Kynosoura peninsula of the island of Salamis and the site of Xerxes' throne on the mainland. I will examine how scholars have approached locating the sites in question, and try to answer the question why Herodotus or his sources believed that events took place there.[14]

4 Psyttaleia

As Herodotus informs the reader about the Persian preparations for the battle, he shifts attention to the island of Psyttaleia (8.76):

> τοῖσι δὲ ὡς πιστὰ ἐγίνετο τὰ ἀγγελθέντα, τοῦτο μὲν ἐς τὴν νησῖδα τὴν Ψυττάλειαν μεταξὺ Σαλαμῖνός τε κειμένην καὶ τῆς ἠπείρου πολλοὺς τῶν Περσέων ἀπεβίβασαν· ... ἐς δὲ τὴν νησῖδα τὴν Ψυττάλειαν καλεομένην ἀπεβίβαζον τῶν Περσέων τῶνδε εἵνεκα, ὡς ἐπεὰν γένηται ναυμαχίη, ἐνθαῦτα μάλιστα ἐξοισομένων τῶν τε ἀνδρῶν καὶ τῶν ναυηγίων (ἐν γὰρ δὴ πόρῳ τῆς ναυμαχίης τῆς μελλούσης ἔσεσθαι ἔκειτο ἡ νῆσος), ἵνα τοὺς μὲν περιποιῶσι, τοὺς δὲ διαφθείρωσι. ἐποίευν δὲ σιγῇ ταῦτα, ὡς μὴ πυνθανοίατο οἱ ἐναντίοι. οἱ μὲν δὴ ταῦτα τῆς νυκτὸς οὐδὲν ἀποκοιμηθέντες παραρτέοντο.

> And when [the Persian generals] believed the messages, they first brought many Persians to the islet of Psyttaleia, which lies between Salamis and the mainland ... And they brought the Persian troops to the islet called Psyttaleia, for when the battle would break out, the men and wrecks would mostly wash up there (for the island lay in the way of the sea-battle that was going to take place), so that they could save some, and kill others. They did this in silence, so that their adversaries would not find out. They prepared their plan at night, not having slept.

Later in his account, Herodotus tells us that the Persians at Psyttaleia were murdered, an event which ended the battle (8.95):

> Ἀριστείδης δὲ ὁ Λυσιμάχου ἀνὴρ Ἀθηναῖος, τοῦ καὶ ὀλίγῳ τι πρότερον τούτων ἐπεμνήσθην ὡς ἀνδρὸς ἀρίστου, οὗτος ἐν τῷ θορύβῳ τούτῳ τῷ περὶ Σαλαμῖνα γενομένῳ τάδε ἐποίεε· παραλαβὼν πολλοὺς τῶν ὁπλιτέων οἳ παρατετάχατο παρὰ τὴν ἀκτὴν τῆς Σαλαμινίης χώρης, γένος ἐόντες Ἀθηναῖοι, ἐς τὴν Ψυττάλειαν {νῆσον} ἀπέβησε ἄγων, οἳ τοὺς Πέρσας τοὺς ἐν τῇ νησῖδι ταύτῃ κατεφόνευσαν πάντας.

---

[14] I will not discuss several other anecdotes with littoral locations: the divine epiphany near the temple of Athena Skiras (8.94); the stranding of the shipwrecks at the beach of Kolias (8.96); and Xerxes' attempt at building an earthen causeway and a pontoon bridge in the strait to gain access to the island of Salamis (8.97); for these see van Rookhuijzen (2018: 214–44).

Aristides, son of Lysimachos, an Athenian, whom I mentioned a little while before these events as a good man, did the following in the chaos that had arisen around Salamis. He took many of the hoplites that had been arranged along the coast of the land of Salamis, Athenians by origin, and landed on the island of Psyttaleia while he led them, and they slaughtered all the Persians who were on that island.

In other accounts of the battle, Psyttaleia is even more prominent: Aeschylus (*Pers.* 447–71) has a vivid description of the island,[15] and in Plutarch (*Arist.* 9.2) it appears as the centre of the fight: 'most of the crashing of the ships and the worst part of the battle seems to have happened around that place: that is why a trophy stands on Psyttaleia'. Pausanias (4.36.6) likewise presents it as well-known because 'the Persians died on it'.

The pinpointing of Psyttaleia on the map has dominated the efforts of historians and archaeologists to reconstruct the battle of Salamis in the modern landscape. It is now generally agreed that it was the island until recently known as Leipsokoutali (and now officially renamed Psyttaleia).[16] In the middle of nineteenth century, Ludwig Ross identified some traces of the trophy which Plutarch (*Arist.* 9.2) mentions on the small peninsula on the northwest side of the island. They were seen again in 1967, but were then beyond description.[17] The current status of the alleged trophy is unknown after the construction of Europe's biggest sewage treatment plant on the island in the 1990s. If Ross was correct, it shows that at some point in antiquity (not necessarily in the fifth century!) the locality was awarded this significance. The monument corroborated the littoral aspect of the battle. Psyttaleia was an important mnemotope in Aeschylus's and Herodotus's time, and we can try to answer the question why and how Psyttaleia had received that status. While it is clear that something happened on Psyttaleia, the exact event is beyond recovery. Nevertheless, the historicity of the massacre seems to have been taken for granted by most scholars.[18] But would a Persian general really station his troops on a small island without any water, in order to kill any Greeks that might wash up there?

We will never be able to reconstruct in full detail what happened in 480 BCE. I nevertheless suggest that the importance awarded to Psyttaleia by Herodotus, Aeschylus

---

[15] The island is not named by Aeschylus. For the identification with Psyttaleia, see Wallace (1969: 298). Georges (1994: 84) explains that Aeschylus portrays Psyttaleia as the 'richest and most concentrated slaughter of the real enemy'.

[16] E.g. Leake (1841: 267), Milchhoefer (1895: 29), Grundy (1901: 375), Judeich (1912), Obst (1913: 145–9), Munro (1926: 308), Wilhelm (1929: 16), Kromayer (1924: 87–9), Burn (1962: 454), Hignett (1963: 402), Pritchett (1959: 256–62), Pritchett (1965: 100–3), Bayer (1969), Wallace (1969: 297–302), Taylor (1997: 119, n. 39), Wallinga (2005: 62–3), Bowie (2007: 165). An alternative identification is Agios Giorgos: Beloch (1908: 477–82), Hammond (1956, 1973). Cf. Wallace (1969: 294–9).

[17] Wallace (1969: 302) (reporting that Ludwig Ross had described a rectangular base at the north side of the island). It is possible that this trophy is hinted at by Pausanias (1.36.1), Plato (*Menex.* 245a), Xenophon (*An.* 3.2.13) and Lycurgus (*Leoc.* 73). Beschi (2002: 70–1) and Proietti (2015a: 159–60) point out that the archaeological evidence is minimal. Cf. Proietti (2015b).

[18] Reflections on the historicity of the event are found in e.g. Macan (1908: II 307), Fornara (1966), Wallace (1969: 293), Wallinga (2005: 91).

and Pausanias may be a result of the island's prominence in the strait between Salamis and Piraeus. On the basis of epigraphical evidence, it has been argued that the confrontation that took place on Psyttaleia was, directly after the war, regarded as a very important encounter during the battle and perhaps even as separate from (though equivalent to) the battle of Salamis proper.[19] It is therefore remarkable that the Psyttaleia episode, as a more convenient 'littoral' encounter, has become exemplary for the battle in the literary tradition, as represented by Aeschylus and Herodotus. In the fifth century BCE, Psyttaleia amounted to the best possible answer to the question 'Where was the battle of Salamis fought?' and 'What happened to the Persians? After all, it was impossible to point out the exact areas of the seas near Salamis where individual ships had sailed.[20]

Several parallels for the indication of a small island as the location for an event during a battle can tentatively be given. They suggest that in narratives of conflict in a seascape setting, small islands can be singled out as the central mnemotope. In particular, they showcase the place where the enemies retreated, and where they might have been (deservedly) slaughtered.[21] For example, during the Trojan War, the Greeks hid their fleet at Tenedos,[22] and the battle for Miletus between Persians and Greeks (494 BCE) was fought near Lade (Hdt. 6.7–8). The Psyttaleia massacre is very similar to the battle of Sphacteria during the Peloponnesian War (425 BCE, Thuc. 4.8–38), in which 148 Spartans were killed by an Athenian force. The similarity between the Sphacteria and Psyttaleia episodes was already noted by Pausanias (4.36.6). Though we must remain open to the idea that these islands were historically important places in the respective battle, it is also possible that the physical prominence led to narrative prominence. And though we can never be sure about the exact workings and significance of such parallels, (the significance of) the narrative about Psyttaleia may have been transposed to Sphacteria.

Psyttaleia's role in the battle narrative is particularly reminiscent of that played by a fourth island, Asteris in Book 4 of the *Odyssey*. Here Penelope's suitors awaited Telemachos in ambush: 'There is a rocky island in the middle of the sea between Ithaka and rugged Samos, Asteris, not big, and there are two ship-sheltering havens in it. There the Achaeans awaited him, lying in ambush.'[23] The idea of enemies lying in ambush on a small, rocky island in a sea strait is common to both texts. Aeschylus structures his verses in a similar way to Homer's: 'There is an island before the places of Salamis, small, difficult

---

[19] Proietti (2015b). The phrase πεζοί τε [καὶ ὠκυπόρων ἐπὶ νηῶ]ν on Lapis A of the Persian war inscriptions (*IG* I³ 503–4) could be a reference to Psyttaleia and Salamis as two separate, but equal battles.

[20] For the idea that the entire battlefield was visible from Psyttaleia, and that this was the justification for its recording, see Hammond (1988: 581), Ray (2009: 84). Wallinga (2005: 87) points out that Psyttaleia was the only part of the original Persian plan that was remembered.

[21] For this scene in terrestrial battles, see e.g. Herodotus's description of the battle of Plataea (9.15) and Mykale (9.96–7).

[22] This story first appears in Vergil (*Aen*. 2.21–4), but could reflect an older tradition.

[23] Hom. *Od*. 4.844–7: 'ἔστι δέ τις νῆσος μέσση ἁλὶ πετρήεσσα | μεσσηγὺς Ἰθάκης τε Σάμοιό τε παιπαλοέσσης, | Ἀστερίς, οὐ μεγάλη· λιμένες δ' ἔνι ναύλοχοι αὐτῇ | ἀμφίδυμοι· τῇ τόν γε μένον λοχόωντες Ἀχαιοί.'

to anchor for ships, where Pan, lover of choral dance, treads on the shores of the sea. There...'[24] In typical ekphrastic manner, both passages start with 'There is an island' and are followed by a short description, after which the presence of the enemies is introduced. I tentatively suggest that the Psyttaleia scene in Aeschylus may have been embellished in oral and/or literary traditions by this reference to a scene from the *Odyssey*. Even if the description of Psyttaleia in Aeschylus's *Persae* is independent of Homer's *Odyssey* and the parallel only coincidental, both attest to the salience given to islands in seascapes of conflict in a more general sense.

Both Aeschylus (in the passage quoted above) and Pausanias (1.36.2, referring to many wooden statues) suggest that there was a cult of Pan on Psyttaleia. The presence of the god normally associated with forested mountain valleys on this the small, barren island seems rather strange. However, the association of Psyttaleia with Pan may have originated with the purely poetic reference in Aeschylus. To say that the island, where Persians were stationed to kill beached Greeks, and where Greeks finally killed the Persians, is sacred to the god of terror and panic is an apt poetic device for this particular narrative.[25] We also imagine that Aeschylus's testimony is revealing of (or inspired?) a real cult of Pan on the island after the battle, as had happened at Marathon.[26] If so, the cult will have further contributed to the designation of Psyttaleia as one of the foremost locations associated with the battle of Salamis.

5 Kynosoura

After stationing some of his men at Psyttaleia, Xerxes directed part of his armada so as to line up between Kynosoura and Mounichia (8.76):

> ... τοῦτο δέ, ἐπειδὴ ἐγίνοντο μέσαι νύκτες, ἀνῆγον μὲν τὸ ἀπ' ἑσπέρης κέρας κυκλούμενοι πρὸς τὴν Ἐλευσῖνα, ἀνῆγον δὲ οἱ ἀμφὶ τὴν Κέον τε καὶ τὴν Κυνόσουραν τεταγμένοι, κατεῖχόν τε μέχρι Μουνιχίης πάντα τὸν πορθμὸν τῇσι νηυσί. τῶνδε δὲ εἵνεκα ἀνῆγον τὰς νέας, ἵνα δὴ τοῖσι Ἕλλησι μὴ διαφυγεῖν ἐξῇ, ἀλλ' ἀπολαμφθέντες ἐν τῇ Σαλαμῖνι δοῖεν τίσιν τῶν ἐπ' Ἀρτεμισίῳ ἀγωνισμάτων. ...

> ... and second, when it had become midnight, they led the western wing in a circle to Eleusis, and those posted around Keos and Kynosoura, and they occupied the entire strait up to Mounichia with their ships. And they directed their ships so that it was impossible for the Greeks to flee. Being trapped in Salamis, they would give recompense for the sufferings at Artemision ...

---

[24] Aesch. *Pers.* 447–50: 'νῆσος τίς ἐστι πρόσθε Σαλαμῖνος τόπων, | βαιά, δύσορμος ναυσίν, ἣν ὁ φιλόχορος | Πὰν ἐμβατεύει ποντίας ἀκτῆς ἔπι | ἐνταῦθα ...'
[25] Cahen (1924: 313). This may also be the reason why Sophocles calls Pan ἀλίπλαγκτος 'sea-roaming' (*Aj.* 695; cf. *Suda* s.v. ἀλίπλαγκτος).
[26] Simon. *FGE* 5; Hdt. 6.105; Paus. 8.54.6; Nonnus, *Dion.* 27.290; *Suda* s.v. Ἱππίας.

This was in an apparent fulfilment of an oracle that Herodotus quotes directly afterwards (8.77):

Ἀλλ' ὅταν Ἀρτέμιδος χρυσαόρου ἱερὸν ἀκτὴν νηυσὶ γεφυρώσωσι καὶ εἰναλίην Κυνόσουραν, ἐλπίδι μαινομένῃ λιπαρὰς πέρσαντες Ἀθήνας, δῖα Δίκη σβέσσει κρατερὸν Κόρον, Ὕβριος υἱόν, δεινὸν μαιμώοντα, δοκεῦντ' ἀνὰ πάντα πιθέσθαι.

But when, with mad hope, they bridge the holy coast of Artemis with the golden sword and the Dog's Tail in the sea, after having sacked splendid Athens, divine Justice will smother strong Arrogance, the son of Hubris, eager and threatening, planning to engulf everything.

Kynosoura ('Dog's Tail') is a long, narrow peninsula of the island of Salamis, pointing towards Piraeus. The coast of Artemis with the golden sword is believed to refer to the temple of the goddess at Mounichia, which is currently the Kastello hill in the eastern part of Piraeus.[27] The identification of Keos is insecure.[28]

Herodotus seemingly does not make much of Kynosoura as a location in the battle. Its appearance in an oracle nevertheless suggests that it was a salient location in the traditions about the confrontation in the fifth century and beyond.[29] This importance coincides with the various ways in which this mnemotope was commemorated. The first instance of commemoration was a trophy mentioned in various literary and epigraphical sources.[30] The trophy was set up at the very tip of the Kynosoura peninsula (which is, perhaps not coincidentally, known as Cape Varvari (Βάρβαρι) today). Here, marble blocks were seen by early modern travelers and interpreted as the trophy mentioned in the texts.[31] Parts of it were probably taken to Venice.[32] One block appears still to be in situ today. The trophy's connection to the commemoration of the battle remains speculative,[33] but clearly the peninsula would be a suitable point to erect such a trophy because this was the point of Salamis closest to Athens. The monument may have been visible to Athenians on the mainland.[34] As a trophy was meant to mark the place where the climax of the battle had taken place, this was the best possible site to put it, close to Psyttaleia. It therefore helped to mark the peninsula and the waters surrounding it as a mnemotope

---

[27] The temple is mentioned by Pausanias (1.1.4). For the localization, see Macan (1908: I 480–1), Hammond (1969: 53), (1988: 574), Papachatzi (1974: 119–22), Müller (1987: 706–7), Papadopoulou (2014: 111; 118).
[28] Various proposals can be found in Lolling (1884: 4–5), Obst (1913: 147), Wilhelm (1929: 30–1), Burn (1962: 472), Hammond (1988: 574), Kromayer (1931: 582–3), Wallinga (2005: 50).
[29] On the oracle, see Kirchberg (1965: 103–5), Maurizio (1997: 326–7).
[30] Timoth. *Pers.* 196; Pl. *Menex.* 245a; Xen. *An.* 3.2.13; Ath. 1.20ff. (mentioning that Sophocles used to dance around it); Lycurg. *Leoc.* 73; Paus. 1.36.1; *IG* I³ 255; *IG* II² 1035.
[31] On the material remains, see Wallace (1969: 299–302), Culley (1977: 296–7), Clairmont (1983: 118), Beschi (2002: 68–9).
[32] *Relazione d'un mio viaggio fatto da Venezia a Costantinopoli* (1802), 467–8 (non vidi) in Stefanini (1977: 162). Cf. Beschi (2002: 69–70).
[33] Proietti (2015a: 158–9).
[34] Hammond (1988: 581), Ray (2009: 84).

for the battle.³⁵ There also exists archaeological and epigraphic evidence for the erection of trophies in Piraeus, on the so-called tomb of Themistocles (where the column had been reconstructed) and on Cape Krakari.³⁶ The trophies helped to define the battlefield, but they also marked the endpoints of the ships mentioned by the oracle, and therefore may have helped visitors to visualize that line of ships before their eyes (though it is inherently difficult to trace whether the oracle had been fabricated before or after the construction of these monuments).

A unique instance of interaction with these monuments appears in inscriptions dating to the second and first centuries BCE that inform us about the existence of the Aianteia festival.³⁷ This event included boat races, as well as sacrifices to Ajax, Artemis Mounichia and Zeus Tropaios at one or more of the trophies. It testifies to the importance of the landscape around Kynosoura as a seascape of war and seems to have been specifically designed to allow the Athenian youth to engage with it.³⁸

The second monument related to the battle on the Kynosoura peninsula is a hill in the middle of the peninsula's north shore, which is currently also the place of a modern sculpture that commemorates the battle. It has sometimes been suggested that this *magoula* was a tumulus containing the victims of the battle, because we hear about a polyandreion in a first-century BCE inscription (*IG* II² 1035).³⁹ Although similar burial mounds existed near Plataea and one still exists near Marathon, there is no further evidence to substantiate this suggestion. It has also been pointed out that only late fifth-century BCE graves have been found in the *magoula*, and that the polyandreion was, instead, near the trophy at the tip of Kynosoura, underneath currently abandoned buildings of the Greek navy.⁴⁰ This is also suggested by the inscription, which seems to mention the grave in relation to the trophy. The *magoula* may instead have been associated with Kychreus, the mythical king of Salamis. He was the son of Poseidon and Salamis and said to have either killed or raised a snake, or to have been a snake himself.⁴¹ We read in Pausanias (1.36.1) and in the above-mentioned inscription (*IG* II² 1035) that the island accommodated a shrine to this hero. There also existed a cave sacred to him (Lycoph. *Alex.* 451). Other sources suggest that the shrine amounted to a hill on the coast.⁴² Excavations of the hill have revealed remains of walls, and possibly an altar.⁴³

It is possible that this mnemotope of the myth of Kychreus acquired a new meaning as the imagined grave of those who had fallen in the battle. From an Athenian perspective

---

³⁵ Cf. Wallace (1969: 302); Clairmont (1983: 118).
³⁶ Beschi (2002: 71–90) (with photographs); Proietti (2015a).
³⁷ *IG* II² 1006; 1008; 1009; 1011; 1028; 1029; *IG* V.1 657.
³⁸ Deubner (1932: 179–80), Culley (1977: 294–5), Taylor (1997: 187), Parker (2005: 456), Proietti (2015a: 158).
³⁹ Another inscription mentions Corinthian graves near Salamis town (retrieved at Ambelakia, *IG* I³ 1143), and Plutarch mentions an epitaph for the Corinthian leader Adeimantos (*De Herodoti malignitate* 870e = Simon. *FGE* 10–1). Cf. Milchhoefer (1895: 29), Pritchett (1965: 95–6), Culley (1977), Jacquemin (2000: 67–8).
⁴⁰ Tsirivakos (1967), Culley (1977: 293–8).
⁴¹ Apollod. *Bibl.* 3.161; Diod. Sic. 4.72.4; Strabo 9.1.9; Steph. Byz. s.v. Κυχρεῖος. Cf. Milchhoefer (1895: 28–9), Wallace (1969: 300–1), Culley (1977: 291–2), Langdon (2007: 112–16).
⁴² Euphorion fr. 30; Steph. Byz. s.v. Κυχρεῖος (on the authority of Sophocles' *Teukros*).
⁴³ Lolling (1884: 8–10), Wallace (1969: 301), Culley (1977: 292–4).

in the post-war period, Salamis was synonymous with the battle. Existing monuments and their cults could then easily have been enveloped in commemoration practices.[44] The burials dating to the later fifth century BCE on the *magoula* could, perhaps, suggest that in this period, the hill was perceived as the last resting place of the Greek soldiers. The modern monument for the battle on the hill, erected in 2006, is an illustration of the same process that the hill underwent in our own time. Even though the original functions of the hill are unclear, it has become a mnemotope for the battle.

There are some other idiosyncratic stories connected to Kynosoura not found in Herodotus. They show how easily anecdotes of the battle could be anchored in the peninsula. Aeschylus (*Pers.* 302–3) mentions the rocky beach of Seliniai at or near Kynosoura where the body of the Persian general Artembares had washed ashore.[45] More fantastically, Pausanias (1.36.1) remarks that Kychreus appeared in the battle of Salamis as a snake. The hero's association with snakes is readily understandable, as the Kynosoura peninsula was as much a dog's tail as an enormous snake. Wallace has therefore suggested that the later belief that the central position of the Kynosoura peninsula in the battlefield has given rise to the story that Pausanias records.[46] It seems that a tradition had arisen in which Kynosoura was imagined as a giant petrified snake. Yet it is difficult to disentangle cause and effect: the story could also be the reason why the hill became a mnemotope connected with the battle.

6 The Aigaleos ridge: Xerxes' throne

The final place appearing in the traditions about the battle of Salamis that I would like to examine is the place from which Xerxes is said to have followed the activities of his armada. The vision of an enraged Xerxes overlooking the fighting has become a quintessential scene of the battle of Salamis: in modern popular illustrations, Xerxes is often pictured as overlooking the battle seated on a throne, and the site is usually marked on maps of the battlefield. Topographical and historical investigations of the battle of Salamis almost traditionally start with the quest of this 'throne'. The scene is described by Herodotus in 8.90:

ὅκως γάρ τινα ἴδοι Ξέρξης τῶν ἑωυτοῦ ἔργον τι ἀποδεικνύμενον ἐν τῇ ναυμαχίῃ, κατήμενος ὑπὸ τῷ ὄρεϊ τῷ ἀντίον Σαλαμῖνος τὸ καλέεται Αἰγάλεως, ἀνεπυνθάνετο τὸν ποιήσαντα, καὶ οἱ γραμματισταὶ ἀνέγραφον πατρόθεν τὸν τριήραρχον καὶ τὴν πόλιν.

For whenever Xerxes, as he sat under the mountain called Aigaleos opposite Salamis, saw one of his men demonstrating a certain achievement in the sea-battle,

---

[44] Cf. Minchin (2016) on reinterpreted 'heroic' tumuli in the landscape surrounding Troy.
[45] Attempts to identify this beach in Milchhoefer (1895: 5), Wilhelm (1929: 70), Wallace (1969: 301), Papachatzi (1974: 461), Hammond (1988: 54).
[46] Wallace (1969: 301).

he inquired about the person who did it, and the scribes wrote down the name of the trierarch, his father's name, and his city.

The scene appears in most other accounts of the battle of Salamis, and also, before Herodotus, in Aeschylus's *Persae* (465–7).[47] Rather surprisingly, neither Aeschylus nor Herodotus mention a throne (or seat), but in later sources, the scene is embellished to include one: in Demosthenes (*In Timocratem* 24.129) we read that Xerxes' silver-footed δίφρος 'seat' was believed to be present in the Parthenon.[48] By the time of Plutarch (*Them.* 13.1), the throne on Mount Aigaleos has become golden.

We cannot reconstruct the precise site of the throne from the accounts of Aeschylus and Herodotus. These texts only allow us to locate the throne under Mount Aigaleos, in modern Perama. Mount Aigaleos is, in fact, a small massif with several different peaks, and there is considerable confusion in ancient and modern scholarship as to which peak it was.[49] Moreover, Herodotus does not speak of a mountaintop, but says that the king was positioned ὑπὸ τῷ ὄρεϊ, 'under the mountain'. The search for the throne continues today in Perama, with locals still calling yet another peak of Aigaleos, between Keratsini and Perama, the Θρόνος του Ξέρξη, and one website even reports plans of local authorities to reconstruct the throne here as a tourist site.[50]

There is no reason to assign particular value to any of the proposed locations of the throne. However, their number reveals an important point: apparently, there is a great demand to localize the throne, as much today as in antiquity. And yet we may wonder, how much closer does this bring us to the historical topography of the battle of Salamis? One 'justification' for the quest for the throne has been and still is its perceived importance in determining the locations of other landmarks of the battle of Salamis: the assumption is that they need to have been visible from Xerxes' lookout point.[51] However, as Macan already pointed out, this particular piece of information does not allow us to reconstruct the battle in more detail.[52]

It thus seems that, through the lack of a possibility to come closer to the historical battle by studying the surface of the water, attention has been deflected to the mountains towering above it. It is my surmise that the quest for this mnemotope depends on the dramatic picture which it paints of the battle. Herodotus himself points out that the

---

[47] For the image of Xerxes on the throne in Aeschylus, see Bridges (2015, 24).
[48] As I have recently argued (van Rookhuijzen 2020: 31) the throne appears in the Classical inventory lists of the Parthenon, which I believe to be the west part of the Karyatid Temple. Cf. Frost (1973), Harris (1995: 205), Proietti (2015a: 163–4).
[49] See e.g. Plut. *Them.* 13.1 (citing Phanodemus (*FGrH* 325 F 24) and Acestodorus); Aristodemus, *FGrH* 104 F1. Discussed in e.g. Leake (1841: 33–4), Hauvette (1894: 418), Grundy (1897: 234–5), (1901: 398); Goodwin (1906: 95–6), Rediadis (1906: 239–44), Beloch (1908: 482–3), Obst (1913: 17; 148), Munro (1926: 312), Myres (1953: 267), Bigwood (1978: 41), Caspari (1911: 103n.12).
[50] At the time of writing, the modern local viewpoint is explained at www.koutouzis.gr/peramiotika.htm (last consulted on 25 August 2020).
[51] Cf. Pritchett (1965: 101–2), Frost (1973), Hammond (1956: 38 with n. 24).
[52] Macan (1908: II 294).

Persians fought better because Xerxes could see them (8.86).[53] Salamis was not the only site where Xerxes had a throne: they also appear at the Hellespont (7.44) and Thermopylae (7.212), while a similar 'look-out scene' is painted at Doriskos in Thrace (7.59). The idea of the monarch on the throne can safely be thought of as a commonplace, as various scholars have noted.[54] It may also be part of a more general topos in which prominent characters watch something from mountains, called *oroskopia* by Irene de Jong, with clear Homeric resonances.[55] More generally, the designation of mountains as the locations of historical or mythical events is common.[56]

While the scene is usually regarded as historically authentic,[57] I suggest that it may just as well have existed only in the minds of later Greeks, desiring to somehow anchor the sea battle in the land. The search for Xerxes' throne will probably continue into the future. I suggest that we nevertheless acknowledge that, even if we take it as historical fact that Xerxes was present at the battle, it may be enough to regard the various sites of Xerxes' throne as mnemotopes. The very act of the search for the actual throne ironically confirms the success of its functioning as such.

7 Conclusion

I have argued that Herodotus's topography of the battle of Salamis can be seen as a collection of mnemotopes that together form a historical 'seascape' of the battle of Salamis. Through a lack of adequate means to designate the surface of the waters between the island of Salamis and Attica, ancient narratives and accompanying commemoration efforts, as well as modern searches have been concentrated on the littoral. The island of Psyttaleia became the emblematic mnemotope of the battle, as it was thought that the Persians were finally defeated here. The Kynosoura peninsula, apparently not very important in Herodotus's narrative, still sported a trophy for the battle. It also featured a hill, possibly sacred to Kychreus, which was interpreted as the grave of the Greeks who had fallen in the battle. And various mountain tops were designated as the site of Xerxes' throne. As our gaze, following Herodotus, is directed to the littoral, the 'real' battle of Salamis slips away in the waters where it was fought.

Rather than offering an answer to the question where the battle 'happened', this approach brings us closer to the beliefs and preoccupations of later visitors to the strait east of Salamis and adds new relief to the agency of the texts of Herodotus and other authors in the functioning of these mnemotopes. We may wonder, does Herodotus's

---

[53] Cf. Grethlein (2009: 207–8).
[54] On the topos of Xerxes' throne in Herodotus, see Immerwahr (1966: 182), Grethlein (2009: 209), Bridges (2015: 54–6, 59) (noting that Darius was pictured in a similar fashion). See Allen (2005) on images of the enthroned Achaemenid king in audience scenes that featured widely in imperial propaganda.
[55] De Jong (2018). Cf. Grethlein (2009: 209–10).
[56] On the importance of mountains in Greek mythology, see Buxton (1994: 81–96); he stresses the frequent association of mountains with Zeus.
[57] E.g. Sancisi-Weerdenburg (1980: 75), Green (1996: 189–90).

account reflect the beliefs and preoccupations of later visitors, or does it also (and perhaps even to a large extent) shape them? My tentative answer to this difficult question is that we can expect the text to have functioned both as a means of reflection and a source of inspiration: on the one hand, we can read Herodotus as a source for how people generally remembered the battle of Salamis by using landmarks; yet his way of arranging the narrative around landmarks also prompted people to search for the sites all through antiquity and up to the present day. It is intrinsically difficult to disentangle Herodotus's influence on the creation of the seascape of the battle from that of the sources on which he relied, as well as from other beliefs and traditions which existed independently of Herodotus in the fifth century. As various different processes seem to have shaped the seascape laid down in their accounts, we should proceed with care as we write the histories of the land- and seascapes in which the Persian wars were believed to have 'taken place'.

Bibliography

Allen, L. 2005. *The Persian Empire*. Chicago: University of Chicago Press.
Assmann, J. 1992. *Das Kulturelle Gedächtnis. Schrift, Erinnerung und Politische Identität in frühen Hochkulturen*. Munich: C. H. Beck.
Azaryahu, M. and K. E. Foote. 2008. 'Historical Space as Narrative Medium: On the Configuration of Spatial Narratives of Time at Historical Sites.' *GeoJournal* 73: 179–94.
Bayer, E. 1969. 'Psyttaleia.' *Historia* 18 (5): 640.
Beloch, K. J. 1908. 'Die Schlacht bei Salamis.' *Klio* 8: 477–86.
Beschi, L. 2002. 'I trofei di Maratona e Salamina e le colonne del Pireo.' *Rendiconti dell'Accademia nazionale dei Lincei. Classe di Scienze morali, storiche e filologiche* 9.13 (1): 51–94.
Bigwood, J. M. 1978. 'Ctesias as Historian of the Persian Wars.' *Phoenix* 32 (1): 19–41.
Bowie, A. M. 2007. *Herodotus: Histories Book VIII*. Cambridge: Cambridge University Press.
Bridges, E. 2015. *Imagining Xerxes: Ancient Perspectives on a Persian King*. London: Bloomsbury.
Burn, A. R. 1962. *Persia and the Greeks: The Defence of the West, c. 546–478 BC* London: Edward Arnold.
Cahen, É. 1924. 'Sur quelques traits du récit de "Salamine" dans les "Perses" d'Eschyle.' *Revue des études anciennes* 26 (4): 297–313.
Caspari, M. O. B. 1911. 'Stray Notes on the Persian Wars.' *Journal of Hellenic Studies* 31: 100–9.
Cawkwell, G. 2005. *The Greek Wars: The Failure of Persia*. Oxford: Oxford University Press.
Clairmont, C. W. 1983. *Patrios Nomos: Public Burial in Athens during the Fifth and Fourth Centuries BC*. Oxford: British Archaeological Reports.
Culley, G. R. 1977. 'The Restoration of Sanctuaries in Attica, II.' *Hesperia* 46 (3): 282–98.
de Jong, I. 2018. 'The View from the Mountain (oroskopia) in Greek and Latin Literature.' *Cambridge Classical Journal* 64: 23–48.
Deubner, L. 1932. *Attische Feste*. Berlin: Verlag Heinrich Keller.
Fentress, J. and C. Wickham. 1992. *Social Memory*. Oxford: Blackwell.
Ferrill, A. 1966. 'Herodotus and the Strategy and Tactics of the Invasion of Xerxes.' *American Historical Review* 72 (1): 102–15.
Fornara, C. W. 1966. 'The Hoplite Achievement at Psyttaleia.' *Journal of Hellenic Studies* 86: 51–54.
Frost, F. J. 1973. 'A Note on Xerxes at Salamis.' *Historia* 22 (1): 118–19.
Georges, P. B. 1994. *Barbarian Asia and the Greek Experience: From the Archaic Period to the Age of Xenophon*. Baltimore and London: Johns Hopkins University Press.

Goodwin, W. W. 1906. 'The Battle of Salamis.' *Harvard Studies in Classical Philology* 17: 74–101.
Green, P. 1996. *The Greco-Persian Wars*. Berkeley and Los Angeles: University of California Press.
Grethlein, J. 2009. 'How Not to Do History: Xerxes in Herodotus' Histories.' *American Journal of Philology* 130 (2): 195–218.
Grundy, G. B. 1897. 'The Account of Salamis in Herodotus.' *Journal of Hellenic Studies* 17: 230–40.
Grundy, G. B. 1901. *The Great Persian War and Its Preliminaries: A Study of the Evidence, Literary and Topographical*. London: John Murray.
Hammond, N. G. L. 1956. 'The Battle of Salamis.' *Journal of Hellenic Studies* 76: 32–54.
Hammond, N. G. L. 1973. *Studies in Greek History*. Oxford: Clarendon Press.
Hammond, N. G. L. 1988. 'The Expedition of Xerxes.' In, *The Cambridge Ancient History, Volume IV: Persia, Greece and the Western Mediterranean c. 525 to 479 BC* edited by John Boardman, N. G. L. Hammond, D. M. Lewis and M. Ostwald, 518–91. Cambridge: Cambridge University Press.
Harris, D. 1995. *The Treasures of the Parthenon and Erechtheion*. Oxford: Clarendon Press.
Hauvette, A. 1894. *Hérodote. Historien des guerres médiques*. Paris: Librairie Hachette.
Hignett, C. 1963. *Xerxes' Invasion of Greece*. Oxford: Clarendon Press.
Immerwahr, H. R. 1966. *Form and Thought in Herodotus*. Cleveland: American Philological Association.
Jacquemin, A. 2000. *Guerre et Religion dans le monde grec (490–322 av. J.-C.)*. Liège: Sedes.
Judeich, W. 1912. 'Psyttaleia.' *Klio* 12: 129–38.
Kirchberg, J. 1965. *Die Funktion der Orakel im Werke Herodots*. Göttingen: Vandenhoeck & Ruprecht.
Kromayer, J. 1924. *Antike Schlachtfelder: Bausteine zu einer antiken Kriegsgeschichte. Vierter Band: Schlachtfelder aus den Perserkriegen, aus der späteren griechischen Geschichte und den Feldzügen Alexanders und aus der römischen Geschichte bis Augustus. 1. Lieferung*. Berlin: Weidmannsche Buchhandlung.
Kromayer, J. 1931. *Antike Schlachtfelder: Bausteine zu einer antiken Kriegsgeschichte. Vierter Band: Schlachtfelder aus den Perserkriegen, aus der späteren griechischen Geschichte und den Feldzügen Alexanders und aus der römischen Geschichte bis Augustus. 4. Lieferung*. Berlin: Weidmannsche Buchhandlung.
Langdon, M. K. 2007. 'Lolling's Topographical Work on Salamis.' In *Historische Landeskunde und Epigraphik in Griechenland. Akten des Symposiums veranstaltet aus Anlaß des 100. Todestages von H. G. Lolling (1848–1894) in Athen vom 28. bis 30. 9. 1994*, edited by K. Fittschen, 109–22. Münster: Deutsches Archäologisches Institut.
Leake, W. M. 1841. *The Topography of Athens and the Demi. Vol. II. The Demi of Attica*. London: J. Rodwell.
Lolling, H. G. 1884. 'Die Meerenge von Salamis.' In *Historische und philologische Aufsätze Ernst Curtius zu seinem siebenzigsten Geburtstage am zweiten September 1884 gewidmet*, 3–10. Berlin: Verlag von A. Asher & Co.
Macan, R. W. 1908. *Herodotus: The Seventh, Eighth, & Ninth Books with Introduction, Text, Apparatus, Commentary, Appendices, Indices, Maps*. London: MacMillan and Co.
Maurizio, L. 1997. 'Delphic Oracles as Oral Performances: Authenticity and Historical Evidence.' *Classical Antiquity* 16 (2): 308–34.
Meyer, E. 1954. *Geschichte des Altertums. Vierter Band, Erste Abteilung: Das Perserreich und die Griechen bis zum Vorabend des peloponnesischen Krieges*. Darmstadt: Wissenschaftliche Buchgesellschaft.
Milchhoefer, A. 1895. *Karten von Attika. Heft VII–VIII*. Berlin: Geographische Verlagshandlung Dietrich Reimer.
Minchin, E. 2016. 'Heritage in the Landscape: The "Heroic Tumuli" in the Troad Region.' In *Valuing Landscape in Classical Antiquity: Natural Environment and Cultural Imagination*, edited by J. McInerney and I. Sluiter, 255–75. Leiden: Brill.

Müller, D. 1987. *Topographischer Bildkommentar zu den Historien Herodots: Griechenland im Umfang des heutigen Griechischen Staatsgebietes*. Tübingen: Ernst Wasmuth Verlag.
Munro, J. A. R. 1926. 'Xerxes' Invasion of Greece.' In *The Cambridge Ancient History, Volume IV: The Persian Empire and the West*, edited by J. B. Bury, S. A. Cook and F. E. Adcock, 268–316. Cambridge: Cambridge University Press.
Myres, J. L. 1953. *Herodotus: Father of History*. Oxford: Clarendon Press.
Obst, E. 1913. *Der Feldzug des Xerxes*. Klio, Beiheft 12. Leipzig: Dieterisch'sche Verlagsbuchhandlung.
Papachatzi, N. D. 1974. *Παυσανίου Ελλάδος Περιήγησις: Αττικά*. Athens: Εκδοτική Αθηνών.
Papadopoulou, C. 2014. 'Transforming the Surroundings and its Impact on Cult Rituals: The Case Study of Artemis Mounichia in the Fifth Century.' In *Locating the Sacred: Theoretical Approaches to the Emplacement of Religion*, edited by C. Moser and C. Feldman, 111–27. Oxford: Oxbow Books.
Parker, R. 2005. *Polytheism and Society at Athens*. Oxford: Oxford University Press.
Pritchett, W. K. 1959. 'Towards a Restudy of the Battle of Salamis.' *American Journal of Archaeology* 63 (3): 251–62.
Pritchett, W. K. 1965. *Studies in Ancient Greek Topography: Part I*. Classical Studies 1. Berkeley: University of California Press.
Pritchett, W. K. 1985. *Studies in Ancient Greek Topography: Part V*. Classical Studies 32. Berkeley: University of California Press.
Pritchett, W. K. 1993. *The Liar School of Herodotos*. Amsterdam: Gieben.
Proietti, G. 2015a. 'I Greci e la memoria della vittoria: alcune considerazioni sui trofei delle Guerre Persiane.' *Hormos* 7: 148–75.
Proietti, G. 2015b. 'War and Memory: The Battle of Psyttaleia before Herodotus' Histories.' *Bulletin of the Institute of Classical Studies* 58 (2): 43–54.
Ray, F. E., Jr. 2009. *Land Battles in 5th Century BC Greece: A History and Analysis of 173 Engagements*. Jefferson: McFarland.
Rediadis, P. D. 1906. 'Τὸ Ἡράκλειον τῆς ναυμαχίας τῆς Σαλαμῖνος.' *Ἀρχαιολογικὴ Ἐφημερίς* 1906: 239–44.
Sancisi-Weerdenburg, H. 1980. *Yaunā en Persai: Grieken en Perzen in een ander Perspectief*. PhD diss., Leiden.
Schudson, M. 1995. 'Dynamics of Distortion in Collective Memory.' In *Memory Distortion: How Minds, Brains, and Societies Reconstruct the Past*, edited by D. L. Schacter, 346–64. Cambridge, MA: Harvard University Press.
Stefanini, R. 1977. 'Giambattista Casti in Troy and Athens, 1788.' *California Studies in Classical Antiquity* 10: 157–68.
Taylor, M. C. 1997. *Salamis and the* Salaminioi: *The History of an Unofficial Athenian* Demos. Amsterdam: J. C. Gieben.
Tsirivakos, E. 1967. 'Μαγούλα.' *Ἀρχαιολογικὸν Δέλτιον* 22: 146.
van Rookhuijzen, J. Z. 2017. 'Thetis in the Ovens: A Reconsideration of Herodotus' Topography of Magnesia.' *Journal of Hellenic Studies* 137: 24–41.
van Rookhuijzen, J. Z. 2018. *Herodotus and the Topography of Xerxes' Invasion Place and Memory in Greece and Anatolia*. Berlin and Boston: De Gruyter.
van Rookhuijzen, J. Z. 2020. 'The Parthenon Treasury on the Acropolis of Athens.' *American Journal of Archaeology* 124 (1): 3–35.
Vansina, J. 1985. *Oral Tradition as History*. Madison: University of Wisconsin Press.
Wallace, P. W. 1969. 'Psyttaleia and the Trophies of the Battle of Salamis.' *American Journal of Archaeology* 73 (3): 293–303.
Wallinga, H. T. 2005. *Xerxes' Greek Adventure: the Naval Perspective*. Leiden: Brill.

Whatley, N. 1964. 'On the Possibility of Reconstructing Marathon and Other Ancient Battles.' *Journal of Hellenic Studies* 84: 119–139.

Wilhelm, A. 1929. *Zur Topographie der Schlacht bei Salamis*. Akademie der Wissenschaften in Wien Philosophisch-historische Klasse Sitzungsberichte 211 (1). Vienna and Leipzig: Hölder-Pichler-Tempsky.

Wilson, N. G. 2015. *Herodoti Historiae*. Oxford: Oxford University Press.

CHAPTER 11
WAR IN A LANDSCAPE: THE DARDANELLES FROM HOMER TO GALLIPOLI
C. J. Mackie

The Dardanelles region of modern Turkey is usually thought of as a kind of maritime boundary between Europe and Asia – part of a waterway that extends northeast up to the sea of Marmara and the Black Sea, and southwest to the Aegean and Mediterranean seas.[1] To control the Dardanelles waterway has been seen through time as providing a crucial strategic military advantage, most recently by Winston Churchill in the ill-fated Gallipoli campaign of 1915. His aim was to get to Constantinople – an intention that seems somewhat bizarre now, given what we know about the limitations of the campaign. The British, French and their allies (including the Anzacs) found out to their cost, both by sea and land, how difficult a landscape (and seascape) the Dardanelles could be to capture in the face of a courageous and determined enemy. As we now know from some significant scholarship in this area, one of the remarkable things about the 1915 campaign is just how 'Greek' it was, how the dominance of the Classical curriculum in the pre-war years entered into the literary discourse of well-to-do British soldiers.[2] The Gallipoli campaign, set as it was within the landscape of ancient Greece, certainly had a different feel to it from the Western Front.[3] Indeed Homer's Troy was a kind of silent witness to a new campaign set in an ancient heroic landscape.

So narratives of war set at the Dardanelles have a long history, and one might even make the claim that the region is defined by war more than any other single area of the ancient Mediterranean world. That is certainly my view, although it is not the purpose of this chapter to argue for it. The European and Asian landscapes of the Dardanelles together have witnessed some renowned conflicts, and they play a major part in the ancient Greek literary narratives. One might think instantly of the Trojan wars, the Persian wars, the Peloponnesian War, not to mention the Macedonian presence in the region in the fourth century BCE (Philip and Alexander). And there were many other renowned conflicts too, most of them connected in some way with the desire to control the waterway.[4] This chapter deals with some of the ancient Greek narratives set at the Dardanelles, and their reception in 1915, and the landscape that they describe. The

---

[1] 'All history has passed through the Hellespont, from the expedition of the Argonauts and the Trojan war down to the recent Great war': Ximinez (1925: 91).
[2] Elizabeth Vandiver (2007, 2010) is a key figure in this scholarly area.
[3] It is worth noting the population statistics of the Gallipoli Peninsula, as set out in Pentzopoulos (1962: 31–2). Based on Turkish and Greek census statistics undertaken not long before the war (1910 and 1912) there were two Greeks living on the peninsula for each Turk.
[4] For one recent survey, see Sagona et al. (2016: esp. 1–35).

chapter takes the broad view and argues that too often scholars are focused on individual texts, or single narratives of a particular war, without any sense of the bigger picture of the region. This does little justice to the collective memory of earlier events, and the dominance of the Dardanelles as the quintessential landscape of war in Greek literature.

We will, therefore, be concerned in the first instance with key narratives of Troy in the *Iliad*, notably Heracles' presence there in the earlier generation of Greek heroes. It will be argued that these Homeric 'para-narratives' are fundamentally important in giving us a sense of the earlier heroic context and how different it was from the world of Achilles.[5] The chapter then moves to two other figures from the main Trojan war who are associated with landmarks on the European side of the waterway – the Greek warrior Protesilaus, who had a hero-cult situated at Elaious at the tip of the Gallipoli peninsula (Cape Helles), and Hecuba in the play *Hecuba* by Euripides, who was associated with the naming of the promontory 'Cynossema' (where a major sea battle was fought in 411, described by Thucydides in Book 8 of his *History*).[6] I am particularly interested in the way that the main Trojan war 'spills across' the Dardanelles waterway in post-Homeric narratives, from Asia to Europe, and the way that landmarks associated with this process have a life of their own in later conflicts. The memory of earlier individuals plays a fundamental role in the emergence of later conflicts.

But we begin on the Asian side with the two struggles for Troy, and the fact that there were *two* conflicts described in the ancient sources, not just one. The poems of Homer and the Epic Cycle of course were concerned primarily with the ten-year war against Priam's Troy, as were many other ancient texts and works of art. The warriors around Agamemnon in the *Iliad* (and also the gods on Olympus) anticipate a Trojan genocide, one which is played out in other texts after the end of the *Iliad*. The emphasis in the *Iliad* itself is on the imminent destruction of the place by fire (e.g. 20.313–17).[7] Hector's body on the pyre at the end of the poem (24.656ff., 778ff.) symbolizes the imminent torching of the city itself. The poem does not need to show the burning city itself, because Hector's body on the pyre is enough.[8] Cremation is significant in the last part of the *Iliad* both in terms of the warriors who are on the pyres (notably Patroclus in Book 23 and Hector in Book 24); but also in terms of the imminent death and cremation of Achilles and the city of Troy itself. The fate of Achilles and the fate of Troy are inextricably linked in the final books of the *Iliad* (cf. 24.131–2, 650ff., 669ff., 778ff.).

References to the sack of the city by Heracles in the earlier generation are a significant inclusion within the *Iliad* (5.265–73, 638–51; 7.451–3; 8.284; 14.249–51; 20.144–8;

---

[5] On Homer and the para-narratives, see Alden (2000).
[6] For references in Herodotus to Protesilaus and the cult site constructed in his honour, see 7.35 and 9.114–21. The site itself has not been identified archaeologically, even though Schliemann had made an attempt, as did the French in the early twentieth century. On this, see Özdogan (1986) and Körpe (2014).
[7] This is often described as Homeric 'foreshadowing', on which see Scodel (2011).
[8] The burning of the river Scamander in Book 21 has the same function as Hector's cremation, in so far as we witness another burning of 'Troy' prior to the actual city itself (a fate which occurs, of course, after the conclusion of the *Iliad*). See the introduction to this volume (3–14, esp. 7–8).

The Dardanelles from Homer to Gallipoli

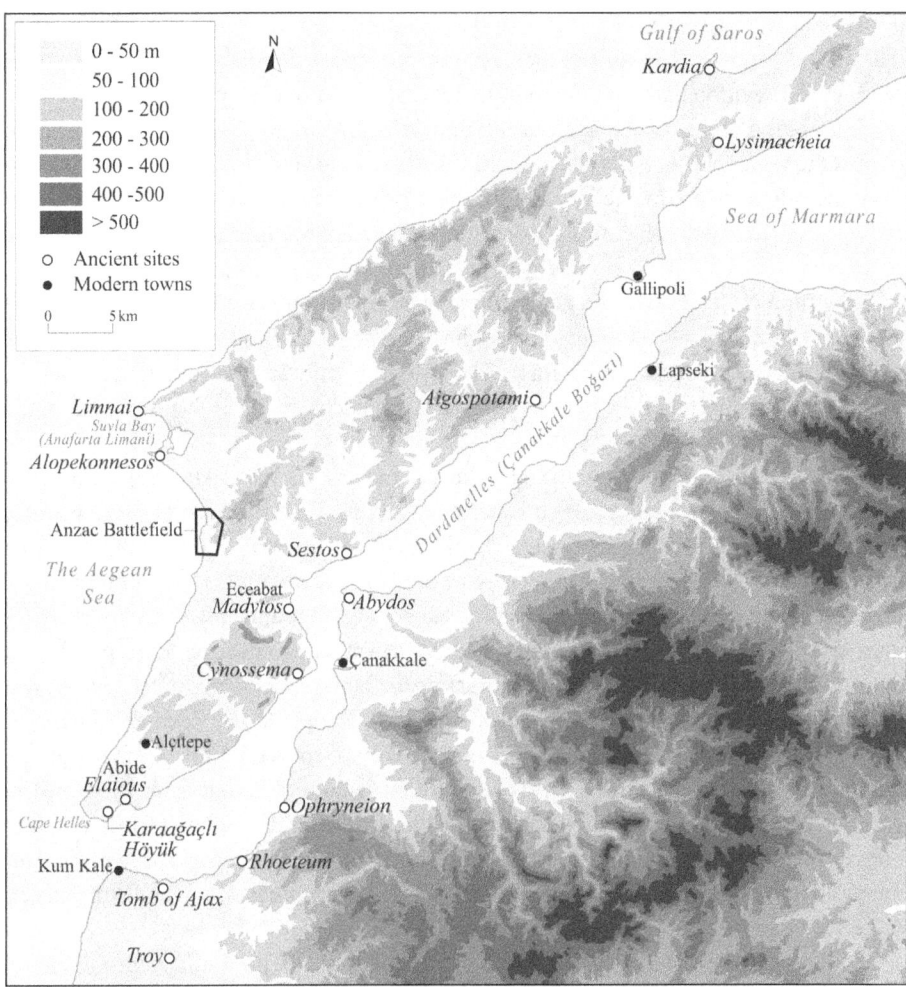

Figure 11.1 Map of the Gallipoli Peninsula showing the main ancient and modern sites. C. J. Mackie, M. Atabay, R. Körpe and A. Sagona, 'Boundary and Divide: The Antiquity of the Dardanelles', in A. Sagona, M. Atabay, C. J. Mackie, I. McGibbon and R. Reid (eds.), *Anzac Battlefield: A Gallipoli Landscape of War and Memory* (Melbourne: Cambridge University Press, 2016), 6. Reproduced with kind permission of Cambridge University Press.

20.231–8; 21.441–60). These Iliadic references obviously predate later, more expansive, accounts of the Heracles-at-Troy story.[9] It scarcely needs to be said that this is the sort of thing that could have been left out of the poem, in so far as it sits well outside of the main narrative of Priam's city. But the fact is that the story is firmly situated in the memory of the participants of the main campaign, most notably Heracles' son Tlepolemus, who tells Sarpedon in *Iliad* 5 (641–2) that Heracles came to Troy 'with six ships and fewer men and

---

[9] Such as Apollod. *Bibl.* 2.5.9.

destroyed (*exalapaxe*) the city of Ilios and made the streets desolate (*chêrôse*)'. The story that Homer appears to know (based on the references above) is that in the earlier generation Poseidon had built the walls of Troy, but had not been paid by the somewhat perfidious king of the day, Laomedon (Priam's father). As a consequence Poseidon sent a monster to torment the city of Laomedon. The wandering Heracles happened to come by Troy and offers to destroy the monster for the Trojans if he receives the immortal horses of Zeus that Laomedon had in his possession. These are the immortal horses that Tros received for the loss of his son Ganymede. Laomedon agrees to the deal, and Heracles kills the monster and saves the girl Hesione, who had been placed outside the walls to appease it. The Trojans, however, renege on the arrangement and so Heracles sacks the city and kills Laomedon. The young girl Hesione is duly married off to Telamon of Salamis, and she becomes the mother of the archer Teucer who is fairly prominent in the *Iliad*, notably in Book 8 (esp. 281ff.).[10]

In the eyes of the Greeks in the poem, Teucer is a *nothos*, a bastard (8.284), because his mother Hesione is Trojan. Teucer's brother Ajax, on the other hand, is high-born because both his father and mother are Greek. The different social status of the two is informed by their characteristic weapons, especially in *Iliad* 8: Teucer with his bow, and Ajax with his great shield and spear (note especially Teucer's eight victims in Book 8 in which he uses Ajax's shield for protection, 266ff.). Hesione's brother Priam survives Heracles' sack of the city and becomes king after his father's death. Homer's audience must have known this story well enough, given the allusive nature of the 'snippets' (as Maureen Alden calls them[11]) within the *Iliad* itself. The earlier sack of Troy, of course, is only one story among many in the *Iliad* of an earlier heroic setting that is quite different from the world of Achilles. Monsters in particular, such as in the heroic life of Bellerophon (6.145–211), are one feature of the heroic landscape that has disappeared from the world of Achilles. This means that the human landscape of cities and towns, are more fundamentally the targets of heroic violence than creatures of the wild.

It seems appropriate in a volume like this to think of the built environment of Laomedon's Troy as the 'landscape' of the city at that time. One feature of the narrative of Heracles' Trojan adventures is that whatever happened to the built environment of Troy seems to have been quite minor. Certainly, the *Iliad* gives us no sense of any major damage or destruction of the physical setting of the place that Heracles sacked. Indeed, this seems to be the core feature of the whole narrative – that it was a comparatively small-scale assault that was dealt with quickly and easily. The language is really one of 'defeat' by Heracles and his men, rather than 'destruction' as such. It is an important difference between the two defeats of the city that runs right through the poem. It is noteworthy that in the *Iliad* Heracles is remembered as an *archer* in a poem where archery is comparatively ineffectual as a weapon. On the Greek side the bow and arrow is a weapon of bastards (as with Teucer above), in contrast to the spear as a fully aristocratic weapon.

---

[10] Gantz (1993: 400–2, 442–4) gives a useful diachronic summary of the sources and the broader story.
[11] Alden (2000: 24).

But the *Iliad* is not in the business of making a negative judgement of Heracles. His use of the bow is appropriate enough given the range of challenges that he faced in his travels. Or to put it another way, the world of Heracles is very different from the world of Achilles. Monsters roamed the earth, even at Troy, very unlike the world of the warrior Achilles. He fights other men with the spear, and wouldn't be seen anywhere near a bow and arrow. Heracles' characteristic weapon, the bow and arrow, is appropriate to his heroic challenges, just as Achilles' weapon is right for his. The Heraclean conflict with Troy sets a context that informs the more acute cruelty of the world of Achilles and Agamemnon. The generational context – the different landscapes of war in the two conflicts – speaks to us about a fundamental transition in the conduct of human affairs in war. We hear the language of defeat in the earlier generation, but that of total destruction of the city in the later one.

So the 'main' Trojan war has a prehistory, and the *Iliad* sets out different layers of conflict which are quite distinct from each other. The Trojans and Athena had built a wall for Heracles in the earlier struggle (20.144–52), one that still survives in the later conflict. The emphasis in Homer and the Cycle is on the total destruction of the built environment of Troy in the main war, and the genocide of the Trojan people. References to Heracles provide a very different context and a very different heroic *modus operandi*. The message is that the world has moved on since Heracles came with his bow and his six ships. The spearmen of the *Iliad*, led by Agamemnon and Odysseus, will deal with the Trojans in a very different way from Heracles.

It is true to say, therefore, that the first sack of Troy, if we can call it that, is an important background episode in the Iliadic context of the war at Troy. One might think of it as the sort of narrative that our poet might have left out, not the least because his audience seems to know the basic storyline well enough (unlike many readers today, who are surprised to hear that Heracles sacked the place in earlier times). But Heracles provides a very different heroic context in the *Iliad*, one that helps to signify the heroic features of Achilles and his world.[12] The poetic advantage in providing a pre-history for the main campaign of Agamemnon and Menelaus is to draw some sharp comparisons between two contexts of war and heroic conduct. It reminds us, in case we were to forget, that the second landscape of war is all about a genocide and total destruction of the landscape.

What we tend to find in various war narratives set in the Dardanelles is a kind of continuity and layering where particular landmarks witness new struggles and new levels of suffering (as with the wall built for Heracles, 20.144–52). This is true both of the built environment (like the two Greek campaigns at Troy, as above), and also of the natural formations of the environment (like Cynossema below). The narrative of Protesilaus is a particularly good example of this. In the Greek myths generally, he was the leader of a contingent from Thessaly, but he saw very little action because he was killed as soon as the war began (usually by Hector, as was told, presumably, in more detail in the *Cypria*).[13] He is renowned in the Greek myths as the first Greek hero to be killed

---

[12] See Martin (1989: *passim*).
[13] West (2003: 77).

in the Trojan War. His name in Greek probably means 'first of the people' and so seems very apposite. Generally speaking, however, the surviving Greek sources for Protesilaus are very limited (although the main Latin sources – Catullus, Ovid and Hyginus – elaborate his myth in some detail).

Homer mentions the death of Protesilaus in the *Iliad*, and the fact that he left behind a young grieving wife and a house that was only half-completed (2.695ff.). When the Trojans manage to set fire to a ship of the Greeks in Book 16 (112–29; 293ff.), it is actually Protesilaus's ship that gets burnt, and therefore is not a very significant achievement on the Trojans' part. Homer seems to use Protesilaus's name to undercut this moment of Trojan triumph.[14] There were other important sources for Protesilaus that have not survived. Sophocles seems to have written a play, *Poimenes*, about the killing of Protesilaus by Hector, and told the story from the Trojan point of view (frr. 497, 500, 501R). Likewise, Euripides wrote a play called *Protesilaus* in which the hero is married for just one day before he goes off to Troy. His loving wife Laodamia seems to be very central to the story of his death at Troy, and this is rather unusual for a Greek casualty of the Trojan War. Later still, in Apollodorus, we are told the version that Thetis had warned Achilles not to disembark straightaway at Troy because it was fated that the first warrior to do so would be killed (*Epit*. 3.29–30). Protesilaus, who knew nothing of the prophecy, thus fell victim to the workings of fate.

The nature of Protesilaus's death as leader of the first charge from the ships at Troy makes him an ideal figure for Greek hero-cult. And this was duly established at some early stage at ancient Elaious on the other side of the waterway from Troy, near to Cape Helles. It then becomes a landmark of contention – a symbol of Persian hubris and Greek piety. Herodotus tells us that the Persian governor of Sestos, Artaÿctes, collected women in the temple of Protesilaus at Elaious and committed various acts of sacrilege (7.33). The revenge of the Athenians, led by Xanthippus after the defeat of the Persians ends the whole *History* of Herodotus. Artaÿctes and some of his people made their escape from the siege of Sestos conducted by the Athenians, but they were captured near Aegospotami. The people of Elaious wanted their revenge on the governor, as did Xanthippus. And so he had him nailed to a plank above the town of Madytos (modern Eceabat) close to where Xerxes had crossed with his fleet into Europe. To add to the governor's agony, he was forced to watch his son being stoned to death before his eyes. Herodotus seems to take some grim satisfaction in ending his whole *History* with this gruesome narrative (9.114–21).

Thus, the hero Protesilaus, and the symbolic significance of his shrine on the European side of the Hellespont, could scarcely be more important than in Herodotus. The figure of Protesilaus takes us back to the Greek world of Homer; and the treatment of his shrine in Herodotus is a defining characteristic of the religious affairs of Greeks and Trojans. The cult site helps to define the boundary between the two continents, and justifies, at least in Herodotus' mind, the treatment of the satrap and his son by Xanthippus and the Athenian forces.

---

[14] Taplin (1992: 173, n. 34).

But the most famous visitor to the shrine of Protesilaus arrived about 150 years later, in the person of Alexander the Great in 334 BCE. Alexander had pilgrimage on his mind on both sides of the Dardanelles (i.e. the tombs of Protesilaus and Achilles), and so he ventured to Protesilaus' shrine at Elaious and then to Troy. Arrian tells us (*Anab.* 1.11) that: 'At Elaious [Alexander] offered sacrifice upon the tomb of Protesilaus, who was supposed to have been the first man of Agamemnon's army to set foot upon the soil of Asia when the Greeks sailed against Troy. His purpose in performing the ceremony was to ensure better luck for himself than Protesilaus had.' Alexander wants to be the new Achilles, not the new Protesilaus, and so he embarks on a kind of personal pilgrimage prior to the campaign in Asia. He crosses to Sigeum from Elaious, whereas his army crosses at the narrows between Sestos and Abydos, where Xerxes had gone in the other direction all those years before. As we have seen, Apollodorus records that Thetis had advised Achilles not to get to Troy first because the first to land would be the first to die. The fates of Achilles and Protesilaus are thus connected both in the post-Iliadic sources on the Trojan War, and Alexander's own landing on the coast near Troy.

The shrine of Protesilaus has not been identified with any precision, although Heinrich Schliemann is meant to have done some exploratory fieldwork on a possible cult site without a permit only to be sent packing after two days. In terms of the Gallipoli landscape in 1915, the shrine is probably located between V and S Beaches, the former of which saw some terrible casualties. One might think of Protesilaus's death as a kind of early Greek leitmotif of the Gallipoli landings, in so far as the emphasis in the Gallipoli record is on the disastrous arrival of the soldiers there. On 25 April 1915 thousands died at Helles much like Protesilaus did – leaping from the boats, or in the water, or on the beaches themselves. There are, of course, some graphic accounts of these landings. Midshipman Drewry of the Royal Naval Reserve, later a VC winner, described his landing at V beach in the following way:

> At last we had the signal at 6.am and in we dashed. At 6.10 the ship struck, very easily – she brought up and I shot ahead and grounded on her port bow. Then the fun began, picket boats towed lifeboats full of soldiers inshore and slipped them as the water shoaled and they rowed the rest of the way. The soldiers jumped out as the boats beached and they died almost all of them, wiped out with the boats' crews.[15]

Likewise Midshipman Berridge on the ship *Albion* wrote that 'the slaughter was awful and you could see them falling on the beach and in the water. They got into dead ground under a bank however and there remained for the whole day'.

In all, thousands died in the Helles landings in a similar human catastrophe to the landings at Anzac. The ancient Greek setting at the tip of the Gallipoli Peninsula allows us now to see the Helles landings in a broader temporal and cultural context. The men in

---

[15] Snelling (2013).

the water and on the beaches met their fate in the vicinity of the ancient shrine of Protesilaus. The very idea of Protesilaus's cult-site silently witnessing the Helles landings has a rather profound and immediate poignancy about it. It must be one of the great topographical coincidences of the First World War (and very rarely noticed too!). It is almost as if his shrine stands nearby as a single heroic memorial of their fates. No setting could quite evoke the collective tragedy of the Helles landings like the adjacent shrine of Protesilaus (even if we don't know for certain where it is).

One individual lone soldier figure worth mentioning in the context of the nearby shrine of Protesilaus is Lieutenant-Colonel Charles Hotham Montague Doughty-Wylie of the Royal Welsh Regiment whose own death has its mythic quality. He spoke Turkish, having been a participant in the Balkan wars of 1912–13 with the Red Cross. On 25 April, the day of the landing at Helles, he was on the *River Clyde* landing steamer (a ship also known as the 'Trojan Horse'!), from where he could see the failure of the British landings. On 26 April he led a charge to the village of Seddulbahir but Doughty-Wylie was killed trying to take the heights above the village. It is said that he loved the Turkish people so much that he refused to carry a gun and only had a walking stick. He is the only soldier to have an individual grave at Helles quite separate from the main cemeteries and memorials. Moreover, it seems to me rather fascinating (given the important part played by the wife of Protesilaus in his myth, as above) that on 17 November 1915 a small boat pulled up at Helles and the solitary figure of Doughty-Wiley's wife Lillian got out. She is the only recorded woman on the allied side to visit Gallipoli.

One might say that a narrative is played out in 1915 that has some extraordinary parallels with narratives from antiquity, notably with the myth of Protesilaus. Upon reflection one can appreciate these parallels today. In his book *Homeric Sites Around Troy* Jonathan Brown writes that 'there was a hill . . . on the southern tip of the Gallipoli Peninsula. However, it was largely destroyed in the First World War, when it was known by its attackers as Hill 141. . . . Nearby is the tomb of a modern hero who died trying to capture the hill [i.e. Doughty-Wylie]. There is no sign of the Tomb of Protesilaus.'[16] There is, however, no reason to think that the ancient parallel played out in the minds of participants in 1915 itself.

It is significant, therefore, that the story of Protesilaus does not remain 'fixed', as it were, on the Asian side of the Dardanelles, as one might have expected. The figure of Protesilaus 'spills across' from Asia (i.e. in Homer) to Europe (in post-Homeric sources) making him a critical individual in narratives on both sides of the waterway. The memory of other Greek heroes such as Achilles has them situated in the vicinity of Troy. But the figure of Protesilaus has a very different afterlife. Indeed, his cult site has a life of its own in a major kind of way on the European side as a *casus belli* in later conflicts at the boundary of the Greek and Persian worlds.

Protesilaus was not the only connection to Homer and the Trojan War that the people of Elaious could claim. There was also a rather curious story about Hecuba, the queen of

---

[16] Brown (2017: 276).

Troy, and her fate after the city fell to the Greeks. Hecuba was the principal wife of king Priam, and (presumably) mother to nineteen of Priam's hundred children, including Hector and Paris (*Il.* 24.495–7). In Homer's *Iliad* she is an imperious but gentle matriarch. When Troy is defeated and sacked she is gathered together with the women and children of the city to be taken back to Greece as a prize of war. The story of the passage of the women from stately luxury in their own land to slavery in Greece is told in two renowned plays by the Athenian poet Euripides (the *Hecuba* and the *Trojan Women*). I have argued in an article focused on *Iliad* 24 that Homer is well acquainted with stories of the fall of Troy, including this version of the fate of the Trojan women.[17]

Both of the Euripidean plays are set immediately after the defeat of the city, as the women await deportation. Within the course of the *Hecuba* the queen loses two further children in addition to all the family she has already lost – her daughter Polyxena and her son Polydorus. Polyxena is a victim of sacrifice, ostensibly to appease the ghost of Achilles, who had previously been promised the princess after the fall of Troy. Because Achilles is now dead, Polyxena is given to him in death by human sacrifice. It is worth noting that again Achilles is associated with the land of the dead, as in Homer and other sources. Hecuba's young son Polydorus is also found dead within the play. He had been given to the Thracian king Polymestor for his protection together with a lot of gold. When Troy falls, the king kills the boy and keeps the gold. Hecuba then conspires her own revenge, despite her captivity and her imminent deportation, by blinding king Polymestor and killing his sons (see also the fate of Artaÿctes, as above).

All of these horrors are meant to take place on the European side of the Dardanelles – the Gallipoli Peninsula where the Greek forces and their Trojan captives are gathered prior to returning to their homelands. *Hecuba* is the only extant play set on the European side. Again we can identify the way that the narrative of Trojan suffering 'spills across' from Asia to Europe at the beginning of new horrors for the Trojans in the Greek world.

In the course of the play and in the wake of what has happened to his sons, Polymestor then makes a rather strange prophecy of what will happen to Hecuba on the way back to Greece: 'I foretell that you shall drown at sea. You shall climb to the masthead and fall . . . You shall climb the mast of your own free will, changed to a dog, a bitch with blazing eyes . . . and when you die your tomb shall be called "Cynossema", the bitch's grave, a landmark to sailors' (*Hec.* 1259ff.). Cynossema ('dog's grave') is – or seems to be – a cape further to the north from Elaious, probably near modern Kilit Bahir (not far from modern Turkish town of Eceabat). It could, however, be further to the south, closer to Elaious.

The word 'Cynossema' is not so much known from this obscure aetiological narrative about how this particular promontory got its name, but rather for a sea-battle fought between the Athenians and their allies and the Spartans and their allies in the vicinity of the promontory in 411 BCE. Thucydides tells us (8.104–7) that the Athenians used Sestos

---

[17] Mackie (2013).

and Elaious (Cape Helles) as their base, whereas the Spartans operated from Abydos on the Asian side of the Dardanelles. He tells us that the seventy-six Athenian ships sailed close to the peninsula heading towards Sestos and the narrows, and that the Spartans and their allies, with their eighty-six ships came out to meet them. It must have been quite something to see 162 ships engaged together in the comparative confines of the Hellespont, although Aegospotami six years later (also at the Dardanelles) had double the number of ships – about 350 in total (what a pity Thucydides cuts out before that battle!).[18] These two great sea-battles (Cynossema and Aegospotami) represent two absolutely crucial struggles in the last part of the Peloponnesian War. The battle of Cynossema in particular was fought not very far from where the British and the French navies tried to force their way through the Dardanelles, but were defeated on 18 March 1915, about five weeks before the similarly ill-fated land assault on 25 April.

What is important is that a narrative of Troy (Hecuba = 'Cynossema') gives its name to the landscape of a new conflict between Athenians and Spartans on the other side of the Dardanelles. Again we can identify the importance and the fluidity of aetiological myths of the Dardanelles nomenclature. Just as little Helle is meant to give her name to the Hellespont when she fell off the ram and the golden fleece into the sea, so a myth of the queen of Troy helps to identify a later landscape (and seascape) of war.

To conclude: the Dardanelles region is a much-contested landscape, both in terms of 'actual' historical warfare in recent times, such as the Gallipoli campaign, and in terms of much earlier Greek narratives of conflict set there (Troy, the Persian campaigns, the Peloponnesian War and the Macedonian campaigns). This chapter has really just touched the surface of the number of struggles that were set there. My own view is that this landscape is defined by war more than any other single area of the Mediterranean world. It is the setting for the genocide of the Trojans in two different struggles; it is the border between the Greek world and the Persian assaults of 480–479, the struggle between Athenians and Spartans during the late stages of the Peloponnesian War, and the site of the Macedonian military venture of Alexander against the Persian world in 334. And that is only a small part of it. Of particular interest to me in this chapter has been the way that the Troy narrative of Homer spills across the Hellespont in antiquity to inform later struggles that take place within the context of the European side of the peninsula. The various landmarks on both sides of the waterway are silent witnesses to new stories and new struggles. The built environment of Troy is witness to and participant in two sacks of the city, not just one; the shrine of Protesilaus at Elaious is the centrepiece of fundamental religious conflicts between Greeks and Persians; and the Cynossema promontory a little bit further up the peninsula plays a key role in the outcome of the battle named after it in 411.

These layers of conflict through time, and the connections with antiquity, of course come to the fore in the discourse of the Gallipoli campaign itself of 1915, particularly some of the literature and private correspondence of the soldiers. Much has been written

---

[18] For *kunos sema*, see Diod. Sic. 13.40.6, Strabo 7 fr. 56.

in recent times on enthusiasts of Greek literature and myth who found themselves in the locality of Homer's Troy, and who were conscious of other stories from Greek antiquity. Rupert Brooke and Patrick Shaw-Stewart are probably the two most famous soldier-bards, but they were not the only ones. My own view is that modern classicists probably have a tendency to overstate the Greek context of what was going on at Gallipoli in 1915. For every member of the classically literate officer class from the great public schools of England (who might have known about Troy or Protesilaus or Hecuba) there must have been hundreds for whom Greek antiquity meant nothing.

Nonetheless it is undeniable that Gallipoli sits within an ancient Greek context and even has an ancient Greek name (Gelibolu = Gallipoli = Kallipolis = 'Beautiful City'). The notion of beauty is embedded in the name Gallipoli, and nothing like that occurs in the nomenclature of the western front. Moreover, the physical remains of the Greek and Roman world uncovered during the campaign itself were a reminder that this was a landscape of war going back a very long way and with many different levels. Indeed, the French forces conducted an entire excavation of the ancient site of Elaious in 1915 itself, a location which, as we have seen above, was the site of the shrine of Protesilaus.[19] Thus the material remains uncovered during the Gallipoli campaign itself complemented what is known about Protesilaus at Elaious from the ancient literature. Archaeology in Turkey essentially came to a halt in 1915 apart from the very place where the battle was being fought. The physical layers in the landscapes of war at the Dardanelles confirmed the ancient literature referred to in this chapter. The Dardanelles is a crowded space, and one that is defined through war like no other in the Mediterranean world.

Bibliography

Alden, M. J. 2000. *Homer Beside Himself: Para-Narratives in the Iliad*. Oxford: Oxford University Press.

Brown, J. 2017. *Homeric Sites around Troy*. Canberra: Parrot Press.

Gantz, T. 1996. *Early Greek Myth: A Guide to Literary and Artistic Sources*. 2 vols. Baltimore and London: Johns Hopkins University Press.

Körpe, R. n.d. '2014 Yili Gelibolu Yarimadasi Sestos Antik Kenti ve Cevresi Yuzey Arastirmasi' *37 Uluslararasi Kazi, Arastirma ve arkeometri Sempozyumu*. Ankara: T.C. Kultur ve Turizm Bakanligi.

Mackie, C. J. 2010. 'Archaeology at Gallipoli in 1915.' In *Philathenaios: Studies in Honour of Michael J. Osborne*, edited by A. Tamis, C. J. Mackie and S. G. Byrne, 213–25. Athens: Greek Epigraphic Society.

Mackie, C. J. 2013. '*Iliad* 24 and the Judgement of Paris.' *Classical Quarterly* 63: 1–16.

Martin, R. 1989. *The Language of Heroes: Speech and Performance in the Iliad*. Ithaca: Cornell University Press.

Özdogan, M. 1986. 'Prehistoric Sites in the Gelibolu Peninsula.' *Anadolu Arastirmalari* 10: 51–67.

---

[19] For the archaeology that took place at Gallipoli in 1915 during the campaign, see Mackie (2010) and Sagona et al. (eds) (2016).

Pentzopoulos, D. 1962. *The Balkan Exchange of Minorities and its Impact upon Greece.* Paris: Mouto.
Sagona, A., M. Atabay, C. J. Mackie, I. McGibbon and R. Reid, eds. 2016. *Anzac Battlefield: A Gallipoli Landscape of War and Memory.* Melbourne: Cambridge University Press.
Scodel, R. 2011. 'Foreshadowing.' In *The Homer Encyclopedia (Vol. 1),* edited by M. Finkelberg, 295. Chichester: Wiley-Blackwell.
Snelling, S. 2013. *VCs of the First World War: The Naval VCs.* Stroud: The History Press.
Taplin, O. 1992. *Homeric Soundings.* Oxford: Clarendon Press.
Vandiver, E. 2007. 'Classics in British Poetry of the First World War.' In *Remaking the Classics: Literature, Genre and Media in Britain 1800–2000,* edited by C. Stray, 37–55. London: Duckworth.
Vandiver, E. 2010. *Stand in the Trench, Achilles: Classical Receptions in British Poetry of the Great War.* Oxford: Oxford University Press.
West, M. 2003. *Greek Epic Fragments from the Seventh to the Fifth Centuries BC.* Cambridge Massachusetts and London: Harvard University Press.
Ximinez, S. 1925. *Asia Minor in Ruins.* London: Hutchinson.

CHAPTER 12
MUTABLE MONUMENTS AND MUTABLE MEMORIES IN LUCAN'S *BELLUM CIVILE* AND THE FORMER YUGOSLAVIA[1]

Jesse Weiner

1 Introduction

Wars occasion struggles over history and memory, struggles which frequently play out in the accumulation and destruction of monuments – landmarks that 'direct attention to specific places and events', thereby '[anchoring] "collective remembering" in material sites that [serve] as rallying points for shared common memory and identity'.[2] With the passage of time, as multiple wars layer over a single landscape, so do the meanings of these mnemonic artefacts and the memories they determine and preserve. Civil war landscapes, for obvious reasons, stand out as particularly divisive Loci of memory production; we need only think of recent controversies over the removal of Confederate monuments in the United States. 'Like lightning rods', as Susan E. Alcock writes, these sorts of objects draw 'energy to select versions of the past'.[3] It should come as no surprise that monuments, landscape and cityscape are major themes in Latin poetry, especially in epic. An epic poem, like a monument, can function as a 'mnemotope', an organizing mnemonic site around which collective memory, history and national identity are formed, performed and reinforced.[4] At the same time, to borrow two terms from Jan Assmann, these artefacts enact both 'cultural repression' and the erasure of 'cultural memory'.[5] This duality reflects the fractured and divisive collective memories generated by civil wars.

---

[1] Like many of the contributors to this volume, I presented a version of this chapter as a paper at the 2017 Celtic Conference in Classics in Montréal. I have also presented portions and versions of the chapter at Hamilton College, Monmouth College, Pacific Lutheran University, University of Arizona, University of Otago, University of South Florida, University of Western Ontario and Virginia Tech University; I appreciate the feedback I received on each occasion. In addition to the editors and anonymous referees of this volume, thanks are due to Stephen Hinds and James I. Porter, who read and commented on early versions of this material. Finally, I am grateful to Jan Kempenaers, who has graciously allowed me to include images of his photography.

[2] Osborne (2001: 50–51).

[3] Alcock (2002: 17), also quoted in Weiner (2020: 191). The complexity of these dynamics and the potential for landscapes to play a role in distorting history and memory are central themes in van Rookhuijzen (in this volume).

[4] Cf. Weiner (2020: 191). See Assmann (1992), Assmann (1995), Assmann (1997), Alcock (2002). For one recent discussion of collective memory and civil war in Latin poetry, see Ginsberg (2017).

[5] Assmann (1995: 366), also discussed by Flower (2006: xix–xx) and Weiner (2020: 191). See also Brockmeier (2002) and Bollig (2009: 19).

In ways that should feel familiar to us and that continue to inform our present, struggles over history and memory are at the very core of Lucan's *Bellum Civile*, which, of course, is a poem about civil war, written as Rome stood at the brink of yet more civil wars. (This perhaps accounts for Lucan's rich representation in the present volume.) As I have previously noted, 'a struggle between often painful acts of remembrance' and their opposite, 'consignment to oblivion', pervades the *Bellum Civile* (which is itself presented as a *monumentum*), especially in the poem's depictions of other monuments, landscapes and their physical and hermeneutic instability.[6] Lucan presents these mnemonic artefacts as coterminous with the project of empire, and he uses monuments to construct and, as I will suggest, unmake social memory.

Many of Lucan's literary predecessors – Augustan authors like Virgil, Horace, Ovid, Livy and Vitruvius – had inscribed monuments in their work, highlighting the shared ability of 'geographical relics' and poetry to determine and replicate memory for posterity.[7] The Augustan poets therefore presented their own literary output as monumental in its own right and joined their imagined afterlives to that of Rome itself.[8] Indeed, the Augustan literary regime tended to imagine a *Roma Aeterna* – Rome as the eternal city that would provide an unchanging showcase for its eternal monuments.[9] This cultural poetics of static monumentality is perhaps paradoxical, given the obvious renewal, refashioning, rededication and destruction of old monuments around them in Augustan Rome. Nevertheless, if Latin poetry uses monuments as a metonymy for empire, this should be familiar to us, too. We need only think about iconic scenes from numerous films in which the preservation of the American republic is represented in its familiar monuments (e.g. *Mr. Smith Goes to Washington*), or where the destruction and decay of monuments present dystopian visions of state collapse (e.g. the iconic final scene of *Planet of the Apes*).

When it comes to Lucan, writing about the civil war that brought about the end of the Republic, the latter image of the Statue of Liberty rising out of the sand (Fig. 12.1) is especially appropriate, since it uses a monument to conjure themes of *libertas* and precipitous and unexpected state collapse. (The monument's beachfront setting, too, is suggestive of Pompey's grave in Lucan, *BC* 8.) These dynamics, present in Lucan, by which civil war landscapes and their mnemonic artefacts serve as volatile Loci of memory production, surround us in our contemporary present. With an eye towards these issues in modernity, I here view Lucan's mutable monuments in tandem with a mutually illuminating bit of material culture. By looking at a fascinating, eerie set of war

---

[6] Weiner (2020: 191) On *memoria* and *oblivio* in Lucan, see especially Thorne (2011), as well as Gowing (2005), McClellan (2019: 115). In a sense, then, this chapter complements that of Zientek (in this volume). Whereas Zientek reads Lucan's agrarian landscapes, I read his monumental landscapes. To adapt Tuan (1979: 131): Lucan forces us to disregard any 'image of rural peace and urban turmoil'; in Lucan, countryside and cityscapes alike become 'landscapes of war'.

[7] Hardie (1993: 17).

[8] See Weiner (2020: 191–3) for discussion of monumentality in Augustan poetry with bibliography.

[9] This dynamic is also present in Augustan prose. See Weiner (2016) on Vitruvius. Propertius 3.2.17–26 claims monumentality over the less durable wonders of the world. It is telling that Propertius offsets his poetry against Egyptian and Greek monuments (pyramids, the tomb of Mausolus and the Temple of Jupiter at Olympia), not Roman ones. On the relation of Propertius 3.2 to Horace *Carm*. 3.30, see Miller (1983).

Monuments in Lucan and the Former Yugoslavia

Figure 12.1 Scene still from *Planet of the Apes,* dir. Franklin J. Schaffner. 20th Century Fox, 1968. Alamy.

monuments in the Balkans, I suggest we might visualize broadly the politicized processes by which monuments and their commemorative referents change in Lucan's poem and appreciate their relevance to our world. Like Lucan's poem and its monuments, these sculptures 'sing of wars more than civil' (*bella ... plus quam civilia | ... canimus*; Lucan, *BC* 1.1–2).[10] As Alcock suggests, 'the former Yugoslavia' stands out as a 'familiar' theatre for 'the politics of memory', a place 'where conflicting, equally strongly affirmed, accounts of the past are sent into battle, much as people are'.[11]

At stake in the present inquiry, then, are not only questions of poetics, politics and philosophy in Lucan's poem but also larger questions about how we view and read. How do texts relate to more manifestly material objects? How do art, material artefacts and the landscapes they occupy preserve and/or determine history and memory? And who gets to determine meaning? The artist or the audience? These questions are as modern as they are ancient, and they have profound consequences, especially, I think, in our newly 'post-truth' and 'alternative factual' culture.

2 Shifting landscapes, shifting memories

I now turn to the eastern provinces of the Roman Empire, albeit quite a few centuries after its collapse. It may seem a stretch to draw deep comparisons between Augustus and

---

[10] For the text of Lucan, I use David R. Shackleton Bailey's Teubner edition, reprinted as Shackleton Bailey (2009).
[11] Alcock (2002: 17).

Figure 12.2 *Monument to the Revolution of the People of Moslavina* (sculptor: Dušan Džamonja) in Podgarić, Croatia. Jan Kempenaers, *Spomenik #1* (2006). © Jan Kempenaers.

the former Yugoslav premier, Josip Broz Tito (1892–1980). Nevertheless, their careers bear a number of striking similarities to one another. Like Augustus, Tito emerged from a period of war and civil war to consolidate power under his person and, despite the fact that his regime was in many respects authoritarian, Tito gained a cult of personality and was largely viewed as a unifying symbol for the nations of the Yugoslav Federation. In both his politics and the symbolism of his regime, Tito was forced to walk a delicate tightrope, celebrating the new Socialist Federal Republic of Yugoslavia and his powerful position in it, while simultaneously downplaying the memories of the violent discord, global conflict and civil wars that gave birth to this new order. Like Augustus, Tito remained in power until his death, serving as supreme commander of the military for four decades. Also like Augustus, Tito amassed a slew of titles and decorations, was celebrated in a Partisan poetry regime (replete with Apollonian pretensions) and, most importantly for our purposes today, left behind thousands of monuments.[12]

One group of these monuments warrants our attention. During the 1960s and 1970s under Tito, Yugoslav landscapes became marked by the construction of thousands of monuments as Second World War memorials. Known as *Spomeniks* – literally 'the monuments' in Serbo-Croatian – these sculptures mark the sites of battles, concentration camps and civil war massacres. For example, Owen Hatherly notes that the *Spomenik* at Petrova Gora (Fig. 12.3) marks the site where '300 barely armed local peasants were killed fighting against the ferociously violent fascist Ustaše militia in 1942'.[13] They were

---

[12] Tanja Zimmerman (2015: 56) suggests that Roman celebration of 'Augustus as a relative of Apollo' provided a template for solar imagery and metaphor in Tito's Partisan poetry regime.
[13] Hatherly (2016). The Ustaše were rivals of Tito's 'multi-ethnic, Communist-dominated Partisans'. The Petrova Gora *Spomenik* originally housed a museum, which was ravaged in the 1990s.

Monuments in Lucan and the Former Yugoslavia

Figure 12.3 *Monument to the Uprising of the People of Kordun and Banija* (sculptor: Vojin Bakić) in Petrova Gora, Croatia. Jan Kempenaers, *Spomenik #2* (2006). © Jan Kempenaers.

meant to convey the strength of the state, and the monuments were a vital part of patriotic education. As they were celebratory icons located upon sites of past atrocities, the *Spomeniks* always sported a dual nature: they were at once mnemonic artefacts and objects of forgetting. Their very forms marked them as such, as the futuristic designs cheerfully looked forward without explicitly conjuring the often painful and divisive past they were built to commemorate.[14]

As Joshua Surtees observes, quoting an interview with Kempenaers:

'Tito couldn't erect figures or busts in honour of generals because he didn't want to be seen to be favouring any ethnic group, for example a Bosnian general or a Serb war hero, so instead they made these things that didn't refer to people'. They were deliberately devoid of identity and built in places where schoolchildren were encouraged to visit to cultivate a sense of national and cultural togetherness.[15]

To anticipate my discussion of Augustus's Palatine Temple in Lucan, Augustus's monument was built to commemorate his victory in civil war, but the form of the monument excised the divisive elements of this history to suggest a pious and harmonious relationship with the god Apollo. In a sense then, both Tito's *Spomeniks* and Augustus's Palatine Temple might be understood as attempts to whitewash history and impose a redirection of social memory.

---

[14] It should be noted that, while I here focus on an abstract non-representational subset, not all of these monuments were abstract and not all were federally commissioned. See Hatherly (2016).

[15] Surtees (2013). See also Neutelings (2010: 17).

Figure 12.4 Monument in Krusevo, Macedonia. Jan Kempenaers, *Spomenik #5* (2007). © Jan Kempenaers.

'Spomeniks are everywhere. You'll see them on strategic outcroppings, lofty passes, and sweeping plateaus: gigantic sculptures, firmly anchored to the rocks.'[16] In the misguided, or perhaps ironic, words of one design journal, 'they are built of *indestructible* materials like reinforced concrete, steel, and granite.'[17] Nevertheless, in the turmoil of the early 1990s, the majority of these monuments were destroyed, dismantled or, at best, abandoned to the natural elements. Today, 'hardly anyone outside of the former Yugoslavia is aware of their existence', and within the ex-Yugoslav nations, 'no one really wants to be reminded that they are there'.[18] As the architect Willem Jan Neutelings observes:

> In the 1980s, these monuments still attracted millions of visitors, but a decade later, their appeal vanished, they have become submerged in a new age, rendered unintelligible to the current generation. Their symbolism has been lost in translation as the visual language has changed, their signals muffled by a shifted world-view. The monuments have been the object of blind fury and now, of indifference. What remains is pure sculpture in a desolate landscape.[19]

When we look at these monuments – here photographed by Jan Kempenaers and published in his 2010 book *Spomenik* (and presented in more recent exhibitions) – I suggest that we gaze at a realization of the vision of Lucan's *Bellum Civile*. Throughout the

---

[16] Neutelings (2010: 16).
[17] Neutelings (2010: 16). My own emphasis.
[18] Neutelings (2010: 16).
[19] Neutelings (2010: 16).

Monuments in Lucan and the Former Yugoslavia

epic, Lucan rejects a Roman imperial rhetoric of eternal monuments and instead couples his assault on the Julio-Claudian principate and its versions of history with the physical and hermeneutic destabilization of its monuments. Augustan poets such as Virgil, Horace and Ovid proclaimed the anticipated longevity of their monuments, and they presented these monuments as metonymy for Rome itself and its promise of empire without end. But what of Lucan, a poet who inherits this tradition, yet is openly inimical to Julio-Claudian *imperium* and who presents a Rome at breaking point, on the verge of tearing itself apart? We might easily ask the speculative question: what if the Pisonian conspiracy (a plot to assassinate Nero for which Lucan himself lost his life) had succeeded? What if Augustus's successors, Tiberius, Caligula and Claudius, had earlier failed to maintain the principate built by Augustus? What if Lucan's side had won?[20] How, then, would posterity have received Augustan monuments? In contrast to the Augustan principate, Tito's Yugoslav federation violently collapsed in the civil wars a mere decade after his death, and the state he built atomistically fragmented into its constitutive parts.

The architects of many of the *Spomeniks* lived well into the 2000s and thereby outlasted their own monuments (Dušan Džamonja, the award-winning sculptor of the *Monument to the Revolution of the People of Moslavina* in Podgarić, Croatia, lived until 2009). Most of the monuments have been destroyed utterly, victims of memory sanctions as it were (Fig. 12.2).

Figure 12.5 Destroyed monument in Kamenska, Croatia. Jan Kempenaers, *Spomenik #21* (2009). © Jan Kempenaers.

---

[20] I mean this in the broadest possible sense to incorporate Lucan's hostility to the Julio-Augustan regime and the *Bellum Civile*'s antipathy towards Nero, at least in its final books. As Martindale (1984) traces, Lucan scholarship lacks consensus on Lucan's Republicanism. For reasons of space I here leave unanswered the question of whether the proem's encomium of Nero should be treated as sincere or subversive, though I do suggest below that Lucan's treatment of the Palatine Temple in *BC* 3 is anti-Augustan, and I elsewhere suggest that the passage may also operate on an anti-Neronian register. See Weiner (2020).

Landscapes of War in Greek and Roman Literature

Others have been overwritten with graffiti (Fig. 12.6), left to crumble and to be reclaimed by their natural surroundings (Fig. 12.7).

These ruins and their desolation conjure the landscapes of the *Bellum Civile*. Lucan tells us at the outset of his epic that Rome has turned its hand against itself (*in te verte manus*; 1.23) and, as a result, its landscapes and structures have been transformed and left desolate to the destructive powers of nature (1.24–9):

Figure 12.6 Graffiti-covered monument in Košute, Croatia. Jan Kempenaers, *Spomenik #12* (2007). © Jan Kempenaers.

Figure 12.7 Crumbling monument in Makljen, Bosnia and Herzegovina. Jan Kempenaers, *Spomenik #15* (2007). © Jan Kempenaers.

> at nunc semirutis pendent quod moenia tectis
> urbibus Italiae lapisque ingentia muris 25
> saxa iacent nulloque domus custode tenentur
> rarus et antiquis habitator in urbibus errat,
> horrida quod dumis multosque inararta per annos
> Hesperia est desuntque manus poscentibus arvis

> But if now walls totter over half-demolished homes in the cities of Italy, great stones lie beneath moldering houses, homes are protected by no guard, and only an occasional resident wanders the ancient cities; if Hesperia bristles with brambles and lies unploughed for many years, and hands are lacking for begging ploughs.

Lucan's apocalyptic vision of Italy after Pharsalus is again one of vacuity and monuments made unmonumental by civil war (7.391–9):

> tunc omne Latinum
> fabula nomen erit; Gabios Veiosque Coramque
> pulvere vix tectae poterunt monstrare ruinae
> Albanosque lares Laurentinosque penates,
> rus vacuum, quod non habitet nisi nocte coacta 395
> invitus questusque Numam iussisse senator.
> non aetas haec carpsit edax monimentaque rerum
> putria destituit: crimen civile videmus
> tot vacuas urbes.

> Then the entire Latin name will be a legend; ruins covered with dust will scarce indicate Veii, Gabii, and Cora, and the houses of Alba and the Laurentian homes – an empty country which no one inhabits save the unwilling senator forced there for a night by the order of Numa. Hungry time did not devour these things and decay did not forsake the monuments of things past; we see civil crime in all these empty cities.

The crime (*crimen*) of civil war has consigned collective memory to the realm of *fabula*. Ruins (*ruinae*) cannot function as mnemotopes (*vix ... monstrare*), and the memorials (*monimenta*) are consigned to decay (*putria*). Lucan's *edax aetas* puts the passage into conversation with Horace (*Carm.* 3.30.3) and Ovid (*Met.* 8.872), and the *Bellum Civile* replaces monumental and mnemonic longevity through political harmony with ruination and oblivion in the aftermath of civil war.[21]

Lucan's Caesar well understands the value of controlling the past through its artefacts. For example, at Book 6.32–51, 'Caesar destroys monumental structures such as city walls

---

[21] Leigh (1996: 89) also connects these passages and notes that Lucan 'savages' these Augustan 'conceits'. Leigh also notes the passage's anachronism: 'Lucan blames on the civil wars the destruction of cities ruined years earlier and by the expansion of Rome'. Cf. Dilke (1960: *ad loc.*).

and homes and repurposes the materials to build fortifications for war that rival the walls of Troy and Babylon'.[22] The general thereby weaponizes ruined monuments, turning them against their own landscapes.[23]

When Caesar tours the ruins of Troy in Book 9, a combination of warfare, decay, and the super-fecundity of nature have robbed – or at least transformed – the landscape and its monuments of their mnemonic powers (9.964–9):

> circumit exustae nomen memorabile Troiae
> magnaque Phoebei quaerit vestigia muri. 965
> iam silvae steriles et putres robore trunci
> Assaraci pressere domos et templa deorum
> iam lassa radice tenent, ac tota teguntur
> Pergama dumetis: etiam periere ruinae.

> He walks round the memorable name of burnt-out Troy and he seeks the great remains of Phoebus's wall. Now the barren forests and rotten trunks of trees press the palace of Assaracus and now their worn-out roots hold the temples of gods, and all Pergama is covered with thorn-brushes: even the ruins have perished.

What monuments 'still stand have been reclaimed by nature and its super-fecundity', and 'grasses, brambles, and thorn-brakes obscure manmade structures and render the monuments unrecognizable and, ultimately, uninterpretable'.[24] Similarly, Tito's *Spomeniks* have become sites of decay caused by civil war – be it through neglect, decay, incidental violence or intentional destruction – and Kempenaers' photographs capture the melancholic ruination of the *Spomeniks*. On Fig. 12.5, one snarky online commenter remarks that there must be some mistake – this monument looks more like a bush. A reader of Lucan might well be reminded of *BC* 9.969, where *etiam periere ruinae* ('even the ruins have perished').[25] It has become virtually impossible to discern what is or was a monument, let alone its intended commemorative value.

Nevertheless, Caesar and his Phrygian guide (*monstrator*; 9.979) are drawn to the ruined Trojan landscape as an organizing site of memory and national identity, and each does attempt to interpret the site through his own political agenda. The ruins have perished, yet 'no stone lacks a name' (*nullum est sine nomine saxum*; 9.973). Lucan presents us with an exercise in reader response. Caesar and his guide perform interpretive interventions on the site coloured by their discursive communities. Caesar, the Roman who traces his own lineage through Aeneas to Venus, 'sees ... the marriage chamber of Anchises' (*aspicit ... Anchisae thalamos*; 9.970–1), while 'the Phrygian guide forbids Caesar to trample the grave of Hector' (*Phryx incola manes | Hectoreos calcare vetat*;

---

[22] Weiner (2020: 193).
[23] On homes as memory theatres and monuments in Roman culture, see especially Bergmann (1994), Bodel (1997), Roller (2010).
[24] Weiner (2020: 194).
[25] Ahl (1976: 215–16) connects Troy's ruins with Italy's ruins after Pharsalus in *BC* 7. Cf. Rossi (2001: 322).

9.976–7), even though nothing was visible besides 'high grass' (*alto gramine*; 9.975–6).[26] As readers, we are not told what, if any, monument once marked Hector's grave. We, along with Caesar, are included among the readers of posterity and, if ever a monument had marked the spot, the tall grass and lapse of years has hidden it from view, like the sands of Pompey's gravestone (discussed below). When he puts his foot in the tall grass, Caesar transforms from *inscius* (9.974) to *securus* (9.975), and the Roman gives no indication whatsoever that he accepts his guide's rebuke. Caesar is overconfident and arrogant but can hardly be proven wrong; he is secure in all its connotations, both positive and negative. Caesar and his guide thus 'challenge each other with divergent readings of the site, none of which, in my reading, are narratologically endorsed or wholly censured by the poem'.[27] If anything, Lucan's narrator is sceptical as well, as, far from chastising Caesar, he concedes that the 'scattered stones lay in ruins, preserving no appearance of anything sacred' (*discussa iacebant | saxa nec ullius faciem servantia sacri*; 9.977–8).[28]

3 Forms of attention

Lucan's monuments point both towards the power of audiences in posterity to impose new commemorative values on monuments and towards the power of war and civil war to provoke these interpretive interventions upon memory, monuments and landscapes. For those *Spomeniks* that still stand, commemorative values have been lost or overturned. Neutelings argues that, in only a decade or two, the sculptures have lost their monumentality altogether and he asks 'whether a former monument can ever function as pure sculpture, an autonomous work of art, detached from its original meaning'.[29] Conspicuously, Kempenaers' photos are devoid of spectators, and, like Lucan's farmers *in absentia* (1.28–9; see Zientek in this volume), the throngs of tourists during the 1970s and 1980s are poignant in their absence. Neutelings' view that the sculptures have ceased to be monuments thereby mirrors the afterlife of Pompey's tombstone as prophesied by Lucan in Book 8 of the *Bellum Civile* (8.867–72):

pulveris exigui sparget non longa vetustas
congeriem, bustumque cadet, mortisque peribunt

---

[26] Ormand (1994: 51) observes that 'Caesar reads the Troy of the *Aeneid*, and misses that of the *Iliad*'. For Ormand, Caesar's 'selectivity ... makes him more powerful'. Cf. Johnson (1987: 119). See also Rossi (2001).
[27] Weiner (2020: 194).
[28] This reading seems to be in agreement with Quint (1993: 6), who writes that the 'historical topography [of Lucan's Troy] is irrecoverable, no matter what labels the local tourist industry may give to individual spots of the landscape in order to turn them into attractions'. Cf. Rossi (2001: 321): 'Neither Caesar's version of the story nor the guide's may control and assert its superiority over the other ... At Troy everyone can create his own story to tell.' It should be pointed out that many readers of Lucan have found the guide's warnings to Caesar to be authoritative corrections. See Ahl (1976: 215), Bartsch (1997: 132).
[29] Neutelings (2010: 17.)

>   argumenta tuae. veniet felicior aetas
>   qua sit nulla fides saxum monstrantibus illud; 870
>   atque erit Aegyptus populis fortasse nepotum
>   tam mendax Magni tumulo quam Creta Tonantis.

A short time will scatter this pile of little dust, the gravestone will fall, and the proofs of your [Pompey's] death will perish. A happier age will come, in which those who point out that stone will not be believed; and perhaps to our descendants Egypt will be as false in Pompey's tomb as Crete in the tomb of Jupiter Tonans.

In this mutually exclusive prophecy, 'Lucan doubly writes the monument out of existence as stone and ash inwardly collapse on the one hand, while the *bustum*'s commemorative referent ("Here lies Pompey" | *hic situs est Magnus*; 8.793) disappears through custom and disbelief'.[30] This *monumentum* for a fallen civil war general will therefore experience both material annihilation and hermeneutic death. Those who point out the stone (*monstrantibus*) will not be believed, and, moreover, Lucan dubs this shift from civil war *memoria* to *oblivio* 'happier' (*felicior*).[31] Lucan invites us to connect this failed mnemotope with Hector's alleged grave in Book 9. Just as Trojan *saxa* fail to preserve anything *sacer*, this *saxum* fails to preserve the *nomen sacrum* (8.792) of its interred general.

Lucan's mnemotopes depend upon the active participation of the audience in creating and performing their own memories when engaging with mnemonic landscapes. Of Pompey's *bustum*, Lucan writes (8.818–22):

>   solitumque legi super alta deorum
>   culmina et extructos spoliis hostilibus arcus
>   haud procul est ima Pompei nomen harena 820
>   depressum tumulo, quod non legat advena rectus,
>   quod nisi monstratum Romanus transeat hospes.

And the name of Pompey, which is accustomed to be read over the tall temples of the gods and arches laden with the spoils of enemies, lies not far above the deep sand, so low on the tomb that a stranger could not read it standing upright, and a Roman visitor would pass by it unless it were pointed out.

On a purely practical level, the small size of the stone, coupled with the imminent threat that it might be overwhelmed by the sand, makes it less likely to be noticed and read by passersby (a connection to the grave of Hector, over which Caesar unwittingly walks at 9.965).[32] The stone cannot recall and memorialize Pompey unless it is read, the likelihood of which is

---

[30] Weiner (2020: 194).
[31] Cf. Malamud (1995: 11): 'In Lucan's happier age, *felicior aetas*, the grave will disappear and with it all proof of Pompey's death ... History will be rewritten – and lies will replace the truth.'
[32] See Mayer (1981: 184). Mayer observes of both episodes that 'the failure to notice a hero's tomb is pathetic' and that 'for this reason, tombs were meant to be conspicuous to travelers'. Also Hardie (2012: 189–90), Fratantuono (2012: 343).

vastly diminished if it must be pointed out by someone already in the know to a prospective spectator who must crouch down to read it. As Henry Day observes, 'the measure of Pompey's ruin is vertical'. Pompey, who 'earlier feared that his name would become *miserabile* or *invisum* (7.120–1)', has his fears realized: the *nomen* once located *super alta deorum | culmina* has been brought low to the point of invisibility.[33] The passive participle, *monstratum*, emphasizes the inability of the monument to signify its referent actively; without the viewer/reader, Pompey's gravestone commemorates nothing and thus becomes a decidedly unmonumental *monumentum*. By contrast, the active forms of *monstare* given to viewers of monuments (in addition to *monstrantibus* at 8.870, cf. *monstrator* at 9.979) emphasize the essential role of posterity in performing and (re)constructing history and memory.[34] Tito's massive *Spomeniks* do not share this problem in stature, yet their geographical isolation and institutionalized neglect – no longer part of public school curricula – effect a similar outcome, largely devoid of a viewership.

The active role of the reader is underscored by *solitum*. Pompey's name is *accustomed* to be read on temples and arches because these are the sorts of structures whose forms are conventionally designated monumental by the Romans. It is custom that nominates the temple, the arch, and the *bustum* as appropriate forms to the makers of intentionally commemorative monuments and, likewise, the habits of the Roman people condition the spectator to see an arch, recognize its form as monumental, pause, and read its inscriptions. Hence, Lucan's narrator fears that the memorial stone will not adequately serve its commemorative function, as its audience is wont to look up rather than down at monuments and at large rather than small objects. The abstract, non-representational forms of Tito's *Spomeniks* similarly frustrate modern monumental expectations. Monumentality is not inherent to the arch, the temple, Pompey's gravestone, or Tito's *Spomeniks*; it is conventionally dependent upon the mores of discursive communities.[35] These mores are perhaps never more fluid and fragile than in the upheaval and aftermath of civil war. *Solitum* thus effects within Lucan's text a hermeneutic model consistent with contemporary reader-oriented literary theories.[36] In his essay, 'How to Recognize a Poem When You See One', Stanley Fish argues for public and conventional acts of recognition, rather than formal characteristics, as the source of constructions of meaning. Meaning is not permanently affixed to a poem or a monument by the artist, but rather we create not only these meanings but also the very taxonomies of poems and monuments 'through interpretive strategies that are finally not our own but have their source in a publicly

---

[33] Day (2013: 220–1).

[34] As we have seen, the *ruinae* of Veii, Gabii and Cora *vix ... poterunt monstrare*. Zwierlein (1986: 469–70) connects Lucan's *monstrator* at 9.979 with Virgil's Evander, who actively 'shows' (*monstrat, Aen.* 8.337, 345) Aeneas the sites of Pallantium. Cf. Ormand (1994: 50), Rossi (2001: 323).

[35] On the mutable significance of monumental architecture in imperial Rome, Edmund Thomas (2007: 18) writes that 'the basic ornamental language of monumental architecture continued to be defined by the classical orders. However, their use and meaning changed.'

[36] Matthew Leigh (1997) argues that Lucan's representation of his narrative as spectacle likens his reader to a member of an audience, yet at times challenges the reader to break from the passivity of this position. Here Lucan affords a particularly active role to readers and viewers, but the poet does not seem particularly optimistic that they will be so active as to break from their culturally determined and normative conventions and habits.

available system of intelligibility'. Monumental artefacts 'are the products of social and cultural patterns of thought'.[37] Two millennia prior to Fish, Lucan's *Bellum Civile* cedes at least partial control over monumentality and commemorative value to posterity and the audience.[38]

In the final analysis, it is viewers, not architects, who make monuments. While the original symbolism of the *Spomeniks* has largely been lost, I suggest that they remain monuments – perhaps with what the Austrian art critic and theorist Alois Riegl would call historical value. 'It is not their original purpose and significance that turn these works into monuments, but rather our modern perception of them'.[39] These monuments are hermeneutically mutable, but poignant and powerful nevertheless. Once symbols of unity, their dilapidated conditions and institutional neglect now reflect the social and historical fracturing of Tito's state. As some considered the civil wars of the 1990s to be an extension of the Second World War, what were intended as symbols of healing and unity instead conditioned violent anger as commemorations of strife and conflict.[40] Wars have layered upon these landscapes and, now forty or fifty years after their creation, these once hopeful sculptures point not to a bright and unified future but instead look backwards, melancholically, at a naïve historical moment which sought to gloss over unhealed social fault lines. The referents of these monuments have been appropriated and overthrown by posterity, and the sculptures have been made to signify the precise opposite of their original intent, despite the fact that many of the sculptors are, or were recently, still alive and well.

These dynamics are present in Lucan's depiction of the Palatine Temple of Apollo, which is turned from a symbol of divine favour for the principate into an emblem of its illegitimacy.[41] The Palatine Temple, built by Augustus adjacent to his home on Rome's Palatine Hill, commemorated his civil war victories at Naulochus (36 BCE) and Actium (31 BCE). The temple was dedicated in 28 BCE and stood as 'the most visible and abiding expression of Augustus's affiliation with Apollo'.[42] The temple therefore functioned as a symbol of Augustus's religious reverence, his divine patronage and the Augustan peace, albeit peace achieved through civil war.[43] This monument, celebrated both in verse and prose, was central to the emperor's self-representation and the regime's attempt to control the memory of its divisive origins.[44] The temple and the building programme at large

---

[37] Fish (1982: 226–32). Cf. Fowler (1996: 60–61). More specific to monumentality, Cecil Elliott (1964: 52): 'monuments are *customarily* overlaid with minutiae and subtleties of symbolism that are meaningless without the viewer's previous knowledge'. My own emphasis.
[38] On Lucan and reader response, see Roche (2005).
[39] Riegl (1982).
[40] See Neutelings (2010: 17).
[41] This reading of Lucan's treatment of the Palatine Temple adapts and condenses my more extensive discussion in Weiner (2020).
[42] Miller (2009: 185). Cf. Babcock (1967: 190).
[43] See Zanker (1988); Syndikus (2006: 308).
[44] See Hor. *Carm*. 1.31; Prop. 2.31, 4.6; Verg. *Aen*. 6.69, 8.720–2. Ov. *Tr*. 3.1.59–62; Suet. *Aug*. 29.1–3; Joseph. *BJ* 2.61; Vell. Pat. 2.81.3. On the Palatine in Augustan poetry, see especially Barchiesi (2005: 282), Welch (2005: 106), Günther (2006: 373–4, 378–9), Syndikus (2006: 208–309), Rea (2007), Fantham (2012: 308–10), Coutelle (2015: 739).

were part of a process by which Augustus 'displaced competing versions of the past ... the image of the benign elder statesman and of his golden age of prosperity displaced the violence and lawlessness of Octavian, the teenage warlord'.[45] The Palatine Temple functioned as a mnemotope around which Roman identity and Augustan memory collected.[46] And, like Tito's *Spomeniks*, the monument simultaneously sought to remember and celebrate civil war victories while also functioning as an object of forgetting, healing, and unification.

Lucan's revisionist and anachronistic revaluation of the Palatine Temple of Apollo constitutes a bold attempt to wrest control of history and its monuments away from their makers. Early in *Bellum Civile* 3, Caesar enters Rome and convenes the senate. Lucan changes historical details to render Caesar's meeting with the senate both unconstitutional and chronologically impossible (3.103–9):

> Phoebea Palatia complet
> turba patrum nullo cogendi iure senatus
> e latebris educta suis; non consule sacrae   105
> fulserunt sedes, non, proxima lege potestas,
> praetor adest, vacuaeque loco cessere curules.
> omnia Caesar erat: privatae curia vocis
> testis adest.

Although there was no authority to call the Senate, a mob of senators were led out from their hiding places and they filled the Palatine Temple of Apollo; the sacred seats did not shine brilliantly with consuls, the praetor (next in power by law) was not present, and the empty chairs of office were removed from the place. Caesar was all of these: the senate was present to bear witness to the authority of a private voice.

Lucan chooses the chronologically impossible Palatine Temple for the setting of the meeting. Elaine Fantham notes that it is a 'deliberate anachronism that Lucan sets the meeting in the Palatine temple of Apollo constructed by Caesar's heir', a full two decades *after* the historical events Lucan describes.[47] Cassius Dio sets the meeting outside the Pomerium (41.15.2), and, irrespective of whether Dio is accurate, the Palatine Temple's presence in Rome two decades before its dedication is a clear instance of temporal disjuncture. Sarah A. Nix observes that 'the temporal disjunction' represented by the temple 'calls attention to the fictive nature of Caesarian claims in both a pre- and post-Augustan world'.[48]

The significance behind the anachronism is intricately interwoven with Lucan's second deployment of poetic licence in his treatment of the episode. Lucan stresses that

---

[45] Flower (2006: 116).
[46] Cf. Newman (1967), Leigh (1997: 18–9).
[47] Fantham (1996: 140). Fantham also observes that Lucan changes the episode to make the meeting unconstitutional. See also (Radicke 2004: 240).
[48] Nix (2008: 292).

the senate met unconstitutionally, which contradicts other historical evidence. Cassius Dio and Cicero each name the two tribunes who convened the meeting and place at least two senators of consular rank at the event.[49] The version presented by the *Bellum Civile*, however, is riddled with imagery and language to the contrary. *Nullo ... iure, non ... sacrae, non ... lege* thrice issues the formulaic assertion (in each case the negative is separated from legal vocabulary by a single word) – reading almost as a magical incantation, willing it to be true – that what Caesar is doing violates the *sacred* laws of Republican Rome. With *omnia Caesar erat*, Lucan remembers the temple as the origin of autocracy rather than as a symbol of a republic restored. 'Caesar is all things', filling and dominating the room and its vacated offices.[50]

As John Henderson suggests, just as wars have historically been fought to claim land and space by force, 'read the *Bellum Civile* as a Black Hole swallowing the coordinates of sense'.[51] Whether we imagine an effacement of a date of construction or the addition of a new one, Lucan strips credit from Augustus for the temple's establishment, as well as the first emperor's agency in determining its meaning and controlling its message. In essence, we are reading a memory sanction, a literary *damnatio memoriae*. Augustus had used his building programme to help sell his regime as a repackaged Republic; Lucan hijacks these same monuments, inverting their authorially intended meanings to commemorate the violent, illegal and sacrilegious end of the Republic and its *libertas*. Lucan thus reconfigures and re-members the Roman cityscape to reorganize the memory of civil wars. It is not that Lucan destroys Augustus's monument. Rather, the *Bellum Civile* relocates and resets the temple in the temporal landscape of Roman history.

Lucan's endeavour to reframe Augustus's monument and to revise historical memory points towards criticisms of Kempenaers' photographs. These criticisms tend to privilege authorial intent and, at times, suggest a tension between aesthetic and political viewing of monuments and landscapes.[52] For example, Hatherly, quoting the architect Dubravka Sekulic, laments that recent attention to these sculptures decontextualizes them from the Partisan battles, uprisings and war crimes they were designed to commemorate, suggesting that 'all the meaning and content of the monuments get wiped out'.[53] Alternately, the photographer Jovana Mladenovic has produced ideologically charged images of these sculptures, which at once aspire to rehabilitate their original meanings and project a polarizing contemporary perspective backwards upon the past: 'I have included a ballerina in the photographs of 6 of the monuments. The ballerina, dressed all in red and pictured together with a Communist star, symbolizes political ideology but also the blood of the victims, and the glory and power of Yugoslavia at that time'.[54]

---

[49] Cic. *Att.* 9.19.2, 10.3a.2, *Fam.* 4.1.1; Cass. Dio 41.15.2; Fantham (1996: 140, n. 7). Gelzer (1968: 208) notes that the meeting had been legally summoned.
[50] Cf. Hardie (1993: 8), Henderson (2010: 474).
[51] Henderson (2010: 484), drawing on Davis (1985: 56).
[52] I explore this tension in Weiner and Benz (2018). See also Apel (2015).
[53] Hatherly (2016).
[54] *Contemporary Balkan Art* (2017).

Monuments in Lucan and the Former Yugoslavia

Like Lucan's Palatine Temple and his landscapes of war, we see struggles over memory and meaning playing out on Balkan mnemotopes. In the aftermath of the terrible civil wars of the 1990s and as much of the West once again flirts with nationalism and fascism, these memory wars not only debate whether and how the past is remembered and in what versions but also the very procedures of memory production and hermeneutics. These sculptures simultaneously commemorate violent conflict and consign it to oblivion, and they provoke debate over author/artist-based and reader/viewer-based interpretive strategies. 'For better or worse, the commemorative and ethical values of monuments are not unalterably affixed by the author or sculptor at the moment of creation', and 'monuments do not simply commemorate the past for the present and future, nor is posterity the inactive recipient of antiquity.'[55] When cultural landscapes undergo radical shifts and rifts in the wake of wars and civil wars, so do physical landscapes and their mnemonic artefacts. Forgetfulness and remembrance each have roles to play in the present's reinvention of the past.[56]

4 Conclusion

Through their monumental landscapes, Lucan and Balkan monuments provoke interpretive interventions of their audiences and ask readers and viewers to choose between competing, mutually exclusive accounts of the past.[57] Together with their commemorative symbols and artefacts, earlier versions of history become revalued. The mutability of collective memory comes into focus even as the unity of such memories fracture. In Lucan's case, the *Bellum Civile*'s capacity to wrest control of the past away from preceding imperial narratives is hampered by the realities of imperial power and the enduring success of the Augustan building programme and literary regime.[58] Augustan monuments and their versions of history and memory often proved more durable than those of Tito's Yugoslavia and those depicted in the *Bellum Civile*. But through the hermeneutic transience engendered by Lucan's model of monumental commemoration and the afterlives of the *Spomeniks* I've discussed, the dominion of the audience over monuments comes to the fore, threatening 'to overthrow the supremacy of the creator as central to the significance' of both art and monuments.[59] The *Bellum Civile* presents a discursive position that readers and viewers make monuments every bit as much as authors and sculptors do. Lucan thus anticipates movements in reader response theory in ways that subvert not only the imperial victors of the civil war but also Roman

---

[55] Weiner (2020: 198–9).
[56] On this process, see Alcock (2002, 16), discussing Assmann (1997: 9), which I quote in Weiner (2020: 198).
[57] This paragraph adapts Weiner (2020: 202–3), where I make similar claims specific to Lucan's treatment of the Palatine Temple of Apollo. Here, I extend this argument to monumentality in Lucan at large and to Yugoslav *Spomeniks*.
[58] Cf. Quint (1993: 133).
[59] Quote is from Zerner (1976: 179), writing on Alois Riegl, whose approach to monumentality I cite above.

aesthetic traditions.[60] These mechanics of monumentality, history and memory have been realized in modernity in the former Yugoslavia (and elsewhere; I again think of Confederate monuments and their afterlives). Like Lucan's poem itself, the civil war landscapes and monuments of the *Bellum Civile* and the *Spomeniks* 'disown [their] patrimon[ies] of knowledge'.[61] Lucan reminds us of the fickleness of collective memory and puts us on guard to the danger that, in our age of post-truths and fake news, history itself is, perhaps, at the mercy of architectural and rhetorical regimes.

The politics of these dynamics are complex and, perhaps, uncomfortable. Even as Lucan warns against the manipulations and abuses of memory through monumental landscapes (Caesar's reading of Troy), the *Bellum Civile* participates in these very processes and invites us to identify with 'alternative facts' (the Palatine Temple, the *felicior* disbelief in Pompey's *bustum*). In the former Yugoslavia, the civil wars remain open scars and the stakes of monumental *memoria* and *oblivio* high. At the time of writing, Slobodan Praljak, a former Bosnian Croat general, was tried and convicted in The Hague for crimes against humanity for his role in the civil wars of the 1990s. (Theatrically, Praljak proclaimed his innocence and committed suicide in the courtroom.) And, reaching back to the original commemorative referents of some of the *Spomeniks*, Hatherly warns against 'forgetting' or revaluing these artefacts when in Croatia 'a right-wing administration openly nostalgic towards the Ustaše' is 'intent on burying whatever anti-fascist legacy might remain today', and when 'real, open fascism is once again mainstream' in much of the world.[62] Lucan's poem and Balkan monuments thereby create interpretive landscapes that mirror the violent instability of the civil wars they commemorate.

Bibliography

Ahl, F. M. 1976. *Lucan: An Introduction*. Ithaca: Cornell University Press.
Alcock, S. E. 2002. *Archaeologies of the Greek Past: Landscapes, Monuments, and Memories*. Cambridge: Cambridge University Press.
Apel, D. 2015. *Beautiful Terrible Ruins: Detroit and the Anxiety of Decline*. New Brunswick, NJ: Rutgers University Press.
Assmann, J. 1992. *Das kulturelle Gedächtnis: Schrift, Erinnerung, und politische Identität in frühen Hochkulturen*. Munich: C. H. Beck.
Assmann, J. 1995. 'Ancient Egyptian Antijudaism: A Case of Distorted Memory.' In *Memory Distortion: How Minds, Brains and Societies Reconstruct the Past*, edited by D. Schacter, 365–76. Cambridge, MA: Harvard University Press.
Assmann, J. 1997. *Moses the Egyptian: The Memory of Egypt in Western Monotheism*. Cambridge, MA: Harvard University Press.
Babcock, C. L. 1967. 'Horace *Carm*. 1. 32 and the Dedication of the Temple of Apollo Palatinus.' *Classical Philology* 62 (3): 189–94.
Barchiesi, A. 2005. 'Learned Eyes: Poets, Viewers, Image Makers.' In *The Cambridge Companion to the Age of Augustus*, edited by K. Galinsky, 281–305. Cambridge: Cambridge University Press.

---

[60] Cf. Zientek (in this volume): 'Lucan displays something like an anachronistic pseudo-modernism'.
[61] Henderson (2010: 457).
[62] Hatherly (2016).

Bartsch, S. 1997. *Ideology in Cold Blood: A Reading of Lucan's Civil War*. Cambridge, MA: Harvard University Press.
Bergmann, B. 1994. 'The Roman House as Memory Theater: The House of the Tragic Poet in Pompeii.' *The Art Bulletin* 76 (2): 225–56.
Bodel, J. 1997. 'Monumental Villas and Villa Monuments.' *Journal of Roman Archaeology* 10: 5–35.
Bollig, M. 2009. 'Visions of Landscapes: An Introduction.' In *African Landscapes: Interdisciplinary Approaches*, edited by M. Bollig and O. Bubenzer, 1–38. New York: Springer.
Brockmeier, J. 2002. 'Remembering and Forgetting: Narrative as Cultural Memory.' *Culture & Psychology* 8 (1): 15–43.
Contemporary Balkan Art. 2017. 'MONUMENTAL FEAR: Interview with photographer Jovana Mladenovic.' 5 May 2017. http://contemporarybalkanart.com/monumental-fear-interview-photographer-jovana-mladenovic/.
Coutelle, E. 2015. *Properce, Élégies, livre IV*. Brussels: Latomus.
Davis, L. J. 1985. *Resisting Novels: Ideology and Fiction*. New York: Methuen.
Day, H. J. M. 2013. *Lucan and the Sublime: Power, Representation and Aesthetic Experience*. Cambridge: Cambridge University Press.
Dilke, O. A. W. 1960. *M. Annaei Lucani De Bello Civili Liber VII*, revision of J. P. Postgate, ed. Cambridge: Cambridge University Press.
Elliott, C. 1964. 'Monuments and Monumentality.' *Journal of Architectural Education* 18 (4): 51–3.
Fantham, E. 1996. '*Religio . . . dira loci*: Two Passages in Lucan *de Bello Civili* 3 and Their Relation to Virgil's Rome and Latium.' *Materiali e discussioni per l'analisi dei testi classici* 37: 137–53.
Fantham, E. 2012. 'Images of the City: Propertius' New-Old Rome.' In *Propertius*, edited by E. Greene and T. Welch, 302–19. Oxford: Oxford University Press.
Fish, S. 1982. *Is There a Text in This Class? The Authority of Interpretive Communities*. Cambridge, MA: Harvard University Press.
Flower, H. I. 2006. *The Art of Forgetting: Disgrace and Oblivion in Roman Political Culture*. Chapel Hill: University of North Carolina Press.
Fowler, D. 1996. 'Even Better Than the Real Thing.' In *Art and Text in Roman Culture*, edited by J. Elsner, 57–74. Cambridge: Cambridge University Press.
Fratantuono, L. 2012. *Madness Triumphant: A Reading of Lucan's Pharsalia*. Lanham, MD: Lexington Books.
Gelzer, M. 1968. *Caesar: Politician and Statesman*, trans. P. Needham. Cambridge, MA: Harvard University Press.
Ginsberg, L. D. 2017. *Staging Memory, Staging Strife: Empire and Civil War in the Octavia*. Oxford: Oxford University Press.
Gowing, A. 2005. *Empire and Memory: The Representation of the Roman Republic in Imperial Culture*. Cambridge: Cambridge University Press.
Günther, H.-C. 2006. 'The Fourth Book.' In *Brill's Companion to Propertius*, edited by H.-C. Günther, 353–96. Leiden: Brill.
Hardie, P. 1993. *The Epic Successors of Virgil: A Study in the Dynamics of a Tradition*. Cambridge: Cambridge University Press.
Hardie, P. 2012. *Rumour and Renown: Representatons of Fama in Western Literature*. Cambridge: Cambridge University Press.
Hatherly, O. 2016. 'Concrete clickbait: next time you share a spomenik photo, think about what it means.' *The Calvert Journal*. 29 November 2016. www.calvertjournal.com/articles/show/7269/spomenik-yugoslav-monument-owen-hatherley.
Henderson, J. 2010. 'Lucan/The Word at War.' In *Lucan*, edited by C. Tesoriero, 433–91. Oxford: Oxford University Press.
Johnson, W. R. 1987. *Momentary Monsters: Lucan and His Heroes*. Ithaca: Cornell University Press.
Leigh, M. 1997. *Lucan: Spectacle and Engagement*. Oxford: Oxford University Press.
Kempenaers, J. 2010. *Spomenik*. Amsterdam: Roma Publications.

Malamud, M. A. 1995. 'Happy Birthday Dead Lucan: (P)raising the Dead in *Silvae* 2.7.' *Ramus* 24 (1): 1–30.
Martindale, C. 1984. 'The Politician Lucan.' *Greece & Rome* 31 (1): 64–79.
Mayer, R. 1981. *Lucan: Civil War VIII*. Liverpool: Liverpool University Press.
McLellan, A. M. 2019. *Abused Bodies in Roman Epic*. Cambridge: Cambridge University Press.
Miller, J. F. 1983. 'Propertius 3.2 and Horace.' *Transactions of the American Philological Association* 113: 289–99.
Miller, J. F. 2009. *Apollo, Augustus, and the Poets*. Cambridge: Cambridge University Press.
Neutelings, W. J. 2010. 'Spomenik: The Monuments of Former Yugoslavia.' *Junk Jet* 4: 16–17.
Newman, J. K. 1967. *Augustus and the New Poetry*. Brussels: Latomus.
Nix, S. A. 2008. 'Caesar as Jupiter in Lucan's *Bellum Civile*.' *Classical Journal* 103 (3): 281–94.
Ormand, K. 1994: 'Lucan's "Auctor Vix Fidelis."' *Classical Antiquity* 13 (1): 38–55.
Osborne, B. S. 2001. 'Landscapes, Memory, Monuments, and Commemoration: Putting Identity in its Place.' *Canadian Ethnic Studies* 33 (3): 39–77.
Quint, D. 1993. *Epic and Empire: Politics and Generic Form from Virgil to Milton*. Princeton, Princeton University Press.
Radicke, J. 2004. *Lucans poetische Technik*. Leiden: Brill.
Rea, J. 2007. *Legendary Rome: Myth, Monuments, and Memory on the Palatine and Capitoline*. London: Bloomsbury Academic.
Riegl, A. 1982. 'The Modern Cult of Monuments: Its Character and Its Origin,' trans. K. W. Forster and D. Ghirado. *Oppositions* 25: 21–50.
Roche, P. 2005. 'Righting the Reader: Conflagration and Civil War in Lucan's *De Bello Civili*.' *Scholia* 14: 52–71.
Roller, M. B. 2010. 'Demolished Houses, Monumentality, and Memory in Roman Culture.' *Classical Antiquity* 29 (1): 117–80.
Rossi, A. 2001. 'Remapping the Past: Caesar's Tale of Troy (Lucan "BC" 9.964–999).' *Phoenix* 55 (3/4): 313–26.
Savage, K. 1997. *Standing Soldiers, Kneeling Slaves: Race, War, and Monument in Nineteenth-Century America*. Princeton: Princeton University Press.
Shackleton Bailey, D. R., ed. 2009. *Marcus Annaeus Lucanus: De bello civili libri X*. Berlin: De Gruyter.
Spencer, D. 2005. 'Lucan's Follies: Memory and Ruin in a Civil-War Landscape.' *Greece & Rome* 52 (1): 46–69.
Surtees, J. 2013. 'Spomeniks: the second world war memorials that look like alien art.' *The Guardian*, 18 June, 2013 (www.theguardian.com/artanddesign/photography-blog/2013/jun/18/spomeniks-war-monuments-former-yugoslavia-photography).
Syndikus, H. P. 2006. 'The Second Book,' trans., C. B. Brown. In *Brill's Companion to Propertius*, edited by H.-C. Günther, 245–318. Leiden: Brill.
Thomas, E. 2007. *Monumentality and the Roman Empire: Architecture in the Antonine Age*. Oxford: Oxford University Press.
Thorne, M. 2011. 'Memoria Redux: Memory in Lucan.' In *Brill's Companion to Lucan*, edited by P. Asso, 363–82. Leiden: Brill.
Tuan, Y.-F. 1979. *Landscapes of Fear*. New York: Pantheon.
Weiner, J. 2016. 'Transcending Lucretius: Vitruvius, Atomism, and the Rhetoric of Monumental Permanence.' *Helios* 43 (2): 133–61.
Weiner, J. 2020. 'Re-Membering the Palatine in Lucan's *Bellum Civile*.' In *Lucan's Imperial World: The Bellum Civile in Its Contemporary Contexts*, edited by M. Thorne and L. Zientek, 191–208. London: Bloomsbury Academic.
Weiner, J. and T. A. Benz. 2018. 'Detroit and the Classical Sublime; Or, in Defense of Ruin Porn.' In *Landscapes of Dread: The Weird and Uncanny in Natural and Constructed Spaces of Classical Antiquity*, edited by D. Felton, 279–302. London: Routledge.

Welch, T. S. 2005. *The Elegiac Cityscape: Propertius and the Meaning of Roman Monuments*. Columbus: Ohio State University Press.

Zanker, P. 1988. *The Power of Images in the Age of Augustus*, trans. A. Shapiro. Ann Arbor: University of Michigan Press.

Zerner, H. 1976. 'Aloïs Riegl: Art, Value, and Historicism.' *Daedalus* 105 (1): 177–88.

Zimmerman, T. 2015. 'Yugoslav Partisan Poetry. Songs for the Leader.' In *Partisans in Yugoslavia: Literature, Film and Visual Culture*, edited by M. Jakiša and N. Gilić, 49–70. Bielefeld: transcript Verlag.

Zwierlein, O. 1986. 'Lucans Caesar in Troja.' *Hermes* 114 (4): 460–78.

INDEX LOCORUM

Epigraphic sources

IG I³
255	220 n. 30
503–4	218 n. 19
1143	221 n. 39

IG II²
1006	221 n. 37
1008	221 n. 37
1009	221 n. 37
1011	221 n. 37
1028	221 n. 37
1029	221 n. 37
1035	220 n. 30, 221

IG V.¹
657	221 n. 37

Literary sources

Aeschylus
Pers.
302–3	222
447–50	218–19
447–71	217
465–7	223

Sept.
587	103
587–8	93

Ammianus Marcellinus
31.7.16	139 n. 39

Anthologia Palatina
6.236	99 n. 26

Apollodorus
Bibl.
2.5.9	231 n. 9
3.161	221 n. 41

Epit.
3.29–30	234

Appian
B Civ.
5.5.46–7	142 n. 53

Mith.
106	166 n. 53

Syr.
33.171	53

Aratus
Phaen.
129–32	97 n. 22

Aristodemus
FGrH 104 F 1	223 n. 49

Aristotle
Rh.
1419a26–30	115

Arrian
Anab.
1.11	235
2.11	206 n. 45

Athenaeus
1.20ff.	220 n. 30

Augustus
RG
13	162 n. 27, 164 n. 45, 164 n. 46, 168 n. 58
13.1	152

Aurelius Victor
Caes.
20.8	207 n. 50

Caesar
BCiv.
1.8	157 n. 2
1.8–9	168
3.2	165 n. 49

BGall.
1.1	177
1.13.5	188 n. 40
4	162 n. 35

Cassius Dio
41.5–6	168 n. 62
41.15.2	255, 256 n. 49
46.33–4	165 n. 48
48.14.5	139 n. 42
63.27.3	206 n. 46
74.4	203 n. 41
74.6.2a	207
74.6.3	198
74.7.1ff.	207 n. 48
74.7.2–3	207
74.7.6–8	203
74.8.3	206 n. 46
74.8.4	206 n. 47
74.10–14	198

Cato
Agr.
praef.	158 n. 5

Catullus
64	93 n. 10

Index Locorum

Cicero			2.72.8	164 n. 39
Att.			4.49	165 n. 47
7.20.1	157 n. 2		Ennius	
7.22.1	157 n. 2		*Ann.*	
8.13.1	157 n. 2		20 Sk.	56 n. 53
9.19.2	256 n. 49		Euphorion	
10.3a.2	256 n. 49		fr. 30	221 n. 42
De or.			Euripides	
2.63	63		*Bacch.*	
Div.			862–76	111 n. 2
1.78	83 n. 42		*Hec.*	
Fam.			1259ff.	237
4.1.1	256 n. 49		Eutropius	
Leg.			8.18.4	207 n. 50
1.5	73		Florus	
2.9	162 n. 29		1.24.17	54 n. 44
2.22.57	139 n. 43		Frontinus	
Leg. Agr.			*Str.*	
2.95	186 n. 33		4.30	54 n. 44
Nat. D.			Hellenica Oxyrhynchia	
2.159	99–100		17.4	116 n. 16
Off.			Herodian	
1.11	161 n. 24, 162 n. 29		1.1.3	194 n. 6
3.30.107–8	161 n. 24		1.1.4	195
Pis.			1.11.2	206 n. 44
50	160 n. 19		2.6.4–14	195
Rep.			2.7.1–2	195
2.5	93 n. 11		2.7.3	195
2.17	161 n. 24		2.8.9–10	195
2.31	161 n. 24		2.9.1ff.	195
Tusc.			2.9.7	202 n. 37
14.31	93 n. 11		2.15.1–5	195
Verr.			2.15.2	202 n. 37
2.3.120–9	98 n. 24		2.15.6	202 n. 38
Coelius Antipater			2.15.6–7	194
FRHist fr. 14B	83		2.15.7	194
Curtius Rufus			3.1.1ff.	195
3.11	206 n. 45		3.1.4	200, 202 n. 35
Demetrius of Phalerum			3.1.5–6	197
Eloc.			3.1.6–7	198
209–20	43 n. 16		3.2.1	199
Demosthenes			3.2.1ff.	195
In Timocratem			3.2.2	195 n. 11
24.129	223		3.2.2–6	199 n. 27
Diodorus Siculus			3.2.6–7	199 n. 27
4.72.4	221 n. 41		3.2.7ff.	195
13.40.6	238 n. 18		3.2.7–10	199 n. 27
13.72.3–73.2	117		3.3.1–2	200–1
17.34	206 n. 45		3.3.2	200
17.37	206 n. 45		3.3.3	195
Dionysius of Halicarnassus			3.3.3–5	199 n. 27, 201
Ant. Rom.			3.3.4–5	201 n. 31
2.72.4	161 n. 24		3.3.7	200 n. 29, 201–2
2.72.6	164 n. 39, 167 n. 56, 169 n. 67		3.3.8	202
			3.3.9	199 n. 27
2.72.6–8	162		3.4.1–5	196

Index Locorum

3.4.2	207	2.695ff.	234
3.4.2–3	203–5	3.79–80	31
3.4.4	204	3.89	33
3.4.4–5	205–6	3.146–244	28
3.4.5	207	4.15	27
3.4.5–6	206	4.33–4	27
3.4.6–7	196	4.68–126	170 n. 70
3.4.7	206	4.427–9	32
3.4.7–9	206	4.431–2	32
3.6.9	199 n. 24, 199 n. 26, 199 n. 27	4.447	33
		4.450	33
3.7.7	206	4.451	31
3.9.3–6	197 n. 16	4.459–62	32
3.9.12	202 n. 37	4.462	32
3.14.5–10	202 n. 34	4.463–72	32
3.14.6–7	197 n. 16	4.473	32
4.2	203 n. 41	4.482	32
4.3.6	202 n. 37, 202 n. 38	4.490	32
5.4.7ff.	206 n. 46	4.493	32
6.7.6–8	202 n. 34	4.495–8	32
8.2.2–6	198 n. 21	4.504	32, 33, 33 n. 34
8.4	202 n. 34	4.518–19	31
Herodotus		4.522–6	32
1.1	65	4.527–8	32
1.8	62 n. 4, 65	4.536–8	32
1.8–10	65–6	5.42	33, 33 n. 34
6.7–8	218	5.136–43	169 n. 64
6.105	219 n. 26	5.222–3	28
7.33	234	5.265–73	230
7.35	230 n. 6	5.499–502	35
7.44	224	5.503	31
7.59	224	5.638–51	230
7.212	224	5.641–2	231
8.55	115 n. 10	6.145–211	232
8.76	216, 219–20	6.433	27
8.77	220	7.22	27
8.86	224	7.60	27
8.90	222–3	7.451–3	230
8.95	216–17	8.47–52	29
8.121–2	215 n. 11	8.106–7	28
9.15	218 n. 21	8.159	33
9.96–7	218 n. 21	8.266ff.	232
9.114–21	230 n. 6, 234	8.281ff.	232
Homer		8.284	230, 232
Il.		8.346–7	33
1.12	27	8.491	34
1.34	27	8.543–4	34
1.306	27	8.545–7	34–5
1.357–8	29	8.549	35
2.86	32	8.558	35
2.87–90	32	9.177–85	28
2.149–51	31	10.13	35
2.457–8	32	10.160	27
2.465–8	9–10	10.189	35
2.469–73	35	10.298	31
2.486	66 n. 14	10.414–16	30

Index Locorum

10.415	12 n. 34	16.459–61	31 n. 26
10.466	30	16.469	31
10.526	30	16.486	31
10.528–9	30	16.565–6	33
11.52–5	31 n. 26	16.639–40	31
11.97–8	32	16.734–5	31
11.163–4	31	16.765–9	32
11.166	12 n. 34, 28	16.774	33
11.166–8	30	16.774–5	31
11.167	27	17.315	31
11.172–6	32	17.360–1	31
11.181–4	29	17.389–95	32
11.372	12 n. 34	17.616–18	32
11.558–62	35	17.651–81	29
11.596	32	17.679–80	32
11.599–601	29	17.736–9	32
11.749	33 n. 34	17.740–1	33
12.154–5	31	17.756	33
12.252	33	17.759	33
12.338	33	18.541–9	35
12.380–1	31	18.550–60	35
12.383–6	32	18.561–72	35–6
12.445	31	18.573–86	36
13.10–14	29	18.587–9	36
13.137–42	32	19.61	33 n. 34
13.187	33, 33 n. 34	19.363–4	33
13.392–3	31	20.53	27
13.393	31	20.144–8	230
13.588–90	35	20.144–52	233
13.655	31	20.151	27
13.834	33	20.156	32
14.60	33	20.164–73	169 n. 64
14.249–51	230	20.231–8	231
14.409–11	31	20.232	12 n. 34
14.409–13	30	20.236	12 n. 34
14.433	27	20.313–17	230
14.433–9	30	21.1–11	4–6
14.418	31	21.8	31 n. 27
15.239–42	30	21.17–18	10
15.424	33	21.20–1	6
15.590	33	21.96	13
15.630–6	32	21.122–7	12
15.658	33	21.136–8	10
15.715	31	21.147–7	10
15.732	33	21.169–72	8 n. 25
16.112–29	234	21.180–1	8 n. 25
16.259–62	32	21.190–3	11
16.293ff.	234	21.202	31 n. 27
16.321–4	32	21.203–4	13
16.352–5	32	21.212–13	7
16.361	33	21.218–20	7
16.373–4	33	21.238–9	10
16.374–5	31	21.254–5	6
16.393	33	21.257–66	8–9
16.467–9	32	21.268–71	11
16.468–9	33	21.279–83	11–12

265

Index Locorum

21.309	10	Josephus	
21.316–23	13	*BJ*	
21.337–8	7–8	2.61	254 n. 44
21.343–4	7	Justin	
21.344	32	*Epit.*	
21.349	7	41.1.1	186 n. 34
21.350–2	7, 31 n. 27	Livy	
21.350–5	8	*praef.* 9	83
21.356	7	*praef.* 10	85
21.361	7	1.19.3	168 n. 58
21.361–4	6–7	1.24.4–9	162
21.363–4	6 n. 22	1.24.6	163 n. 37, 169 n. 66
21.365	7	1.24.7	169 n. 67
21.441–60	231	1.24.7–9	164 n. 43
22.25	29	1.25.2	83 n. 43
22.26	29	1.32.6	169 n. 67
22.38–91	29	1.32.6–7	164 n. 39, 167 n. 56, 169 n. 67
22.145	28		
22.146	33	1.32.8	169 n. 65
22.147–56	34	1.32.10	164 n. 39, 164 n. 45
22.153–6	9 n. 27	1.32.12	161 n. 24, 170
22.208	34	4.17–19	170 n. 70
22.330	31	4.39.6	41 n. 10
22.402–3	31	5.25.7	169 n. 65
22.405	31	7.7.5	169 n. 65
22.447–61	29	7.10	85
22.463	29	7.26	85
22.463–5	29	7.33.15	41 n. 10
23.365–6	31	6.8.7	41
24.23	29	6.24.2	56 n. 53
24.131–2	230	6.28.5	190 n. 45
24.322–447	28	6.32.6	41
24.349	12 n. 34, 30	6.32.7–9	41
24.349–51	8 n. 26	8.1.4–5	42
24.350–3	30	8.1.6	42 n. 12
24.495–7	237	8.9–10	85
24.650ff.	230	8.14.5	163 n. 37
24.656ff.	230	9.5	162 n. 29
24.692–4	30	10.9.8	56 n. 53
24.738	33 n. 34	10.28–9	85
24.778ff.	230	10.32.5–8	55–6
Od.		10.45	162 n. 29
4.844–7	218	21.4.10	80
23.358	125 n. 39	21.25.9	56 n. 53
Horace		21.35.6–37	39
Carm.		21.58.3–11	39
1.31	254 n. 44	21.63.5–9	165 n. 48
2.1.29–31	141 n. 49	22.1.4	78
2.1.29–36	94	22.1.4–7	165 n. 48
2.1.34–5	101	22.1.8–13	80
3.30	242 n. 9	22.2.2	79
3.30.3	249	22.2.5–6	78
4.15.9	164 n. 45	22.2.5–9	78–9
Sat.		22.2.10–11	79
1.8.14–16	139 n. 39	22.3.1–2	80 n. 39

Index Locorum

22.4.5–7	81–2	Lucan	
22.5.4	82–3	***BC***	
22.5.8	83	1.1	161 n. 20
22.6.2	84	1.1–2	243
22.6.3	84	1.2	159, 161 n. 20, 172
22.6.8–9	44–5	1.4	171
22.14	58	1.11	190 n. 42
22.28.3	56 n. 53	1.12	160 n. 17
23.44	39–40	1.23	248
23.44.6–45.3	40	1.24–9	248–9
26.8.5	43 n. 15	1.28–9	92, 98, 251
26.11.1–3	42–3	1.29	104
30.43	162 n. 29	1.72	101 n. 30
30.43.10	169 n. 66	1.126–7	172
32.1	165 n. 47	1.158–9	103 n. 37
32.6–10	162	1.182–5	159
32.10	169 n. 67	1.183–235	157–72 *passim*
33.3.11–4.3	51 n. 35	1.186–9	159–60
33.3.12	51 n. 35	1.190–2	160–1, 167 n. 57
33.6–10	45–51, 46 n. 20, 56 n. 55	1.192–4	161
		1.195–200	163–5
33.7.3	48 n. 27	1.200	166, 167
33.7.5	51 n. 36	1.200–3	167–8
33.7.7	50 n. 33	1.202	164
33.7.8	50 n. 33	1.204	169
33.7.8–11	84 n. 44	1.204–5	168
33.8.3	50 n. 34	1.205–7	104
33.8.5–6	51 n. 35	1.205–12	169, 169 n. 64
33.9.6	50 n. 34	1.213–22	170 n. 72
33.10.3–4	50 n. 34	1.223–5	166
33.22.9	49	1.225–7	170–1
37.39–44	51–4, 54 n. 47	1.228–30	171
37.39.7	52	1.248–57	171 n. 77
37.39.7–8	52	1.277	172 n. 78
37.39.9	52	1.286–9	160 n. 16
37.39.9–10	52	1.348–9	172 n. 78
37.39.12	52 n. 39	1.483–4	171 n. 77
37.40.1	52	1.582–3	100, 102
37.40.12	52	1.615	102
37.40.4	52	1.618	102
37.41.2–4	53	1.619	102
37.41.5–12	54	2.162–4	106 n. 40
37.42.1	54 n. 47	2.209–20	158 n. 4
37.42.1–6	54	2.439–45	98–9
37.42.7–43.5	54	2.444–5	107
41.2.1	56	2.592	160 n. 18
41.2.2	56	2.602	99 n. 25
41.2.4–7	56–7	3.103–9	255–6
41.2.10	57	3.150	103 n. 37
41.2.11–13	57	3.261ff.	190 n. 44
41.4.3–4	57	3.450–2	99
42.47.8	161 n. 24	3.509–672	158 n. 4
Longinus		4.255	106 n. 42
Subl.		4.308–13	105
15	43 n. 16	4.319	105

267

Index Locorum

Reference	Page
4.410–4	105
4.549–56	102–3
4.581–2	106
4.588	106
4.590	106 n. 40
4.602	106
4.605–6	106
4.629–30	106
4.660	106
4.793–5	103–4
5.349	160 n. 18
5.400–2	165
5.416	190 n. 43
5.654–71	158 n. 4
6.32–51	249–50
6.395	103 n. 37
7.120–1	253
7.191	106 n. 42
7.253	172
7.254–60	160 n. 16
7.264–6	172
7.292–4	106 n. 43
7.391–9	249
7.728	104
7.728–9	106
7.786–91	106–7
7.794–5	106–7
7.823–4	101–2
7.844–6	100–1
7.846	104, 106 n. 40
7.851	102, 142 n. 54
7.851–4	100–1
7.853–4	103
7.855–9	107
7.859	101, 103
7.861	107
7.862	107
7.862–3	107
7.864–5	107
7.866–7	107–8
8.33–4	187
8.202–40	165
8.211–14	186–7
8.217	188 n. 36
8.218–20	164 n. 42, 165–6
8.260–327	165 n. 51
8.262–3	165
8.266	106 n. 40
8.289–94	187–8
8.290–4	188 n. 36
8.292	188 n. 36
8.315	188 n. 36
8.322	166
8.335–7	187 n. 35
8.337	188 n. 36
8.363–76	185–6
8.385	186
8.431–9	158 n. 4
8.431–41	189–90
8.477	104
8.526	104
8.712–822	158 n. 4
8.792	252
8.793	252
8.818–22	252–4
8.822	189 n. 41
8.851–8	189 n. 41
8.867–72	251–2
8.870	253
9.161–3	99
9.235–6	166
9.281	160 n. 18
9.420–3	104
9.423	104
9.426–30	99 n. 26
9.696–9	104
9.964–9	250
9.965	252
9.969	92, 250
9.970–1	250
9.973	250
9.974	251
9.974–5	14
9.975	251
9.975–6	251
9.976–7	250–1
9.977–8	251
9.979	250, 253
9.1073	106 n. 40
10.219	104
10.330	166 n. 54

Lucian
Hist. conscr.

19	194 n. 9
27	194 n. 5
57	194 n. 6, 194 n. 9

Lucretius

5.1289–91	93 n. 11

Lycophron
Alex.

451	221

Lycurgus
Leoc.

73	217 n. 17, 220 n. 30

Macrobius
Sat.

1.9.16	164 n. 45
1.16.16	165 n. 47
3.20.3	170

Manilius

4.674–5	186 n. 34
4.802–5	186 n. 34

Index Locorum

Menander Rhetor
  1.346.27–31   197 n. 19
Nonnus
  Dion.
  27.290   219 n. 26
Orosius
  7.17   207 n. 50
Ovid
  Fast.
  3.707–8   139 n. 39
  4.825–6   93 n. 11
  5.581–2   179, 183
  Her.
  1.51–6   95–6
  1.55–6   101
  Met.
  3.101-26   103 n. 36
  7.653   99 n. 25
  8.872   249
  11.35   99 n. 25
  Tr.
  3.1.59–62   254 n. 44
Pausanias
  1.1.4   220 n. 27
  1.32.4   151 n. 95
  1.36.1   217 n. 17, 220 n. 30, 221, 222
  1.36.2   219
  2.31.7   215 n. 11
  4.36.6   217, 218
  5.11.5   215 n. 11
  8.54.6   219 n. 26
  10.14.5   215 n. 11
Phanodemus
  FGrH 325 F 24   223 n. 49
Pindar
  Isth.
  4.52–4   106 n. 40
Plato
  Menex.
  245a   217 n. 17, 220 n. 30
Pliny the Elder
  HN
  1.1.70   163 n. 37
  3.68   165 n. 47
  5.86   189
  16.74   170
  16.176   170
  22.2–3   162 n. 29
  22.3   169 n. 66
Plutarch
  Arist.
  9.2   217
  Artax.
  9.1   206 n. 45
  Caes.
  22.4   162 n. 34
  Cat. Min.
  51.1–2   162 n. 34
  Comp. Nic. et Crass.
  4.3   162 n. 34
  Crass.
  18.4   186 n. 32
  19.2   180 n. 15
  20.2   180 n. 15
  22.1–2   179–80, 183–4
  22.5   184–5
  22.6   186 n. 33
  24.1–2   186 n. 31
  25.4–5   180 n. 12
  25.9–10   180 n. 13
  29.1–5   180 n. 14
  De glor. Ath.
  347A   62 n. 2
  De Herodoti malignitate
  870e   221 n. 39
  Mar.
  21.3   96
  Num.
  12.3–5   162 n. 29
  Pomp.
  39.3   166 n. 53
  Them.
  13.1   223
  15.3   215 n. 11
Polybius
  1.2.1   62, 75
  1.4.1   75
  1.4.2   75
  2.56   74
  2.56.10   75 n. 29
  2.56.13–14   76
  3.25   164
  3.47.6   78 n. 35
  3.47–8   78
  3.48.10–12   78
  3.48.12   78 n. 35
  3.78   77
  3.78.6   77
  3.78.7   77
  3.78.8   79
  3.79.1–5   77
  3.79.6   81
  3.79.6–12   77
  3.81.2   80
  3.81.3   80
  3.83   80
  3.84.2   81
  3.84.5   81
  3.84.6   84
  3.84.9   81
  9.6.5–6   43 n. 14
  18.19–27   46 n. 20

Index Locorum

18.20.7	46	4.3.33–40	181–3
18.20.8–9	47	4.3.63–72	181
18.20.9	48 n. 27	4.6	189, 254 n. 44
18.21.1	47	4.6.15–16	151 n. 96
18.22.2	46	4.6.83–4	189
18.24.6–7	50	4.10	132, 145–8, 149 n. 84, 152
18.25.4–5	50 n. 34	4.10.23–6	145–6

Propertius

1.1	139, 142 n. 50	4.10.27–8	147 n. 73
1.1.1	133 n. 11	4.10.27–30	146–8
1.19.1–4	139 n. 44	4.10.37–8	148 n. 81
1.20	133		
1.21	132, 133, 134–6, 139, 142 n. 56, 148, 149, 150		

Quintilian
Inst.

3.7.26	197 n. 19
6.2.29–33	43 n. 16
8.3.61–71	43 n. 16

Rhetorica ad Herennium

4.68.55	43 n. 16

Sallust
Cat.

2	158 n. 5
10–13	158 n. 5
55	56 n. 53

Iug.

17.5	104 n. 38

Scholia on Aristides

172.1 Dindorf	117 n. 20

Scriptores Historiae Augustae
Pesc. Nig.

5.8	199 n. 27, 206 n. 46, 207 n. 50

Sev.

8.12	199
9.1	207 n. 50
9.7	199

Seneca the Elder
Suas.

2.7	186 n. 34

Seneca the Younger
Clem.

1.11.1	102 n. 35

Oed.

41–2	101 n. 31
49–51	101 n. 31

QNat.

5.18.10	186 n. 34

Servius

1.62	162 n. 29
9.52	163 n. 37
9.52–3	162 n. 29
10.14	162 n. 29
12.120	163 n. 37, 169 n. 66

Simonides

FGE 5	219 n. 26
FGE 10–11	221 n. 39
FGE 12	215 n. 11

Propertius (continued)

1.21.1–4	134
1.21.2	140
1.21.5–10	134–6
1.21.9–10	144
1.21.10	140
1.22	132, 133, 134, 136–43, 148, 149
1.22.1	144
1.22.1–2	136–7
1.22.3	144
1.22.3–5	137–8, 140
1.22.3–10	94–5
1.22.6	140
1.22.6–8	138–40, 143
1.22.8	144
1.22.9	144
1.22.9–10	140–3, 144
1.22.10	144
2.1	148–9
2.1.27–36	148–9
2.1.29	150 n. 90
2.10	189 n. 41
2.15	132, 149–51
2.15.43–6	149–51
2.16	132
2.16.37	151 n. 96
2.16.37–8	151
2.16.39–40	150 n. 90
2.31	254 n. 44
2.34.61	151
3.2	242 n. 9
3.2.17–26	242 n. 9
3.11	132
3.11.69	150 n. 90
3.11.71–2	151 n. 93
4.1	132, 133, 143–5, 148
4.1A.63–4	143
4.1A.67	143
4.1B.121–8	143–5
4.1B.127–8	138 n. 37
4.3	180–3
4.3.7–10	180–1

Index Locorum

Sophocles		1348	124
Aj.		1492–5	115
695	219 n. 25	1556–78	115 n. 11
OC		1600–1	125 n. 41
14–18	112	*OT*	
16–17	124	1138	125 n. 39
17–18	124	*Poimenes*	
36–40	125	fr. 497	234
38–44	125 n. 41	fr. 500	234
53-6	125 n. 41	fr. 501R	234
78	124	Statius	
91	117 n. 19	*Silv.*	
150–68	125 n. 38	2.7.65	139 n. 39
155–60	112–13, 125 n. 38	Stephanus Byzantius	
389–94	112	s.v.	
398–406	116–17	Κυχρεῖος	221 n. 41, 221 n. 42
399	117 n. 19	Strabo	
409–11	117	7 fr. 56	238 n. 18
411	117 n. 21	9.1.9	221 n. 41
469–70	113	*Suda*	
616–23	117	s.v.	
668-9	125	ἁλίπλαγκτος	219 n. 25
668–706	113–15	s.v.	
668–719	115 n. 11	Ἱππίας	219 n. 26
669	125 n. 39	s.v.	
671–3	124	Σιμωνίδης	215 n. 12
675	124–5	Suetonius	
676	124	*Aug.*	
676–8	124	22	164 n. 45
678–80	125	29.1–3	254 n. 44
680	124 n. 37	*Claud.*	
681–4	126	22	162 n. 29
682	125 n. 42	25.5	162 n. 29
685–6	125 n. 42	*Iul.*	
685–8	126	24.3	162 n. 34
685–91	126	*Ner.*	
686-7	124	48.1	206 n. 46
688	125, 125 n. 42	Tacitus	
689	124 n. 37	*Ann.*	
690	124	1.61	139 n. 39
691	124	2.2–3	186 n. 34
691–3	125	Theocritus	
694–9	115 n. 10	*Id.*	
698	115 n. 10, 125 n. 42	10.47	94
701	124 n. 37	Thucydides	
704	125 n. 42	1.2.5	126 n. 43
704–6	125	1.22.3	68, 70
707–15	125 n. 41	1.22.4	62, 70
714	125 n. 40	4.8–38	218
716–17	125 n. 40	6.91	116 n. 17
716–19	125 n. 40	7.19.2	116
1044–95	115 n. 11	7.27.5	116
1070–95	125 n. 41	7.28.2	116 n. 18
1157–9	115	7.28.4	116 n. 17
1211–48	115 n. 11	7.70–1	67–72
1326–48	112 n. 6	7.87.6	71 n. 22

Index Locorum

8.67.2–3	115	8.345	253 n. 34
8.104–7	238	8.720–2	254 n. 44
Timotheus		9.792–6	169 n. 64
Pers.		11.190	190 n. 43
196	220 n. 30	11.823	135 n. 25
Valerius Flaccus		12.4–8	169
Arg.		12.4–9	169 n. 64
3.587–9	169 n. 64	12.13	169 n. 65
Varro		12.36	139 n. 39
Ling.		12.118–20	169 n. 66
5.41	164 n. 41	12.158	169 n. 65
5.86	162 n. 29, 169 n. 65	12.197–202	169 n. 67
5.143	93 n. 11	12.200	169 n. 67
6.25	165 n. 47	12.202–3	171 n. 74
Rust.		12.206–7	170
praef. 1–2	158 n. 5	**Ecl.**	
2	158 n. 5	1.71–2	145 n. 65
Vegetius		**G.**	
Mil.		1.50	93 n. 6
4.44	150 n. 91	1.99	93 n. 6
Velleius Paterculus		1.104	93 n. 6
2.81.3	254 n. 44	1.145	93 n. 6
Vergil		1.160	93 n. 6
Aen.		1.299	102
1.159	56 n. 53	1.491–2	94, 141
1.441	56 n. 53	1.491–7	92–3, 92 n. 3
1.530	56 n. 53	1.492	95, 104
2.21–4	218 n. 22	1.493–7	93 n. 6, 100, 139 n. 41
2.50–2	170 n. 70		
2.268–97	160 n. 15	1.494	100
3.163	56 n. 53	1.496–7	101
3.349–50	14 n. 37	1.497	94, 100
5.496–7	170 n. 70	2.54	99 n. 25
5.755	93 n. 11	2.184–7	95 n. 17
6.69	254 n. 44	*Vita Pindari*	
6.781–7	160 n. 15	2.21	215 n. 12
7.157–9	93 n. 11	Xenophon	
7.506–21	99 n. 26	**An.**	
7.563	56 n. 53	1.4.4	207 n. 49
7.601–17	162 n. 31	3.2.13	217 n. 17, 220 n. 30
8.326	101 n. 31	Zonaras	
8.337	253 n. 34	9.20	54

INDEX

Page numbers in **bold** refer to figures.

Abydos **231**, 235, 238
Achaemenids 178, 224 n. 54
Achilles 4–14, 28–30, 33–6, 230–7
Actium 17, 99 n. 26, 132, 148–52, 150 n. 89, 254
Aegean Sea 229
Aegospotami **231**, 234, 238
Aeneas 86, 160 n. 15, 164, 167 n. 55
    ancestor of Caesar 164, 250
    as tourist 14 n. 37, 253 n. 34
    treaty with Latinus 157, 169–71
Agios Giorgos **215**, 217 n. 16
agricultural implements 93, 96, 99, 103, 147
    hoes 92, 103
    mattocks 8–9
    oxen 93 n. 8, 95–7, 99–100, 106
    ploughs 92–3, 95–6, 99–101, 106–7, 147, 249
    rakes 103
    sickles 95
    wagons 99
agricultural metaphor, *see under* metaphor
agriculture; *see also* agricultural implements, farmers, fertility, sterility
    arable land 95, 98, 104–6
    association with conquest 91–4, 96
    association with peace 9, 16, 91–3, 97, 99 n. 26, 100
    destruction of crops 16, 98, 116
    harvest 35–6, 95–6, 99–100, 101 n. 31, 103, 146–7
    irrigation 8–9, 103–4
    ploughing 35, 91–3, 95, 97, 99–101, 104, 107, 147
    reaping 35, 147
    seeding/sowing 93 n. 11, 103–4, 106
    tilling 101, 104
    unploughed land 98, 249
    vineyards 35, 96
    as violence against the earth 147
    as war 93
    war-recovery cycle 16, 91–108, 158
Aianteia festival 215, 221
Ajax 29–31, 35, 221, 232; *see also* Aianteia festival
Albinus, *see* Clodius Albinus
Alexander the Great 19, 178, 178 n. 5, 181 n. 19, 204–7, 229, 235, 238
Alps, crossing of
    by Caesar 159, 168
    by Hannibal 39, 69 n. 19, 77 n. 34, 78

Amanus (Nur) Mountains 207
Ambracian gulf 150; *see also* Actium
ambush 39, 46–7, 51, 54–9, 218
American Civil War 96–7, 108
Andromachus 180
Anio 42, 100, 102
anthropocentric perspective 91, 132 n. 5
Antioch 195, 199 n. 27
Antiochus III of Syria 51–4
Antium 42
Antonius, Lucius 135, 138–9, 142 n. 53
Antonius, Marcus 105, 150–1, 162, 164, 171 n. 73, 172
Antony, *see* Antonius, Marcus
Anzac Battlefield **231**, 235
Anzacs 229
Apennines, crossing of (by Hannibal) 39
Aphrodite 114, 125; *see also* Venus
apocalypse 98–9, 101 n. 30, 108, 249
Apollo 8 n. 24, 30, 125 n. 41, 245
    Actian 150, 189
    Augustus's relationship with 244 n. 12, 245, 254
    Palatine Temple of 245, 254–5, 257 n. 57
Apulia 94, 101
Asisium 137 n. 30, 140, **141**
Aquae Sextiae 96
Aquileia 198 n. 21, 202 n. 34
Araxes 158 n. 4, 182, 190
Archidamian War 116
Ariamnes 180, 183–6
Ariminum 171
arrows 33, 35, 171, 179, 181, 190, 232–3
Artaÿctes 234, 237
Artembares 222
Artemis 8 n. 24, 125 n. 41, 220, 221
Artemision 219
Athena 8 n. 24, 115, 125, 216, 233
Athenagoras 45
Athens 112, 116–17, 124 n. 35, 127 n. 45, **215**, 220
atmospheric phenomena, *see* weather
Attalus 54
Attica 111–17, 123–8, 213, **215**, 224
Augustus 86, 133 n. 9, 143, 147, 152, 164; *see also* Octavian
    building projects 147, 242, 244–5, 247, 254–8
    (*see also under* temples)

Index

comparison with Tito 243–5, 247
conflict with Marcus Antonius 164, 172
and fetial ritual 162, 164–5
peace of 17, 133, 147 n. 79, 152, 164, 168, 254
relations with Parthia 177, 179
autochthony 93, 103
autopsy 62, 66, 73–4, 78
autumn 202

Bacchus 143; *see also* Dionysus
Bactra 180–1
Bagrada 106
Balkan wars 236, 257–8
barbarians 65, 166, 171, 179 n. 11, 184–6
barrenness, *see* sterility
battles
   Actium 17, 99 n. 26, 132, 148–52, 254
   Allia 190 n. 45
   Aquae Sextiae 96
   Carrhae 177, 178 n. 8, 179–80, 188–90
   Caudine Forks 55 n. 48, 64
   Cynoscephalae 45–51, 46 n. 20, 48 n. 26, 55, 57–8, 84 n. 44
   Cynossema 230, 233, 237–8
   Cyzicus 195, 195 n. 11, 199–200, 199 n. 27, 207
   Fredericksburg 96–7, 108
   Issus 18, 195–6, 199 n. 27, 203–7
   Lake Trasimene 15, 44, 57–9, 63, 76–86, 144
   Lone Pine 25–6, **26**, 27 n. 9
   Magnesia 51–5, 59
   Marathon 219
   Miletus 218
   Mutina 148–9
   Naulochus 254
   Nicaea-Nicomedia 199 n. 27, 200
   Nola 40
   Pharsalus 3, 100–4, 106–8, 141, 157, 172, 185, 187, 249, 250 n. 25
   Philippi 103, 132 n. 6, 138, 141, 148
   Plataea 218 n. 21
   Psyttaleia 216–20, 224
   Salamis 3, 19, 213–25, **215**
   Sphacteria 218
   Syracuse 67–72, **71**, 86
   Zama 53
Bean, Charles 25 n. 1, 26 n. 4
Berytus 195, 199 n. 27
Bithynia 196
Black Sea 229
blindness 15, 44–5, 53–4, 66, 76, 79–86, 112, 180, 237; *see also* disorientation, vision
blood 4, 12, 31 n. 26, 42, 98, 157, 185, 256
   and agricultural fertility 92–7, 100–4, 106–8, 132, 141–2
   and dust 31, 103–4
   in rivers 107, 158 n. 4, 205

bodies, *see* corpses
bogs, *see* marshes
bones
   and agriculture 92, 95–6, 100–2, 107, 146–7
   and barrenness 140, 142–3
   gathering of 13, 144, 135–6, 138–44
   as monuments 142, 149–51
   skulls 106
   unburied 95, 132, 135–6, 149–51
   of Veii 146–7
borders 2, 116–17, 119, 138, 144, 158, 184, 194, 238; *see also* boundaries
   military and agricultural 95–6, 140–1, 144
   rivers as 160, 167, 179
boundaries 1–2, 5–6, 12 n. 34, 32 n. 30, 66, 70, 143, 146–7, 157 n. 2, 236; *see also* borders
   continental 229, 234
   legal 18, 158, 161, 163, 166–7, 169
   rivers as 18, 146, 158, 161, 170
Brooke, Rupert 122–8, 239
Broz, Josip, *see* Tito
bucolic, *see* pastoral
built environment 232–3, 238
burial, *see* funeral rites
burial grounds 107, 112, 116–17, 148
burial mounds, *see* tombs
Byzantium 18, 195, 197–200, 205

Caesar, Gaius Iulius 14, 17, 18, 98–102, 105–7, 148 n. 81, 157–72, 177–8, 185, 187–90, 249–52, 255–6, 258
Caligula 247
Campania 58, 140 n. 47, 184–6
Cape Helles 230, **231**, 234–8
Cape Krakari **215**, 221
Cape Varvari 220
Cappadocia 196, 200–1
Capua 40, 43 n. 15
Carrhae 177, 178 n. 8, 179–80, 188–90
Cato, Marcus Porcius (= Cato the Younger) 160 n. 18, 162
Cephisus 114, 124–7
Ceres 101 n. 31, 105; *see also* Demeter
characterization 39, 46–51, 55 n. 48, 59, 69 n. 19, 78 n. 36, 100, 171, 182, 193–208
   of Caesar 99, 157 n. 2, 168
   of the Parthians 183–6
Churchill, Winston 229
Cilicia 187, 196, 202
Cilician Gates 200 n. 28, 207
Cilician-Syrian Gates 207
civil war 148, 152, 158, 206, 241
   and agriculture 91–108, 139 n. 41, 158
   battlefields 3, 91–7, 102–3, 107–8, 132, 141, 142 n. 54
   as contaminant 102, 108, 142, 187

commemoration of 3, 20, 151, 242–3, 245, 250–4, 256–7
as crime 107, 172, 249
Greeks' natural propensity for 199 n. 27
justifying 157–72
and memory 3, 20, 241–2, 256
and monuments 20, 107, 132, 142, 206, 242–58
Claudius 247
Cleopatra 151, 162, 164
climate 38, 124, 126, 178, 183, 201, 202 n. 36
in ethnography 180 n. 13, 183, 185–6
Clodius Albinus 195–6, 199 n. 26, 206
cognitive collage 14, 32–3, 36, 182
cognitive psychology 14, 27, 29 n. 19, 31
Colonus 111–17, 123–8
Columna Bellica 162
commemoration 3, 12–13, 18–20, 111 n. 5, 115 n. 12, 204, 241–58
of civil war 20, 111 n. 5, 241–58
of defeat 191
of naval battles 19, 149–51, 213–25
Commodus 195
conquest 59, 150, 152, 167, 181 n. 19
and agriculture 93, 96, 147–8
commemoration of 159–60, 188, 191
deforestation and 99 n. 26
emotional experience of 71
environmental resistance to 17–18, 56–7, 114, 115 n. 10, 125 n. 42
failure of 101–2, 177–91
of Italy 17, 142, 145–8, 150, 165
of Rome 160
tied to geographical knowledge 18, 177–9
Constantinople 229
contamination, see pollution
control 10–12, 54, 66
author's over text 30, 65
of events 48–9, 201
of landscape 10–11, 17–18, 48 n. 26, 50 n. 30, 57, 59, 132, 158, 177–91, 229
of memory 249, 251 n. 28, 254–7
Cora **141**, 146, 249, 253 n. 34
corpses 32, 34, 42 n. 12, 49, 119, 122, 158 n. 4; see also blood, bones
abused 29, 31, 119, 190
agency 101–2, 123, 132
burial 97, 139 n. 43, 158 n. 4
contests over 32
cremation 7, 13, 230
disposal 139
fate 152
and fertility 92–7, 101–3, 106–7, 119–25, 127, 141–2
headless 190
and mud 11, 25

from naval battles 150–2, 158 n. 4, 222
of pack animals 77, 79
and pollution 7, 100 n. 29, 142
as poison 101
and rivers 4, 7, 10, 12–13, 124, 158 n. 4, 190
recovery 12, 135–6, 138, 150
unburied 127 n. 47, 132, 135–6, 138–43, 150–1, 152
of Veii 147
Corvus, Marcus Valerius 85
Cossus, Aulus Cornelius 145–6, 170 n. 70
Cotswolds 119–20, 122–4, 128
Crassus, Marcus Licinius 158 n. 4, 177, 179–80, 183–5, 189, 190
Crassus, Publius Licinius 180
cremation 7, 13, 230
cults 117, 222
hero-cult 12, 222 n. 44, 234
of Jupiter *Latiaris* (Mons Albanus) 165
of Pan (Psyttaleia) 219
of Poseidon Hippios (Colonus) 115
of Protesilaus (Elaious) 230, 234–6
Curicta 105
Curio, Gaius Scribonius 103–6, 171 n. 73
Cynossema 230, **231**, 233, 237–8
Cyzicus 195, 199–200, 207

Dardanelles 19, 229–39, **231**
Darius 203–7, 224 n. 54
darkness 30, 41 n. 10, 45–7, 57, 171, 185; see also blindness, night
dead, the, see corpses
death 105, 125, 138, 142 n. 52, 152; see also corpses
in battle 31, 33, 58, 85, 96, 105, 121–3, 127, 136, 138, 147, 169, 190
by beheading 148 n. 81, 190
of cities 147, 230
in civil war 152
common fate of all humankind 134
Death (personified) 118–19
in *devotio* 84–6
by drowning 6, 11 n. 33, 15, 144, 150–1, 237
elegiac theme 133
execution 143
and fertility 93–4, 96, 121–3
foreshadowing of 31 n. 26, 190 n. 45, 230
hermeneutic 252
human sacrifice 148 n. 81, 237
inglorious 11–12, 105
landscapes associated with 19, 33, 58, 144
of oxen 93 n. 8
punishment for treachery 164
by stoning 234
by suicide 103, 258
trauma 136
at unknown hands 135–6

275

Index

Deceleia 111, 116–17
Deceleian War 16, 111–17, 125–8
deforestation 16, 99 n. 26
Deiotarus 165, 187
Delphi 215
Demeter 125 n. 41; *see also* Ceres
Didius Julianus 195
Dionysus 114, 115 n. 12, 124 n. 37, 125; *see also* Bacchus
  Theatre of 112 n. 9
dioramas 25–7, 28, 31, 33, 36
diplomacy 147, 159, 161–3, 167–8, 177, 179, 189
disorientation 6, 15, 47–8, 57, 140; *see also under* sensory experience
Doughty-Wylie, Lt.-Col. Charlie Hotham Montague 236
Ducarius 84–5
dust 33 n.34, 35, 122–3, 185, 252
  and blood 31, 103–4, 142, 185
  dominant feature of Trojan plain 10, 31
  Etruscan (*puluis Etrusca*) 94–5, 138–43
  and ruins 249
  as weapon 180
dystopian visions 242

earthquakes 83–4
Eceabat **231**, 234, 237
ecocentric perspective 132 n. 5
ecocriticism 15–17, 132–3
Ekbatana 178
Elaious 230, **231**, 234–9
emotions 14, 38
  anger 7, 10, 20, 76, 103, 170, 254
  anxiety 68, 78 n. 35, 205
  astonishment 62 n. 2, 63, 78
  fear 10–11, 14, 46, 49–51, 57, 67–9, 78, 253
  grief 95, 145, 148–50, 159–60, 234
  and historiography 39, 46 n. 20, 48–51, 62 n. 2, 63, 68–72, 74, 85
  joy 49–50, 68, 135
  panic 5–6, 8, 30, 49–50, 54, 57, 219
  rage 4, 6, 14, 169, 222
  of readers/viewers 26–7, 39, 62–3, 69–72, 74, 147 n. 75
  terror 57, 82, 190 n. 45, 219
enargeia 15, 39, 43, 48, 50 n. 30, 62–88
environmental impact of war 7–10, 15–17, 58, 91–108, 131–2
epigraphy 140 n. 47, 189 n. 41, 218, 220–1; *see also* inscription
ethnography 17, 18, 106, 177–8, 183–6, 188, 191, 194
Etruria 77–8, 80, 132, 133–48, **141**, 150–2
Eumenes 52
Euphrates 166, 178–80, 183–4, 186–90
evidentia, *see enargeia*
eyewitness, *see* autopsy

farmers 8–9, 93, 99, 102, 170 n. 72
  compared to soldiers 93, 106
  death of 98, 106
  discover relics of past battles 92, 100, 139 n. 41
  displaced by war 93 n. 10, 97–100, 106–7, 108 n. 44, 251
  mourning 99–100
  ploughmen 35, 108 n. 44
  Rome as community of farmer-citizens 158
farming, *see* agriculture
feelings, *see* emotions
Feriae Latinae 165
fertility 33 n. 35, 112, 119–23, 126, 170, 184 n. 27, 186 n. 33, 250; *see also* sterility
  agricultural 16, 91–108, 140–2, 158
festivals, *see* rituals
filth, *see* pollution
fire 16, 35, 99, 150 n. 91, 234; *see also* cremation
  burning of Perusia 139, 149 n. 84
  burning of Scamander 4, 6–8, 230 n. 8
  burning of Troy 230, 250
  in similes 6–7, 32, 34
  ritual use 42 n. 12
First World War 1, 3, 11 n. 33, 19–20, 108, 131, 236; *see also* Gallipoli
  galleries at Australian War Memorial (AWM) 15, 25–7
  poetry 11 n. 33, 16, 59, 111, 117–28
Flamininus, Titus Quinctius 45–8, 50–1
Flaminius, Gaius 59, 76, 84–6, 165 n. 48
flight, *see* retreat
flowers 9, 97, 123, 126–7; *see also* vegetation
focalization 15, 32, 43–6, 64, 65 n. 11, 69, 83, 91, 184, 198 n. 20
  external 80, 82
  internal 39, 44, 58, 85
foreshadowing 31 n. 26, 71, 190 n. 45, 198, 208, 230 n. 7; *see also* prefiguration
foresight 71, 77–82, 201
forgetting 3, 14, 18–19, 97, 120, 142, 233, 245, 255–8
fountains, *see* springs
frontiers 99 n. 25, 163, 194 n. 7
funeral rites 12–13, 31, 95, 135, 137–8, 139 n. 44, 150 n. 91; *see also* cremation

Galatia 165, 196
Gallipoli campaign 19–20, 229, 235–6, 238–9; *see also under* battles
Gallipoli Peninsula 25–6, 229 n. 3, 230, **231**, 235–9
Gates of War 162, 164, 168 n. 58
Gaugamela 204
gaze 66, 75
  littoral 149 n. 86, 213–14, 224
  readers' 39, 44, 46, 85 (*see also* focalization)
  Roman 44
  spectators' 67–9, 72

Index

genocide 230, 233, 238
geography 17–18, 78, 102–4, 133, 138, 142, 165–9, 177–88, 191, 242
grass 112, 121–2, 124, 127, 184
    destroyed by war 25, 105, 184
    discoloured 102, 142 n. 54
    obscuring ruins/monuments 95, 250–1
graves, *see* tombs
graveyards, *see* burial grounds
Grenfell, Julian 120–8
Gurney, Ivor 16, 119–28

Hades, *see* Underworld
Hannibal 39, 42–4, 53, 55 nn. 48–9, 59, 69 n. 19, 76–86
Hatra 197 n. 16
hearing 6–7, 14, 35, 48 n. 24, 66, 68, 82–3, 151
    auditory confusion 82–3
    auditory deceit 57
    birdsong 108, 124
    less trustworthy than sight 62, 65–6
    soundscapes 26 n. 5, 33, 35–6
    sounds of war 6, 9, 26, 33, 35–6, 63, 70, 94, 146, 151
Hecuba 29, 230, 236–9
Hekatompylos 178
Hellespont 224, 229 n. 1, 234, 238
Hephaestus 4, 6–8, 13, 35
Hercules 106; *see also* Heracles
Hera 4–8, 8 n. 24
Heracles 230–3; *see also* Hercules
hills 38, 44–6, 48, 56, 82, 107, 180, 184, 221–2, 224, 236; *see also* mountains
    Callicolone 27
    Cynoscephalae 45–50 (*see also under* battles)
    Kastello 220 (*see also* Mounichia)
    Palatine 3, 254 (*see also under* temples)
historical accuracy 39, 62 n. 5, 72, 163 n. 38, 193, 206, 255
homelands 111, 117–23, 126–8, 142–4, 237
Hopkins, Pvt. Thomas S. 96–7, 108
household gods, *see* Lares, Penates

idealized landscapes 16, 58, 97, 101 n. 31, 108, 111–12, 117–28
    locus amoenus 184
idylls, *see* idealized landscapes
immersive experience, 14–15, 26, 36
infection, *see* pollution
inscription 25 n. 1, 134, 142 n. 56, 242, 253; *see also* epigraphy
internal audience 25, 64, 69 n. 19, 70, 74, 76, 80, 86
invisibility 1, 19 n. 49, 65, 77, 80, 253
irrigation 8–9, 103–4
Issus 18, 195–6, 199 n. 27, 203–7
itineraria 182, 184 n. 27

Janus (Quirinus) 163–4, 168, 169 n. 67
Juba 103, 106
Julianus, *see* Didius Julianus
Julio-Claudian dynasty 167
Julius Caesar, *see* Caesar, Gaius Iulius
Jupiter 163–6, 169 n. 67; *see also* Zeus
    Feretrius 145
    Latiaris 165, 166
    Tonans 163–4, 166, 252 (*see also under* temples)
just war (*bellum iustum*) 157, 161–2, 168, 170

Kamenska **247**
Kastello hill 220
Keos 219–20
Keratsini **215**, 223
Kilit Bahir 237
Kosute **248**
Krusevo **246**
Kynosoura peninsula **215**, 216, 219–22, 224

Lade 218
Lake Trasimene 15, 44, 57–9, 63, 76–86, **141**
landmarks, *see under* topography
Laodicea 195, 199 n. 27
Lares 144–5, 249; *see also* Penates
Latium **141**, 146, 163–6, 167 n. 55
law 18, 93, 139 n. 43, 157–72, 255–6
    lex Cornelia de maiestate 160
    lex Porcia 160 n. 19
    natural 132
lawlessness 18, 255
Leipsokoutali 217
Lentulus (= Lucius Cornelius Lentulus Crus?) 166–7, 185–6, 187 n. 35, 189–90
Lepidus, Marcus Aemilius 54
locus amoenus, *see under* idealized landscapes
Lone Pine 25–6, **26**, 27 n. 9

Macedonian campaigns 19, 229, 238
Madytos 234
Maecenas 148, 149 n. 84
Magnesia 51–5, 59
Makljen **248**
Mantinea 74
maps 137, 146, 178, 182, 217, 222
    and control of space 178 (*see also* geography)
    mental 28–9, 32, 140, 146, 182 (*see also* cognitive collage, spatial mental model)
Marathon 151 n. 95, 219, 221,
Marcus Aurelius 86
Marcellus, Marcus Claudius 40
Marius, Gaius 100, 102–3
Mark Antony, *see* Antonius, Marcus
marshes 17, 77–81, 180, 197 n.16, 202 n.34
Mars Ultor 179; *see also* Ares

Index

massacres 148 n. 81, 162, 196, 201 n. 31, 206, 217–18, 244
Massilia 96, 99–100, 157, 158 n. 4
Mediterranean Sea 229
memorials, *see* monuments
memory; *see also* commemoration, forgetting, mnemotopes, monuments
    collective 18–19, 230, 240, 241, 249, 257–8
    cultural 18–19, 241 (*see also* mnemotopes)
    layering 19, 34, 136, 233, 238–9, 241, 254
    loci 20, 28, 241–2
    and orality 28–36
    overwriting 17, 19, 108, 248
    visual 30
Mesopotamian plains 179, 184
metaphor 6, 17, 18 n. 45, 75, 108; *see also* metonymy, personification, simile
    agricultural 102–4
    'cognitive collage' 32–3
    'enslavement' of spectators' judgment 70
    solar 244 n. 12
    of vision 65, 70, 80
metonymy 137, 142, 242, 247
Mevania **141**, 144
mimesis 63, 74
mnemotopes 19–20, 30 n. 22, 213–14, 217–18, 220–4, 241, 249, 252, 255, 257
monuments 20, 85–6, 92, 98 n. 23, 131, 236, 241–58; *see also* commemoration, memory, mnemotopes, monumentality, temples
    Australian War Memorial (AWM) 25–7, **26**, 31–3, 36
    Ara Pacis 86
    Columna Bellica 162
    Confederate 241, 257
    of defeat/loss 142, 188–91
    destruction of 13, 241–2, 246–51, 256 (*see also* ruins)
    in former Yugoslav nations 3, 20, 111 n. 5, 244 (*see also* Spomeniks)
    funerary 12–13, 189, 190 n. 45, 242 n. 9, 251–3 (*see also* tombs)
    memorial artefact 142
    of *nefas* 107
    'shadow memorials' 151
    at sites of naval battles 19, 149–51, 217, 220–2
    Statue of Liberty 242
    of victory 99 n. 26, 132, 149–51, 188, 204, 206, 217, 220–2, 245 (*see also* trophies)
monumentality 86, 242, 251, 253–4, 257–8
morale 40, 42, 70
Mounichia **215**, 219–21
mountains 38, 39, 56, 82, 179, 186, 219; *see also* hills
    Alps 39, 69 n. 19, 77 n. 34, 78, 159, 168
    Amanus (Nur) Mountains 207
    Apennines 39

Mons Albanus 165
Mount Aigaleos **215**, 222–4
Mount Taurus 18, 195–6, 199–203, 207
oroskopia 224
peaks 29, 223
ridges 48–50, 121, 185, 203–4, 207, 222–4
mourning 12, 100, 132, 144, 147, 150, 159; *see also under* emotions
mud 11 n. 33, 13, 25, 77, 79, 105, 119–20, 122
mutation 19, 92, 100–2, 106–7
Mutina 148–9

narratology 5 n. 18, 15, 64, 74, 251
natural world 36, 119, 124, 132 n. 5
    element of landscape 2, 131–2
    relationship to war 3, 7–10, 15–17, 91
naval battles 67–72, 149–51, 158 n. 4, 216, 222–4, 230, 237; *see also under* battles
Nero 206 n. 46, 247
Nicaea 195, 199 n. 27, 200
Nicomedia 195, 199 n. 27, 200
Nicopolis 150
Niger, *see* Pescennius Niger
night 30, 34–5, 41–2, 46–7, 121, 159, 171, 180, 182, 187, 201, 205–6, 216, 219; *see also* darkness
Nile 99, 104, 148–9, 166 n. 54
Nomentum **141**, 145–6

Octavian (= Gaius Octavius); *see also* Augustus
    brutality of 132, 142 n. 53, 148 n. 81, 255
    commemorates victory at Actium 99 n. 26, 150–2
    land confiscations of 95, 132 n. 6, 138, 140, 143, 145
    in Perusine War 132, 135 n. 23, 136, 138–40, 142–3, 148 n. 81, 149 n. 84, 152
omens 39, 86, 100, 102, 180, 194, 198, 202 n. 38
oroskopia 224
Owen, Wilfred 16, 118–23

Palatine Hill 3, 254
Pannonia 195
Parthenon 223
Parthia 18, 166, 177–91
Passchendaele 25
pastoral 9, 11 n. 33, 58 n. 58, 64, 94, 119 n. 25, 147; *see also* idealized landscapes
pathos 26, 33–4, 36, 38, 65 n. 11, 85, 92
patria 94, 137–8, 143–4, 147, 159 n. 10, 165, 167; *see also* homeland
Patria (personified) 157–72
patriotism 127, 245
Patroclus 4, 13, 29, 31, 230
Peloponnesian War 19, 111, 116–7, 125, 128, 218, 229, 238
Penates 136, 163; *see also* Lares
Peneus 187

Perama **215**, 223
perception 3, 6, 14–15, 38, 44–5, 57–9, 64, 66, 68–9, 72–3, 75, 77, 79–86, 131, 202, 254
Perinthus 198
Persian campaigns 19, 238
Persian Wars 215, 225, 229
personification 8 n. 25, 17, 132–3, 139–40, 142–5, 147, 148–51; *see also under patria*
Pertinax 195–6, 203 n. 41
Perusia 133–43, **141**, 148 n. 81, 149 n. 84, 151–2
Perusine War 17, 132, 136–40, 142–5, 148, 152
Pescennius Niger 18, 195, 195 n. 11
Petrova Gora 244–5, 244 n. 13, **245**
Philip II 229
Philip V of Macedon 45–51, 58–9, 84 n. 44
Phylarchus 74–6
Piraeus 218, 220–1
plains 18, 38, 45, 82, 102, 114, 116, 127, 203, 205
    Parthian 179–80, 183–6, 189
    Trojan 3–6, 9–10, 13–14, 25, 27–36
    Umbrian 95, 144
Plataea 218 n. 21, 221
ploughs, *see under* agricultural implements
Podgaric **244**, 247
poison 101, 104, 108; *see also* pollution, toxicity
pollution 7, 16, 100–2, 105, 116, 140, 142, 152, 187
Pomerium 255
portents, *see* omens
Poseidon 8 n. 24, 29, 106 n. 40, 115, 124–5, 221, 232
Pozières 25
prefiguration 8 n. 25, 39–43, 48, 51, 53, 161, 167; *see also* foreshadowing
priests
    fetiales 161–71
    flamen Dialis 162
    Pontifex Maximus 162–3
Protesilaus 230, 233–6, 238–9
psychology 1, 15, 25 n. 2, 50–1, 58, 81, 116
    cognitive 14, 27, 29 n. 19, 31
Psyttaleia **215**, 216–20, 224
Pylos 69–71, 86

Quirinus, *see* Janus (Quirinus)

realism 16, 72–4, 77, 80, 85, 132, 152
    'reality effect' 63, 65, 73
    verism 83 n. 42, 84 n.44
reception 20, 64–5, 111, 229
retreat 5, 8, 10, 29, 35, 41, 57, 85, 150 n. 90, 185, 187, 200, 203, 206, 218
rhetoric 40, 43, 52 n. 38, 62–5, 72, 74, 78, 82, 84, 132, 193–4, 202–3, 247, 258
rituals 86, 151 n. 92, 157, 159, 235; *see also* cults, funeral rites, priests, sacrifice
    Aianteia festival 215, 221
    dedication of *spolia opima* 145

deditio 162
devotio 85–6
feriae Latinae 165
fetial 18, 157, 159, 161–72
indictio belli 163, 171
rivers 9 n. 27, 10–11, 17, 38, 86 n. 47, 94, 120, 131, 157 n. 2, 158, 169, 170; *see also* streams
    Aesis 158 n. 10
    Allia 190 n. 45
    Anio 42, 100, 102
    Araxes 158 n. 4, 182, 190
    Bagrada 106
    bloody 107, 205
    as boundaries 5–6, 18, 146, 158, 161, 170
    Cephisus 114, 124–7
    of England 119–20, 123–7
    Euphrates 166, 178–80, 183–4, 186–90
    Nile 99, 104, 149, 166 n. 54
    of the *orbis Romanus* 187
    of Parthia 179, 187, 190 (*see also* Araxes, Euphrates, Tigris)
    Peneus 187
    Rubicon 3, 17–8, 102, 157–72
    Scamander 3–14, 17, 27, 30, 31 n. 27, 34, 36, 157 n. 2, 230 n. 8 (*see also* Xanthus)
    Simois 10, 13
    Tiber **141**, 146, 158 n. 4
    Tigris 185, 187, 190, 206 n. 47
    Timavus 56, 58
    of Troy 13 (*see also* Scamander, Simois)
    Xanthus 5, 7, 9, 14 n. 37 (*see also* Scamander)
Roman civil wars 3, 92, 102, 111 n. 5, 137–8, 142 n. 54, 151–2, 172, 242, 249 n. 21; *see also* particular battles
routes 28–9, 77–8, 115 n. 11, 178, 182 n. 24, 184 n. 27, 200, 214; *see also itineraria*
Rubicon 3, 17–8, 102, 157–72
ruins 92, 94–5, 147–8, 198, 248–51, 253

sacrifice 25 n. 1, 35, 45, 48, 120, 165, 221, 235
    human 148 n. 81, 237
Salamis 3, 19, 213–25, **215**
Samnite War (Third) 55–6, 58, 140
Satricum 41–2
Schliemann, Heinrich 230 n. 6, 235
Scipio (= Publius Cornelius Scipio Africanus) 44, 69 n. 19, 106
Sea of Marmara 229
seascapes 149–51, 213–25, 229, 238
seasons 9–10, 35, 38, 96, 100, 102, 105; *see also* particular seasons
Second World War 3, 20, 111 n. 5, 244, 254
Seddulbahir 236
Seleucids 178
Seleukia 178
Seliniai **215**, 222

279

Index

senses, *see* hearing, smell, taste, touch, vision
sensory experience 6, 14, 63, 76 n. 32, 83, 146, 151
    sensory deprivation 83–4
    sensory disorientation 15, 47–8, 82–3
Septimius Severus 18, 194–208
    civil wars of (193-7 CE) 196
Sestos **231**, 234–5, 237–8
Severus, *see* Septimius Severus
Severus Alexander 196, 202 n. 34
shrines, *see* temples
sieges 78, 91, 160
    Aquileia 198 n. 21, 202 n. 34
    Byzantium 18, 195, 197–200, 205
    Capua 40, 43 n. 15
    Hatra 197 n. 16
    Ilerda 105
    Massilia 96, 99–100, 157, 158 n. 4
    Mount Taurus 200–3
    Perusia 134–5, 137–40, 142–3
    Sestos 234–5, 237–8
    Troy 5, 32
Sigeum 235
sight, *see* vision
simile 75 n. 31; *see also* metaphor
    in Homer 6–7, 9, 11–12, 14, 31 n. 26, 32–5
    in Lucan 99 n. 25, 101 n. 30, 103 n. 36, 169–71
Siwa oasis 104
slings 53–4, 171, 181
smell 6–7, 33 n. 34, 118
    of war 26 n. 6
Somme 25
spatial mental model 14, 28–30, 33 n. 37
spears 8 n. 25, 10, 33, 50 n. 34, 53, 92, 114, 181, 232–3
    in fetial ritual 162–3, 170–1
spectacle 54, 62, 67, 74–6, 77, 80, 85, 253 n. 36
spectators 5 n. 19, 111–12, 117, 128, 251, 253
    and *enargeia* 62–86
    internal 64, 80 (*see also* focalization, internal audience)
Spomeniks 20, 244–8, **244, 245, 246, 247, 248,** 250–1, 253–8
spring 35, 77, 119 n. 24, 123–6
springs 9, 34, 113, 114, 124, 184, 189
Statue of Liberty 242
sterility 104–5, 140, 142–3, 170, 219, 250
strategy (military) 15, 55 n. 49, 77–81, 85, 165, 177 n. 3, 197, 200, 202, 215, 229
    and control of terrain 59, 180, 183, 191
    and diplomacy 163
    impact of terrain on 2, 17
    and leadership 50 n. 32, 51
streams 14, 83, 112–13, 119–20, 124, 125 n. 38, 184, 200–2; *see also* rivers
Sulla, Lucius Cornelius 100, 158 n. 10, 160
summer 34, 96, 126, 144, 185
suspense 15, 39–43, 58, 68

swords 6, 10, 12, 33, 53, 82, 121, 135, 220
symbolism 17–18, 51–4, 132, 244, 246, 254

tactics 14, 17, 58, 177 n. 3, 194, 199 n. 24
Tarpeian Rock 163–4
taste 33 n. 34, 146 n. 70
Taurus, *see* Mount Taurus
temples 250, 252–3
    of Apollo (Palatine Hill, Rome) 245, 247 n. 20, 254–8
    of Artemis (Mounichia) 220
    of Athena Skiras (Salamis) 216 n. 14
    of Janus Quirinus (Rome) 164 (*see also* Gates of War)
    of Jupiter (Olympia) 242 n. 9
    of Jupiter Feretrius (Rome) 145
    of Jupiter Tonans (Rome) 164
    of Kychreus (Salamis) 221
    Parthenon 223
    of Poseidon 106 n. 40
    of Protesilaus (Elaious) 234–6, 238–9
Thebes 93, 103, 111 n. 2, 112, 116–17
Themistocles 221
Thermopylae 224
Tiber 145–6, 158 n. 4
Tiberius 158 n. 10, 247
Tigris 185, 187, 189–90, 206 n. 47
Timavus 56, 58
timelessness 71, 125–6, 128
Tito (= Josip Broz) 20, 244–5, 247, 250, 253–5, 257
tombs 12–13, 92, 94–5, 107, 141 n. 49, 142 n. 56, 149, 221–2, 224
    of Achilles 235
    of Crassus 189–90
    of Lt.-Col. Charles Hotham Montague Doughty-Wylie 236
    of Hector 250–2
    of Hecuba, 237
    of Ilus 12, 28, 30
    of Jupiter Tonans 252
    of Marius 100, 102
    of Mausolus 242 n. 9
    of Oedipus 112, 117 n. 19
    Perusine 95, 137–8
    of Pompey 242, 251–3, 258
    of Protesilaus 235–6
    of Themistocles 221
    of Veii 132
topography 3, 4, 18 n. 45, 19, 48 n. 27, 56 n. 54, 78, 117, 143, 183, 194, 197, 204, 236
    and experience 5, 14, 25, 27, 36, 38
    historical 214, 223–4, 251 n. 28
    and identity 158–9
    landmarks 3, 5, 14, 27–31, 36, 46, 182, 213–16, 223, 225, 230, 233–4, 237–8, 241 (*see also* monuments)

of naval battles 19, 149, 213–16, 222–4
understanding of 178
and weather 15, 38, 58
Torquatus, Titus Manlius 85
touch 26 n. 6, 142, 144, 146 n. 70
tourism 12, 14 n. 37, 25–6, 97, 125, 131, 151 n. 95, 189, 235–6, 252
　Caesar at Troy 14, 190 n. 45, 250–1
　Salamis 221, 223, 224–5
　Spomeniks 245–6, 251
toxicity 16, 100–1
treaties 157, 159, 161–72, 177, 190
trees 7–8, 25, 27, 31, 34, 116, 131, 184, 250; *see also* deforestation
　forests 131, 219, 250
　groves 99, 112–13, 114, 125 n. 38
　in Julian Grenfell's 'Into Battle' 121–2, 124, 127
　orchards 119–20, 122
triumphs 149–52, 159–60, 181, 204, 206
Trajan 177
trophies 17, 149, 188, 206, 215, 217, 220–1, 224; *see also under* monuments
Troy 231
tumuli, *see* tombs
Tyre 195, 199 n. 27

Umbria 94–5, 132–45, **141**, 151–2
Underworld 115 n. 11, 115 n. 12, 142, 169 n. 67, 189 n. 41

valleys 56, 112–13, 121, 219
　Euphrates 180, 184 n. 27
vegetation 115, 122, 124–6, 131; *see also* flowers, grass, trees
Veii 17, 132, **141**, 145–8, 150, 152, 170 n. 70, 249, 253 n. 34
Venus 250; *see also* Aphrodite
Vesta 164
vineyards 35, 96
violence 13, 16, 35, 76, 96, 147 n. 79, 158 n. 9, 162, 244, 255
　against nature 7, 58, 147
　and civil conflict 170, 172, 194–5, 244, 247, 256–8
　and conquest 145, 152, 170
　cycle of 102–4
　disruption of agriculture 100, 102
　heroic 232
　incidental 250
　in nature 11, 39, 202
　reiterative 172
visibility 54–5, 62–3, 75, 81–5, 116, 207–8, 218 n. 20; *see also* invisibility
　of landmarks/monuments 85, 116, 220, 223, 250–1, 254
　of the past 74

of war's physical traces 131, 139, 150, 205
vision 33, 57, 121, 151, 190; *see also* autopsy, blindness, focalization
　more trustworthy than hearing 62, 65–6
　double-vision 106–7
　historians' use of 43–4, 62–86
　metaphorical 65, 80
　visual confusion 82–3
　visual deceit 55–7
　visual environment 84
　visual experience 14, 26–7, 38, 63–4, 68, 85
visuality 26, 38, 43, 46, 50, 52, 75–7, 82, 159
visualization 27–30, 32 n. 28, 64, 66, 74–5, 78, 80, 208, 221; *see also* cognitive collage, spatial mental model
visual language 246

waterways 115, 124, 126; *see also* rivers, springs, streams
　Dardanelles 229–38
weapons 32, 43, 45, 52, 99 n. 26, 149, 167, 172; *see also* arrows, slings, spears, swords
　analogous to farming tools 93, 106
　characteristic (of nations) 52, 54, 171
　characteristic (of individual heroes) 232–3
　landscapes as 56, 179–80, 187
　monuments as 250
　and war dead 49–50, 100–1, 139 n. 41
weather 15, 17, 38–59, 76 n. 32, 124, 126, 202
　clouds 6, 45, 47, 53, 180
　fog/mist 5, 15, 17, 38–9, 44–58, 65, 76, 80–4, 144
　hail 34, 42–3, 58
　heat 38, 44, 104, 180, 182
　rain 17, 31, 32 n. 30, 38–43, 46–7, 54–5, 58, 86, 96, 101, 114, 120, 124, 139, 186
　snow 34, 38–9, 115 n. 11, 185–6, 201
　storms 9 n. 27, 31, 32 n. 30, 39, 40–3, 47, 114, 115 n. 11, 120, 124, 201–3
　sun 44, 57, 69 n. 19, 97, 101, 108, 114, 121, 123–4, 144
　Troy as 'weatherless space' 10 n. 28, 31 n. 26
　wind 32, 35, 40–1, 44, 53, 114, 115 n. 11, 120–1, 124, 139, 150, 182
winter 11, 77–8, 96–7, 102, 182, 201, 202 n. 36

Xanthippus 234
Xerxes 216 n. 14, 219, 222–4, 234–5
　throne of **215**, 216, 222–4

Yugoslav War 20, 244, 247, 257–8

Zeugma 180
Zeus 4–5, 11, 29, 31 n. 26, 114–5, 125, 221, 224 n. 56, 232; *see also* Jupiter

281

www.ingramcontent.com/pod-product-compliance
Lightning Source LLC
Chambersburg PA
CBHW072127290426
44111CB00012B/1811